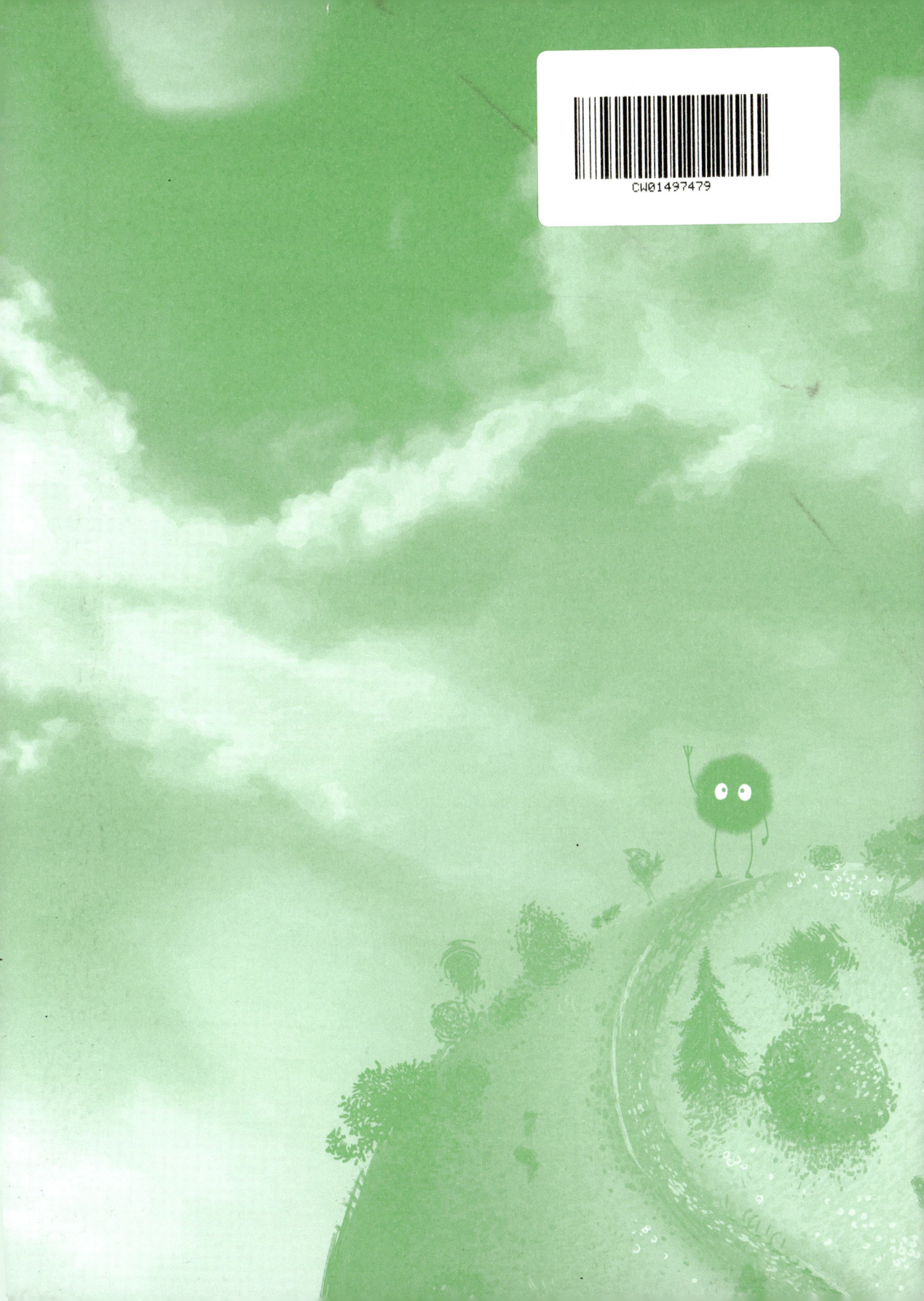
CW01497479

The Animation Atlas

The Ghibliotheque Guide to the
World of Animated Film

Copyright © 2025 Michael Leader and Jake Cunningham

The right of Michael Leader and Jaking Cunningham to be identified as
the Authors of the Work has been asserted by them in accordance with the
Copyright, Designs and Patents Act 1988.

First published in 2025 by Welbeck Illustrated
An Imprint of HEADLINE PUBLISHING GROUP LIMITED

1

Apart from any use permitted under UK copyright law, this publication may
only be reproduced, stored, or transmitted, in any form, or by any means,
with prior permission in writing of the publishers or, in the case of reprographic
production, in accordance with the terms of licences issued by the Copyright
Licensing Agency.

Cataloguing in Publication Data is available from the British Library

ISBN 978-1-03542-729-1

Printed and bound in Dubai

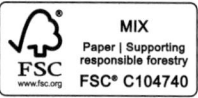

Editor: Ross Hamilton
Design: Russell Knowles
Picture Research: Giulia Hetherington
Production: Marion Storz

Headline's policy is to use papers that are natural, renewable and recyclable
products and made from wood grown in well-managed forests and other
controlled sources. The logging and manufacturing processes are expected to
conform to the environmental regulations of the country of origin.

HEADLINE PUBLISHING GROUP LIMITED
An Hachette UK Company
Carmelite House
50 Victoria Embankment
London EC4Y 0DZ

The authorised representative in the EEA is Hachette Ireland,
8 Castlecourt Centre, Dublin 15, D15 XTP3, Ireland (email: info@hbgi.ie)

www.headline.co.uk
www.hachette.co.uk

Cover credits: Clockwise from top right: TCD/Prod.DB/Alamy
© Dream Well Studio/Sacrebleu Productions/Take Five; Photo
12/Alamy © Rita Productions/Blue Spirit Productions/Gebeka
Films; Everett Collection/Alamy © IFC Films/Arenamedia/Screen;
Australia/Snails Pace Films; Photo 12/Alamy © Comenius
Film; TCD/Prod.DB/Alamy © AppleTV+/Cartoon Saloon
(Wolfwalkers) Ltd/Mélusine Productions; TCD/Prod DB/Alamy ©
Ustredni Pujcovna Filmu/Loutkovy Film Praha/ Studio Kresleneho
a Loutkoveho Filmu; Courtesy GKIDS © 2013 Filme de Papel;
Shawshots/Alamy © Apple Corps/King Features Syndicate/
Subafilms; Cinematic/Alamy © Aardman Animations; Photo 12/
Alamy © Films Armorial/Argos Films; Prod DB/Alamy © Aparte
Film/Sacrebleu Productions/Minds Meet; TCD/Prod DB/Alamy
© Miyu Productions/Dolce Vita Films; TCD/Prod DB/Alamy ©
Arcadia Motion Pictures/Lokiz Films/Noodles Production/Les
Films du Worso; Allstar Picture Library/Alamy & Album/Alamy ©
Studio Ghibli/Tokuma Shoten/Nibariki. Background: AM-art/
Shutterstock; trimitek/Shutterstock

The Animation Atlas

The Ghibliotheque Guide to the
World of Animated Film

MICHAEL LEADER & JAKE CUNNINGHAM
Hosts of the GHIBLIOTHEQUE podcast

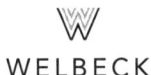

WELBECK

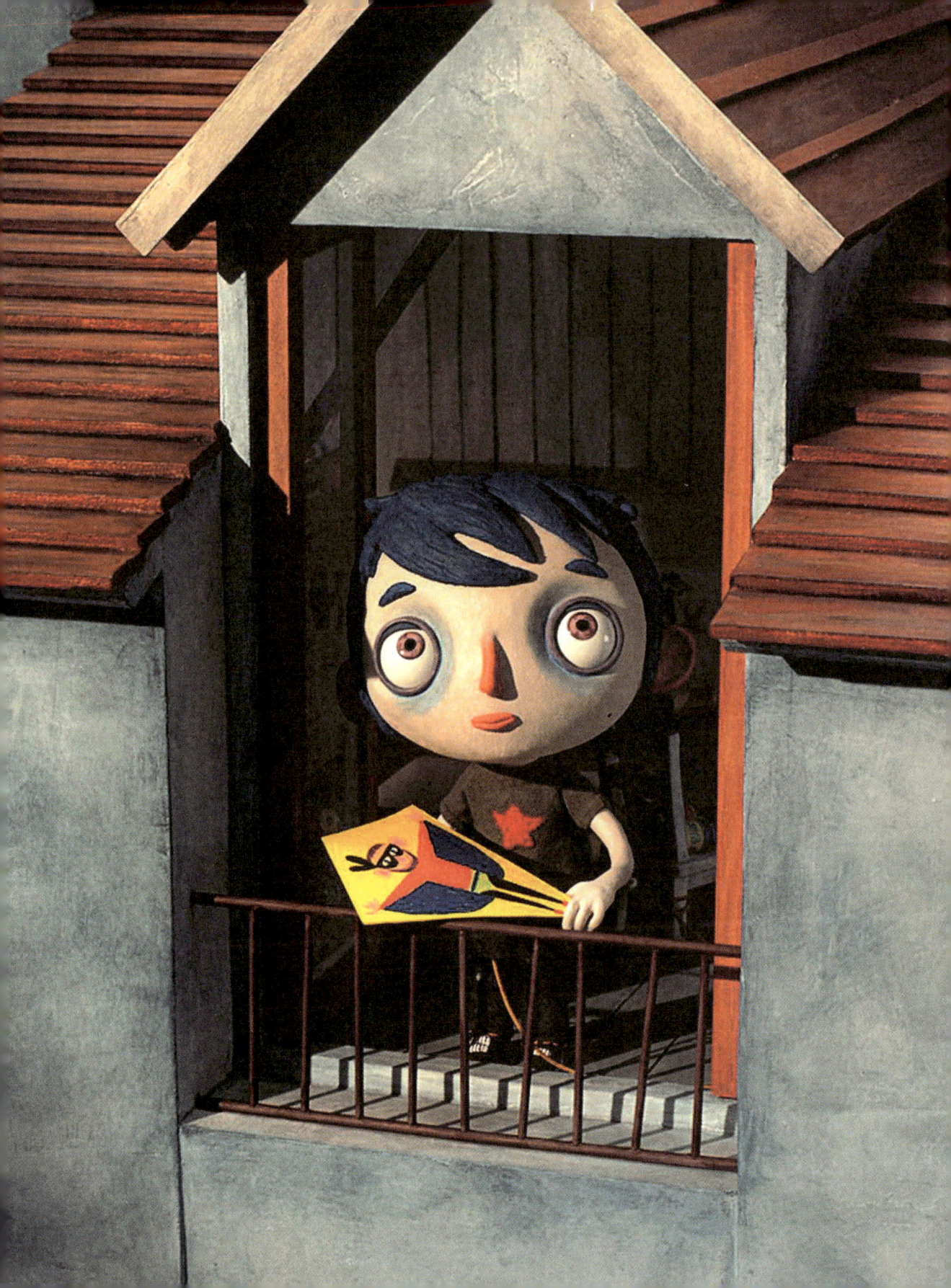

Contents

Icon Key

 Film

Further viewing

Director

Studios

Drawings

Introduction

Pack your bags, folks. We're about to go on a round-the-world trip like no other.

First, though, let's get one thing straight: animation is many things, but it is not a genre. This is a common misconception, one fomented by the likes of IMDb and Letterboxd – where you'll often find *Animation* sitting alongside the likes of *Drama*, *Comedy*, *Horror*, *Musical* or *Documentary* in separate genre categories.

Frankly, this has never sat right with us, and within this book you'll find animated films that are dramatic, funny and horrifying; you'll find animated musicals and documentaries, too, in dozens of languages or in no language at all.

Animation can be anything: it is an art form that can approach any style of storytelling, or it can abandon storytelling completely. From the most ultra-detailed and realistic illustrations to the most minimal, stylized or abstract art, animation can take countless forms – about as many as there are individual artists creating it. Animation has also given us some of the most universally adored, box office record-breaking films of all time, while, at its experimental extremes, there are radical and cutting-edge visions that challenge us and provide us with the shock of the new.

And yet, animation can sometimes be treated as separate from, or subordinate to, live-action cinema. At the Academy Awards, some of the year's greatest films are ring-fenced within the Best Animated Feature category – and only three animated films have ever been deemed worthy of a nomination for Best Picture: *Beauty and the Beast* (1991), *Up* (2009) and *Toy Story 3* (2010). Thanks to decades of Disney dominance, the bias still lingers that animation is merely kids' stuff. It certainly can be, but it is also so much more than that.

Think back: what was the first film or TV series you remember watching? It's very likely that it was animated. Our very first impressions of the delights of the big and

Below: Disney's pioneering feature-length fairy tale *Snow White and the Seven Dwarfs* has epitomised family-friendly animated filmmaking for close to a century.

Opposite above: Tight Crew. 2024's Oscar-winning adventure *Flow*, made independently on a small budget by a close-knit team, points toward exciting, uncharted waters for animation.

Opposite below: How do you 'do'? Kenyan-American director Ng'endo Mukii's *Yellow Fever* uses animation to address themes of identity and imperialism.

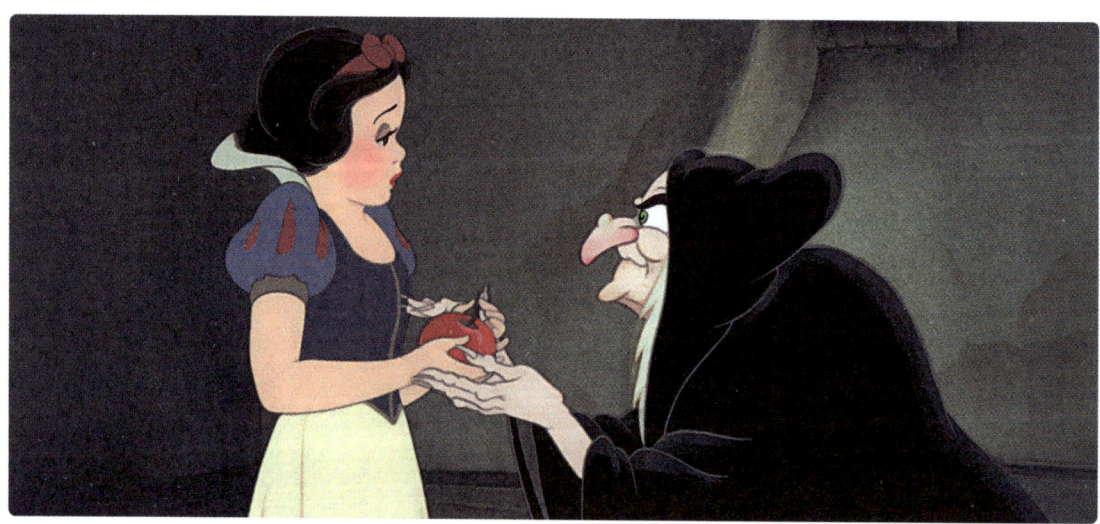

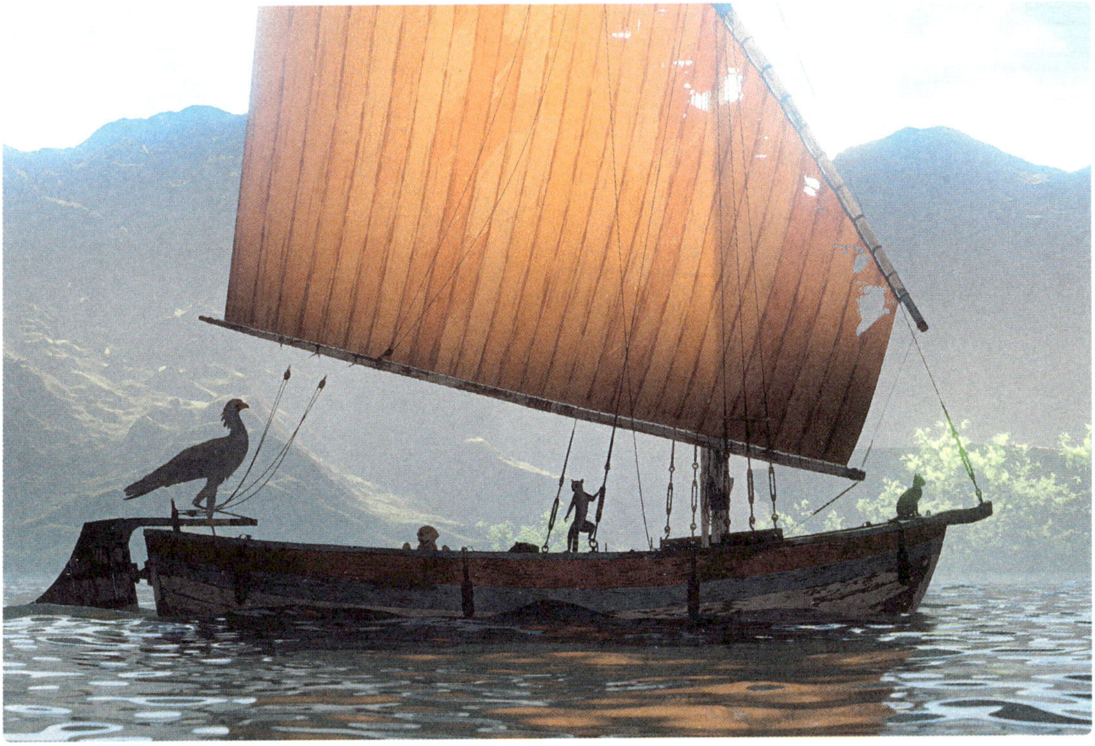

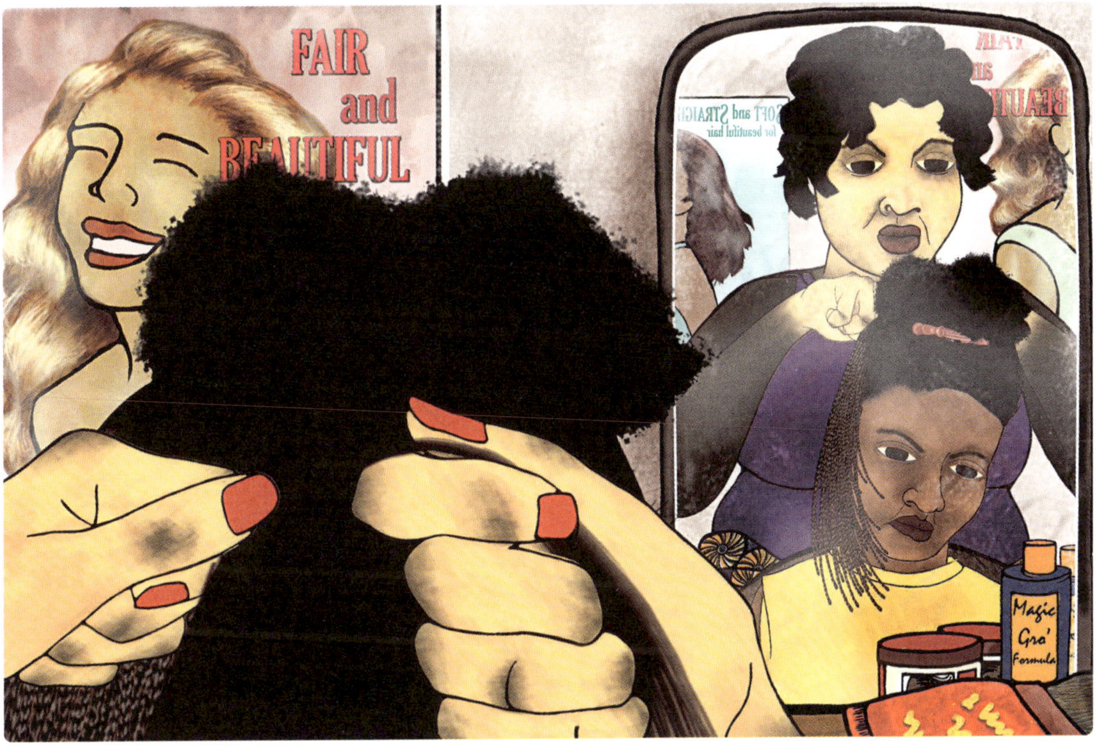
FAIR
and
Magic
Gro'
Formula

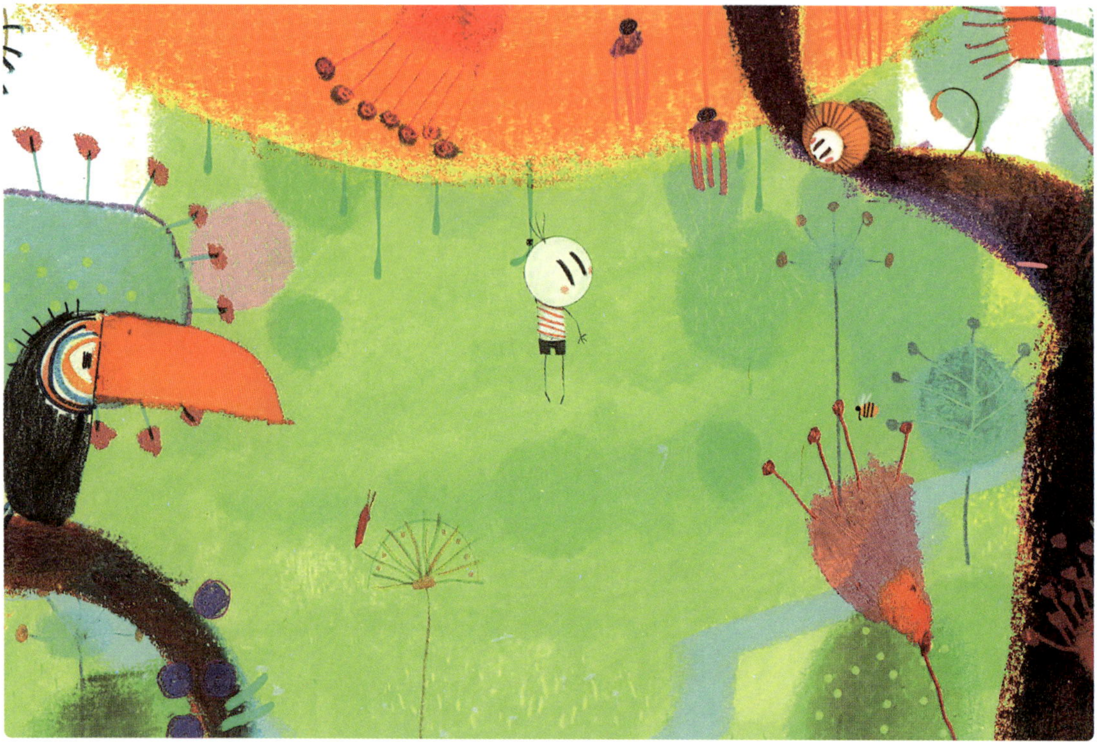

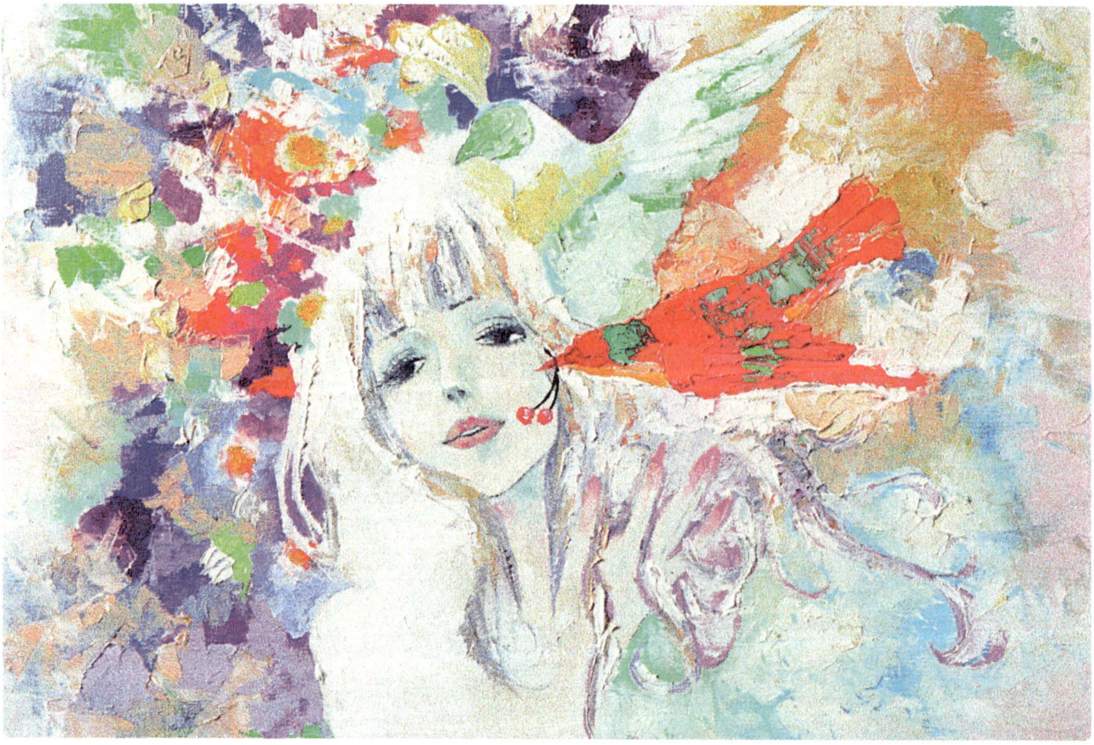

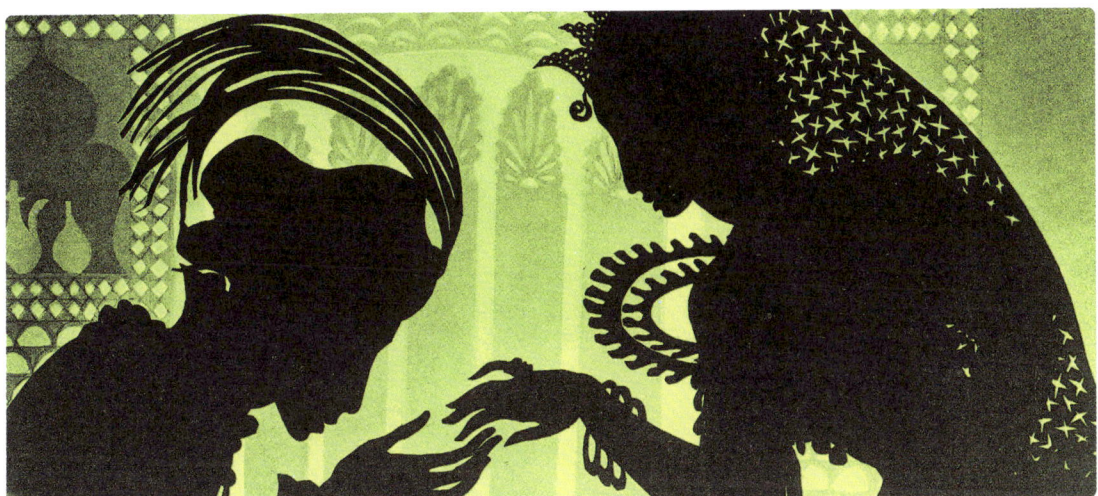

small screen were shaped by animation, and at its best this wonderful art form taps into that childlike sense of curiosity and imagination. Unbound by expectation, animation is a space of pure expression: films rendered in pencil, paint, paper, plasticine or pixels, painstakingly laid out, frame by frame, and brought to life by the magic of the moving image.

And so, here it is: *The Animation Atlas*. In our previous books, we have dived head first into areas of film history that we felt deserved further exploration and consideration, starting with the animation titan Studio Ghibli, then Japanese anime at large, and most recently the vibrant world of Korean cinema. This book returns us to animation, and it is our most ambitious expedition yet. Where we have previously used 30 key films to light the way through a certain strand of cinema, this book takes us around the world of animation in 30 *countries* – with us highlighting key films, filmmakers and studios at each stop along the way.

This international scope was important to us from the off. Despite what you may think from the box office charts, where Hollywood and anime tend to dominate, animation is a truly worldwide phenomenon, with artists making distinctive and creative work in all parts of the planet. So, while we were plotting our journey, we were keen to embrace work from all continents, encompassing countries with long and pioneering animation traditions as well as those that are, comparatively speaking, still finding their feet.

Now, this was sometimes easier said than done. Picking representative films and animators from countries with long and varied histories – from Czechia to France, the USA to Russia – was a task and a half in itself. Trickier still was navigating the inherently international nature of the animation industry, with filmmakers emigrating in search of opportunities, or projects bringing together financing and creative teams from multiple countries in the journey from pitch to screen.

Ultimately, this is a celebration of art made by human hands – something more important than ever, thanks to the rise of AI. Within these pages, you will find recommendations and reviews for hundreds of films: films that come in all shapes, sizes, styles and, yep, genres, all united by that very human urge to create and communicate, to interrogate the world around us and dream of something new. This is only the tip of the iceberg of over a century of innovation, but we hope that this trip is just the first of many.

Animation isn't a genre, it's a whole world. Let's explore it together.

Opposite above: It's a *Boy's World*. Animation is a globe-spanning art form that comes in many colours. Case in point: Brazil's vibrant and unique *Boy and the World*.

Opposite below: State of the Art. The Japanese erotic fantasy anime, *Belladonna of Sadness*, is a lush, painted marvel.

Above: Even a century after its release, Lotte Reiniger's paper cutout epic *The Adventures of Prince Achmed* still looks magical.

Michael and Jake
One in the attic, the other in the basement
December 2024

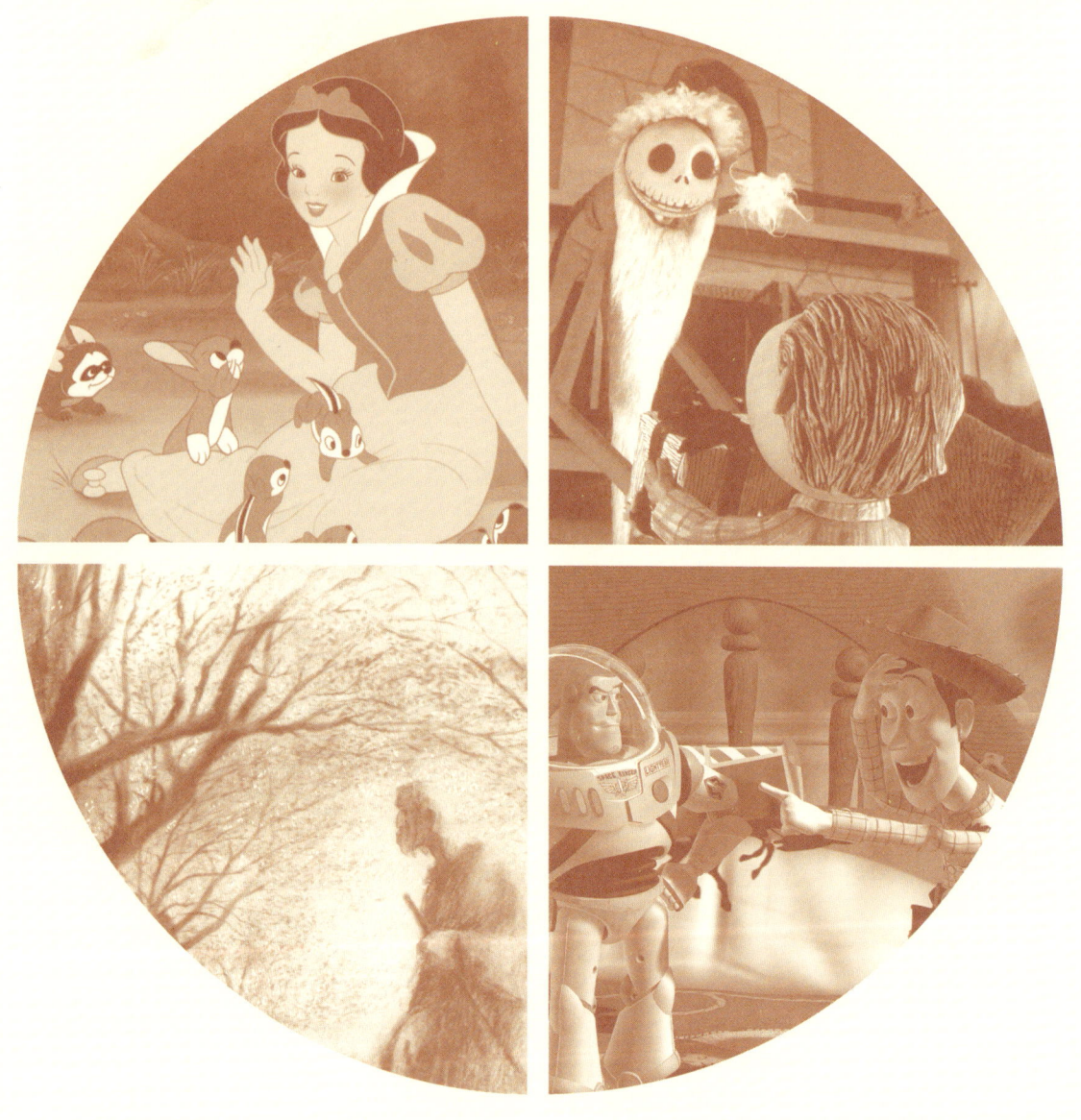

North America

Canada

Shorts Don't Get Much Bigger

🎥 The Man Who Planted Trees

Director: Frédéric Back
Released: 1987

When Studio Ghibli co-founding director Isao Takahata was asked to lead a TV documentary about a place that inspired him (*Journey of the Heart*, 1999), he picked Canada. There, he could not only revisit sites that inspired his pre-Ghibli TV series *Anne of Green Gables*, but also meet the man he considered one of the greatest animators in the world: Frédéric Back.

Born in 1924 in Germany – well, what was technically at the time the Territory of the Saar Basin – Back moved with his family to Paris at the start of the Second World War. There he'd go on to study art, before emigrating to Canada in 1948. After working as a farmer and a teacher at a Montreal art school, he was asked to provide titles for TV shows for public broadcaster Radio-Canada in 1952. He would work there for the rest of his career.

Back's first short as director, *Abracadabra* (1970), is a vibrant vision in which multiculturalism and collaboration help save the sun from a dark thief. It has a psychedelic storybook quality, lavishly painted with the feathered tail end of the hippy era, but it was his 1978 film *All Nothing* that began his streak of more internationally acclaimed work. Telling an Eden-like tale of human vanity and violence in the face of a deity and their creations, *All Nothing* overflows with fluid, constantly shifting natural life and colour, while simplifying the Almighty to pristine curves and sharp angles (not dissimilar to the heavenly counsellors in Pixar's *Soul*). It scored Back his first Oscar nomination for Best Animated Short, but he left empty-handed, a fact his next film *Crac* (1981) would change.

Emblematic of Back's interest in cycles of life, the Oscar-winning *Crac*'s protagonist is a rocking chair. First the wood is felled, then it is lovingly crafted into a chair that passes through eras of domesticity before being abandoned and eventually landing in a gallery.

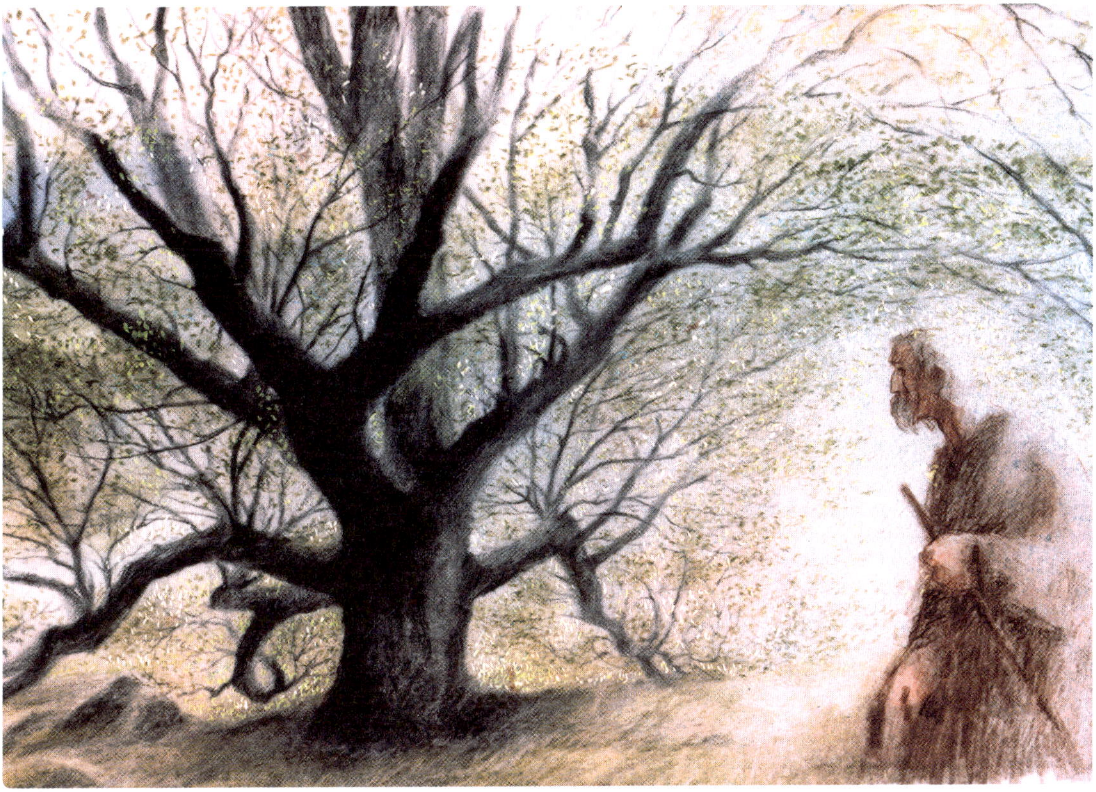

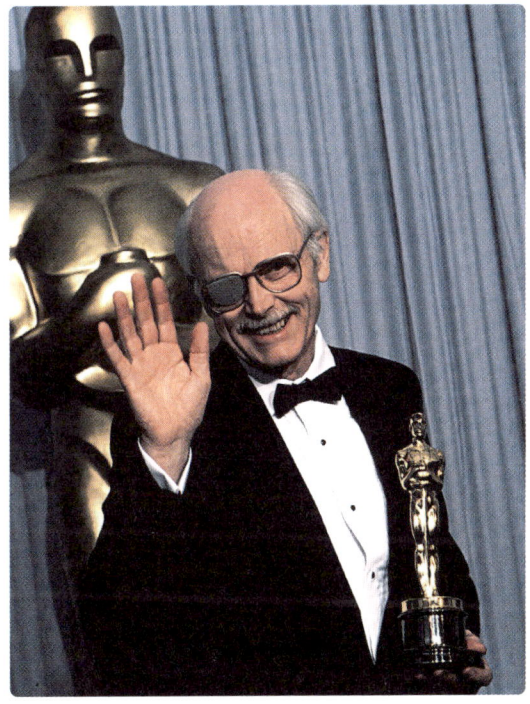

Softly illustrated and emanating warmth, Back's chair is a gift from nature to man and carves out a joyous and tragic silent fable about environmental responsibility and respect. While that film began with a tree being cut down, his next, also an Oscar winner and Back's finest work, is all about growing them.

Based on a 1953 novel of the same name, *The Man Who Planted Trees* (1987) is an extraordinary animated experience. Embracing voiceover, it tells the story of a French man who spends decades turning barren wasteland into a thriving forest by planting seeds, all by himself. Drawn delicately, it feels like it could be blown off the screen: blank space dominates the early chapters of the story, with barely shaded characters surviving through the arid minimalism. Constantly flowing between states, caught in the winds of its Provençal setting, characters, places and times disappear and evolve

Above: *The Man Who Planted Trees*. In a filmography of remarkable achievements, this is Back's masterpiece.

Right: The Man Who Won Trophies. Frédéric Back with one of the two Academy Awards he won.

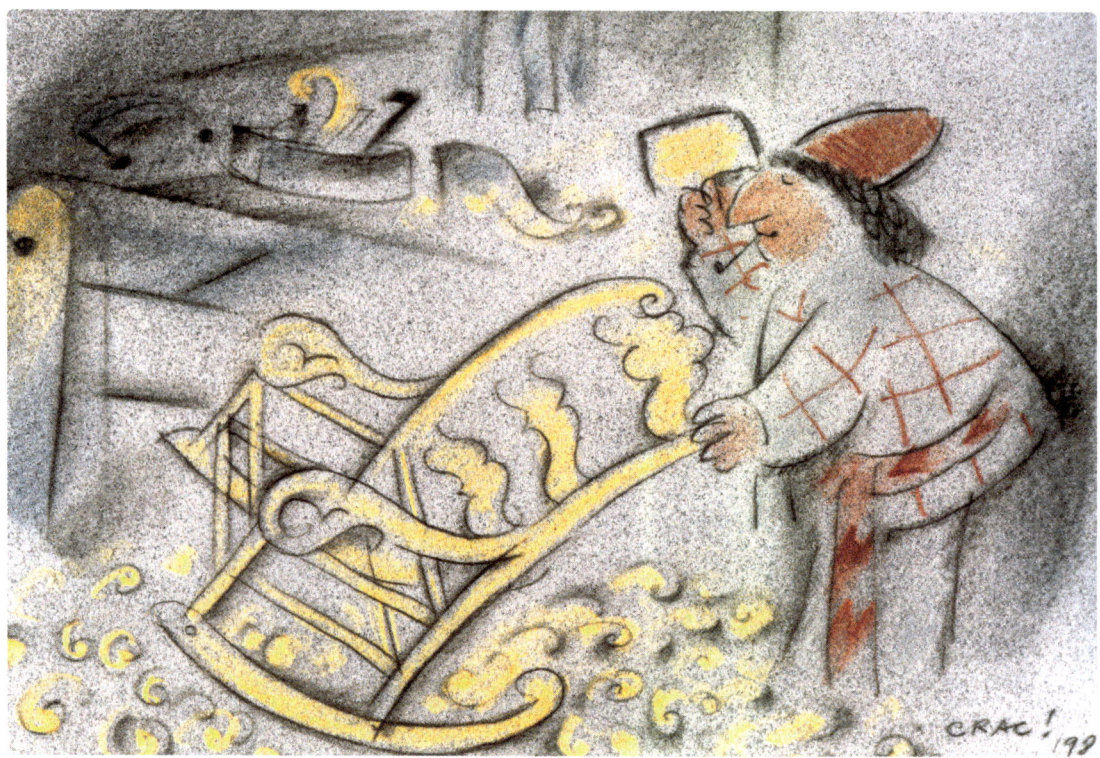

in moments, with the brief arrival of war dramatically thickening lines and stuttering that harmony. Eventually, as the forest begins to grow, Back's page begins to fill in, with life and colour enlivening the parched screen. The short, pulsing strokes evoke Pointillism and become a natural carnival in celebration of a humble act of environmental kindness – one that Back himself took on in reality.

Embracing the lessons of his film, Back actually planted over 26,000 trees himself. And, when Isao Takahata travelled to Canada for his documentary, after first corresponding via mail years earlier, he was able to plant a tree with the man who so inspired him – a tradition Back had with all his guests. Conversing, the two masters of the form spoke interchangeably about art and nature; Back's statement that "nature's beauty is often the work of farmers" could easily be Takahata talking about his agriculturally underscored (and underrated) *Only Yesterday* (1991), while Takahata's belief in the "tremendous life force of trees" is key to Back's life and work.

Back would make one more film before retiring, *The Mighty River* (1993), an animated documentary about Canada's St. Lawrence River, which explores its biological and topographic history, its symbiotic relationship to humanity and eventually its exploitation. After expressing his philosophy through fable and suggestion, he signed off from filmmaking more directly, maintaining his signature animated flow in which time, space and geography can collapse in an instant, but asking (via an English-language voiceover from Donald Sutherland) if the literal flow into environmental disrepair can be avoided. It's a question still asked three decades later. Back died in 2013, but the power of his films endures, creatively and politically, with the internet (and perhaps this book) allowing more people to discover him, share his work and become even more trees in his forest.

Above: What's the *Crac*? Back's 1981 short film follows the unlikely protagonist of a rocking chair through its lifecycle.

Opposite: Across the Board. The National Film Board of Canada is home to a wildly diverse library of short films, from Richard Condle's *The Big Snit* (left) to stop-motion Amanda Strong's *Inkwo for When the Starving Return* (right).

👁 Further Viewing

Canada's standing in animation history rests on its peerless tradition of short filmmaking, and the haven that it has provided for animators over the decades via the National Film Board of Canada (Office national du film du Canada).

In fact, Canadian animation is so closely associated with short films that even one of its most enduring cult features, the wild, and wildly uneven comic book adaptation *Heavy Metal* (1981), is a collection of shorts handled by multiple studios and animators, some in Canada and others abroad (such as the UK's Halas & Batchelor studio). *Heavy Metal* director Gerald Potterton was born in the UK and cut his teeth on Halas & Batchelor's *Animal Farm* (1954) but emigrated to Canada to work on productions funded by the National Film Board, including the Oscar-nominated *My Financial Career* (1962) and *Christmas Cracker* (1963).

He wasn't the only one: many great filmmakers moved to Canada to work with the NFB, including world-renowned innovators and pioneers such as Norman McLaren (*Neighbours*, 1952), Caroline Leaf (*The Street*, 1976), Ishu Patel (*Bead Game*, 1977) and Co Hoedeman (*The Sand Castle*, 1977). The NFB has also supported filmmakers around the world, including many mentioned in other chapters in this book, such as Georges Schwizgebel (*The Man With No Shadow*, 2004), Claude Barras (co-director of *Land of the Heads*, 2008), Kōji Yamamura (*Muybridge's Strings*, 2011) and Joanna Quinn (*Affairs of the Art*, 2021).

Working through the NFB filmography is essentially an immersion course in animation history and practice. Contained within, you'll find experiments in drawn-on-film animation (*Begone Dull Care*, 1949), pixilation (where human subjects are manipulated frame by frame), sand and paint-on-glass animation, stop-motion and early computer animation (*Hunger*, 1974). These overtly experimental works sit alongside a treasure trove of more conventional but no less distinctive films made in hand-drawn 2D and CG-animated styles, including gems by Richard Condie (*The Big Snit*, 1985) and Alison Snowden and David Fine (*Bob's Birthday*, 1993).

Making animated shorts rarely makes financial sense, and so the NFB's cherished status as a government-funded public body gives it the freedom to fund innovation and to showcase under-represented voices and viewpoints, most recently with films such as *Inkwo for When the Starving Return* (2024), directed by stop-motion filmmaker Amanda Strong, the latest in a growing body of works that foreground Indigenous stories and experiences.

If you find yourself with a spare afternoon, you could do much worse than diving into the NFB's website and exploring the scores of animated films they have supported. Start with the above and continue through its enviable library of 6 Oscar winners and 38 total nominees. That second number is significant: only Disney has produced more Oscar-nominated animated shorts, and the gap is closing by the year.

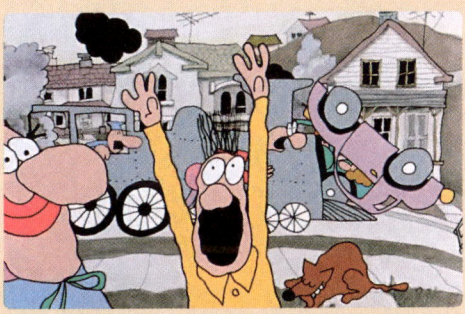

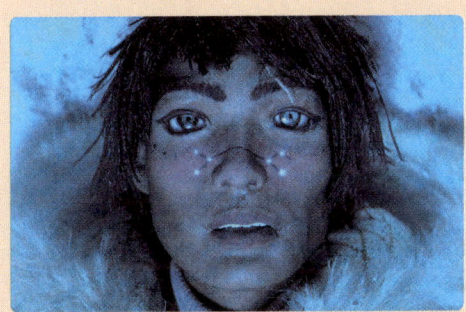

USA

Once Upon a Dream

🎬 Snow White and the Seven Dwarfs

Supervising Director: David Hand
Released: 1937

And so, we come to Disney. If this book were written in the style of a sweeping fairy tale, our grand villain may well be the great Disney empire. The Walt Disney Company has had a chokehold on family entertainment for decades, so much so that the company's own fortunes have an impact on mainstream animation as a whole.

Today, they're the imperialists of cinema, harvesting intellectual property and crowding out the competition with their spectacular, merchandisable franchises filled with sequels, prequels, remakes and spin-offs. Pixar, Star Wars, Marvel and Walt Disney Animation Studios itself are load-bearing pillars in this monolithic, ever-present cathedral of content.

For many of us, our first film experiences were watching Disney films, and for much of culture at large, Disney *is* animation. However outdated that notion may be, it has proved to be useful to have such a totemic presence

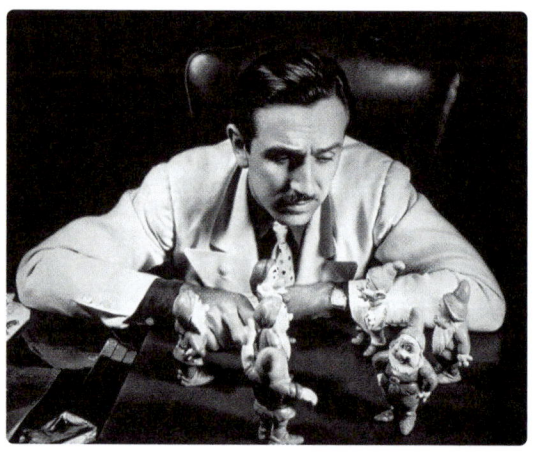

Right: The Founder. Walt Disney, a titan of world animation, pictured with miniature models of his iconic dwarf characters.

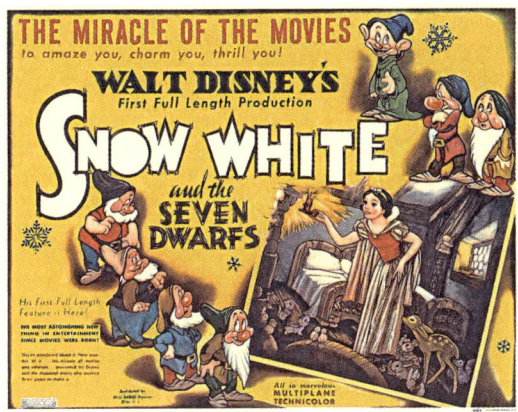

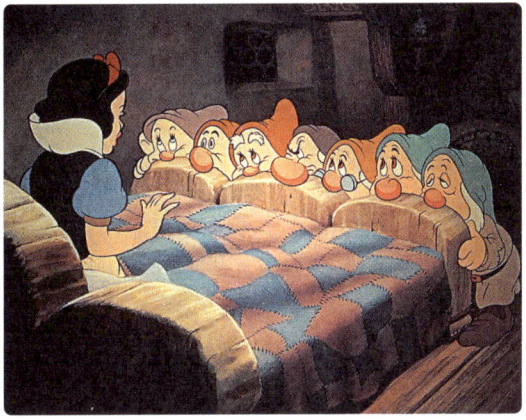

looming over animation history: an accepted norm to co-opt, compete with, fight against or deviate from. Many filmmakers in this book have been christened (or cursed) with the shorthand of being their country's answer to Disney: dream weavers beloved by audiences of all ages. Disney cracked the formula and epitomized a certain style of popular animation, one that's by turns magical, emotionally engaging, stylistically safe and ultimately conservative.

But in this corner of our Atlas let's wind back the clock to the 1930s, when Walt Disney's dream of making a feature-length animation was anything but a safe bet.

These were the days of the Golden Age of (American) Animation, an era of great innovation and huge popular success, with household name characters including

Above left: The Miracle of the Movies. This poster for the initial release of *Snow White* promised a whole new, magical world of animated cinema – and the film delivered.

Above right: Magnificent Seven. The gang of dwarfs are now household names, but there were several alternate characters left on the drawing board, including Jumpy, Wheezy and Baldy.

Below: With a Smile and a Song. *Snow White* is the source of many Disney traditions, including the long-running line of Disney Princesses.

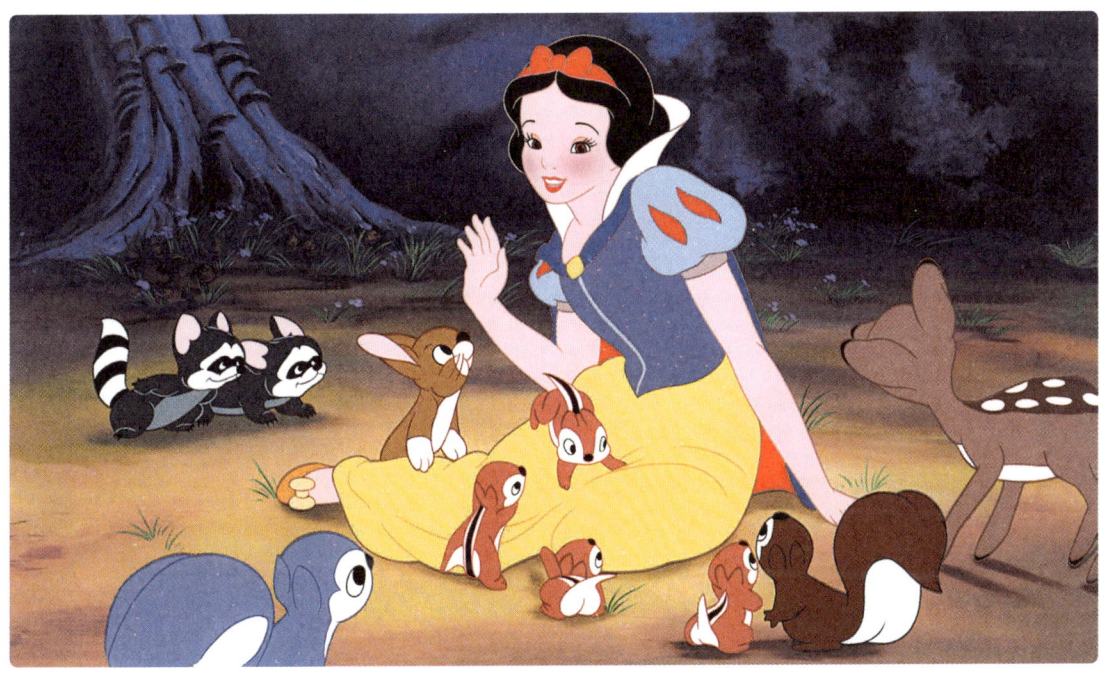

Mickey Mouse, Popeye and Bugs Bunny among many others. Crucially, these miniature marvels were all short films, and despite their clout with the public, they were still standing in the shadow of live-action cinema.

Walt Disney started developing what would become *Snow White and the Seven Dwarfs* in 1933, settling on the German fairy tale popularized by the Brothers Grimm as a compelling, magical story. "[*Snow White*] has every element that makes for great entertainment. It has comedy galore, romance, pathos, excitement, and suspense," Disney later said. It also had the potential to travel around the world. A tour through Europe in 1935 confirmed to Disney that the studio's brand was strong enough to make the leap to features: in certain cinemas, Disney's one-reel shorts were receiving top billing on cinema marquees, above their live-action counterparts, or they were being compiled into all-Disney feature programmes.

Back home, teams of "storymen" and story sketch artists were fleshing out the plot, its characters and world: finding a more uplifting, positive tone than the notoriously dark Grimm original. As production began in earnest, upwards of 500 crew members were brought on board (although some sources put that number north of 750), so team structure proved to be pivotal for such an ambitious production. David Hand, a veteran director of Disney shorts, was given the role of Supervising Director, leading a team of five Sequence Directors, while characters themselves were placed in the care of several senior artists, credited as Supervising Animators.

Over the course of the three-year-long production, budgets spiralled and the project became known as "Disney's Folly" – a sure-fire box office bomb that would send the creator of Mickey Mouse back to shorts with his tail between his legs. How wrong they were! A popular anecdote, shared by Walt himself, tells of a tense visit from the Bank of America executive Joe Rosenberg when the budget had ballooned to six times the original estimate. Disney pulled out all the stops to impress the reticent Rosenberg, who barely batted an eyelid all day – before saying to Walt, as he climbed into his car to leave, "Walt, that thing is going to make a hatful of money."

Below: Queen Witch. The original iconic baddie, the Evil Queen set the standard for countless compelling Disney villains.

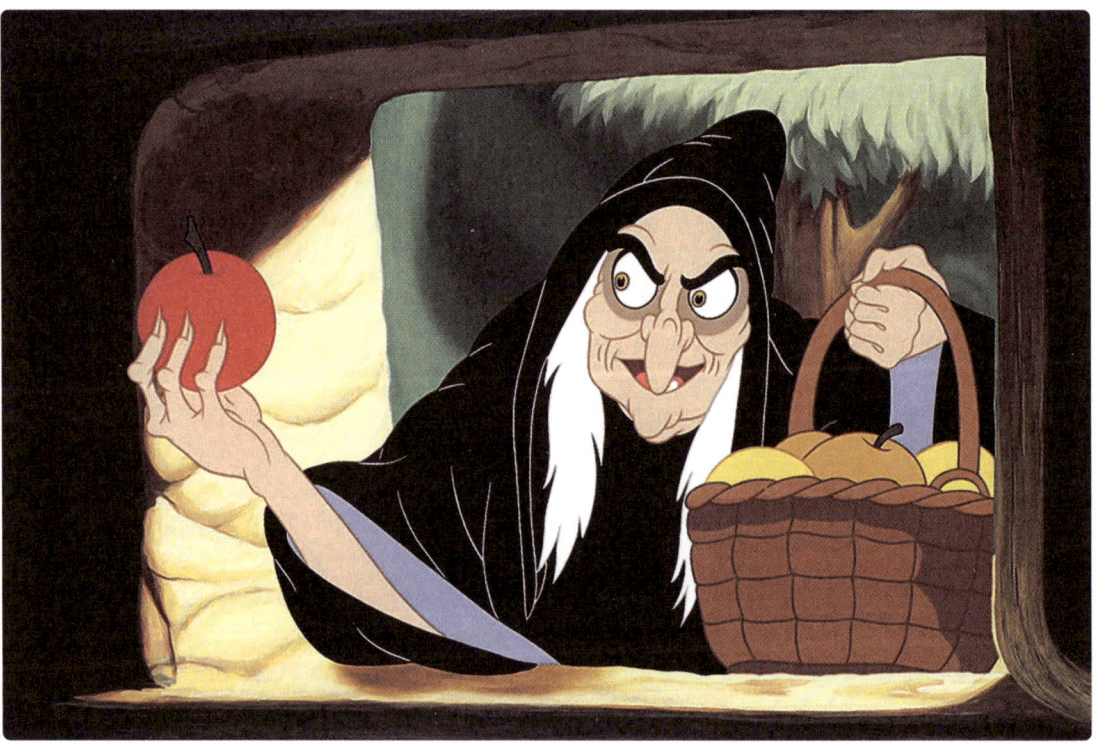

Snow White was a worldwide smash. For all its innovations in sumptuous production design, vivid colours and painted backgrounds, catchy songs and divine dance sequences, its major success lies in the remarkable consistency of its world, tone and look. Despite being divided up into separate sequences and crafted by scores of individual artists, *Snow White* is convincing as a feature film – one that invites you to lose yourself in it. And within it, there are standout scenes that still impress today, from the playful characterization of the dwarfs themselves, to the Evil Queen's tempestuous transformation into the aged witch, to the perilous, expressionistic sequence of Snow White's frightful flight through the haunted forest (which is partly to blame for the film's "A" rating on its UK release in 1938 – requiring kids under 16 to be accompanied by an adult).

Snow White was not the first animated feature – in this book alone, we have Lotte Reiniger's *The Adventures of Prince Achmed* (1926), which predated it by more than a decade (see page 70) – but it might as well have been. Disney had perfected a fresh, new, exciting art form on first try, and that "Disney Magic" was developed across a golden streak of now classic films, before the United States' entry into the Second World War put a pause on feature production. Across *Pinocchio* (1940), *Fantasia* (1940), *Dumbo* (1941) and *Bambi* (1942), we see a consolidation of the studio's house style, principles put in place by Disney's core animators, a group now known affectionately as the Nine Old Men, and passed down from generation to generation. And yet, watch these films with unclouded eyes, and you'll find them to be more experimental and innovative and *risky* than nostalgia and corporate narratives would have us believe.

It's easy to take Disney for granted, and hard to see past the parks, the cruises and the endless content. Yet, venturing through their library is a journey worth taking. And, since our history as animation lovers started with a podcast, it's only fair that we recommend one to lead the way: Disniversity, a delightful romp through the peaks and troughs of the Disney Animation story, hosted with infectious enthusiasm by Ben Travis and Dr Sam Summers.

Below: Kiss Alive. Whether it makes you swoon or cringe, Disney's depiction of a true love's kiss cemented the trope for generations to come.

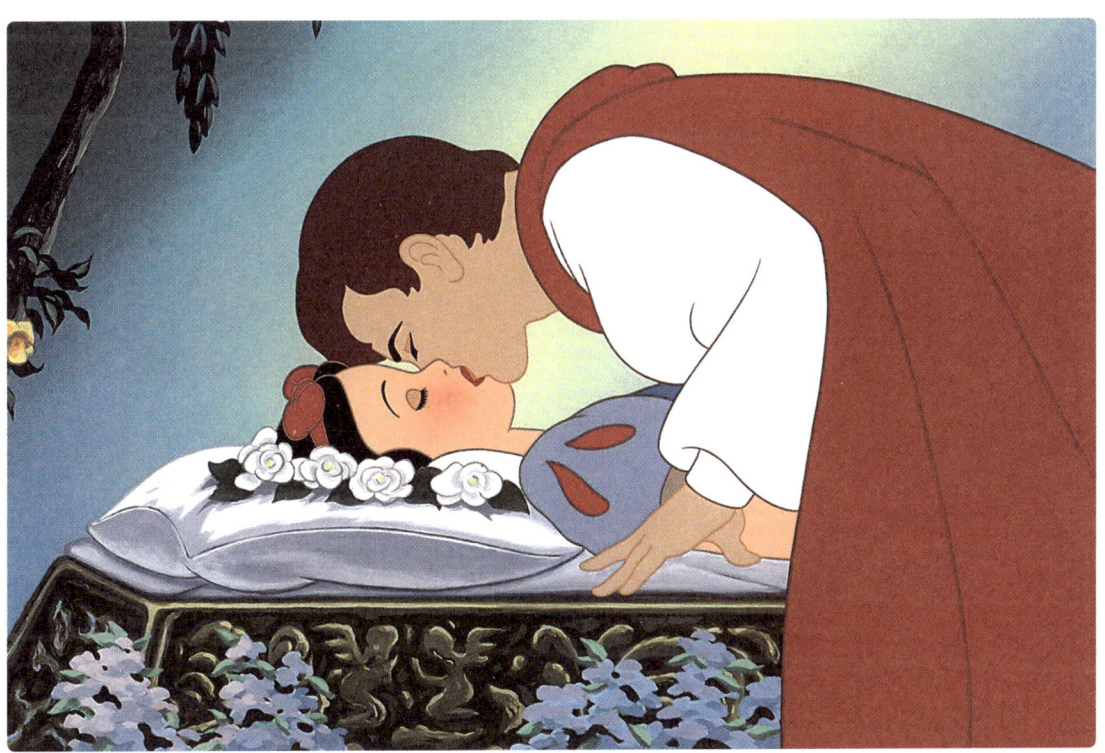

🎥 The Nightmare Before Christmas

Director: Henry Selick
Release date: 1993

First, let's get that possessory credit out of the way. Yes, it's *Tim Burton's The Nightmare Before Christmas*: he drew some initial sketches, wrote a poem, and pitched the idea to Disney when he was still an unknown quantity in the early-mid 1980s.

Years later, it was a different story. By that point, Burton had jumped ship and made a name for himself with *Beetlejuice* (1988), *Batman* (1989) and *Edward Scissorhands* (1990). Literally so: "Tim Burton" was turning into as much of a brand and overarching aesthetic as it was a simple filmmaker's name. And so, Disney wanted a piece of Burton.

But you could make the argument – and many have – that this *Nightmare* belongs just as much to director Henry Selick, screenwriter Caroline Thompson, composer and songwriter Danny Elfman or "visual consultant" (read: initial model designer, storyboard and concept artist) Rich Heinrichs. There are many fingerprints all over this perennial classic. Yet more than anything, the film's enduring appeal is down to its ability to cross over between holidays, generations and demographics, and to be embraced by endless waves of spooky kids and stop-motion fans alike.

It's testament to the riches of the Disney Renaissance period that, while they were on a roll with blockbusters like *The Little Mermaid* (1989), *Beauty and the Beast* (1991) and *Aladdin* (1992), studio bosses Jeffrey Katzenberg and David Hoberman found space in the slate for this offbeat project: its title is a pun on the opening of Clement Clarke Moore's festive poem, "A Visit from St. Nicholas" (often called "The Night Before Christmas" after the first line), and its form a spin on seasonal specials, such as Rankin-Bass's stop-motion *Rudolph the Red-Nosed Reindeer* (1968).

Like Jack Skellington, the King of Halloween Town who finds himself dreaming of a more festive vocation,

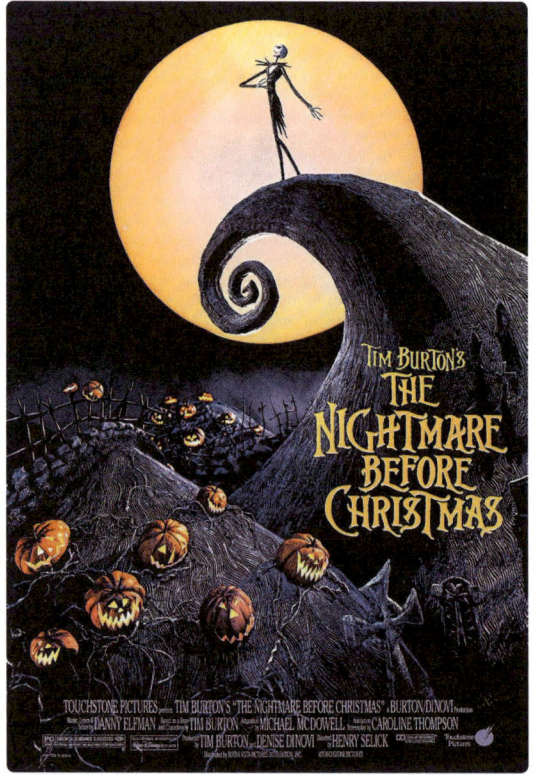

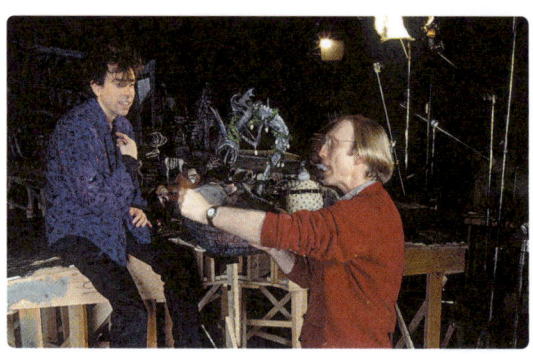

Above right: Welcome to My Nightmare. The addition of producer Tim Burton's name to the film's title is still controversial today.

Right: Tim & Henry's 18 million dollar movie. The former CalArts buddies reunite to revolutionize mainstream American animation.

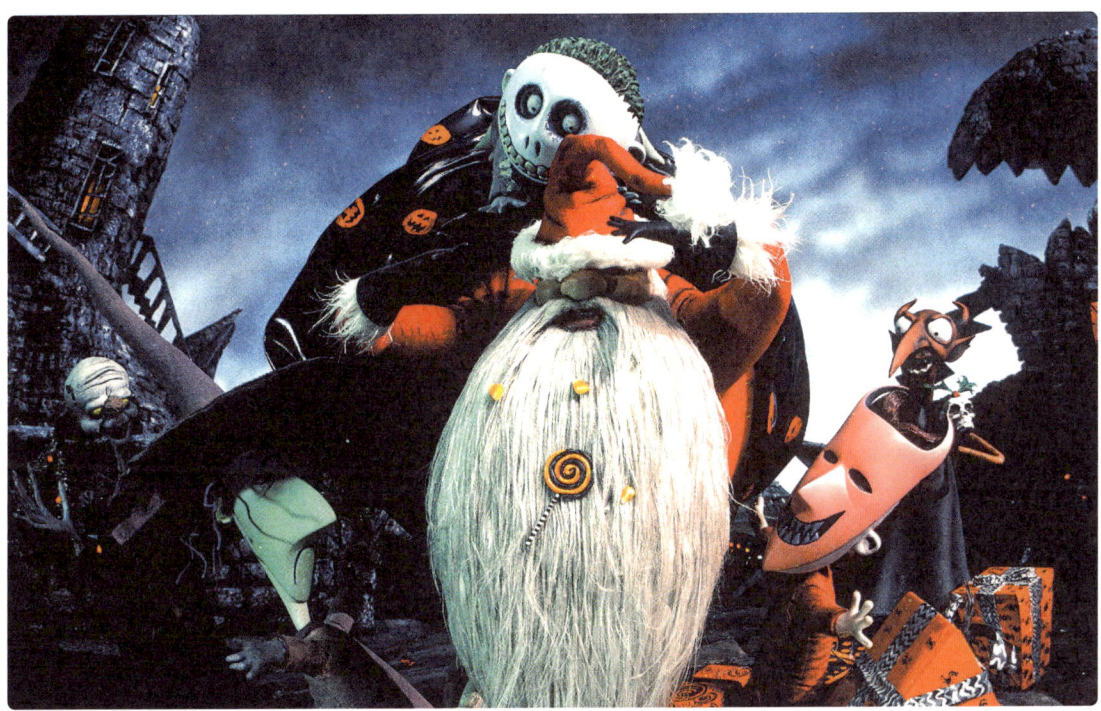

The Nightmare Before Christmas drew from well-worn tradition while pushing into new territory. It found its filmmakers at a creative turning point, too: Burton shuffling out of the shadows and into the mainstream; Elfman abandoning the hyperactive new wave of his band Oingo Boingo in favour of no-less-eccentric orchestral scores for film and television; and Selick, emerging as a filmmaker after years working on the fringes in a more experimental vein. (Track down his gloriously grotesque idents for MTV, or the wildly creative, mixed-media short Slow Bob in the Lower Dimensions.)

Burton and Selick met as students at the California Institute of the Arts. After graduating, both were funnelled into staff jobs at Disney, but neither was an ideal fit for the production line: they needed freedom to be themselves. But whereas Burton brought together influences including kitsch Americana, Universal monster horror and the twisted sensibilities of Charles Addams and Edward Gorey, Selick was deeply immersed in

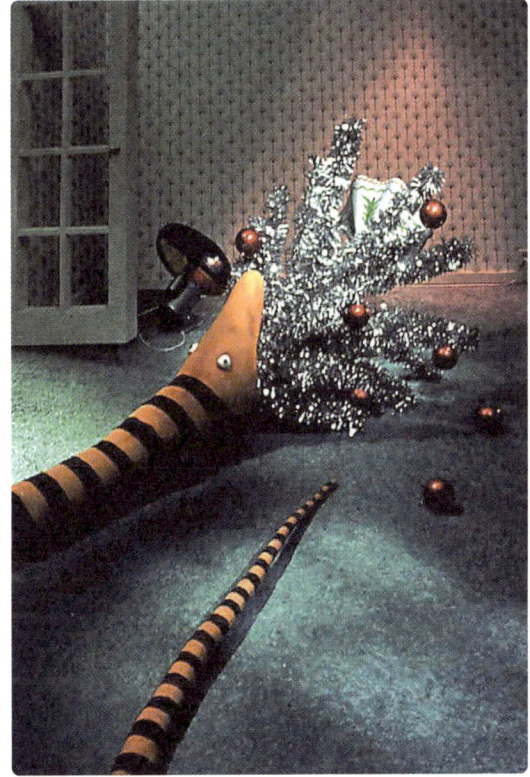

Above: Season's kidnappings. At the heart of Nightmare's unique appeal is the collision of Halloween fear and Christmas cheer.

Right: Wreck the halls. Scenes in which Halloween Town's vision of Christmas goes awry are a devilish delight.

animation as a form of artistic expression, from the cut-out silhouettes of Lotte Reiniger's *The Adventures of Prince Achmed* (1926) to the eerie Czech stop-motion of Jan Švankmajer's *Jabberwocky* (1971) and Jiří Trnka's *The Hand* (1965), and the off-kilter weirdness of Raoul Servais's *Harpya* (1978).

All of that and more is stirred into the style of *The Nightmare Before Christmas*, from its expressionistic set design to its delightful cast of weird and wonderful characters. Even as a devout stop-motion fan, Selick wanted the film to feel like more than just "toys on a table top with two glaring lights", and he was assisted in that aim by a crew of over one hundred, working with hundreds of models and sets to create a consistent world rich in detail. Looking back, decades on, it's easy to forget that, on top of all its creative innovations, *The Nightmare Before Christmas* was a quietly groundbreaking technical marvel, using smaller, computer-assisted cameras to give the proceedings a new sense of scale, dimension and cinematic flair. Director of cinematography and visual effects supervisor Pete Kozachik and his team garnered an Oscar nomination for Best Visual Effects – a rare honour for an animated film – but ultimately lost to Steven Spielberg's gargantuan hit, *Jurassic Park* (1993).

Jurassic Park famously pointed to a predominantly digital, computer-generated future for mainstream cinema – and animation too – but *The Nightmare Before Christmas* set the mould for a new kind of stop-motion feature. Over a decade and a half later, the production company LAIKA picked up the baton, and brought in Henry Selick to direct *Coraline* (2009), which, like *Nightmare*, epitomized this spooky corner of stop-motion animation for another generation.

Yet, despite LAIKA's efforts across several productions, including *ParaNorman* (2012) and *Kubo and the Two Strings* (2016), and the advocacy of live-action filmmakers who always seemed destined to turn their hand to animation, such as Wes Anderson (*Fantastic Mr Fox*, 2009) and Guillermo del Toro (*Pinocchio*, 2022), feature-length stop-motion animation has never attained the crossover mega-success enjoyed by major studio animation in 2D or 3D CG styles. It remains more of a cult concern, and the preserve of artists and visionaries: nightmares, dreams, and all that lies in between, hand-crafted with care and imagination.

Below: Scary Christmas. Pumpkin King Jack Skellington tries his best to be a convincing Santa Claus.

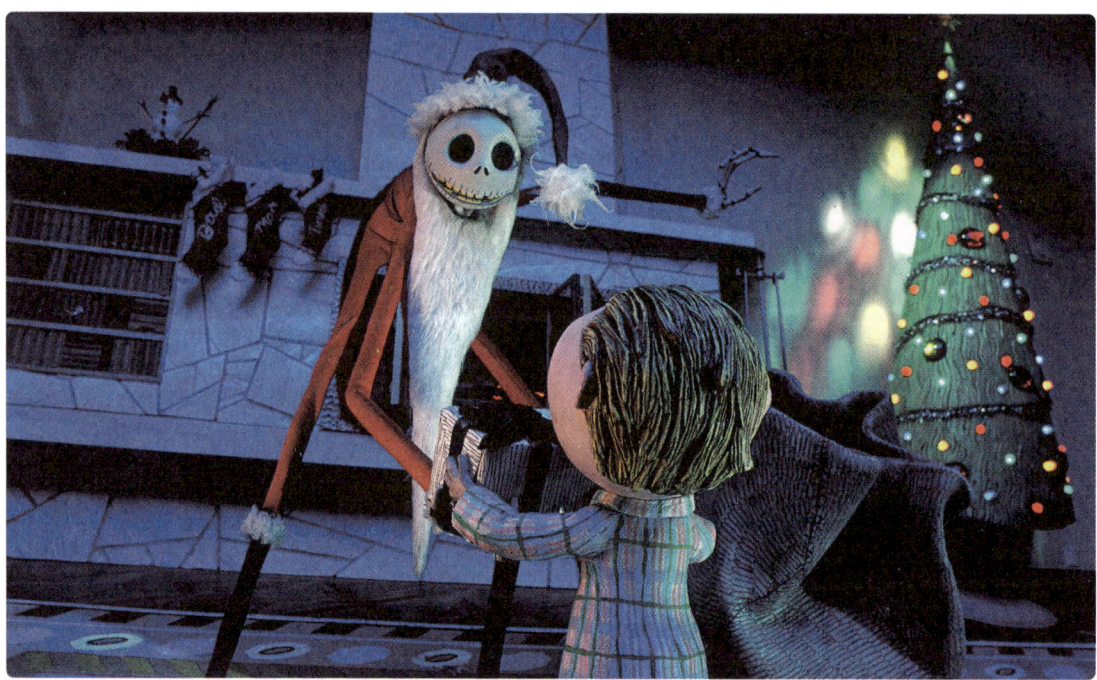

🎬 Toy Story

Director: John Lasseter
Release date: 1995

Inanimate objects coming to life – that's animation. So, when an upstart tech company wanted to prove that their computer-generated images could be used to tell a feature-length film, one which dispelled the myth that digital couldn't work alongside digits and that CG could actually rival the hand-drawn animated greats, they told a story about exactly that. Inanimate objects coming to life – *Toy Story*.

If you're reading this book about animation, you're probably familiar with the talking cowboy toy Woody, his relationship with fresh out of the box Space Ranger action figure Buzz Lightyear, and their rivalry, friendship and love for their pre-teen owner Andy. But, there's more than one story here that tells Pixar's tale, both past and future, so we need to first take a short detour, into, well, shorts. In an early scene of *Toy Story* (1995), Woody stands in front of a bookshelf, and behind him rests the spine for a title called *The Adventures of André & Wally B.* This is a reference to a short of the same name which was the studio's first ever film, before they were even a studio (and some original *Toy Story* viewers may have seen it in what became the traditional short film before the Pixar feature). Made in 1984, it's a plodding comedic battle between a humanoid figure and a bee. They're made of smooth, basic, computerized shapes that look more like an infant's set of building blocks, let alone something with a pulse; and while it might struggle to lift a big response from viewers now, it had a big, big buzz. Created by what was then known as the Lucasfilm Computer Graphics Project (yep, that Lucasfilm), *André* paved the way for their next short, featuring a character who appears in every Pixar film – a lamp. *Luxo Jr.* (1986) is the story of a big desk lamp and its small counterpart (who loves playing with a yellow and blue ball with a red star on it), and now that little lamp hops up onto the top shelf of the capital "I" in the Pixar logo in the studio's ident, playing ahead of all their features. Their following

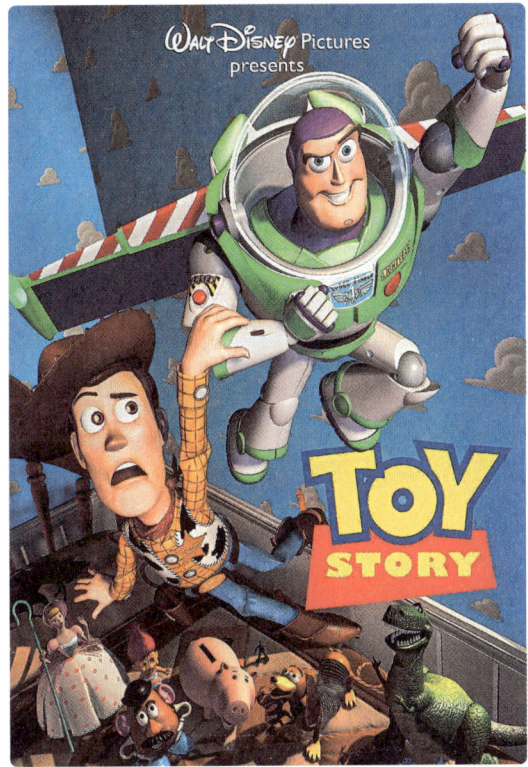

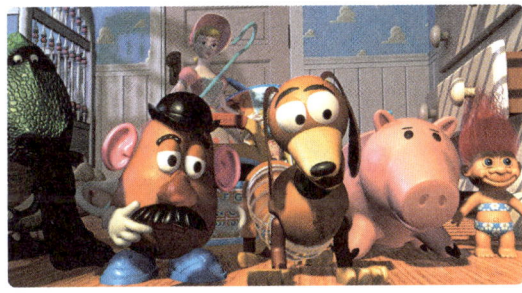

Above right: To infinity and beyond. Woody and Buzz take off, launching a franchise with them.

Right: Toys club. Although the cowboy and Space Ranger get the spotlight, *Toy Story*'s supporting characters are key to its enduring popularity.

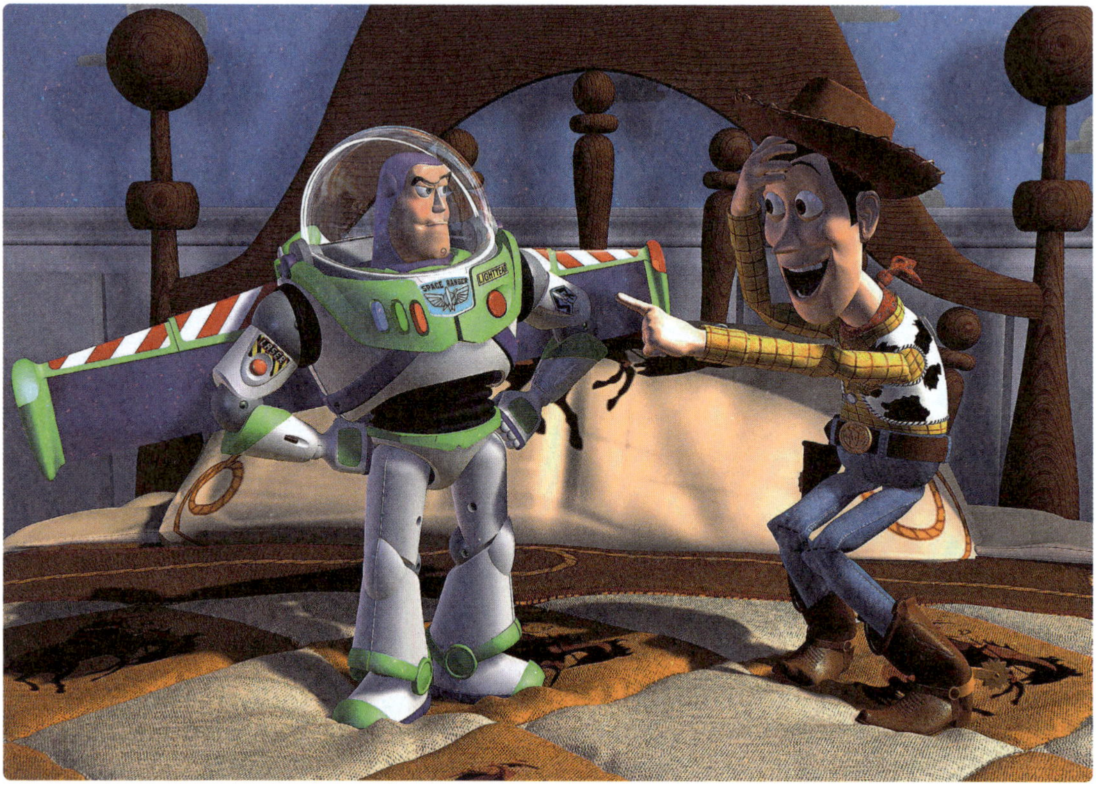

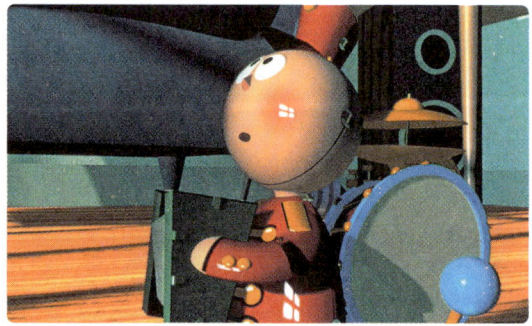

short *Red's Dream* (1987), about a unicycle who wants to be a star, continued an interest in personalized, anthropocentric devices, which was furthered by *Tin Toy* (1988), about a baby's terrorized musical plaything. The latter won the Academy Award for Best Animated Short Film, and while *Tin Toy*'s heavy-limbed and pinch-lipped baby character now creates nightmares for anyone who stumbles upon them while browsing Disney+, they marked the infancy of Pixar's feature film life.

Tin Toy's success led to discussions about a 30-minute special, expanding on ideas in the short, and with financing secured (having Steve Jobs on board often helped with that) and the completion of 1989 short *Knick Knack*, they transitioned the idea into what would become their first feature.

It wasn't perfect right away, though: early versions of their concept had a bawdy sense of humour, with Woody operating as a snarky, unlikeable figure; but thankfully, after a marathon rewriting session, the *Toy Story* story came together. Animators and computer processors worked tirelessly, and seven years after *Tin Toy*, that now familiar cloudy sky wallpaper first

appeared, Randy Newman started singing and a phenomenon had arrived.

As Andy's room was initially an alien landscape to Buzz, so it could have been to audiences. This was a shiny new world that looked like it had just had its plastic wrap peeled off, but toys, with their naturally vacant,

Top: Child's playthings. In early drafts of *Toy Story* Woody was a far less likeable character, becoming more sympathetic with later drafts.

Above: Pixar's fascination with toy stories began with *Tin Toy*, a short from 1988, which won the Academy Award for Best Animated Short.

hard-shelled exteriors, were the perfect prospectors to leap into the waxy ravines of the uncanny valley – and viewers were happy to join them. Made for $30 million, *Toy Story* made over 10 times that and ultimately created a lot more than just box office receipts. Pixar's follow-up, the insect adventure *A Bug's Life*, arrived in 1998, swiftly chased the next year by the chaotically constructed but stunningly successful *Toy Story 2*; and in a few short years Pixar had gone from potential IT folly to filmmaking heavyweight.

Three decades on from its first entry, the *Toy Story* series continues with theatrical sequels, streaming shorts, video games and endless merchandise; and since they first lit up the screen for toys, Luxo Jr.'s bulb has put (among others) bugs, monsters, fish, superheroes, cars, rats, robots, old people, young people, dead people, fish people, dinosaurs, pandas, elements, emotions and even souls in its spotlight. It's not just inanimate objects anymore.

Below: Toy racers. Buzz, Woody and RC give chase in *Toy Story's* unforgettable finale.

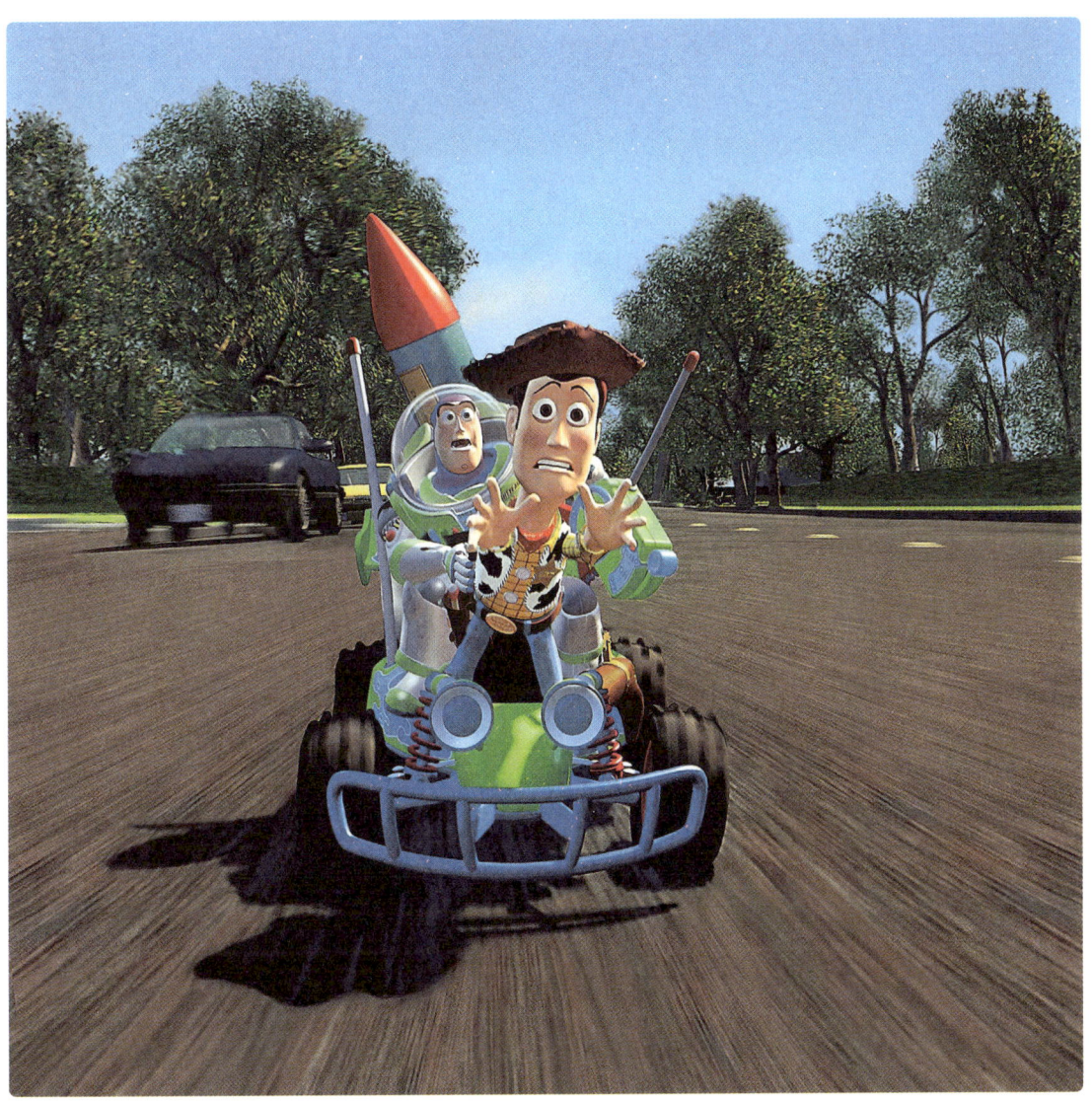

👁 Further Viewing

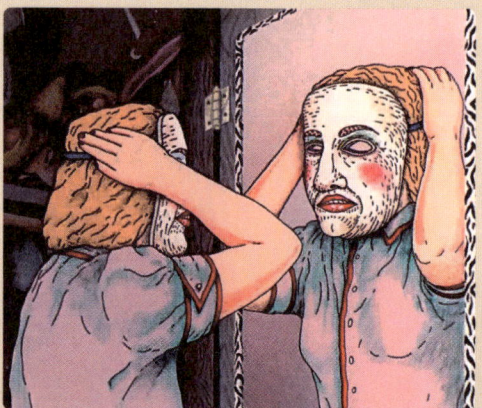

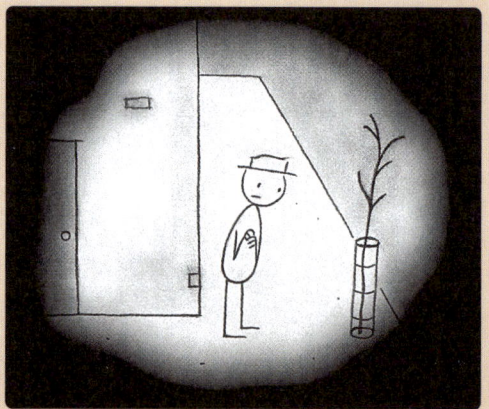

This is where we have to admit defeat. Like with French, Japanese and Czech animation, we have no hope of capturing the full sweep of American animation in just one chapter. You'd need a whole book for that. (Maybe one day...)

For now, we can only provide a whistle-stop tour. In this chapter, we chose to focus on features that epitomized three distinct production styles: hand-drawn 2D animation, 3D CGI animation and stop-motion. Follow each of these art forms down their respective rabbit holes and there is so much to discover.

Our chosen format for this book has led us to neglect some real titans of animation, past and present, including *Looney Tunes* legend Chuck Jones (*Duck Amuck*, 1953), Faith and John Hubley (*The Hole*, 1962), Ralph Bakshi (*Fritz the Cat*, 1972), Brad Bird (*The Iron Giant*, 1999) and Genndy Tartakovsky (*Primal*, 2019), and to leave out some personal favourites from the small screen like *It's the Great Pumpkin, Charlie Brown* (1966), *Over the Garden Wall* (2014) and *Scavengers Reign* (2023).

American animation is dominated by Disney and the mainstream studio blockbuster, and we'll admit we've perpetuated that a little here. Let us carve

out space, then, to salute some of the independent mavericks, such as Don Hertzfeldt (*It's Such a Beautiful Day*, 2011), Suzan Pitt (*Asparagus*, 1979), Bill Plympton (*Your Face*, 1987), Sally Cruikshank (*Quasi at the Quackadero*, 1975) and Kirsten Lepore (*Bottle*, 2010).

Away from the world of intellectual property and franchise filmmaking, there is a spirit of invention and innovation in American animation that dates all the way back to Windsor McCay's pioneering experiments *How a Mosquito Operates* (1912) and *Gertie the Dinosaur* (1914). It's ironic, then, that American animation's greatest tribute, and perhaps its greatest achievement, comes in the form of Robert Zemeckis's *Who Framed Roger Rabbit*, a live-action hybrid film that salutes the characters and creativity of mid-century cartoons – and which was animated in Britain by Canadian expat Richard Williams, no less!

Above left: Eat Your Greens. The colourful, surreal style of animator Suzan Pitt is seen in full effect in *Asparagus*.

Above right: Experimental, offbeat and devastatingly sad, Don Hertzfeldt's *It's Such a Beautiful Day* is a masterpiece of independent animation.

Elsewhere in North America

Mexico is North America's second-largest country by population, but while its animation industry has produced popular popcorn films for local audiences, it is yet to fully emerge on the international stage. However, signs point to that changing in the very near future.

Hits at home include the egg-based antics of Huevocartoon and the CG franchises of Ánima Estudios, including their retooling of the classic Hanna-Barbera character Top Cat for Latin American audiences (*Don Gato y su Pandilla*, 2011). Smaller companies like Cinema Fantasma have straddled borders, making idents for Cartoon Network and Adult Swim, and producing the stop-motion miniseries *Frankelda's Book of Spooks* (2021) for HBO Max Latin America.

Cinema Fantasma founders Roy and Arturo Ambriz were mentored by Guillermo del Toro, a Mexican filmmaker who found great success in Hollywood. Director Jorge Gutierrez has also built his career in the States, with projects such as *El Tigre: The Adventures of Manny Rivera* (2007), *The Book of Life* (2014) and *Maya and the Three* (2021), but while those are made by US-based studios, Gutierrez seeks to share his distinctly Mexican storytelling and worldview with global audiences.

For del Toro's part, he has sought to stimulate and promote the Mexican community, setting up scholarships and founding the studio El Taller del Chucho in Guadalajara as an incubator for local talent. Then, when production was underway on his long-gestating and ultimately Oscar-winning stop-motion feature *Pinocchio* (2022), he made space for the Taller team to contribute to the project, alongside ShadowMachine in the USA and Mackinnon & Saunders in the United Kingdom.

Mere months after *Pinocchio*'s Oscar success, the Annecy International Animation Film Festival announced that their 2023 edition would include a deep focus on Mexican animation, featuring workshops and screenings with del Toro and Gutierrez, and several programmes collecting shorts charting the whole history of Mexican animation, from 1935 to a present day full of promise.

Elsewhere in the region, you can find some real curios, such as Juan Padrón's Cuban animation *Vampires in Havana* (1985) – a bawdy tale of clashing cultures and caricatures as European bloodsuckers and Chicago mobsters descend on Cuba to fight over an experimental formula that can allow vampires to survive in the daylight.

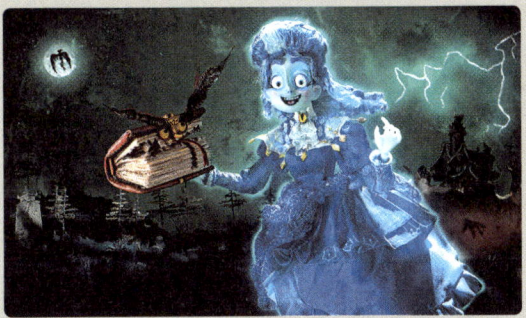

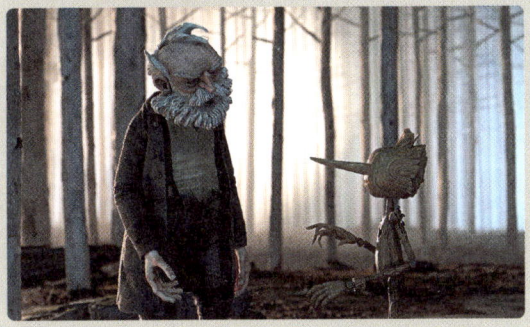

This odd offering played at the London Film Festival in 1986, where programmer Sheila Whitaker predicted that it "could well become a cult".

Flash forward to 2024, and the London Film Festival shone the spotlight on another, very different feature from Latin America, Tomás Pichardo Espaillat's dazzling debut *Olivia & the Clouds*, which received a special mention from the First Feature Competition jury. Looking at a romantic relationship from different perspectives with a light magic realist twist, the film adopts a dizzying array of animation styles (from claymation and cut-outs to photography and collage, alongside more conventional hand-drawn and digital techniques) as it weaves its story through the hazy, unreliable narration of memory. If you ask us, it's impossible to watch this film and not leave the cinema flush with excitement for the future of animation as an art form.

Above top: The stop-motion series *Frankelda's Book of Spooks*, produced by Cinema Fantasma, points to a bright future for Mexican animation.

Above below: Who nose? Guillermo del Toro's magnificent adaptation of *Pinocchio* offered a deeply philosophical take on the fairy tale.

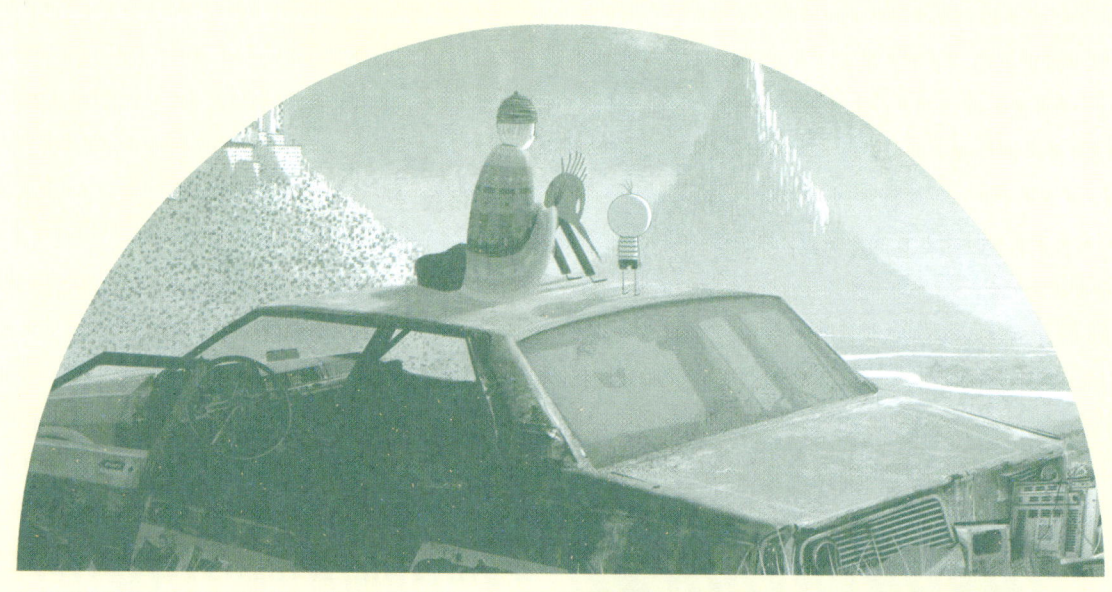
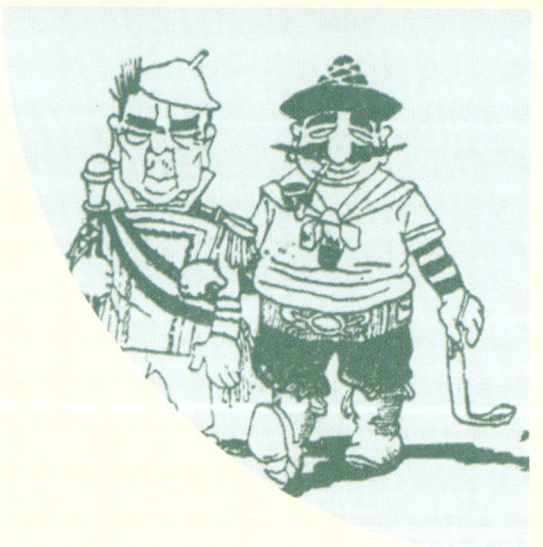
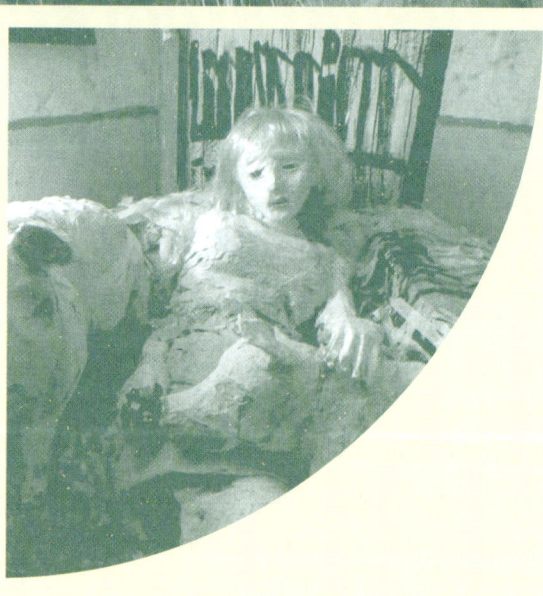

South America

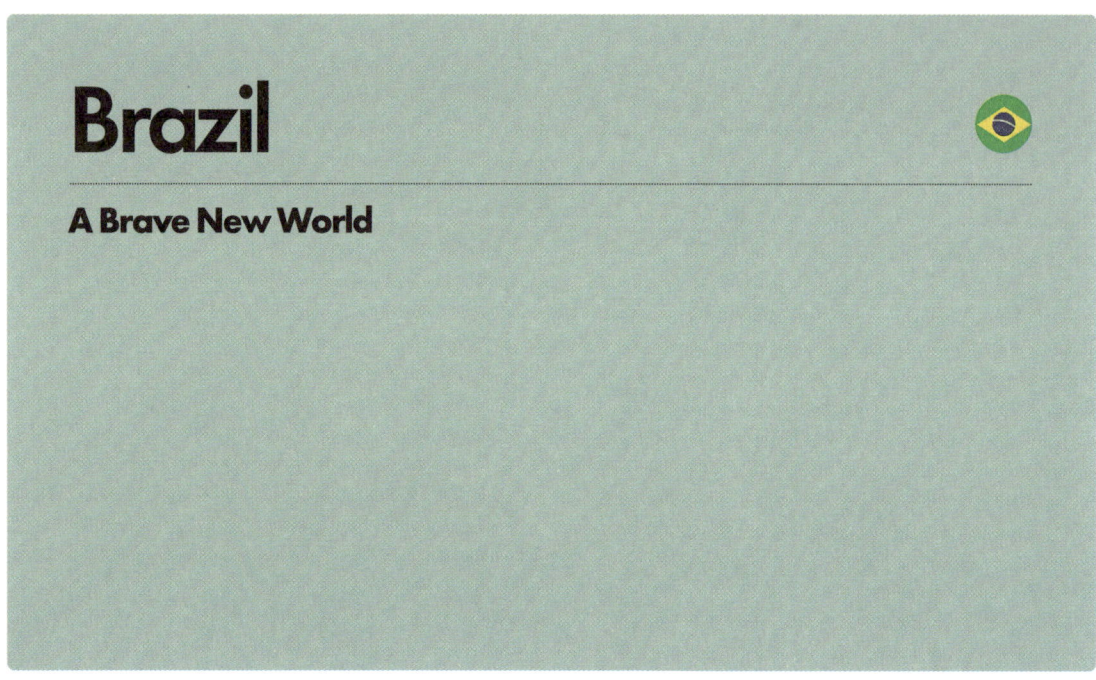

Brazil

A Brave New World

Boy and the World

Director: Alê Abreu
Released: 2013

While some hyper-real and flashy animation might be reductively described as being made for kids, there aren't many animated films that feel like they're made by kids, something which makes *Boy and the World* (2013) so special.

Brazilian director Alê Abreu's second film isn't actually made by children, but its scratchy pencil lines, colourful squiggles of crayon and dappled drags of pastel do feel like they could've been lifted from the liberated sketchbook pages of youth; and while the images and characters they form are beautiful, the idea that young viewers might see styles comparable to their own bouncing into life, is even more so. This isn't just animation as a storytelling device, it's an intergenerational call to take up the pencil, and celebrate the artistry of life.

Told silently, albeit with some gibberish made from reversed Portuguese dialogue, Abreu's film is specific and everyday, universal and eternal. Opening and closing with kaleidoscopic spinning mandalas that are as cellular as they are galactic, the story between follows

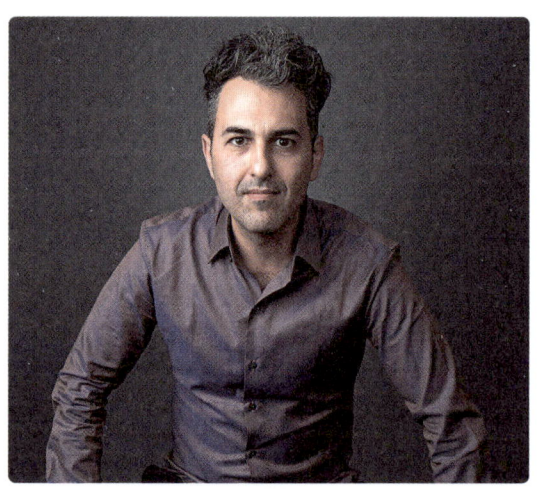

a young boy, made up of a few crude lines for a body and a simple face, like an unsewn button, resting on top. The boy spends his time frolicking in a brilliant green patchwork of natural wonders, cherishing his loving family life and the music they share together, the notes of which float through the air like bubbles of Fanta; until one day his father takes the train to work and the boy begins a journey to find him. Taking him across fields, oceans and cities, the boy's quest could be a face-value race to catch the commuter train, but in Abreu and his team's hands it takes on the form of a metaphysical epic. *Boy and the World* tackles loss at its most painful (his father's skull-shaped head surely not a coincidence) and a lifetime spent trying to navigate it – as well as the stunning but terrifying world in which that loss resides.

The boy's adventure sees him first swept into working in a cotton field with an old man. One of the highlights

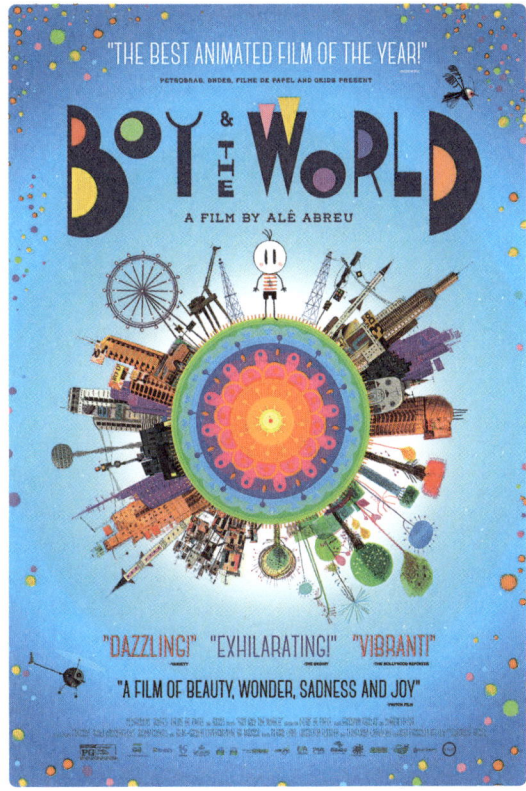

Opposite: Boy in the world of animation. Director Alê Abreu brought this expressive, universal tale to vibrant life.

Right: Although acclaimed, *Boy and the World* lost out at the Academy Awards, where *Inside Out* took the Animated Feature prize in 2016 instead.

Below: Beats, roots and leaves. Abreu's film uses music and rhythm to bring together themes of heritage and independence.

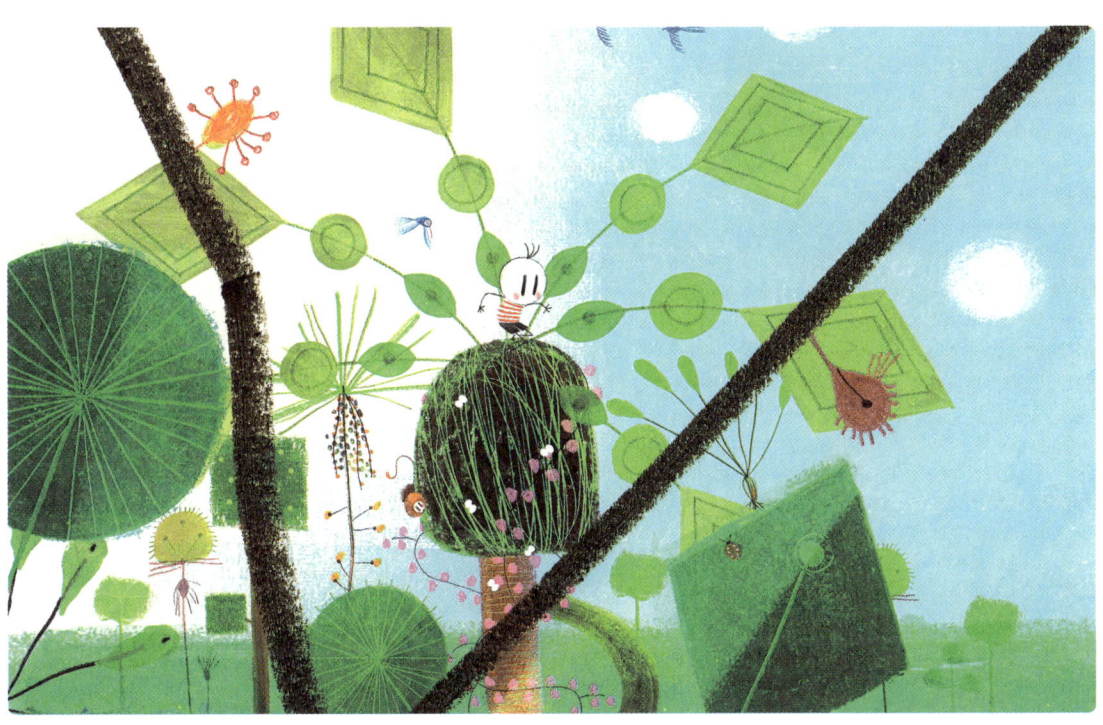

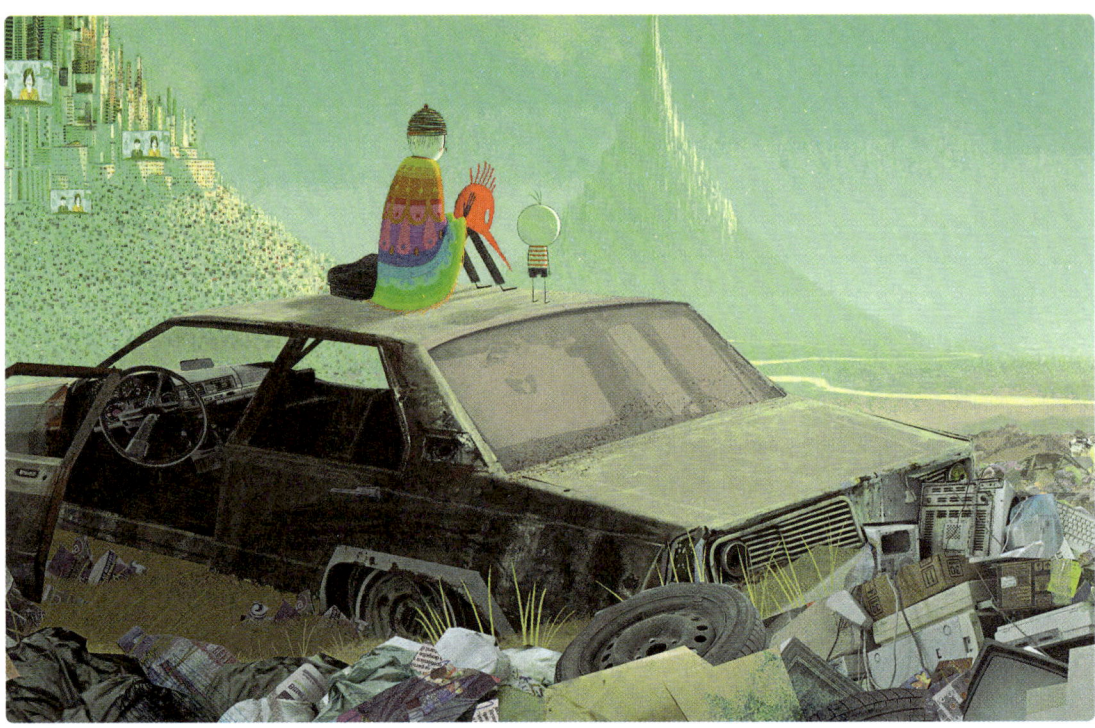

of the chapter is a musically charged sequence where agriculture is choreographed with satisfying symmetry – the harmony between nature and worker briefly enjoyed, before the lockstep march of industry stifles the waltz. A straight road out of the farm offers a reprieve of stability, until the line of the road wobbles and swiftly morphs into a crashing sea (how's that for a metaphor?) and the boy eventually arrives on the shores of a city. Here, the film stretches its visual ambition to great effect, with the boy's innocently sketched life consumed by a nightmarish city. Here, the bricks of buildings are made from newspaper clippings and the people have mismatched, cut-and-pasted facial features that feel like the work of a plastic surgeon making a ransom note.

Throughout his odyssey the boy occasionally encounters the luminescent, rambling sound of a musical procession, whose bright sound offers spiritual and literal light, the musical plumes following in its tracks as a reminder of his father. In the city, however, the marching is far more dystopian, with puffs of suffocating black smog spilling from the rigidly choreographed – and rigid-sounding – band that pounds its sharply angled streets. Accompanied by unsettling, metallic contraptions that are the shape of elephants but which wield the cannons

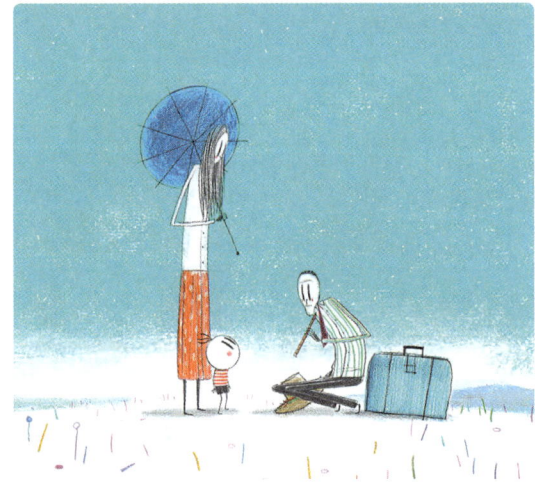

Above top: Points of reflection. The landscapes and narrative pace of *Boy and the World* asks viewers to consider their own horizons.

Above: On the case. A father leaving for work sends the film's protagonist on a metaphorical and literal journey of a lifetime.

Opposite above: Collage education. As the boy grows up and enters an urban environment, the film's textures start to change and overlap.

Opposite: *Rio, Ferdinand.* Despite directing both for Blue Sky Studios, Carlos Saldanha has a Brazil football shirt signed by Pelé in his office, rather than one from a former Manchester United defender.

of gunships, it's a haunting reminder of the bastardizing trajectory that industrialization can have on culture and nature, sapping their individuality and prejudicing them against difference. This environmentalist messaging is explored most dramatically in a striking sequence of live action montage, as the expressionistic world of the boy becomes our own and images of global devastation flood the screen, urgently collapsing the distance between the abstract and reality. But, as the reprieves with the roaming carnival remind us: freedom, inspiration and beautiful colour can be found by listening to the artists outside of the dominant systems. This film is a prime example.

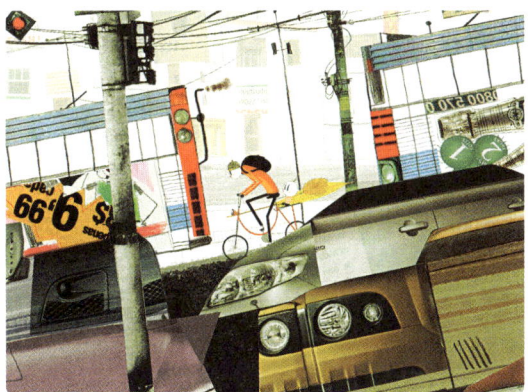

👁 Further Viewing

Brazil's animation industry dates back over a century to a now-lost political short, *Kaiser* (1917), directed by the cartoonist Álvaro Marins, also known as Seth. In the 2013 documentary, *Luz, Anima, Ação*, which traced the history of Brazilian animation back to this starting point, a group of artists were brought together to recreate the film in their own image, with a list of contributors that acts as a who's who of the country's animation industry. Alongside *Boy and the World* director Alê Abreu, contributors included Marcos Magalhães, a veteran of the industry whose simple yet profoundly political cartoon *Meow* (1982) offers a cat's-eye view of social upheaval, empty-calorie consumerism and American influence, to Cannes prize-winning

effect. His film *Animando* (1987), made during an apprenticeship at the National Film Board of Canada, is even better: a wildly creative and virtuosic short that breaks down and recreates a simple animation of a character walking across a dizzying array of different styles, from pencil, to ink, to paint, to paper cut-out, to sand, to clay, to etches on the film itself. Also involved in the *Kaiser* project was Carlos Saldanha, the Brazilian-born filmmaker with perhaps the furthest-reaching international reputation, thanks to his time working at Blue Sky Studios, where he directed a handful of commercially successful films in the *Ice Age* and *Rio* franchises, as well as the Oscar-nominated *Ferdinand* (2017).

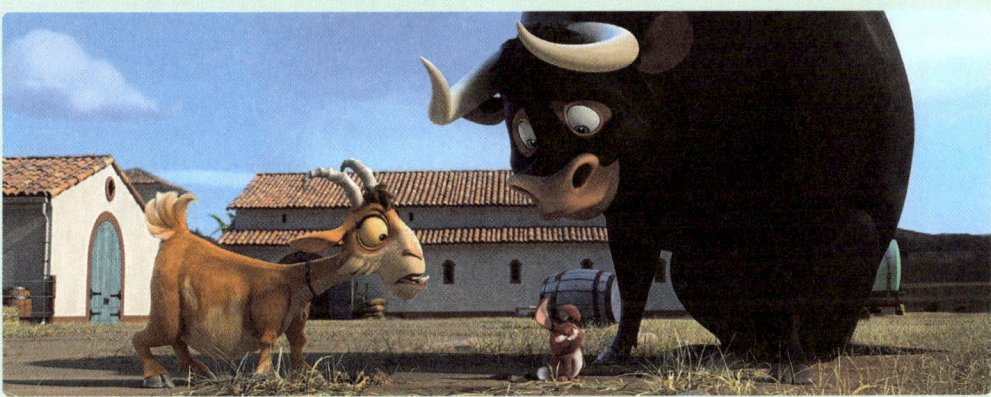

Chile

Innovation Finds a New Home

📷 The Wolf House

Directors: Cristobal León and Joaquín Cociña
Released: 2018

There might be a young girl in the woods, a family of pigs and a looming, lupine threat, but don't mistake *The Wolf House* for a bedtime story, unless you're after a sleepless night.

The debut feature by Cristobal León and Joaquín Cociña – who'd previously made shorts, music videos and gallery work – is an unsettling creation untethered by style or narrative, which brings viewers inside a phenomenally haunting house, locks the door and reveals a frightening and fresh take on the animated form.

The film is inspired by a real, secretive Germany colony, which was founded in Chile in the 1960s and became a torture centre during Augusto Pinochet's dictatorship over the country. *The Wolf House* begins as a live action propaganda film for a version of the camp, but this grainy "reality" is soon dispensed with and the rotten fairy tale beneath emerges. A young woman called Maria – blonde, blue-eyed, blue-dressed – escapes the colony and is pursued by a wolf, finding

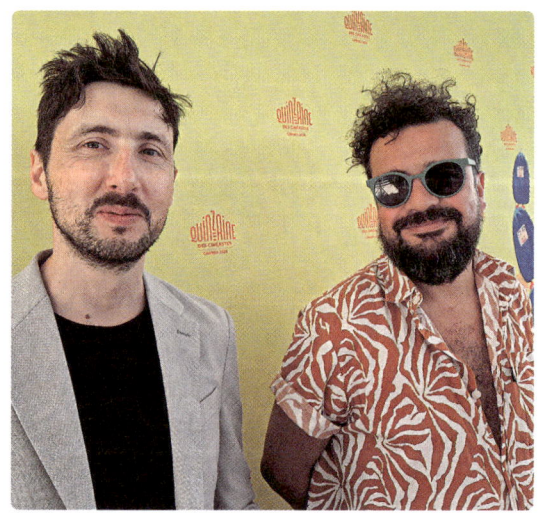

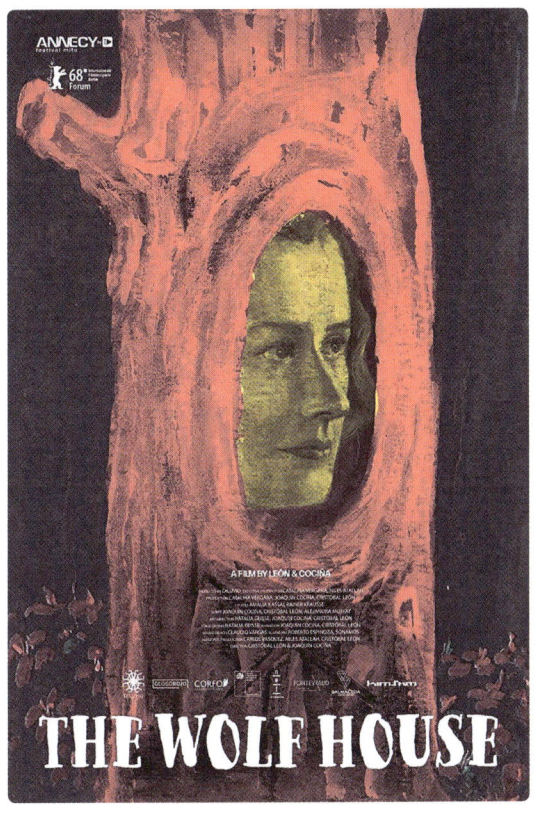

THE WOLF HOUSE

A FILM BY LEÓN & COCIÑA

refuge in an abandoned house. Within its queasy walls, however, there are no rules of structure, time or material. Like a possessed version of an illusion-cake based game show, here, anything can be animated. Solid walls and doors appear as such, and are then covered over and repositioned, with coats of paint warping perspectives and turning rooms into labyrinths; Maria herself may be an oily 2D figure on a glass plane, interacting with a 3D background, before popping into rigid papier mâché depth and then disintegrating into a tangle of masking tape and foam; piles of dirt flow into rooms, building or destroying furniture with their tide; and the wolf, heard but unseen, remains omnipresent and oppressive. As viewers, we are positioned in an almost spectral manner, floating through this dark, swelling space, like a slasher in a horror film, the frame constantly stuttering, as if with the knowledge that every inch of our surrounding is far scarier than us.

Opposite: The Wolf Pack. Directors Cristobal León and Joaquín Cociña.

Left: Family Tree. *The Wolf House* follows a young woman's distorted maternal journey inside a noxious new home.

Below: Puppet masters. León and Cociña use many forms, including puppets, to tell their nightmarish tale.

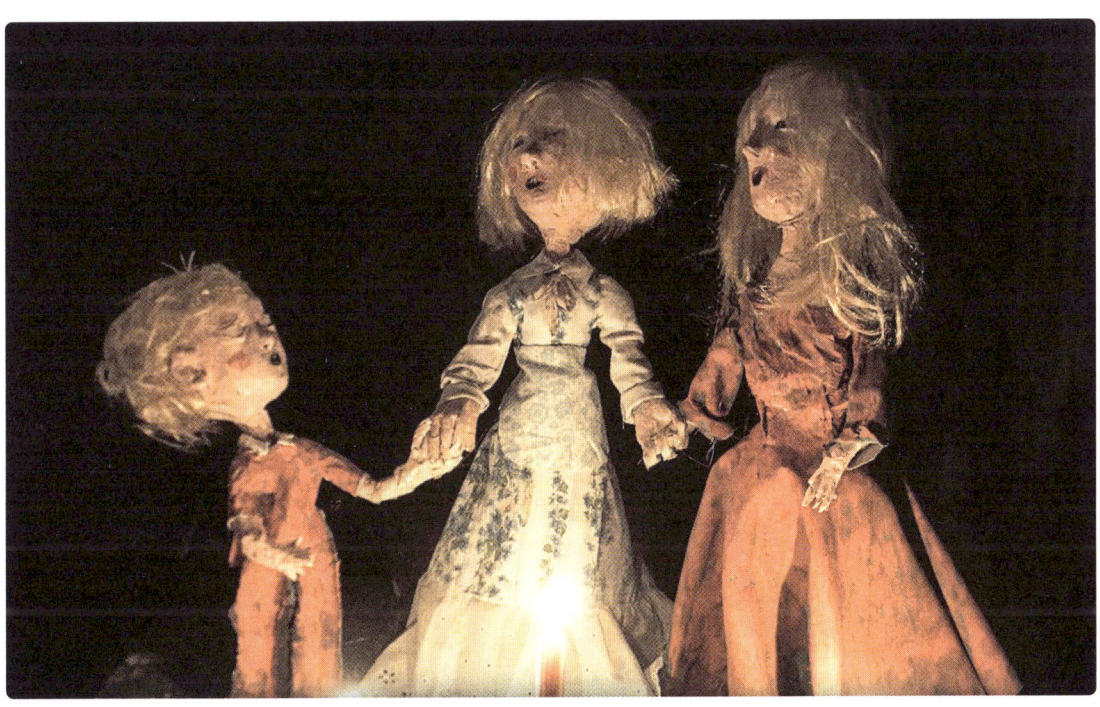

Then come the pigs. Dreamed up by Maria to stave off her isolation, these demonic creations allow the directors' experience in puppetry, stop-motion and 2D animation to shine brightly (or darkly, more appropriately). Initially existing in a form of constant disintegration, their paper and tape exteriors fluttering between frames like a child's forgotten art project, the pigs transition into semi-humanoid form and eventually into blonde and blue-eyed figures – to anyone still afraid of the porcine-morphing buffet in *Spirited Away* (2001), don't try this. Maria's life with her "children" becomes a twisted domestic tale of inverting power dynamics and unpredictable transformation, with innocent moments at toilets and dining tables lacquered in treacly thick paint, swarmed with bugs and stabbed with metastasizing paper stalagmites (a visual found in the directors' other work, notably their video for 'Thin Thing', the song by Radiohead spin-off The Smile) and scored to what sounds like the gurgling panicked foghorns of a sinking armada.

Although the full context of *The Wolf House* is never made explicit, León and Cociña do point to the tale's background: the Nazis who notoriously found safety in South America after the Second World War. The bordered cross of one of the house's windows forms

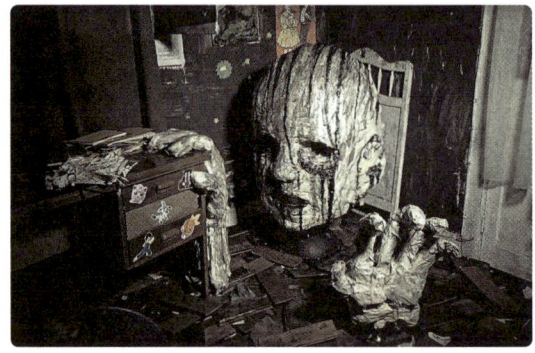

a swastika and scenes of Aryan unity among Maria's "family" feel disconcertingly angelic, appearing mere moments from previous scenes of flesh being burned alive. If not allegorical in every moment, there is a poisonous echo to the film's visuals, which in their ambiguity allow themselves to be transported to modernity. Under the guise of a propaganda film for one direction, it's an evocative warning in the other.

Above: Face your fears. One of the dark, unsettling designs that lurks throughout the walls of *The Wolf House*.

Below: María and her porcine children, the disquieting family in this historical and political tale that goes the whole hog.

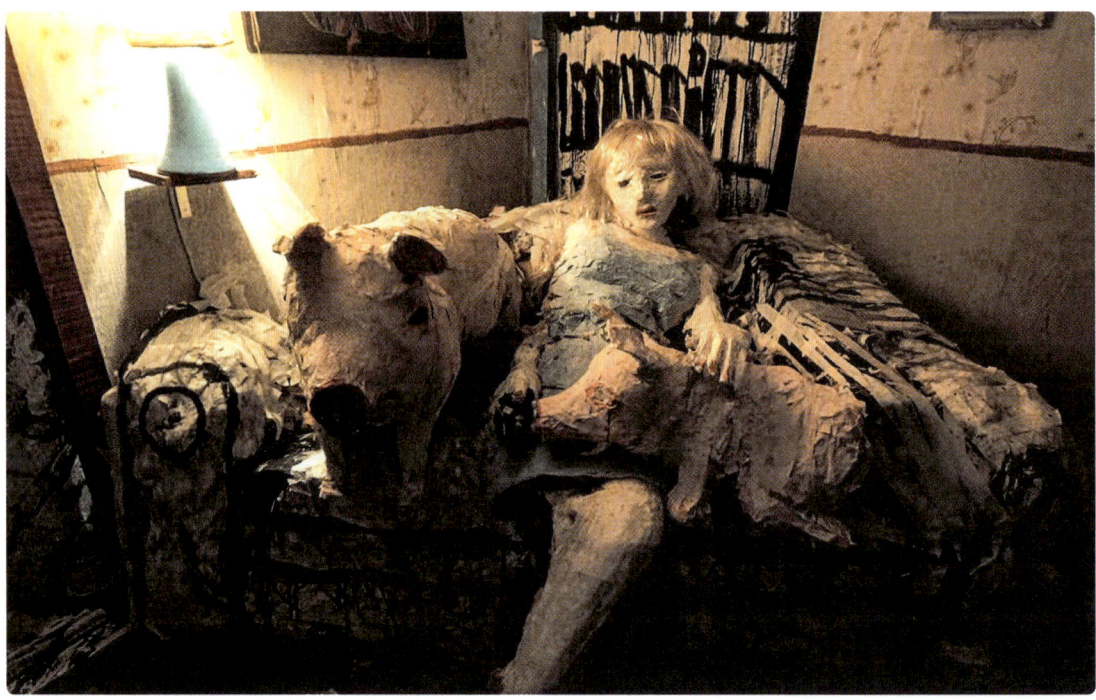

Maria's journey is unsettling, upsetting even, but there is always a playfulness to be found in the directors' craft. Because of the multifaceted nature of the animation styles being used, it's never clear at any given moment *where* the animation will come from. In *The Wolf House* characters, setting, background and foreground can all exist in the same plane, and as the same matter or object; they are all entwined and all at play, ready to wrongfoot viewers with where or what will breathe with life next.

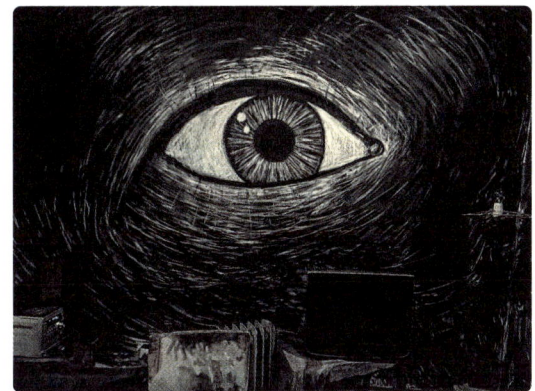

Right: What big eye you have. A fleeting appearance of what might be the titular wolf glancing inside their house.

👁 Further Viewing

If the haunting style of *The Wolf House* has you hankering for more from Cristóbal León and Joaquin Cociña, you're in luck. They contributed animated sequences to Ari Aster's indulgent surrealist saga *Beau Is Afraid* (2023), and later made the labyrinthine live-action/animation hybrid *The Hyperboreans* (2024).

We recommend tracking down their 2021 short, *The Bones*: a phantasmagoric maze of a movie, playful yet political, which hinges on the (fictional) discovery of the world's first stop-motion film, one crafted using a morbid technique, in tribute to animation pioneer Ladislas Starevich (see page 102). "Stop-motion is born resurrecting corpses like Victor Frankenstein, thus sealing the technique's necromantic destiny," León and Cociña told Mubi. "In [*The Bones*] we wanted to make an exaggerated version of Starevich's insects, replacing them with human corpses."

Elsewhere, there are two recent Chilean films that use animation to re-examine the horrors of the country's violent history: Hugo Covarrubias' *Bestia* (2021), a semi-fictionalized, stop-motion portrait of the notorious secret police agent Ingrid Olderöck, and *Bear Story* (2014), an allegorical tale inspired by the imprisonment and exile of director Gabriel Osorio Vargas's grandfather, which won the Oscar for Best Animated Short.

Below: Family Pawtrait. The Oscar-winning short *Bear Story* uses anthropomorphised animal characters to explore horrific national history.

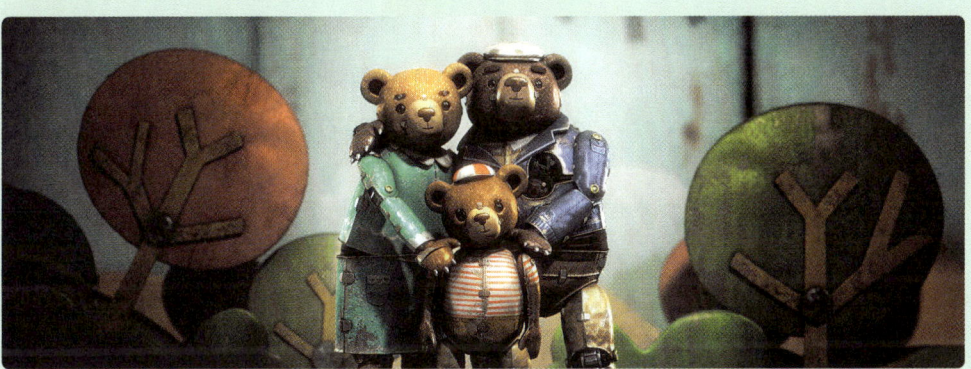

Argentina

Feature-length Animation is Found... and Lost

📽 El Apóstol

Director: Quirino Cristiani
Released: 1917

In this book there might be some films you've seen hundreds of times, some you've never seen, and some you've watched once and never need to put yourself through again – looking at you _When the Wind Blows_ (1986).

This one is different: you'll never be able to watch it. A paper cut-out political satire, Quirino Cristiani's _El Apóstol_ (1917) was the first feature-length animated film ever made – but in 1926, a fire broke out at producer Federico Valle's studio, and the only known copy of it was destroyed.

So, if you're planning a globe-trotting watchalong of _The Animation Atlas_, consider this an Argentinian flyover, where we'll look from over a century's distance at one of the most significant films ever made and be resigned to wonder what it looked like up close.

Before they got together to revolutionize screen storytelling as we know it, Valle was making newsreels and Cristiani provided comic portraits for a daily paper (his parents wanted him to be a doctor, he declared

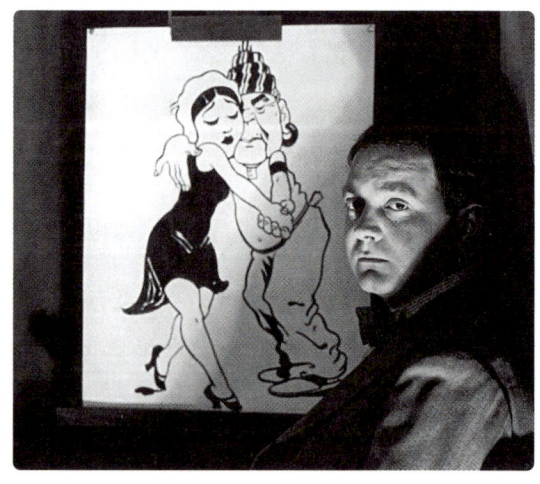

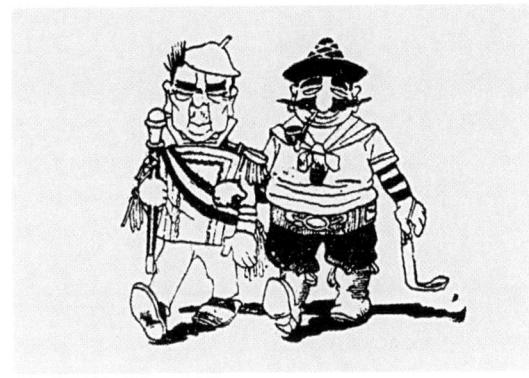

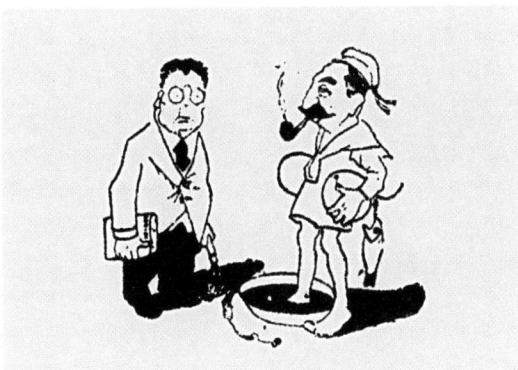

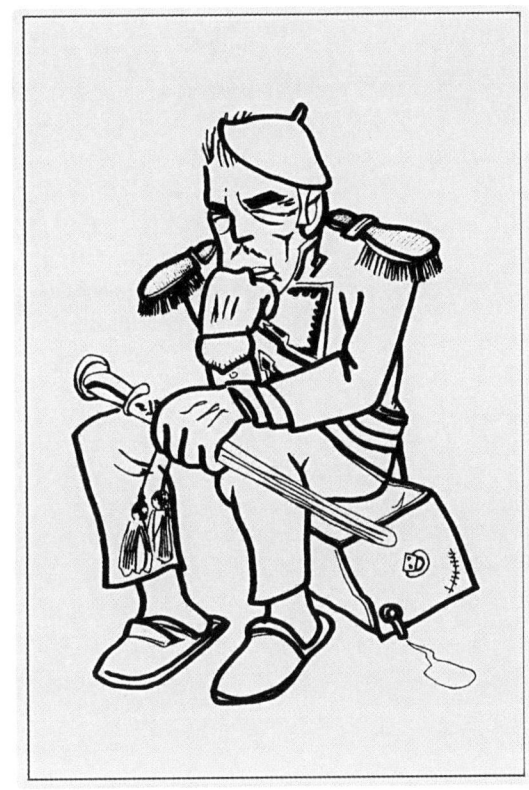

he was to be an artist, then even worse... a cartoonist). Both Italian-Argentine immigrants, Valle asked Cristiani to put graphics on his reels, then one day asked him if he could make those graphics move. The illusion of life had begun. Maintaining Cristiani's reputation for political caricatures, they used the new technique to make a short comedy about a local governor. They had a good time, so they embarked on a feature: a 70-minute satire about Argentina's president at the time, Hipólito Yrigoyen, who climbs Mount Olympus to borrow an almighty lightning bolt from Zeus and strike Buenos Aires to rid the capital of corruption.

It's not exactly *The Thick of It* or *Veep*, but it created a commotion and brought in local crowds. Inspired by the works of French filmic innovator Émile Cohl (another cartoonist turned animator), Cristiani's film was formed of around 58,000 frames of scything paper cut-outs. But despite that sizeable undertaking, *El Apóstol* took less than a year to make – and it paid off: Cristiani's film was shown multiple times a day for six months, before eventually being banned for how it caricatured the political system. Although the film is impossible to fully

imagine, a small selection of surviving imagery from *El Apóstol* (and Cristiani's 1931 effort *Peludópolis*) lets us discover morsels of the director's style. Big-headed, distinctly featured and costumed with precise detail, these fleeting frames suggest a heightened, cartoonish and sharp vision that states on arrival that animation is not just inane toddler fodder.

Although pulled from cinemas and eventually, tragically, destroyed, the motion of motion had been voted in and eventually the entire world would fall under its power.

Opposite: Quirino Cristiani, an early apostle for the feature-length animated film.

Above: Artwork and surviving imagery for *El Apóstol* and Cristiani's 1931 film *Peludópolis*, showing the director's caricatured, satirical style.

While we're on the subject of animation that you're unlikely to ever see, let us highlight a few other lost works. Quirino Cristiani is particularly unfortunate in this regard. The fires in the storage facilities that contained his films also claimed *Peludópolis* (1931), which is commonly considered to be animation's first feature film with sound. Other pioneering productions now lost to us include the first animated film produced in Brazil, the political sketch *Kaiser* (1917), and one of the first feature-length animated films made in Mexico, the sci-fi adventure *Roy del Espacio* (1983) – although, by all accounts, that one in particular is no great loss.

Nowadays, filmmakers need not fear censors or fire damage as much as the whims of their studio backers, who may decide to write off a production for tax reasons and leave them shelved indefinitely, as was the case with *Scoob! Holiday Haunt* (2022) and *Coyote vs. Acme* (2023). Chin up, though. Some films thought lost forever have eventually been found and surprise (re)discoveries still happen even today. For decades, it was thought that Japan's first animated feature, the propaganda film *Momotaro: Sacred Sailors* (1945), had been destroyed during the post-war American Occupation, but a print was unearthed in the 1980s; likewise, *The Story of Hong Gil-dong*, Korea's first animated feature, was lost even after a remarkably successful release in 1967. More than 40 years passed before it was restored and re-released, after a 16mm print was discovered in a small cinema in Osaka, Japan.

Elsewhere in South America

We could easily fall down a rabbit hole when looking at animation from South America. There is so much to discover, ranging from the cute kids' claymation of Venezuelan director Alberto Monteagudo (*El Cuatro de Hojalata*, 1978) to work created by a young generation of animators striking out with distinctive styles of their own.

One standout film from the region that found acclaim at festivals around the world is *Virus Tropical* (2017), a vivid coming-of-age animation from director Santiago Caicdeo. This adaptation of Colombian-Ecuadorian cartoonist Power Paola's graphic memoir of growing up as a rebellious kid in a strict, religious society, told in rough-and-ready, DIY black-and-white style, would make a perfect double bill with Marjane Satrapi's *Persepolis*. This is just the tip of the iceberg when it comes to Colombian animation, which has a tradition dating

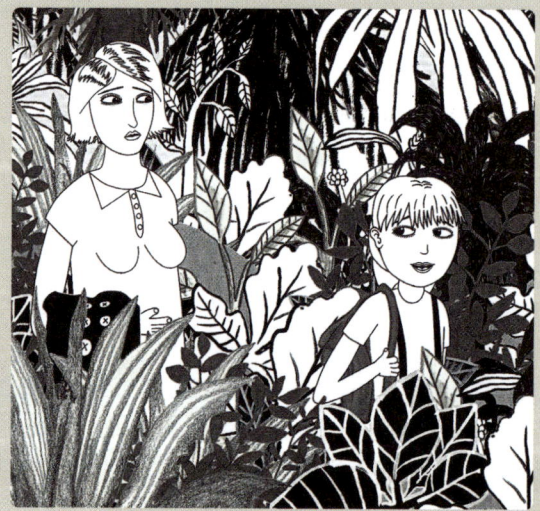

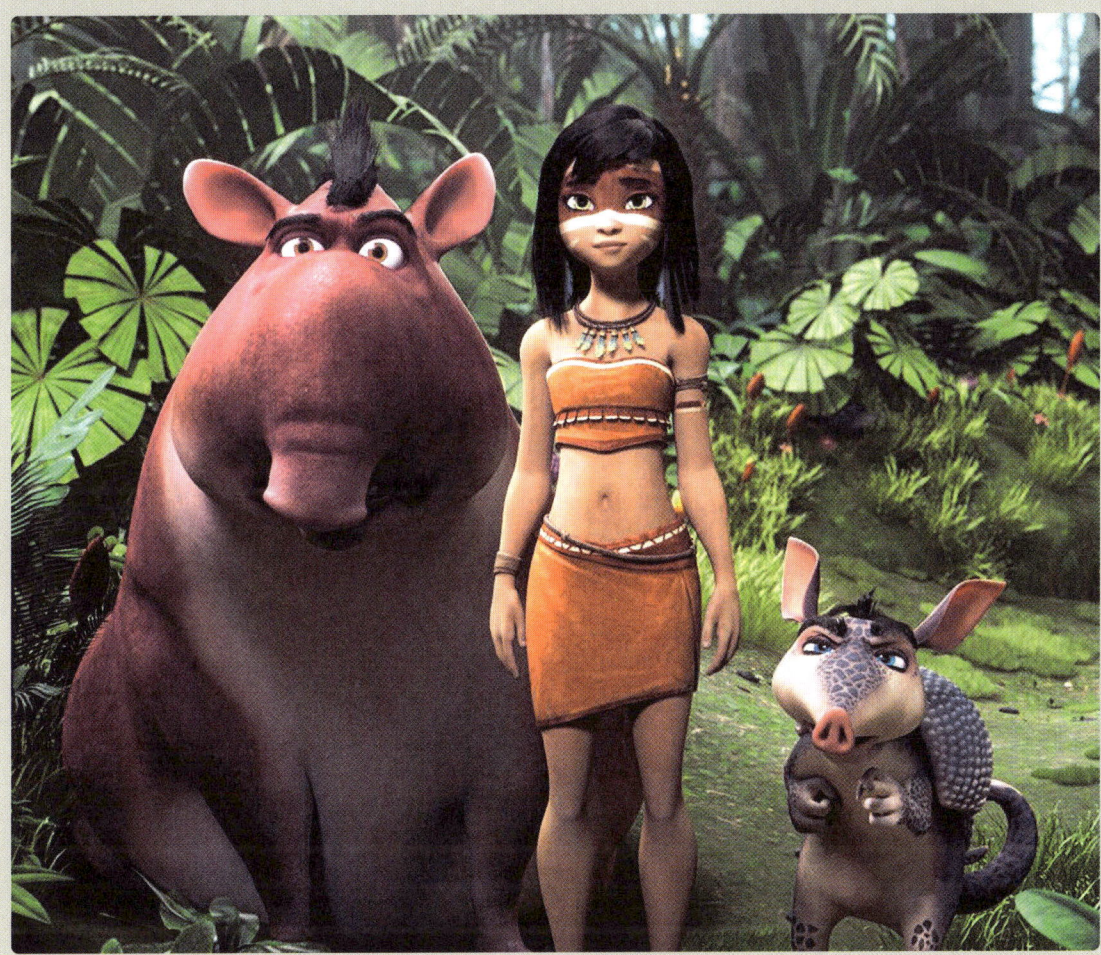

back to the stop-motion animation of director Fernando Laverde (*Cristóbal Colón*, 1983), and thrives today thanks to young artists working in a variety of styles, from Carla Melo Gambert's grotesque, painterly *La Perra* (2023), to the crayon colours of Catalina Matamoros's animated documentary short *Antes de las 4* (2022), to the unsettling, psychological textures of *Gloria* (2022), hand-crafted by the experimental art collective Residuo.

Meanwhile, in Peru, there's a burgeoning industry of computer-generated family entertainment, spearheaded by director Eduardo Schuldt, whose films *The Illusionauts* (2012) and *Condorito: la película* (2017) received international distribution (the latter under the risible English-language title *Space Chicken*; Condorito is an anthropomorphic condor). Many of these films tackle local themes or draw inspiration from indigenous culture, such as José Zelada and Richard Claus's *Ainbo: Spirit*

of the Amazon (2021), a magical adventure filled with mythological creatures from Amazonian folklore, which also travelled around the world. At the other end of the budgetary scale is artist Eliana Otta Vildoso's *Eight Constructions Imagined by Eight Construction Workers* (2012), a simple but profound short that animates the sketches of labourers in Lima, who were asked as they left the site at the end of the day the question: what would you build if you could build anything you wanted?

Opposite: Zine Girls. Power Paola's scrappy coming-of-age animation *Virus Tropical* is an indie gem worth seeking out.

Above: Amazon Prime. The CGI sheen of *Ainbo* anticipates a blockbuster future for South American stories.

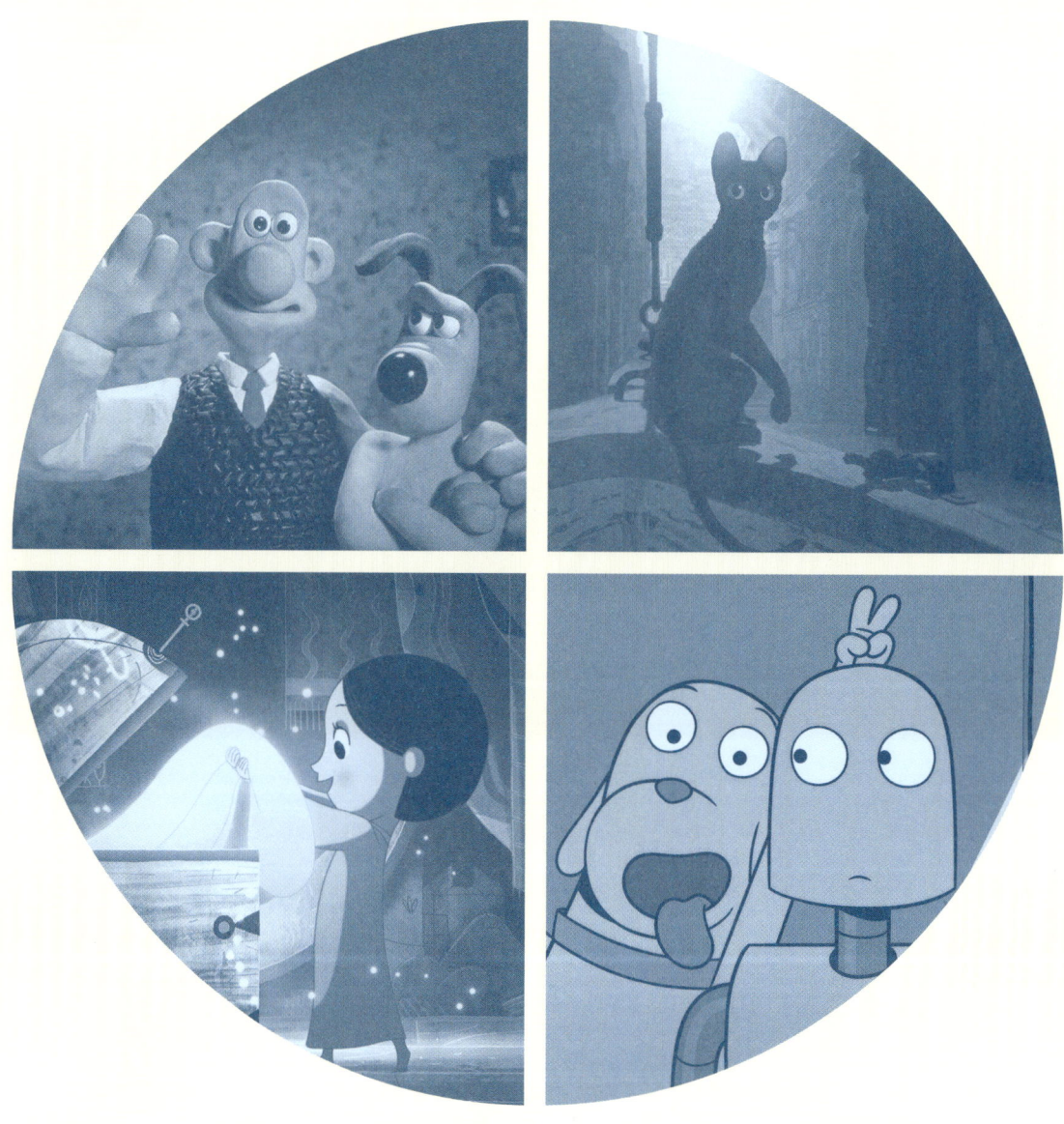

Europe

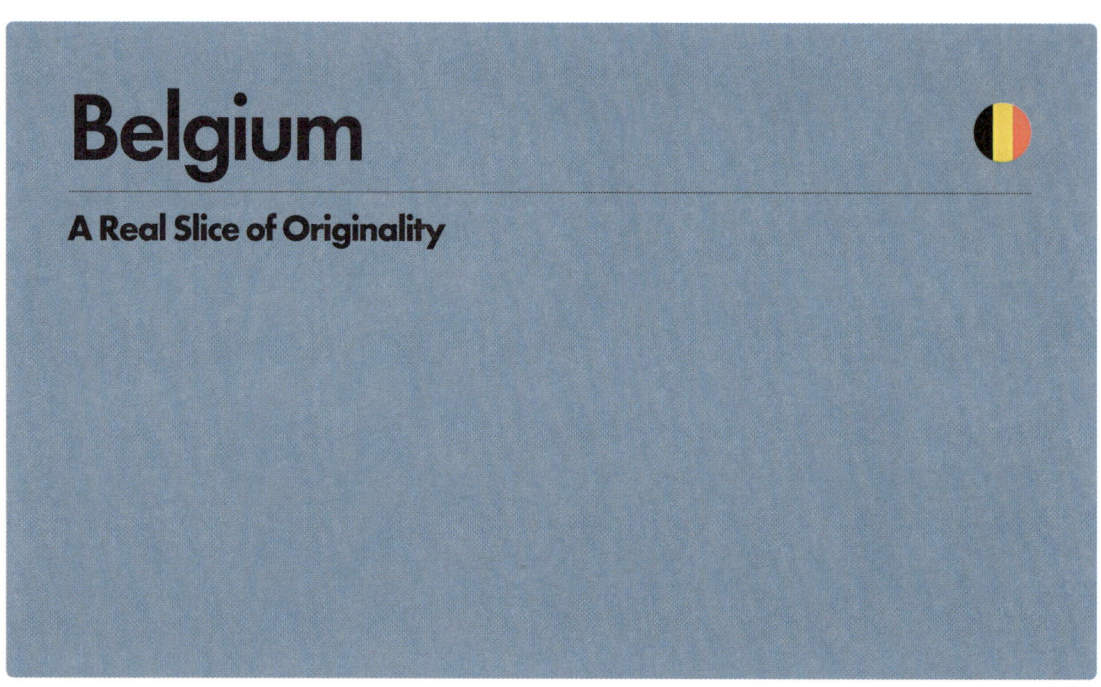

Belgium

A Real Slice of Originality

🎥 This Magnificent Cake!

Director: Marc James Roels and Emma de Swaef
Released: 2018

In animated stories, the Grim Reaper doesn't swing a scythe, but instead throws a piano. It's the musically explosive alternative to the anvil, and *Looney Tunes'* (1930 to present) Wile E. Coyote, Yosemite Sam and Sylvester the Cat all faced its music (or got a face full of it).

Tex Avery threw one at a bullying bulldog in *Bad Luck Blackie* (1949) and so many more since have been squashed by a Steinway that by 1988 and *Who Framed Roger Rabbit*, death-by-piano was a trope that had become a punchline.

Thirty years later, in *This Magnificent Cake!* and its setting of the Belgian colonization of the Congo, the potentially stale stunt gets superbly freshened-up by directors Marc James Roels and Emma de Swaef. But should you really laugh at it? The moment occurs when the outburst of a loud, spoiled, white child sends a grand piano tipping over the stairwell railings of a soulless mansion, crushing a smiling, Black servant who has been forced to wear an ashtray as a hat. Doesn't read like a gag, does it? But, in the moment, the familiarity

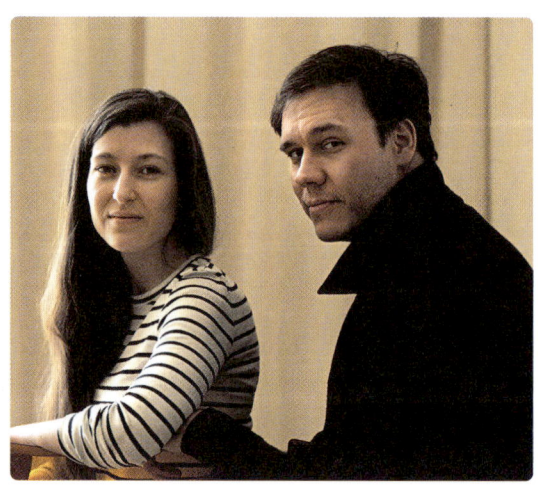

of the joke and the shock of its new deployment do create a quickly stifled laugh. It's the viewer's subsequent questioning of their own reaction that intrigues Roels and de Swaef, and makes *This Magnificent Cake!* such a clever work.

Roels' background is in documentary while de Swaef is a textile artist. They first explored the possibility of working with wool in a short (*Oh Willy*, 2012), and their collated vision is remarkable, with a stark, static and observational look presiding over the most outlandish, beady-eyed and stubby-limbed wool puppets. It's an arresting creative combination that gives a weighty story a new texture. Taking their cue from Belgium's King Leopold II, who referred to the "magnificent African cake", Roels and de Swaef craft a web of stories set in royal palaces, luxurious ships, tangled jungles, vast caves and even more cavernous hotels, delivering a film

Opposite: Marc James Roels and Emma de Swaef, the directing duo behind *This Magnificent Cake!*

Right: From minute musical instruments to petite paintings, Roels and de Swaef's film is full of magnificent miniatures.

Below: Belgium's King Leopold II, uniquely depicted in the centre here, whose reference to the "magnificent African cake" gives the film its title.

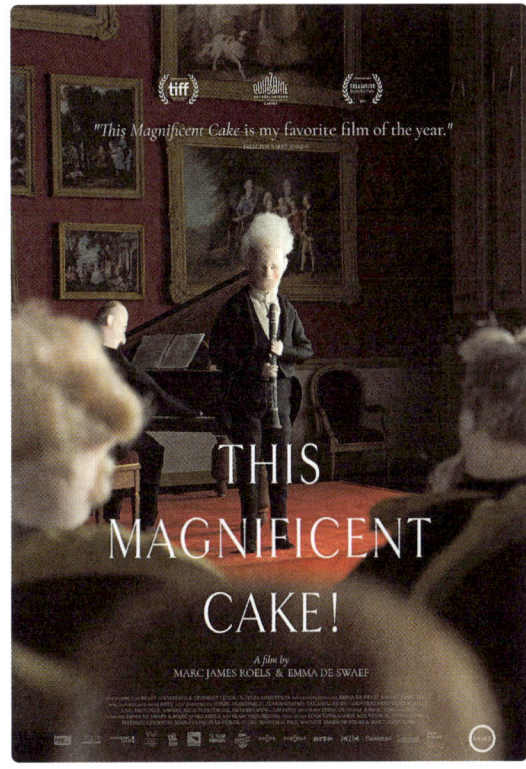

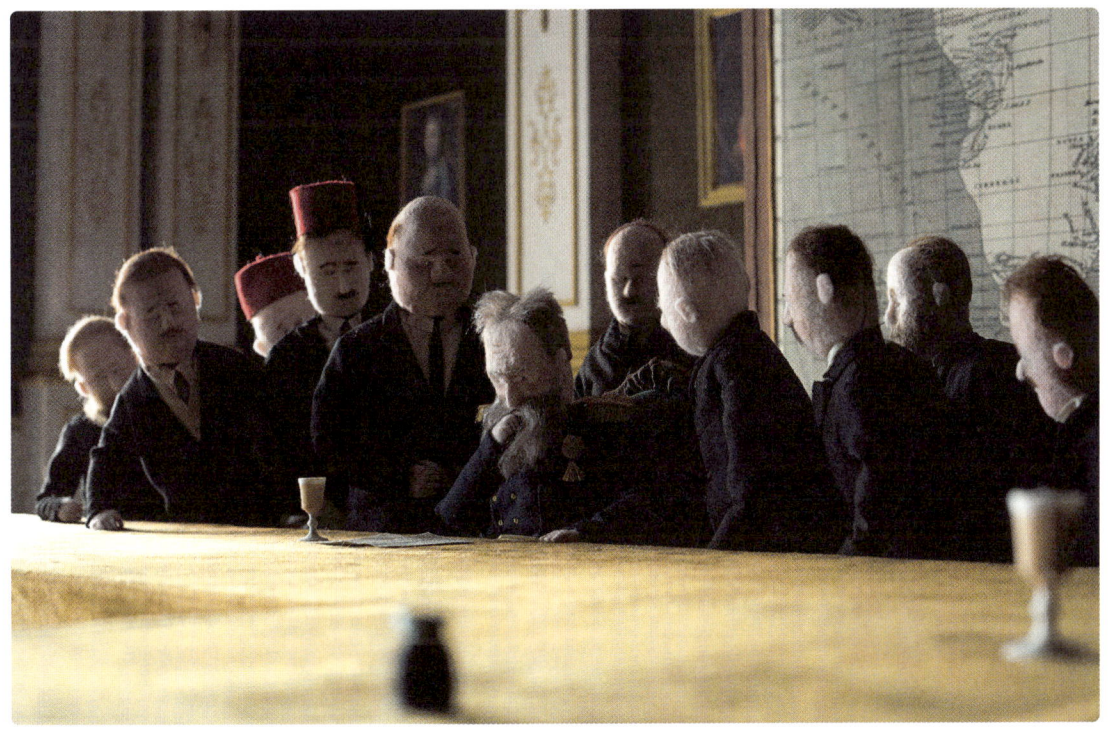

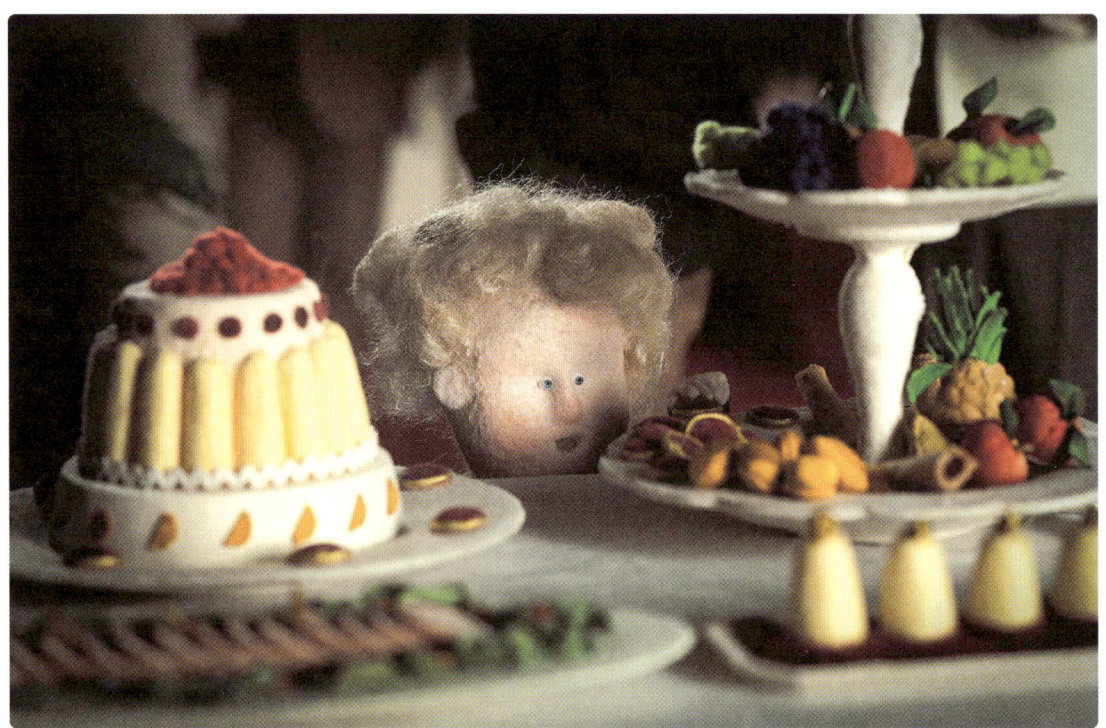

that eschews any white-saviour trappings and positions its subjects as vain and violent fools. These are people who wet the bed while demanding war, live off imported beer and profess their love to snails wearing toupees; it's world domination by farce, not force. And it's the local Congolese who are at the mercy of their boorish bravado, slain by rogue banana skins and jump-scare toots on clarinets, the satire constantly emphasizing the hapless fortune of the invaders, rather than any tactical nous.

The film took six years to complete from when the idea was first stitched in the filmmakers' minds, and the attention to detail (and wrangling with different French, Belgian and Dutch companies to make it) shows why. Backgrounds, whether of thick greenery or great halls, are diligently realized, even down to the miniature framed paintings that fill the palatial walls. The most exquisite work is reserved for the characters, though. De Swaef has emphasized the importance of her puppets having been made by a person, and it's the nature of the material that they've been crafted from that gives them such life. Wool isn't a hugely popular tool for animation, as its minute dusty fibres can change frame by frame, but it's exactly this quality that gives the film so much life. Fluttering moment to moment, like the rollick of a boiling

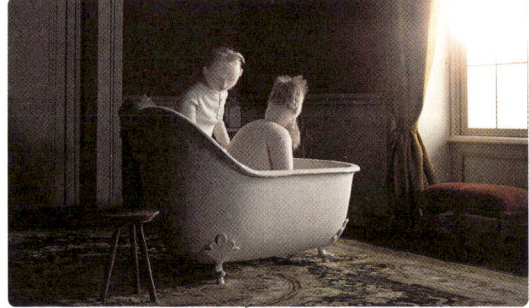

line in 2D animation, these puppets and their actions read at once as alien and distinctly, ashamedly human.

If you're still not convinced to give it a shot, director Barry Jenkins (*Moonlight*, *If Beale Street Could Talk*) described *This Magnificent Cake!* as "so damn extraordinary" and named it his favourite film of 2018. If he's taken the cake, you should too.

Above top: A visual feast. *This Magnificent Cake!* is full of aesthetic delights, ranging from its soft woollen faces to its delicately detailed dining spreads.

Above: Let it wash over you. Although only 44 minutes long, the film creates a distinct world that quickly becomes immersive.

◉ Further Viewing

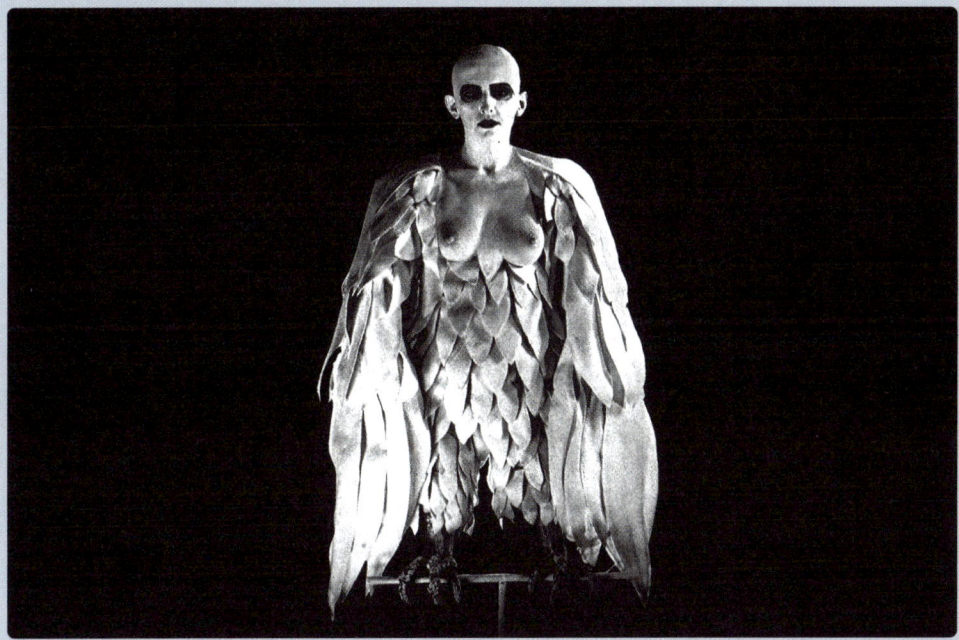

You can find more of Emma de Swaef and Marc James Roels' fuzzy-felt animation in an eerie Netflix anthology film, *The House* (2022). Otherwise, it's common to see Belgian companies as co-producers on films that cross borders with other European countries (most often France), but Belgium is home to its fair share of visionaries and virtuosos. Comic book publisher Raymond Leblanc founded the studio Belvision in Brussels in 1954 and produced animated adaptations of popular Franco-Belgian comic series such as *Tintin*, *Asterix* and *Lucky Luke*. Another crossover between comics and animation was the cartoonist Picha, whose adult animated comedy spoof *Tarzoon: Shame of the Jungle* (1975) arrived in the wake of Ralph Bakshi's *Fritz the Cat* (1972). Despite an English-language dub featuring a cast of Saturday Night Live-adjacent, rising-star comedians,

including John Belushi, Bill Murray and Christopher Guest, the film was received poorly internationally. However, Picha's one-time collaborator, Nicole Van Goethem, fared better with her wonkily designed, grotesque, lightly feminist tale of three old women holding up the crumbling edifice of a dying civilization, *A Greek Tragedy* (1985), which won the Academy Award for Animated Short. If you seek out just one film, however, make it Raoul Servais's Short Film Palme d'Or winner, *Harpya* (1979). This darkly comic and utterly strange hybrid of live action and animation is a phantasmagorical mix of myth and magic realism, with a man discovering a Harpy (half-bird, half-woman) who begins to take over his life – with violent consequences. Once seen, never forgotten.

Above: Harping on. Raoul Servais's eerie short film *Harpya* has had an impact on many filmmakers, including Henry Selick.

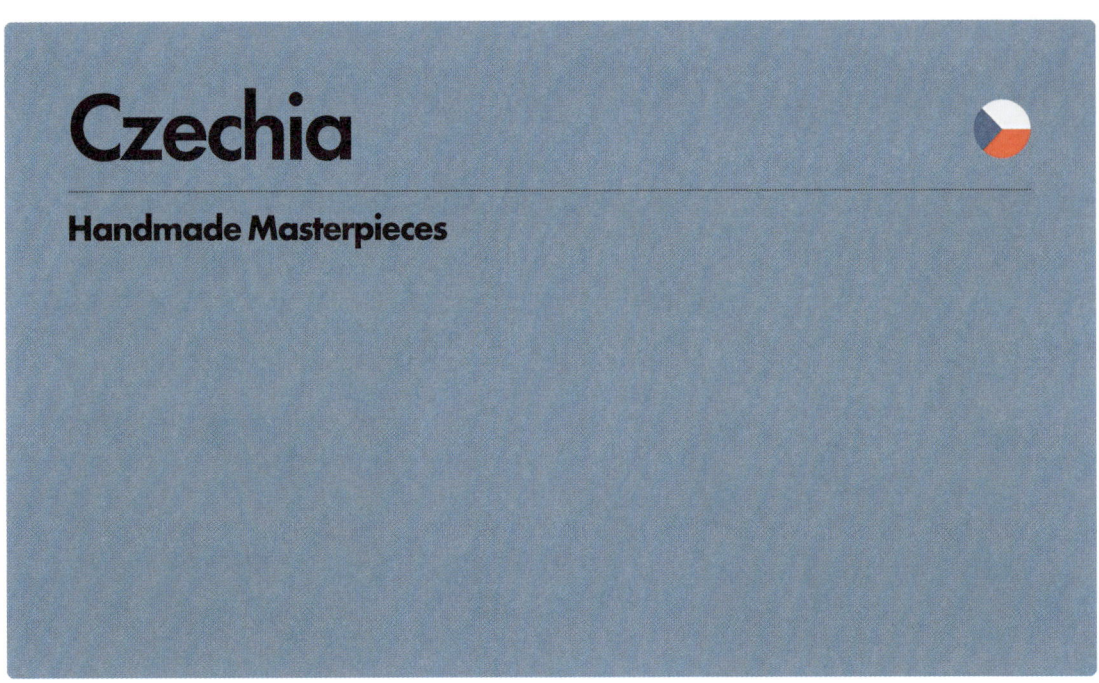

Czechia

Handmade Masterpieces

🎥 The Hand (Ruka)

Director: Jiří Trnka
Release date: 1965

Jiří Trnka was a legend in his own lifetime. A talented puppet maker and artist, he also illustrated over a hundred books for children – including tales from the Brothers Grimm, William Shakespeare, Hans Christian Andersen and Lewis Carroll.

As a filmmaker, he enjoyed acclaim both at home and abroad. His stop-motion puppet films are beloved by generations of Czech audiences and at his creative peak in the 1950s he was heralded as the Walt Disney of Eastern Europe. And yet, mere months after he died in 1969, his final film, *The Hand*, was banned by the authorities and suppressed for two decades.

The Hand marked a stylistic shift for Trnka. For years, he created works that tended towards the pastoral, with beautifully crafted adaptations of literary works, folk stories and fairy tales. The likes of *The Czech Year* (1947), *The Emperor's Nightingale* (1949) and *A Midsummer Night's Dream* (1959) were screened across Europe and won plaudits at film festivals in

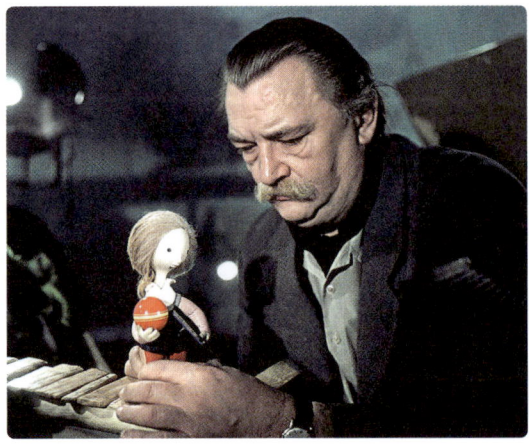

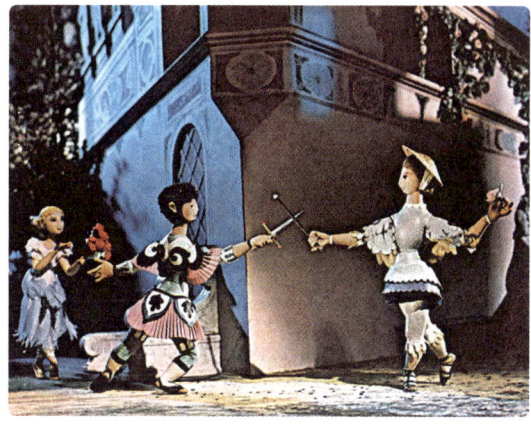

Locarno, Venice and Cannes. *The Hand*, meanwhile, was a pointed allegory that critics immediately linked to the totalitarian political landscape of the Soviet Bloc, and more specifically Communist Czechoslovakia – the state that had been funding and vetting Trnka's work for years.

Deeply pessimistic yet fuelled by an anger against the powers that be, the film is rooted in the potent visual metaphor that gives it its title. A silent potter character – styled like a *harlequin* with sharp facial features and large, vulnerable eyes – plies their trade in their run-down garret apartment. On waking, they skip and pirouette out of bed, before sitting down to mould plant pots at their wheel – until a sharp rat-tat-tat at the door interrupts their calm, artistic solitude. It's the Hand, a human-sized, white-gloved invader here to encourage the potter to make hand-shaped ornaments instead. At first seemingly polite and well-mannered, the Hand's methods of persuasion soon turn to terror as the poor artist is hounded and harried – ultimately, to death.

You can see why the authorities might have been

spooked. *The Hand* wears its allegory on its sleeve, clearly commenting on the friction between the joy of free artistic expression and the pressure to create purposeful work for the state. It's a miracle that it was even granted a release in the first place, let alone that it was allowed to travel to the Annecy International Animation Film Festival, where it picked up a prize from the jury in 1965. Historians now put the film in a continuum with the Prague Spring, a brief period of political upheaval and radical reform in 1968 that was squashed when Soviet tanks rolled in and re-established the status quo – not long after which *The Hand* was banned.

Taken out of its immediate political context, *The Hand* is a chilling and symbolically rich film that explores the artistic urge and the outside forces that get in the way. The Hand itself is an eerie, unsettling creation, a human invasion into this hand-crafted world that, in this context, couldn't look more alien. When it insinuates itself into the harlequin's daily routines, the Hand brings with it technology and organs of mass communication. Telephones, newspapers and the television set: all anchors to a wider society that disrupt a bohemian ideal of living for art and art alone. Later, the harlequin is subjected to a propaganda film that proclaims the

Opposite: Master at work. A legend of Czech, European and world animation, Jiři Trnka.

Above left: Earlier in his career, Trnka turned his hand to adapting works of literature, such as Shakespeare's *A Midsummer Night's Dream*.

Below left: Hands on. The menacing, gloved hand asserts its influence over the harlequin artist.

Below right: The harlequin receives a troubling phone call: plant pots are out; Hand sculptures are in.

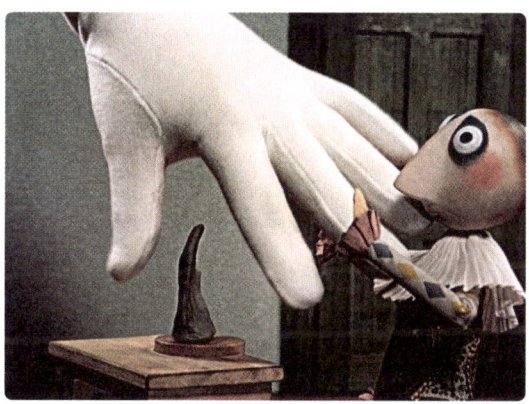

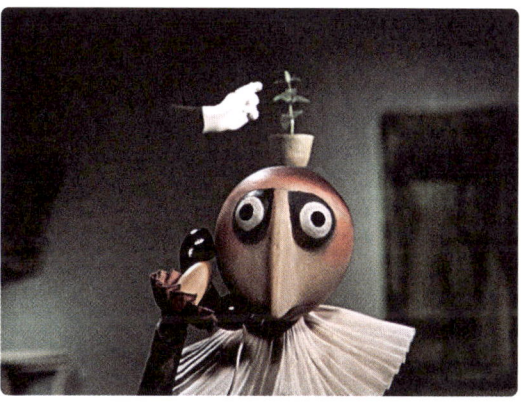

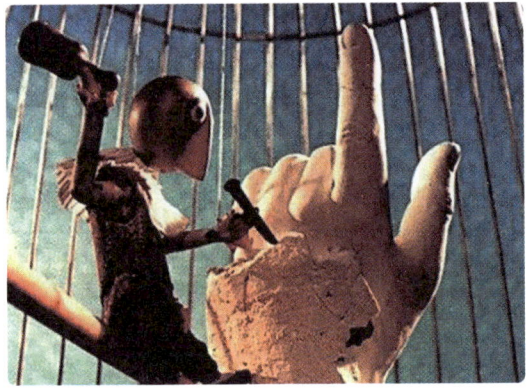

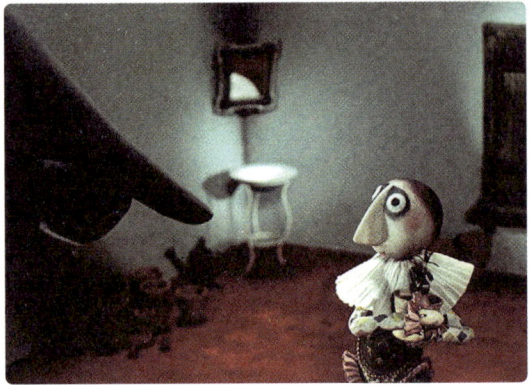

omnipotence and omnipresence of the Hand throughout history: the Statue of Liberty holding her torch aloft; Lady Justice balancing the scales; Napoleon tucking his hand into his waistcoat.

Hands threaten, condemn and harm, but they also *make*. In one of the film's more horrifying moments, the harlequin is bound up in nooses and turned, momentarily, into a puppet manipulated by the Hand itself – a dizzying, multilayered image that offers not just a visual metaphor for coercion and control, but a reflexive comment on the act of animation itself.

The Hand might be a world away from the likes of

Duck Amuck (1953), the classic Chuck Jones short that sees Daffy Duck waging war against the artist's pen as it draws, erases and redraws the action around him, but both films call attention to the unseen hands that lie just out of frame. Animation is a handmade art form, one created with an intentionality that infuses every frame. Without the artist's hand, where would we be?

Above: Through terror and coercion, the harlequin is forced to make art that supports the ideology of the Hand.

Below: Wooden puppets from Trnka's films on display at a retrospective exhibition at the Gallery of the Central Bohemian Region.

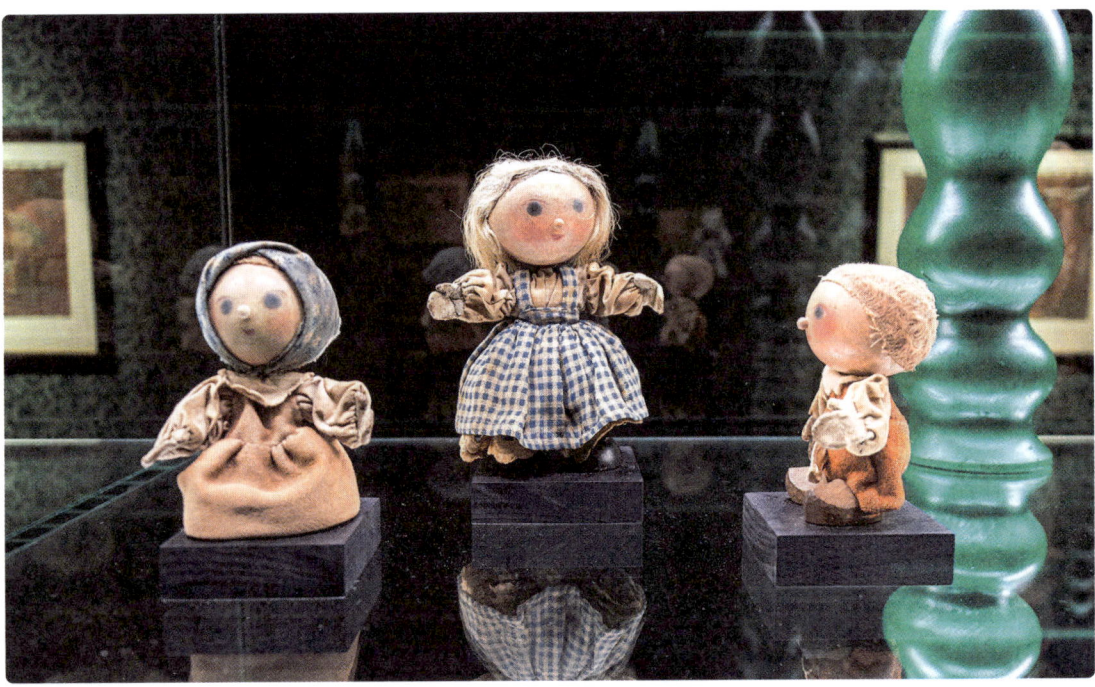

🎬 Alice (Něco z Alenky)

Director: Jan Švankmajer
Released: 1988

On the promo trail for Disney's billion-dollar-grossing, live-action *Alice in Wonderland* in 2010, lead actress Mia Wasikowska was asked time and again about her familiarity with the work of Lewis Carroll – and, more specifically, with Disney's previous 1951 adaptation of the novel.

Press and fans were surprised to hear that, no, Disney's version of the story didn't loom large over her childhood; instead, she was exposed at a young age to a very different telling of the tale from the Czech filmmaker Jan Švankmajer. "We used to be kind of disturbed by it," she recalled in conversation with *W Magazine*. "But we could never walk away, because it was so fascinating and odd."

Fascinating and odd, that's the work of Jan Švankmajer. Born in Prague in 1934, Švankmajer emerged from an avant-garde, politically subversive, Surrealist tradition. He used stop-motion techniques and tactile objects to bring the inanimate to life, exploring the irrational through puppetry, transformation and dream logic in arresting short films such as *Jabberwocky* (1971) and *Dimensions of Dialogue* (1982). Hollywood directors such as Tim Burton and Henry Selick drew deep inspiration from Švankmajer while finding their own voices as mainstream filmmakers; yet Selick himself still points to the Czech master as the epitome of a true artist.

1988's *Alice* was Švankmajer's first feature film, and brought his distinctive style to a wider international audience. It received a theatrical release in America and the UK, won the top prize at Annecy, and even had a UK television broadcast in the re-edited form of a miniseries, thanks to British co-funders Channel 4.

"Now you will see a film made for children," narrates Alice at the start of the film. "Perhaps." The film's Czech title, *Něco z Alenky*, or *Something from Alice*, might give a better impression of what's to come. Not quite an adaptation or a retelling, Švankmajer's *Alice* is more of

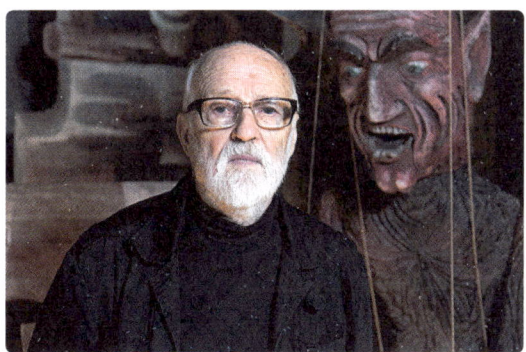

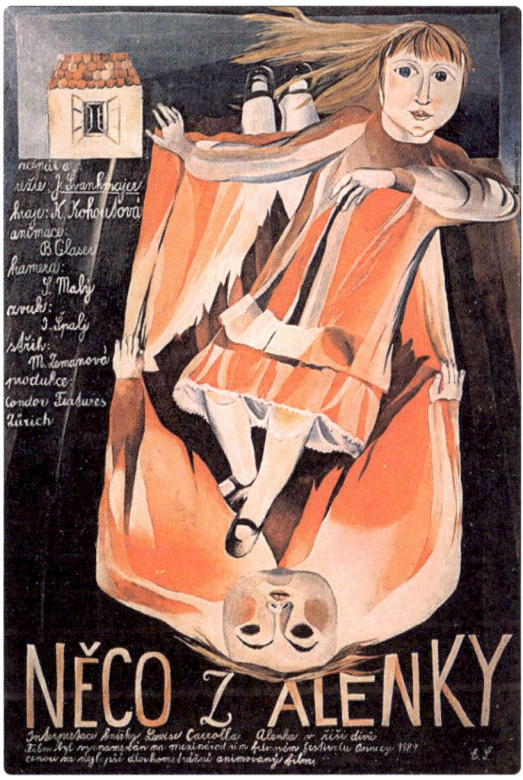

Right above: Jan the Man. The inimitable artist and filmmaker Jan Švankmajer: master of surreal, stop-motion filmmaking.

Right: The Czech poster for *Alice*, complete with its more poetic and elusive title, *Something from Alice*.

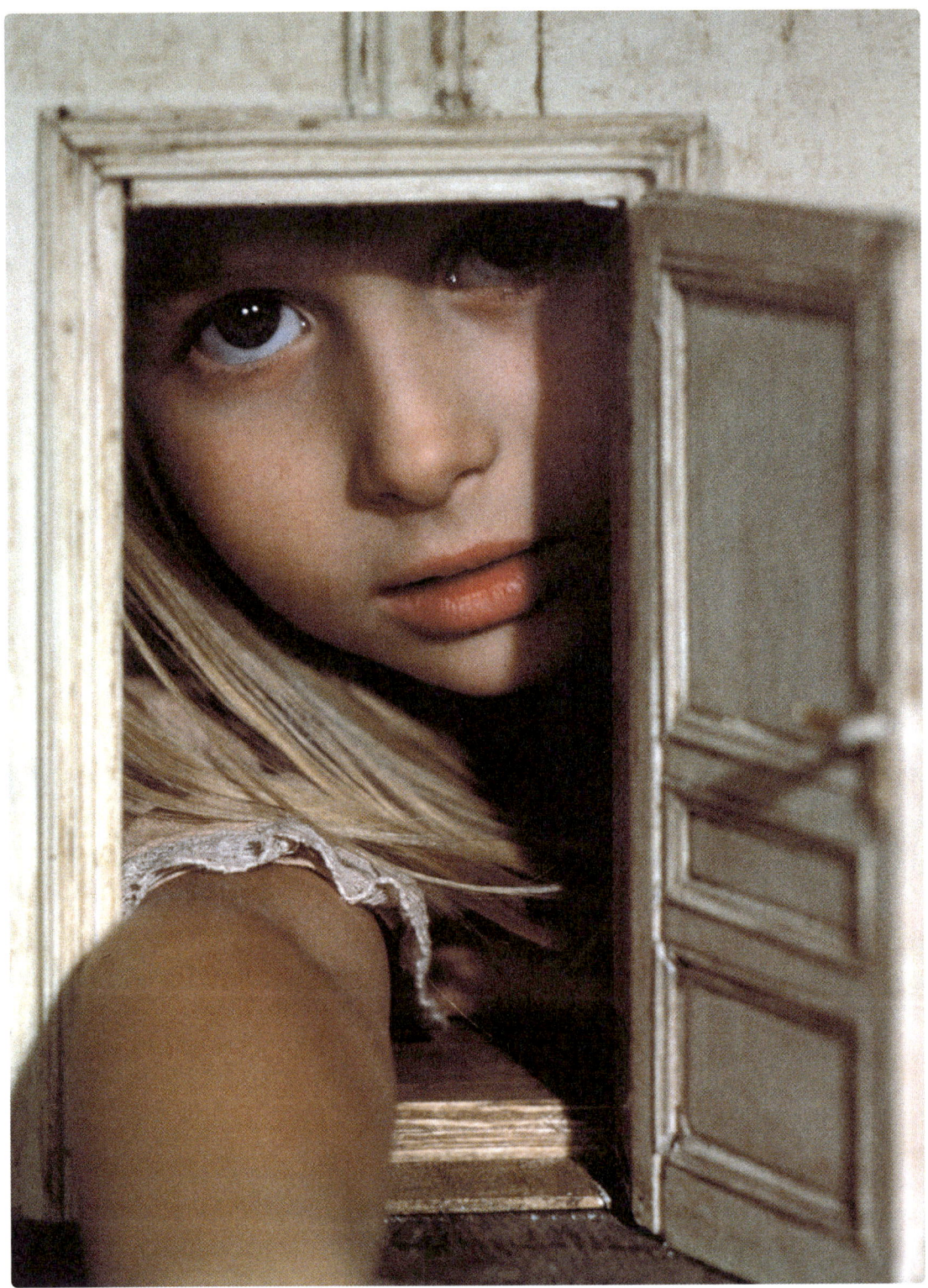

an artistic evocation of Carroll's work in a dark, surrealist vein – reappropriating Wonderland from the world of fairy tale, and returning it to the bizarre, menacing, unpredictable form of a dream.

Most of the gang's present and accounted for: Alice, the White Rabbit, the Hatter and the March Hare. And if you squint, you'll find a familiar route through the surreal maze of the story: drinks that shrink and cakes that enlarge; tea parties that never end; croquet with the Queen of Hearts. The key difference here is that Alice (the very human Kristýna Kohoutová) is adrift in a world of strange, stop-motion creatures: taxidermied animals that split at the stitches and spill sawdust on the floor; skulls and skeletons cobbled together into unholy creations; hunks of raw meat and cans of cockroaches. In Švankmajer's hands, the Caterpillar is transformed into a sinister sock-puppet fitted with large false teeth – all the better to unnerve you with.

The world of *Alice* is messy like the mind, and as transfixing as the most vivid of dreams. Every scene is crammed with an overwhelming accumulation of *stuff*, recalling the cabinets of curiosity where collectors would bring together disparate objects (pieces of art, furniture, ornaments, knick-knacks and assorted natural ephemera) and display them for all to see. But where those *kunstkammern* might have been designed to delight, inspire and show off, Švankmajer uses this accumulation to create a total, inescapable immersion in this eerie, undeniably hand-crafted setting.

Likewise, where other filmmakers might strive to imbue their puppets and models with a soul or a kind of humanity – a point that Guillermo del Toro, for example, stressed with his *Pinocchio* (2022) – we watch *Alice* and

Opposite: The Door of Perception. In contrast to previous adaptations, Švankmajer sought to return Alice to the surreal realm of dream logic.

Below: Feed Your Head. Švankmajer's take on Alice in Wonderland surrounds a real-life actress with unnerving, hand-crafted creatures.

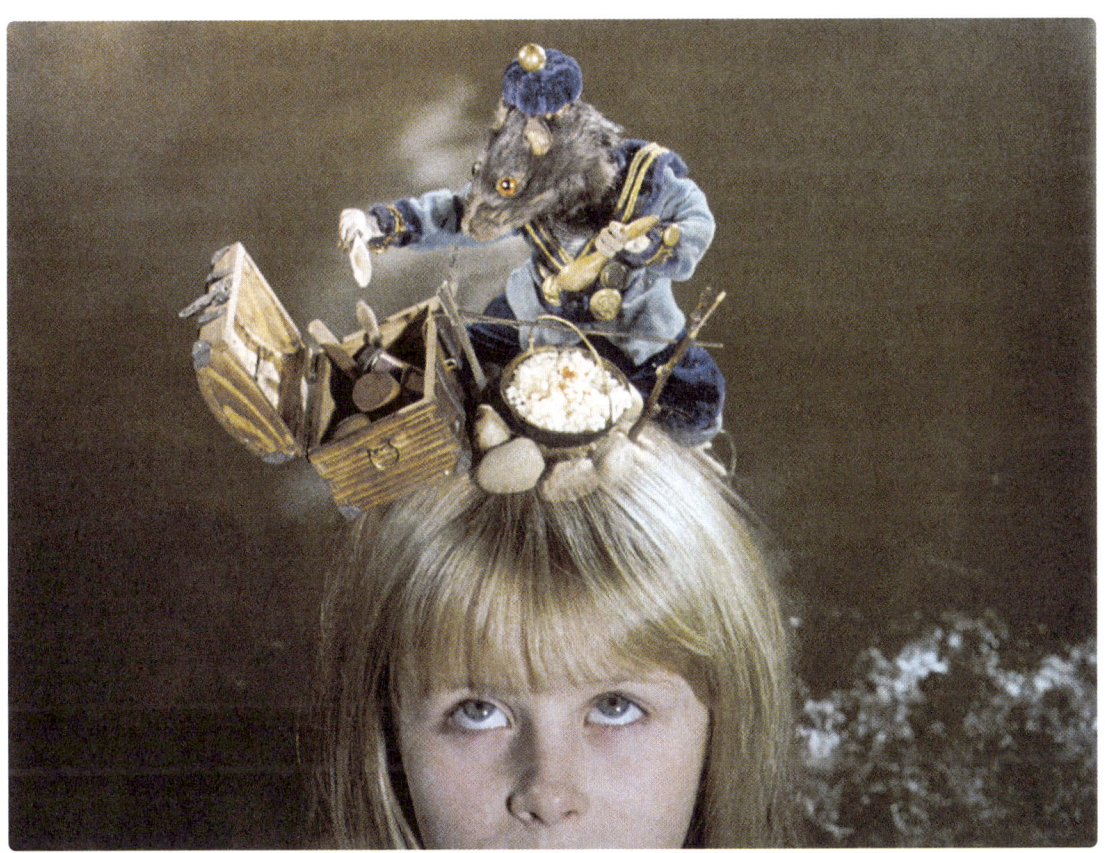

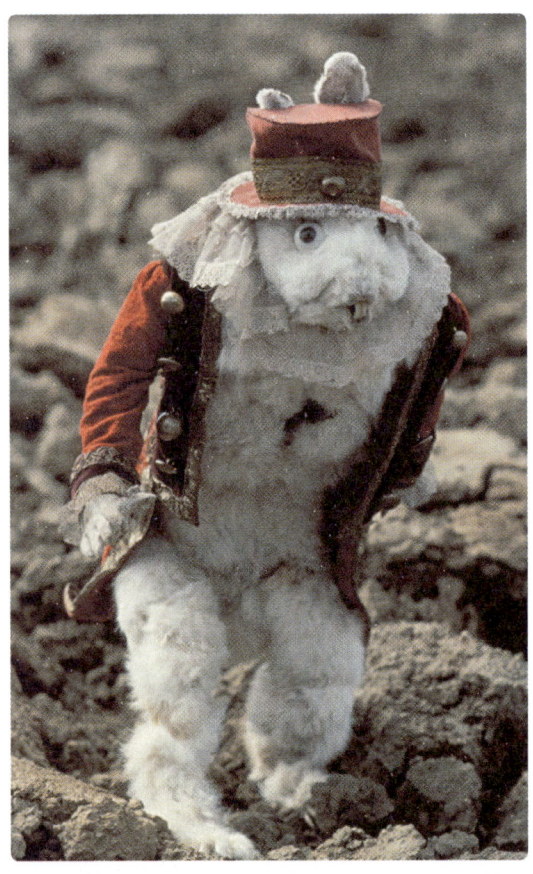

never forget that these carcasses, china dolls, clockwork toys, all brought to life by the artist's hand, are nothing but nightmarish.

In fact, Švankmajer resists the label of "animator" entirely. His explanation is often quoted: "Animators tend to construct a closed world for themselves, like pigeon fanciers or rabbit breeders. I never call myself an animated filmmaker because I am interested not in animation techniques or creating a complete illusion, but in bringing life to everyday objects."

While Švankmajer returned to short films following *Alice*, with the likes of *The Death of Stalinism in Bohemia* (1990) and *Food* (1992), he soon dedicated his efforts to features, further exploring a live-action/animation hybrid style in strange, challenging, blackly comic films such as *Conspirators of Pleasure* (1996), *Little Otik* (2000) and *Surviving Life* (2010).

And so, *Alice* feels poised between this late period of feature filmmaking and the short form work that came before – making it the perfect rabbit hole through which to tumble down and discover Švankmajer's disturbing Wonderland.

Left: Runny Bunny. The White Rabbit is one of the many Wonderland residents given the Švankmajer treatment.

Below: We're All Made Here. Continuing the hand-crafted theme, Švankmajer's Hatter is a carved wooden puppet.

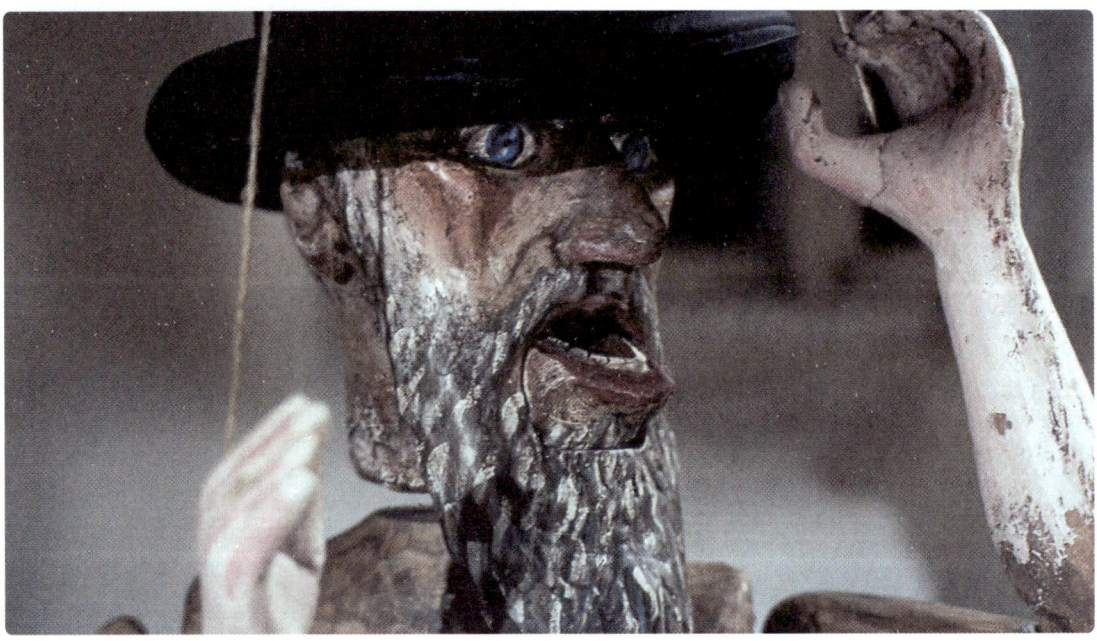

◉ Further Viewing

Czechoslovakia in the twentieth century was a hotbed of groundbreaking animation: a country filled with pioneers and visionaries whose influence is still felt today. Karel Zeman has been described as a successor to Georges Méliès thanks to his innovative technical wizardry in creating his spellbinding fantasy films that combined live action and animation, including *Journey to the Beginning of Time* (1955), *Invention for Destruction* (1958) and *The Fabulous Baron Munchausen* (1962). Zeman's name crops up today as a foundational influence on the work of Terry Gilliam, Tim Burton and Wes Anderson.

Then there's Hermína Týrlová, "the mother of Czech animation", whose stop-motion work across several decades spanned from whimsical children's cartoons, such as the delightful, woolly textures of *The Snowman* (1966) and *Christmas Tree* (1968), to more allegorical fare that takes everyday objects on poetic journeys, such as *The Knot in the Handkerchief* (1958) and *The Blue Apron* (1965).

Břetislav Pojar, a talented puppet animator and protégé of Jiří Trnka, found great acclaim after emigrating to Canada and making hand-drawn films with the National Film Board, such as *To See or Not to See* (1969) and the Cannes prize winner *Balablok* (1972). Jiří Barta also got his start at Trnka's studio, before directing the ambitious, German Expressionist-style stop-motion fairy tale, *The Pied Piper* (1985).

Criss-crossing with many of those mentioned above is the career of the great female animator Vlasta Pospíšilová, who worked on *The Pied Piper* as well as Trnka's *A Midsummer Night's Dream* (1959) and *The Cybernetic Grandma* (1962) and Švankmajer's *Jabberwocky* (1971) and *Dimensions of Dialogue* (1982). Pospíšilová also directed films of her own, including a long series of fairy tales adapted from the writing of Czech actor and author Jan Werich.

We're only scratching the surface here. Director Michaela Pavlátová explained that animation served as "small islands" of free spirit and freedom during the days of the Czechoslovak Socialist Republic. "We made films as pieces of art. The studios didn't care about the market, because there was no market." Since we're giving Pavlátová the last word, it's only fair, then, to finish with a recommendation to track down her 1991 short, *Words, Words, Words*, a witty, visually inventive exploration of language, communication and human connection across one evening in a bustling bar.

Below left: Ball Games. In Hermína Týrlová's delightful short, *The Glass Marble*, various stop-motion animals vie for ownership of the shiny bauble.

Below right: Czech Mate. The King plays chess in *The Hat and the Little Jay Feather*, Vlasta Pospíšilová's contribution to the anthology film *Fimfarum: The Third Time Lucky* 3D (2011).

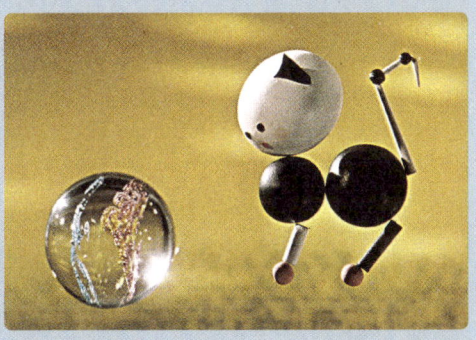

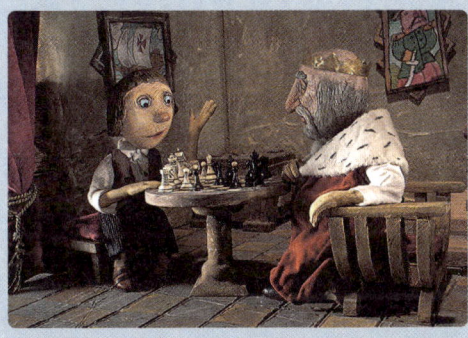

Denmark

Where Animation Meets Reality

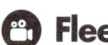 **Flee**

Director: Jonas Poher Rasmussen
Released: 2021

If you were to watch some of the biggest titles in the North America section of this book, each film would probably start with one or two logos for the studios or production companies that funded the project.

Over in Europe, however, you'll regularly encounter a full slideshow of idents and names before the story kicks in, and Jonas Poher Rasmussen's 2021 film *Flee* is no exception, with more than ten different groups playing a part in getting this story told. Watch it, and you'll be very glad they did.

A Danish production, but one scraped together with cultural funding from its home nation, as well as Sweden, Norway, France, various private ventures and the European Union, *Flee* is a rare, always intriguing, surprise in animation: it's a documentary. It tells the story of an anonymous refugee – here renamed Amin – who escaped war-torn Afghanistan to Denmark, while also navigating his homosexuality. It's also about the telling of that story, with the real Amin's audio testimony providing

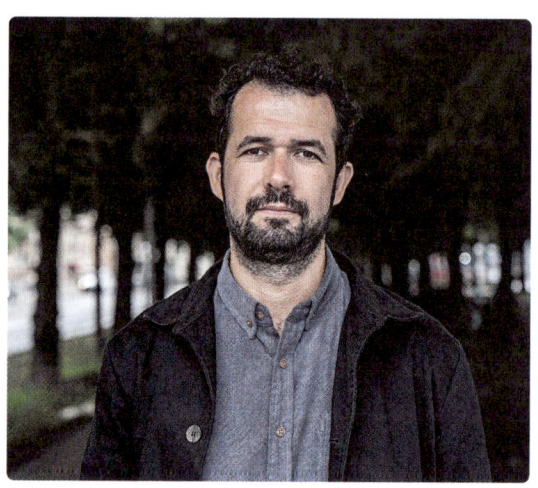

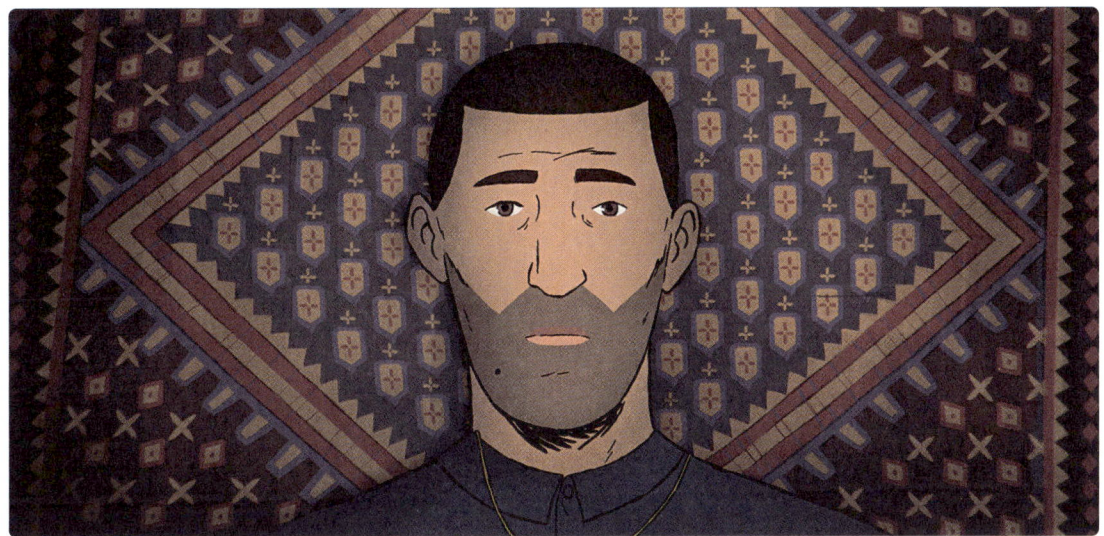

the narration, and the animated avatar of Rasmussen appearing as a recurring character throughout.

Amin's journey is tense, shocking and amazingly joyous. It's framed by Rasmussen and Amin's conversations, staged like a Hollywood therapy session, with Amin lying back on a bed and sinking into memory. These sessions and the reprieves between them are the most reflexive, with clapperboards, focus pulling and the presence of the director all drawing audiences into Amin's experience via familiar non-fiction cinematic techniques. This smartly immerses viewers into feeling the reality of his story, despite its 2D form and its anonymous protagonist. Once that connection is established, the film

can leap into vividly coloured reconstructions of Amin's childhood memories and from there into abstracted charcoal fugues, and still a deep, human empathy and link to the present remain constant.

Flee doesn't use its animated form as a means to push away from reality, instead using it to try and get closer to it. Amin has an everyman look, with his anonymity

Opposite: Jonas Poher Rasmussen, director of *Flee*.

Above: Eye catching. Amin, the subject of *Flee*, meets the viewer's eyeline in one of his many therapy-like interviews.

Below: All bottled up. Switching between past and present, *Flee* is a powerful and intimate outpouring of emotion.

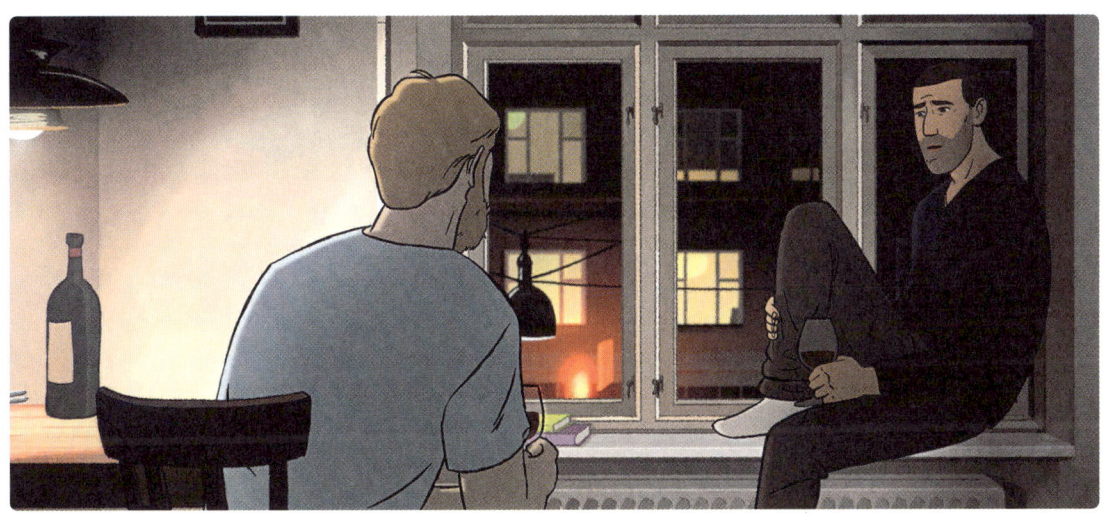

breeding universality – he could be anyone. In the present, and as his remembered young self, he is flat, simple and smoothly lined, at times an unknowable figure that is never as elastically reactive as one might expect of a cartoon, considering the intensity of the emotional burdens on him. When we spoke to Animation Director Kenneth Ladekjær about the film's stylistic approach, he said he wanted to be as "subtle as possible and try to really avoid telling the audience [Amin's emotions] and really force them to try and empathize with him instead". Through both realist and abstract actualization, the film achieves that goal. While some memories are brought to life with bright colour, minute gestures and subtle looks, others are so traumatic that their colours, backgrounds, even faces are erased, leaving only a chalk outline on a harsh, empty void, scrawled on screen. Despite these dramatic aesthetic shifts, the force of empathy remains, first constructed with precision detail, then with loose, panicked scribbling. These moments are perhaps the film's strongest. The fragility of collective refugee lives is reflected in the transience of the fine lines, and the minimalist, almost unfinished nature of the sequences feels like a direct representation of Amin's trauma as it is memorialized and gradually shaded in.

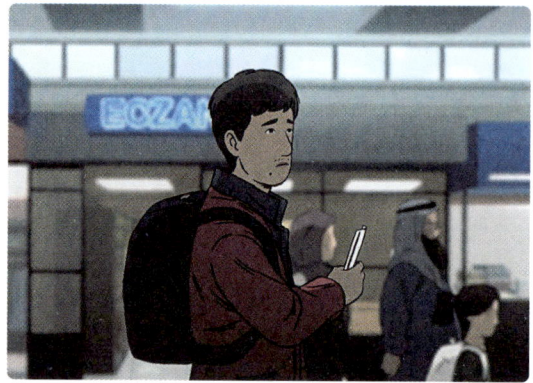

Considering the darkness, both literal and emotional, in those moments, it's remarkable how wonderful *Flee* can be as a viewing experience. During one of the monochrome memories, terrifying flashes of red start to slice through the screen. These could be the bulbs of law enforcement, but instead shift into something more heartening. As the film

Above: Fleeing the past. A teenage Amin has to navigate confusing feelings in a confusing new world as an immigrant.

Below: Amin sits against a window, with the skyline of New York behind him, one of many international locations *Flee* moves between.

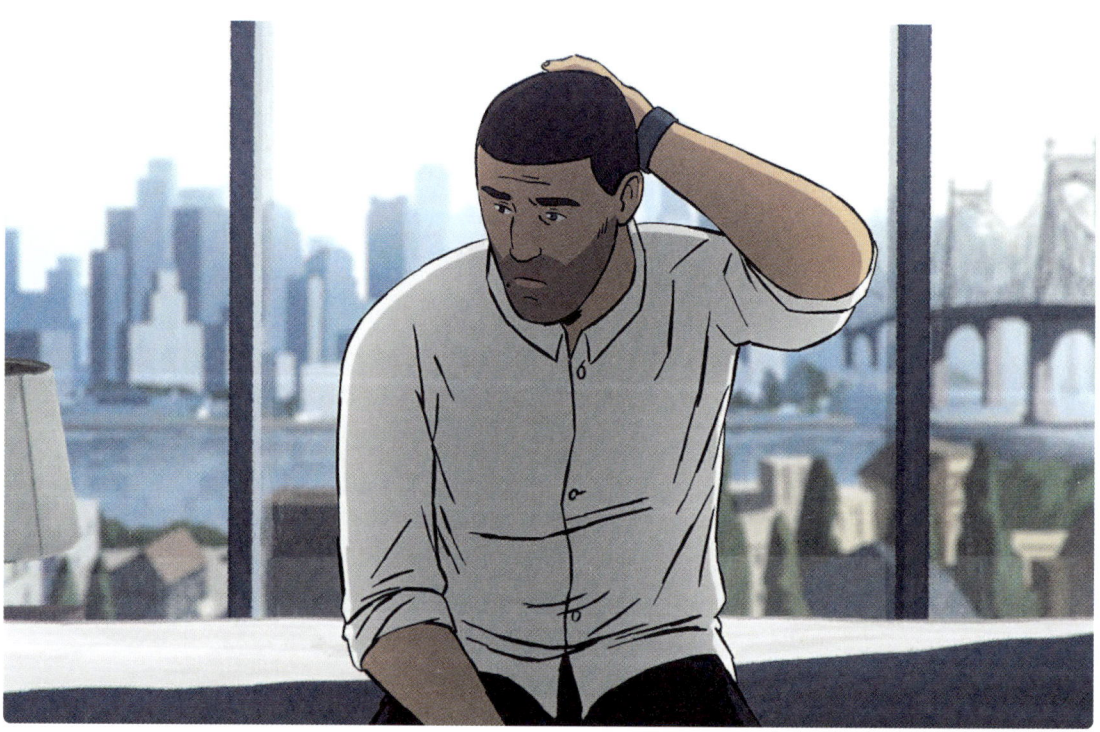

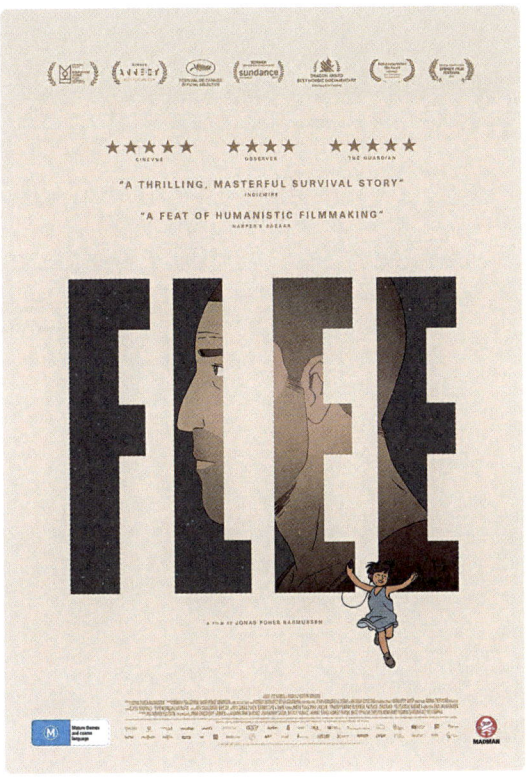

progresses, the lights in Amin's eyes transform, the sirens of trauma engulfed by the flashing joy of a nightclub. He embraces art as its own refuge, from the youthful discovery of Jean-Claude Van Damme (and his films), to the melodramatic escape of Mexican soap operas, to the cathartic pleasure of dancing to Daft Punk, surrounded by a community that embraces him. Film, TV and music are underlined as escapist, restorative powers, even in the most extreme circumstances.

Those powers were felt by the Academy of Motion Picture Arts and Sciences too, rewarding the film with a record-breaking collection of Oscar nominations. It became the first film to score nods for the International Feature, Animated Feature and Documentary Feature prizes all at the same time. Ultimately, it didn't win any of those (*Drive My Car*, *Encanto* and *Summer of Soul* did), but don't let that put you off. *Flee* remains a film you should run towards.

Left: *Flee* was nominated for Best Documentary Feature, Best International Film and Best Animated Feature at the 94th Academy Awards, the first film to do so.

◉ Further Viewing

While the Copenhagen-based studio Sun Creature haven't produced another feature on the scale of *Flee*, their talents are in demand across short form and commercial work, including contributing animation to campaigns for video games such as *Apex Legends*, *Genshin Impact*, *Clash of Clans* and *Marvel's Midnight Suns*. However, to our minds their most impressive and intriguing work comes in the form of a series of tourist films made for Travel Oregon, titled "Only Slightly Exaggerated", which captures the landscape of the Pacific Northwest in a magical style that intentionally evokes the films of Hayao Miyazaki.

In 2006, the Danish Ministry of Culture organized a grand project to form discrete canons of the country's contributions to a range of art forms, from architecture to literature. In the film selection, alongside works by world cinema titans such as Carl Th. Dreyer, Bille August, Thomas Vinterberg and Lars von Trier, there was one animated film: Jannik Hastrup and Flemming Quist Møller's freaky, 41-minute children's odyssey *Benny's Bathtub* (1971). Hastrup's work in animation spans several decades and encompasses both TV series and feature film work, often exploring subversive, anti-capitalist and environmentalist themes. *Benny's Bathtub* is a real head-trip, following a young boy submerged and guided through a colourful underwater wonderland by a magical tadpole, backed by a wild psychedelic-jazz score.

France

Liberté, Egalité, Animé

📽 The King and the Mockingbird (Le Roi et l'Oiseau)

Director: Paul Grimault
Released: 1952/1980

In 2014, the British Film Institute donated a collection of 35 celluloid drawings to the Cinémathèque Française. They had been found, decades before, in a box on the side of the road by a passer-by.

They had been left to rot, but the BFI and the Cinémathèque knew that these pieces of art were of great importance to the history of world animation: they were from *The King and the Mockingbird* (*Le Roi et l'Oiseau*), the landmark French animation from director Paul Grimault.

The story of *The King and the Mockingbird* is one of grand ambition and hard-won rediscovery. Production was first started in the late 1940s by Grimault, already a veteran of French animation and co-founder of the commercial studio Les Gémeaux, and the poet-screenwriter Jacques Prévert, who had previously worked together on the short film *The Little Soldier* (1947). Like that film, they drew influence from the short stories of Hans Christian Andersen for their next project, *The*

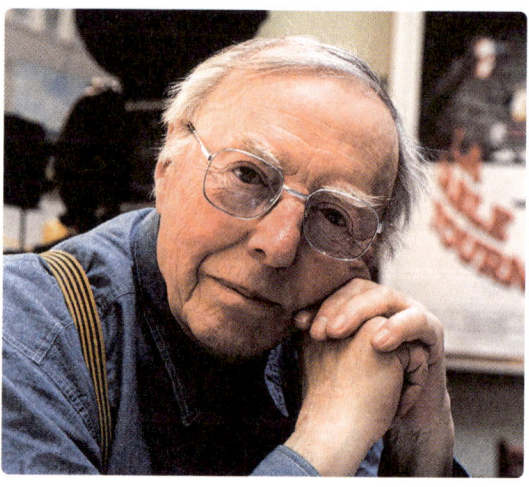

Shepherdess and the Chimney Sweep (La Bergère et le Ramoneur). The film was well resourced with a crew of over a hundred artists working at peak production – pushing forward on what was mooted to be France's first hand-drawn animated feature. However, tensions arose as costs started to spiral. Whole teams of artists were laid off, and eventually Grimault himself was ousted from his own project. Producer André Sarrut took the reins, releasing the film in unfinished form in 1952.

This initial version of the film was warmly received: it won a Jury Prize at the Venice Film Festival and, on the other side of the planet, it became something of a touchpoint for a generation of young Japanese animators, such as Hayao Miyazaki and Isao Takahata. Nevertheless, Grimault disowned *The Shepherdess and the Chimney Sweep* (also known as *The Curious Adventures of Mr. Wonderbird* in English-speaking territories) and he fought to regain ownership of the project in order to capture his vision fully. That process took almost three decades, until the film was finally unveiled in 1980. "They say it took me 35 years to make *The King and the Mockingbird*," Grimault told *Le Figaro*. "In reality, it took me five years (in two parts) to make it – and thirty to find the money!"

This new version of the film reused around two thirds of the 1952 release cut, and then added 40 minutes of extra scenes with help from both new and returning artists. Grimault likened this approach, with material from the 1940s and 1970s sitting side by side, to viewing two paintings of the same landscape by the same artist on different days: familiar, yet different, with new meanings and textures arising from the juxtaposition.

Screenwriter Jacques Prévert was also involved in this second version of the film, although he died in 1977 before production began in earnest. On release, *The King and the Mockingbird* was dedicated to Prévert, and that is the best way to view it: a poet's film. The previous version had been screened at the International Animated Film Festival in London in 1957, where films

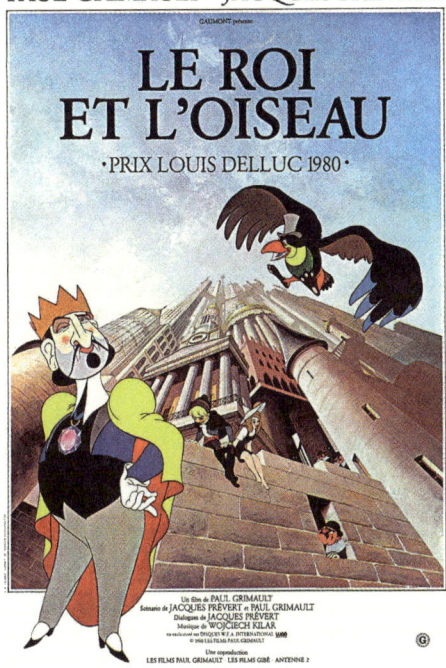

Opposite: Kingmaker. Paul Grimault was a pioneer of French animation, and strove to make the country's first feature-length animated film.

Right top: Take two. The poster for the completed 1980 version of the film, retitled *Le Roi et l'Oiseau*.

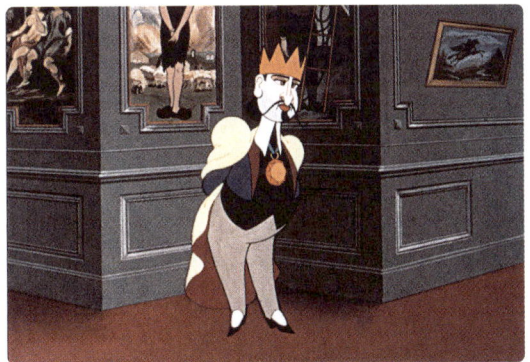

Right middle: Conceited and pompous, the King is a pointed parody of power-hungry despots and their empty vanity.

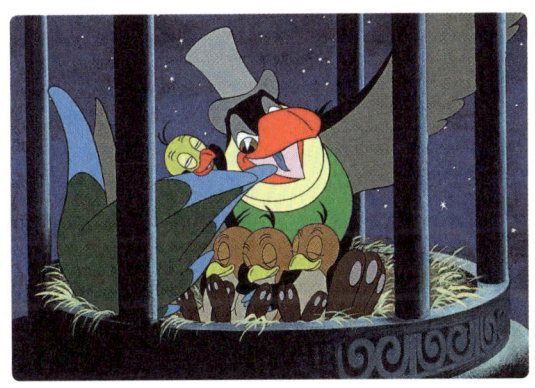

Right: Top Flock. The Mockingbird and his family in their castle nest.

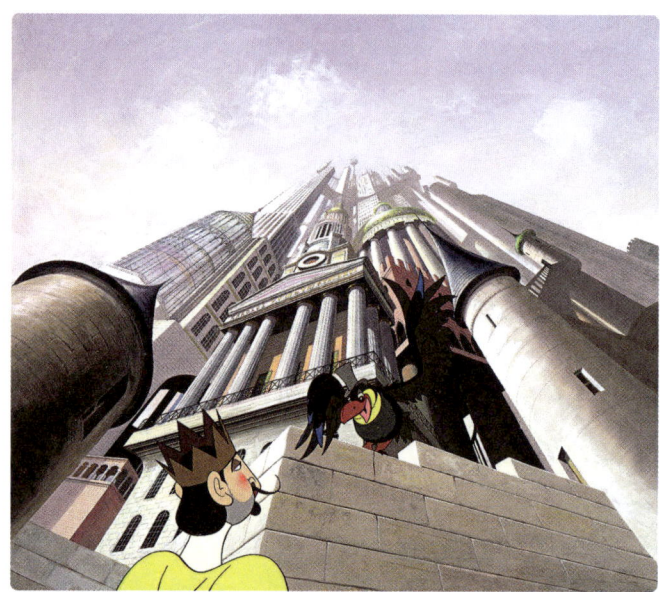

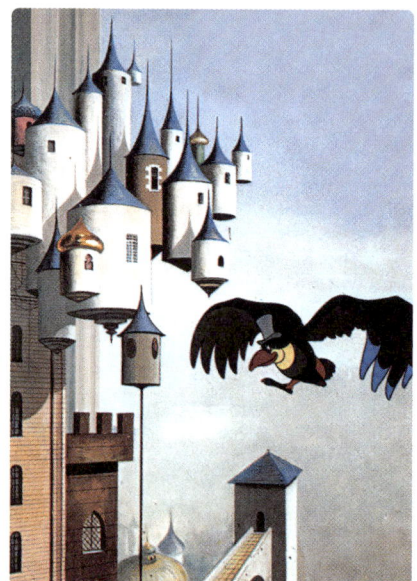

were categorized under themes such as "puppets", "caricature" and "satire", and *Mr. Wonderbird* (as it was then billed) was classed as "philosophy" – standing out in contrast to the likes of *Dumbo* and *Snow White and the Seven Dwarfs*.

Grimault is sometimes referred to as France's answer to Walt Disney, but *The King and the Mockingbird* is no straightforward fairy tale: it pushes Andersen's story into more allegorical territory. The Shepherdess and Chimney Sweep characters, here reimagined as paintings come to life, are let loose in a sprawling castle kingdom of a conceited tyrannical ruler – himself overthrown by his own portrait. There's a superficial similarity in the character designs to contemporary films from Disney and the Fleischer Brothers – the classical romantic figures of the heroes, the bulky streetwise buffoons in the King's policemen – but *The King and the Mockingbird* has a beguiling quality all of its own: loose, exploratory and ultimately profound.

At the centre of it all is the King's 296-storey palace: a skyscraping mishmash of architectural styles that evokes Bruegel's *The Tower of Babel* in its colossal commentary on human hubris. It has a dizzying verticality that grows in meaning as the characters venture from penthouse to poverty-stricken underbelly, presenting us with an animated answer to both Fritz Lang's *Metropolis* (1927) and Charlie Chaplin's *Modern Times* (1936), captured in a retrofuturistic fashion that sees gleaming elevators pass by towers of stone, marble and glass.

When our heroes scurry down vast staircases that surround the castle's exterior, it's possible to see the chains of influence spreading out through the decades, and imagine Chihiro perilously scampering around the edges of the bathhouse in Hayao Miyazaki's *Spirited Away* (2001), or Sophie and the Witch of the Waste scaling the steep stairs up to the Royal Palace in *Howl's Moving Castle* (2004). It's also likely that the mind of young Miyazaki was set alight by another of Grimault and Prévert's creations: a gigantic robot, made by the King to tyrannize and subdue, but turned against its maker and his domain.

A final sequence added by Prévert before his death offers a perfect crystallization of the film's themes of freedom, resistance and revolution. As the dust settles on the new, open landscape left behind by the destruction of the King's empire, we spy one of the Mockingbird's rebellious chicks caught in a trap set by the castle guards. The giant hand of the robot delicately unlocks the trap's mechanism to let the chick fly free, before clenching into a formidable fist, and coming down with great force on the cage – shattering it, decisively, for good.

Above: The dizzying verticality of the King's palace is one of the many enduring, influential aspects of *The King and the Mockingbird*.

📽 Fantastic Planet (La Planète sauvage)

Director: René Laloux
Release date: 1973

"Take a trip to the Odeon St. Martin's Lane for an hallucinatory experience that will blow your mind," read the newspaper ads when René Laloux's animated sci-fi headtrip *Fantastic Planet* opened in London on Halloween night in 1974.

On arrival, the film's place in the canon of stoner movies was already assured. When it had been released in the States the previous year by Roger Corman's notorious distributor of B-movie schlock and international arthouse flicks, New World Pictures, the publicists had reportedly recommended that the film was best enjoyed – and understood – with a side order of psychedelics.

In a way, you can't blame them. *Fantastic Planet* is a strange and dreamy film that looks like a space-rock album cover come to life, and tells the story of giant blue aliens ("Draags") and the tiny humans ("Oms") that they treat alternately as insects and pets. Its bizarre allegory plays out across a beautiful yet forbidding landscape,

as the Oms rebel against their oppressors and weather their violent retaliation, before stealing a source of ultimate knowledge and seeking new life among the stars. *Fantastic Planet* is visually dense, at times glacially paced, and it's backed by a soundtrack packed with mild jazz-funk jams, courtesy of Alain Goraguer, the regular Serge Gainsbourg collaborator. It's weirdo sci-fi at its best.

Below left: Double act. Director René Laloux and designer Roland Topor pose on the famous Promenade de la Croisette in Cannes.

Below right: Om and Draag. A poster for *Fantastic Planet* foregrounds the relationship between giant blue aliens and their tiny humanoid pets.

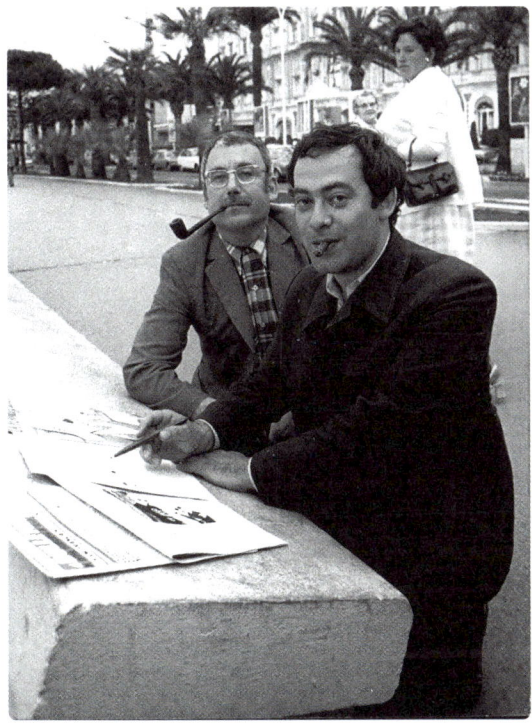

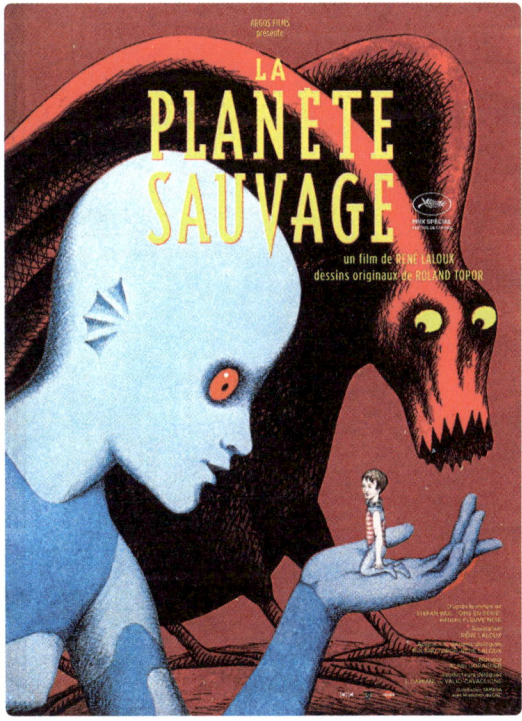

Critics at the time, through the thick marijuana fug, noted the film's potential commentary on the contemporary Civil Rights Movement and the Cold War. Director René Laloux, on the other hand, described the film in its press book as "a sort of hymn to education" – no doubt drawing from his experiences organizing painting and shadow puppetry workshops for residents at psychiatric clinics and troubled children.

Laloux's closest collaborator on the feature was illustrator, designer and co-writer Roland Topor, following their work on short films like *Les Escargots* (1965) – an odd and beguiling monster movie where gigantic carnivorous snails roam the rural landscape. A multitalented eccentric, Topor took many left turns through his long career, including creating a surrealist art-theatre collective with Alejandro Jodorowsky, writing the novel that inspired Roman Polanski's *The Tenant* (1976), and later appearing as an actor in Werner Herzog's *Nosferatu the Vampyre* (1979) – but it's his inimitable work on *Fantastic Planet* for which he's most remembered.

To animate Topor's otherworldly designs, Laloux had to look outside of France. "We immediately thought of Prague," he explained in the film's press book, "which

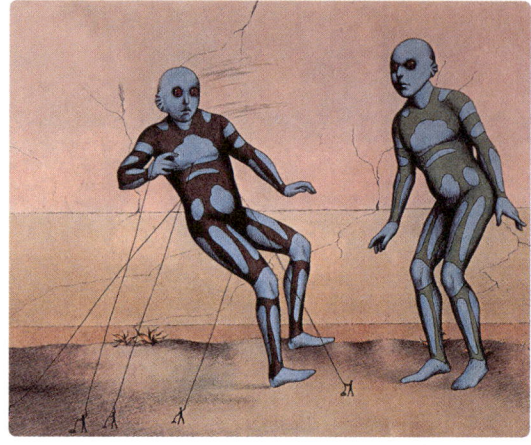

is the European capital of animation." Specifically, the project was undertaken by animators at Jiří Trnka Studio, the company founded by the Czech stop-motion pioneer (see page 48). That tradition would come in handy,

Above: Born Trippy. The minuscule Om creatures successfully topple a giant Draag.

Below: Blue Bloods. The war between the two species takes a gory turn.

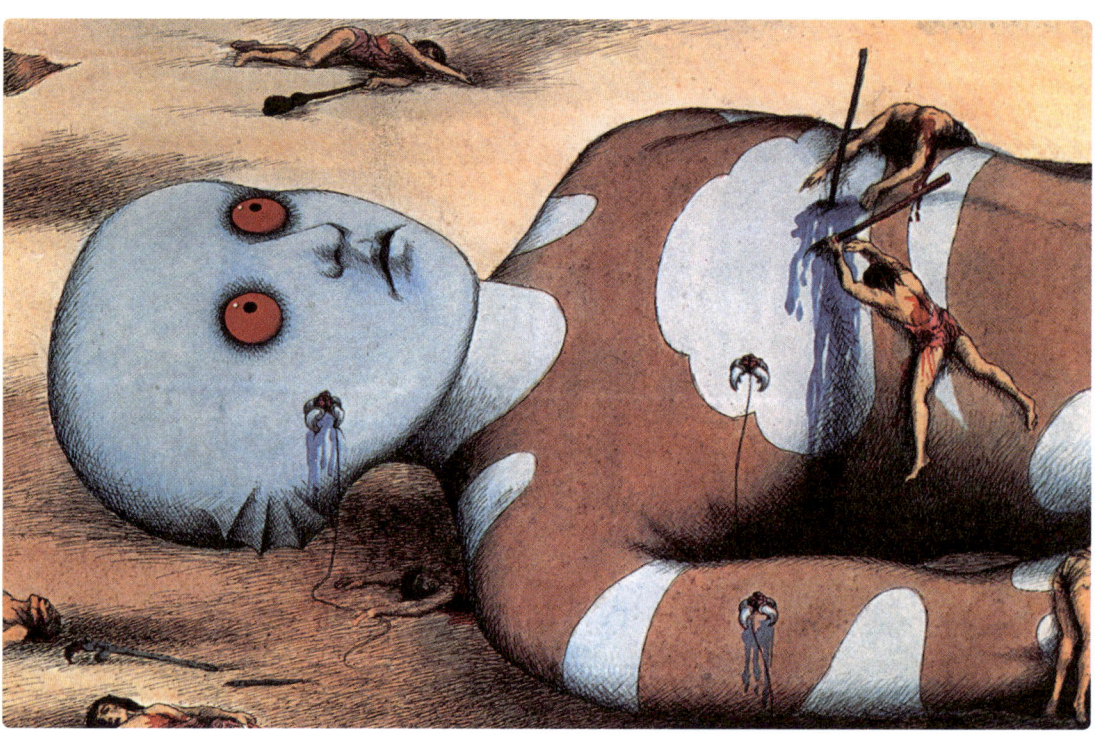

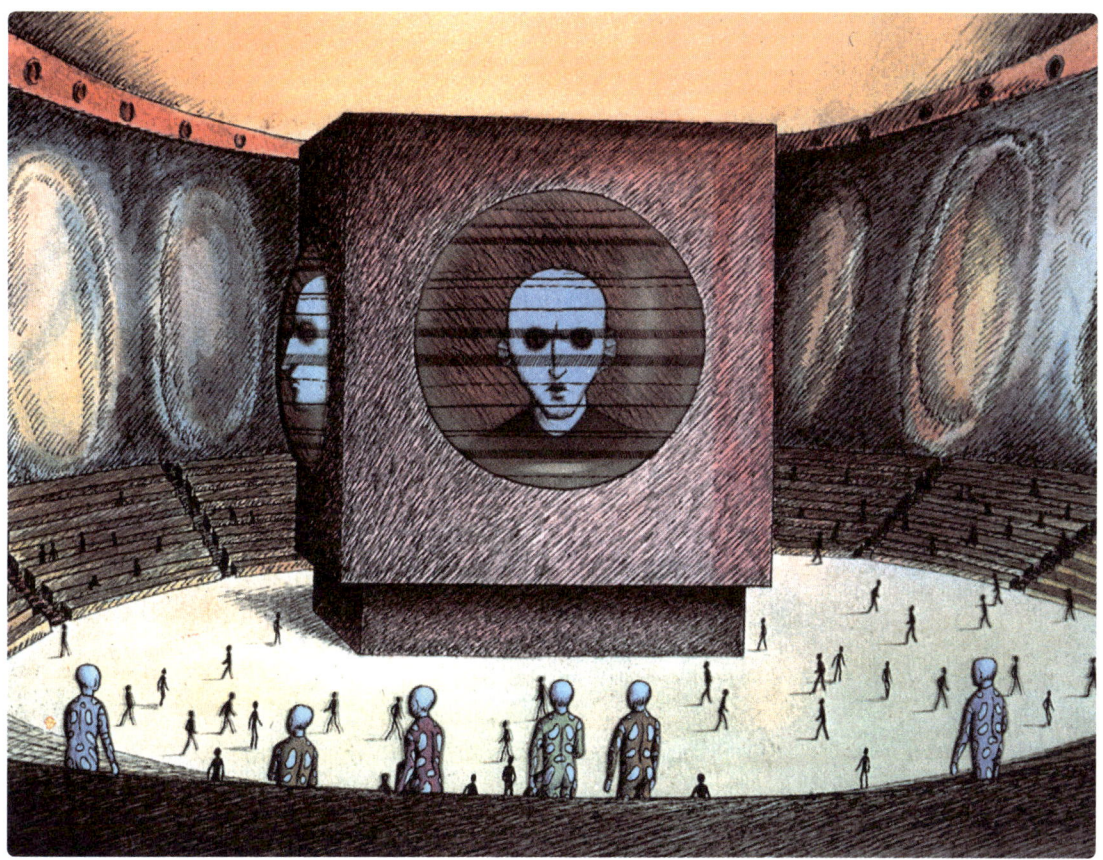

because Laloux wanted to use a paper cut-out animation technique. In contrast to what he described as the American, Disney style of hand-drawn animation, which was fluid but visually poor, Laloux argued that animating cut-out designs retained "a great graphical richness" and brought the film into more of an artistic tradition, like the films of Polish graphic artist-animator Jan Lenica.

In keeping with its more artistic ambitions, *Fantastic Planet* premiered at the Cannes Film Festival in 1973 and won a Special Jury Prize. Over 50 years on, it remains one of the very few animated features picked to compete for the coveted Palme d'Or at Cannes. Other members of this very select club include *Dumbo* (1941), *Make Mine Music* (1946), *Peter Pan* (1953), *Shrek* (2001), *Shrek 2* (2004), *Ghost in the Shell 2: Innocence* (2004), *Persepolis* (2007), *Waltz with Bashir* (2008) and, most recently, *The Most Precious of Cargoes* (2024).

Still, its influence endures, and can be seen across graphic art, independent comics and animation, with the 2023 series *Scavengers Reign* picking up the baton

and pushing even further into the surreal and unsettling depths of extraterrestrial flora and fauna. You can even find traces of *Fantastic Planet* in the world of video games, too. When Nintendo was looking to move away from the familiar imagery of Mario and Zelda for a new game called *Pikmin*, which would be set on an alien planet filled with tiny creatures fighting for survival, they knew where to look. "I wanted to take a bold step and depict a somber, mature, and mysterious world," recalled game director Shigefumi Hiro. "So, we said, 'Let's watch a movie together for inspiration!' and the choice was an animated movie called *Fantastic Planet*. We all had puzzled looks on our faces while watching it [laughs]." Much like those Londoners were promised back in 1974, the minds of the team at Nintendo had been blown.

Above: Strange New Worlds. The rich designs of *Fantastic Planet* brought the visual language of sci-fi novel artwork to the cinema screen.

🎥 Chicken for Linda (Linda veut du poulet!)

Director: Chiara Malta and Sébastien Laudenbach
Release date: 2023

This exuberant feature is the culmination of over 20 years of friendship and collaboration between the Italian live-action filmmaker Chiara Malta and the French animator Sébastien Laudenbach.

The story is all there in the title: our 8-year-old protagonist Linda has a hunger for chicken. Not just any kind of chicken, though: the specific dish of chicken with peppers that was often cooked by her father, who died when she was a baby. The problem is, her mother Paulette is useless at cooking. And, worse still, a general strike has shuttered shops across town.

What ensues is something of a wild chicken chase, captured in a vibrant artistic style. An entire animated world is created out of splashes of colour and free-form line work that seem to breathe along with the action. Characters are swathed in unique colours – yellow for Linda, orange for Paulette, red for the chicken – that bleed outside of the lines, like a child's haphazard colouring-in exercise. Like in *The Tale of the Princess Kaguya* (2013) or

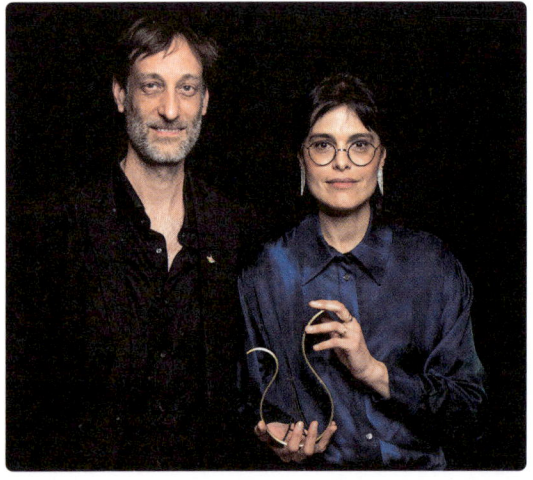

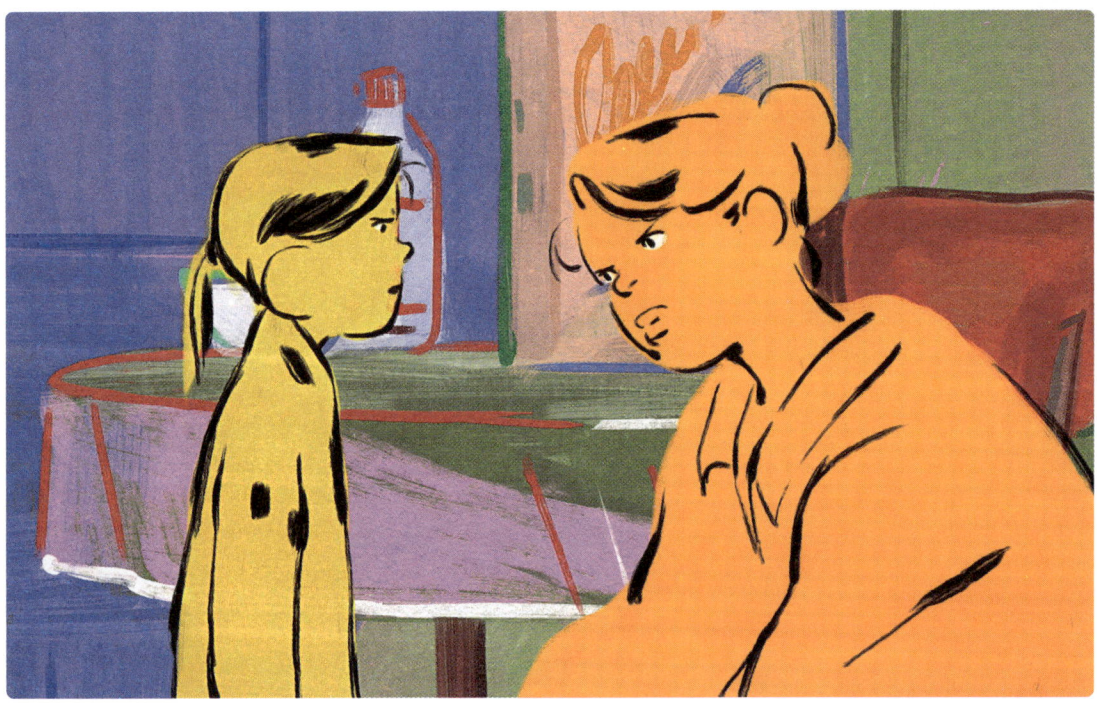

the work of Frédéric Back (see page 12), this is cinema that foregrounds the movement of shapes, the twisting of lines and characters that transform between recognizable figures and abstracted forms. Animation at its most expressive: miraculous and alive.

Nevertheless, the directors are quick to confess that despite working in animation, they wouldn't call themselves animation *fans*. Even Laudenbach, a filmmaker with an impressive back catalogue of shorts and music videos to his name, alongside his lush, feature-length Grimm fairy tale adaptation *The Girl Without Hands* (2016), admits that he only turned to animation after "failing" to make it as a comics artist. Both he and Malta approached *Chicken for Linda* as an opportunity to craft a film in which children could "recognize themselves", and find "value in the way they think and

Opposite: The directors behind this wild, colourful celebration of childhood, Chiara Malta and Sébastien Laudenbach

Opposite below: At the heart of *Chicken for Linda* is the relationship between the young girl and her single mother, Paulette.

Right: The US poster for *Chicken for Linda* shows off the film's bold colour scheme – with characters rendered in unique colours.

Below: The chaos of the film's wild chicken chase spills over into the courtyard in front of Linda's apartment building.

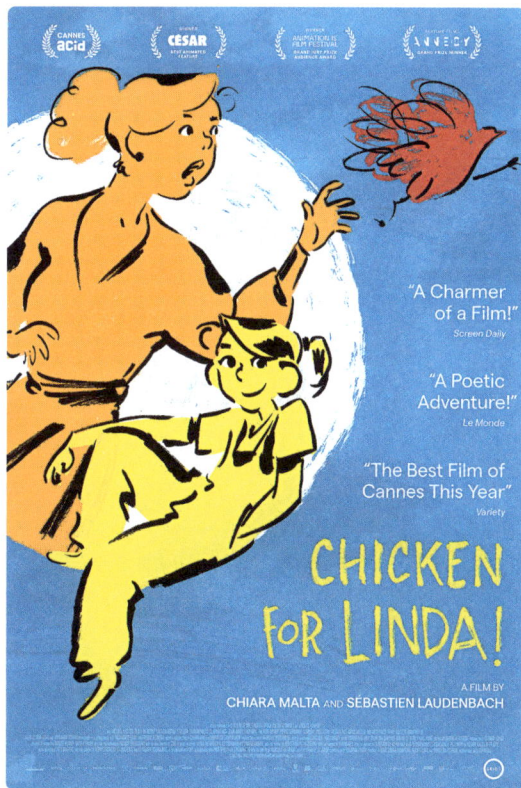

"A Charmer of a Film!"
Screen Daily

"A Poetic Adventure!"
Le Monde

"The Best Film of Cannes This Year"
Variety

CHICKEN FOR LINDA!

A FILM BY
CHIARA MALTA AND SÉBASTIEN LAUDENBACH

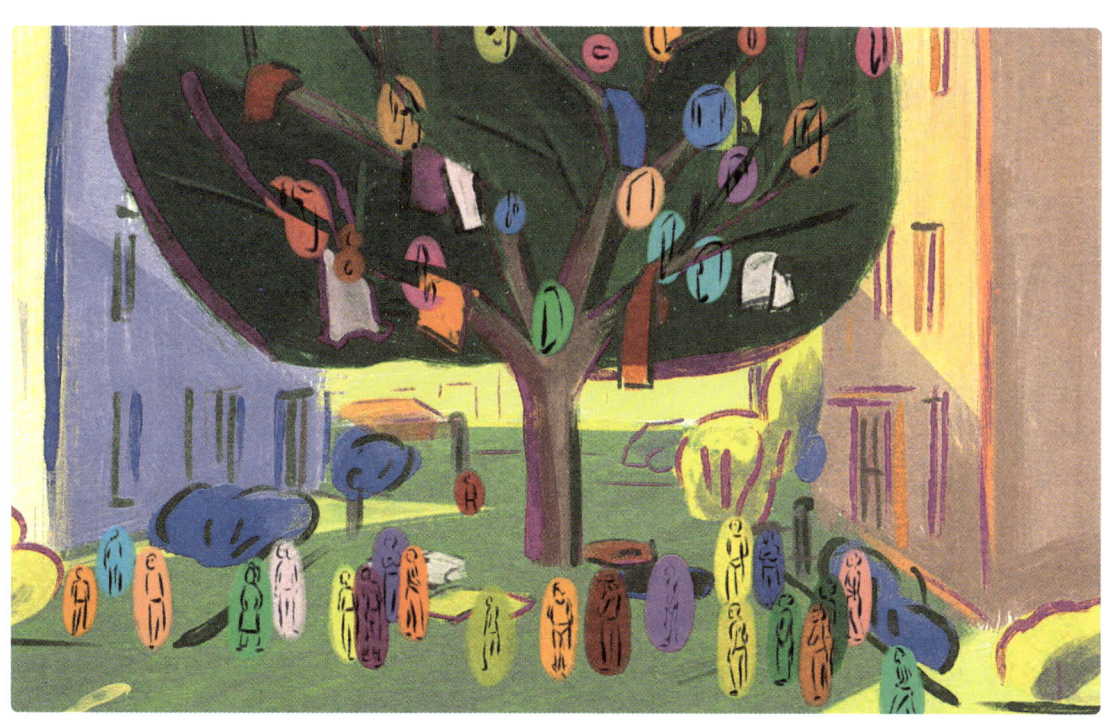

see the world", as well as a chance to delve into themes that they feel are underexplored in films for children: memory, melancholy and, above all, rebellion.

In pursuit of this goal, they were inspired by films that are dedicated to or inspired by free-spirited children, such as Peter Bogdanovich's New Hollywood gem *Paper Moon* (1973), Louis Malle's riotous *Zazie dans le Métro* (1960) and François Truffaut's *Small Change* (1976, known as *Pocket Money* outside the US). The latter film features a sequence with images of children bursting out of their houses, like corks popping from bottles, and invading the streets, which informed *Linda's* anarchic energy and freewheeling storytelling: what begins with one child's mournful craving soon snowballs into a carnivalesque revolt that shakes the foundations of her Parisian neighbourhood.

Rather than telling their story in live action, though, the directors chose animation, and there's no better medium to capture the vibrancy and chaos of childhood. Liberated from filming real children on camera, Malta

and Laudenbach were able to record the voices of children as they improvised and played on location in schoolyards and out in the urban wilderness – and then their small team of animators and artists were able to bring it to stunning life.

As a result, *Chicken for Linda* is one great big colourful swirl of feeling. It's wild and it's wise, and it uses animation to its fullest potential. "We're interested in animation," explains Laudenbach, "because it's a good way to tell the truth." In the absence of live human characters, the action on screen consists only of lines and colour. "But the movement and rhythm of the drawings," he continues, "are a good way to speak about people, and speak about the world."

Below top: Kind of Blue. Over the course of their adventure, Linda and Paulette cross paths with a put-upon cop and an amorous truck driver.

Below bottom: Winner Winner. After the chicken dinner has finally been served up, Paulette and the truck driver, Jean-Michel, share a meaningful glance.

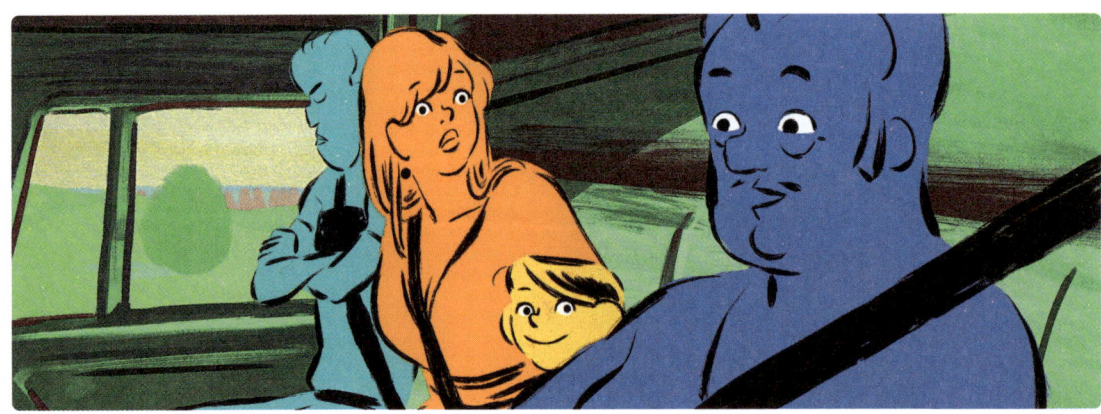

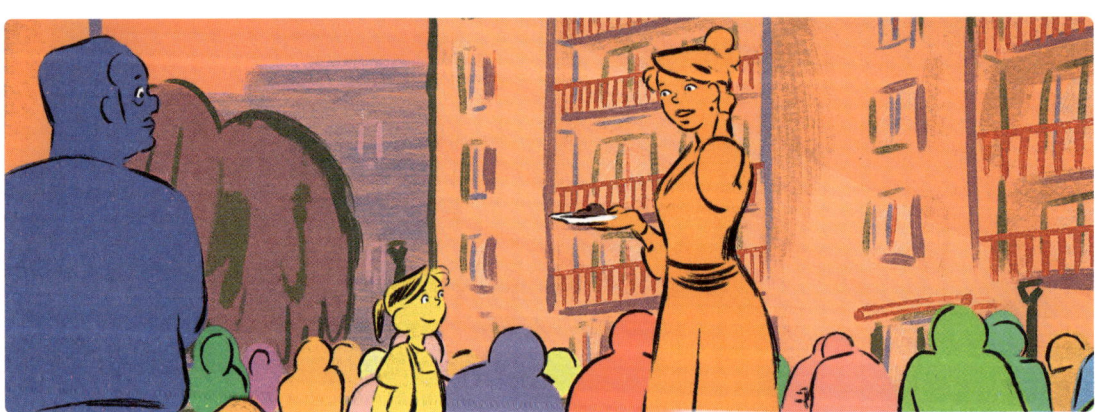

⊙ Further Viewing

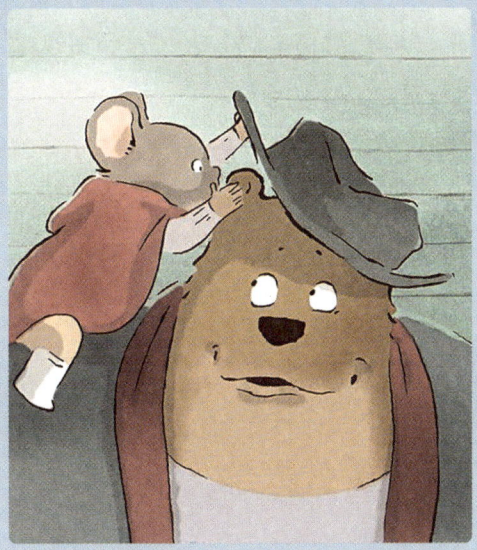

France is undeniably one of animation's global superpowers – and not just because it is home to the Annecy International Animation Festival, possibly the most important date in the calendar for the industry and art form. French companies are also major backers for animated projects from around the world, several of which we've included in other chapters. Like with comics, French society at large considers animation to be an integral component of a broad cultural diet – to an extent that makes us in the English-speaking world green with envy. For our three picks for this chapter, we prioritized personal favourites, but left out two of the most widely recognized *auteurs* of French animation. Sylvain Chomet garnered international renown and several Oscar nominations for his wonkily designed, endearingly odd films *The Old Lady and the Pigeons* (1996) and *Belleville Rendez-Vous* (2003), and his dual homage to both the city of Edinburgh and the French comedy legend Jacques Tati, *The Illusionist* (2010). He later received what might be the highest honour in animation: the chance to redesign the opening

"couch gag" sequence of *The Simpsons*. And then there's Michel Ocelot, a veteran of the industry who has worked across traditional hand-drawn animation, cut-out silhouettes and 3D CG techniques in his career-long exploration of global traditions of fairy tales and folklore, in such films as *Kirikou and the Sorceress* (1998), *Azur & Asmar: The Prince's Quest* (2006) and *Tales of the Night* (2011). It seems that every year brings several new gems from France, so here are a few more recent recommendations: the heartwarming *Ernest & Celestine* (2012), the unexpectedly moving tale of one disembodied hand's crosstown odyssey, *I Lost My Body* (2019), the genre-splicing sci-fi thriller *Mars Express* (2023), and the mesmerizing, abstract short *Genius Loci* (2020), from Cartoon Saloon alum Maya Merigeau.

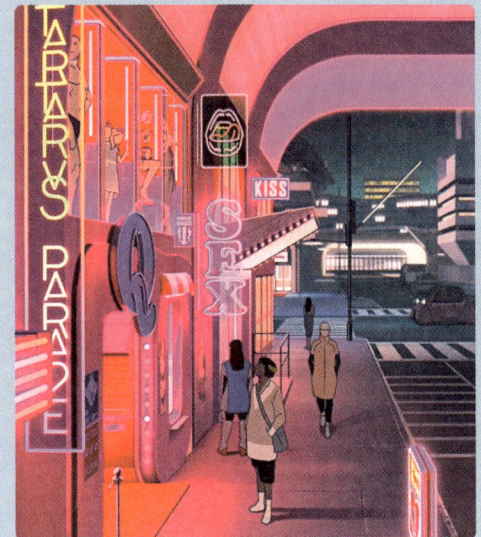

Top left: A game of Bear and Mouse. Adapted from Gabrielle Vincent's children's books, *Ernest and Celestine* is a watercolour-style wonder.

Above: Neon Nights. Jérémie Périn's *Mars Express* mixes futuristic sci-fi and noirish thrills.

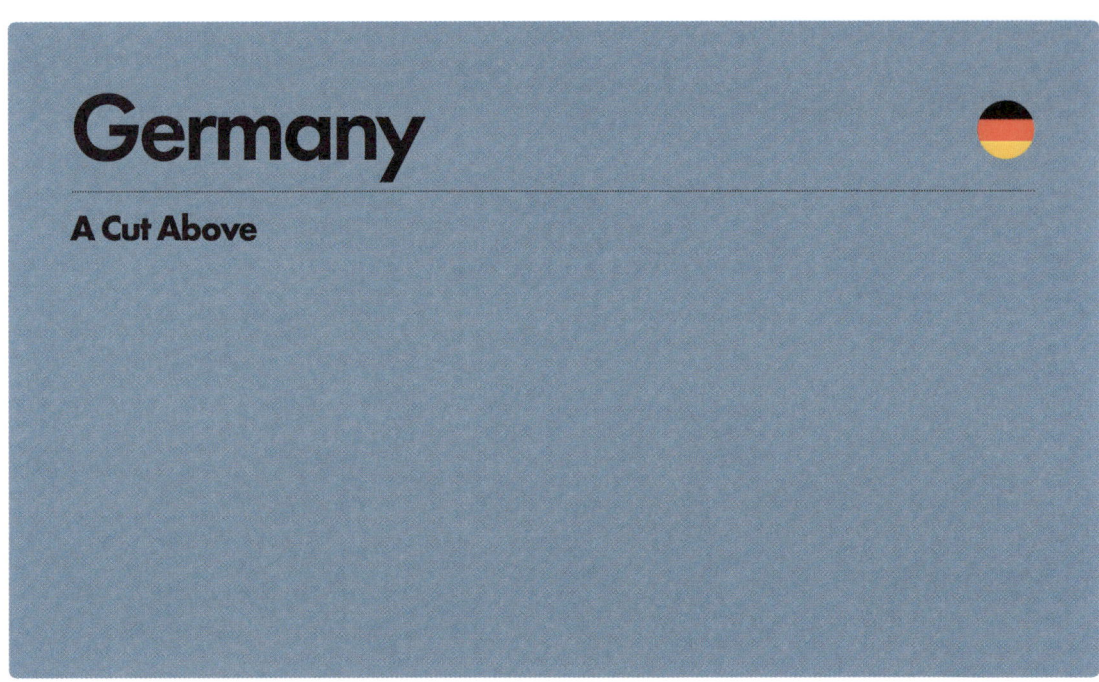

Germany

A Cut Above

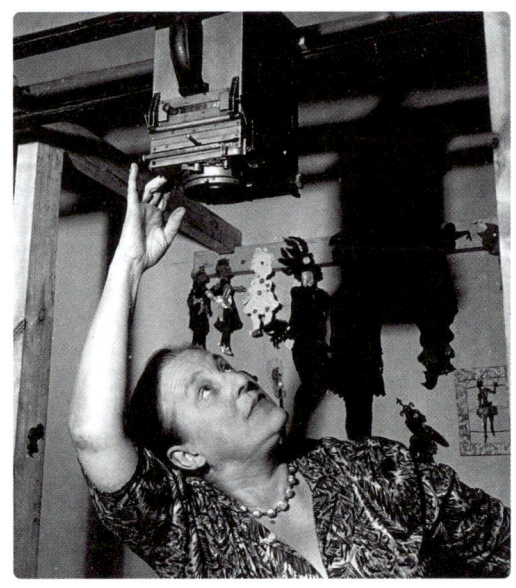

📽 The Adventures of Prince Achmed (Die Abenteuer des Prinzen Achmed)

Director: Lotte Reiniger
Released: 1926

First unveiled in 1926, *The Adventures of Prince Achmed* is an adaptation of tales from the *One Thousand and One Nights*. Told in silhouette, paper cut-out style, it is the oldest surviving feature-length animated film.

Director Lotte Reiniger was only 27 when her film premiered to the public, and the medium of animation itself was young, too. "At this time animation was still walking in its infant shoes," Reiniger wrote in 1972. "There was no Mickey Mouse yet. We had to experiment and try out all sorts of inventions to make the story come alive. The more the shooting of Prince Achmed advanced, the more ambitious he became. But he was lucky."

We're lucky we're even able to watch Prince Achmed today. The original negative of the film was destroyed during the Battle of Berlin at the end of the Second World War, but it was later discovered that the British Film Institute had made a copy, setting the scene for a revival of interest in the 1970s, and then a full restoration undertaken by the Deutsches Filmmuseum in Frankfurt in 1999.

But the luck to which Reiniger alluded was a confluence of circumstances that allowed Prince Achmed to fly, such as the community of collaborators that clustered around the project. Reiniger herself cut out tens of thousands of pieces of paper and assembled them into wire-hinged characters and sets, while the colourful, spectacular backgrounds, weather and magic effects were created by two men who were innovative filmmakers in their own right: Walter Ruttmann (*Berlin: Die Sinfonie der Großstadt – Berlin: Symphony of a Metropolis*, 1927) and Berthold Bartosch (*The Idea*, 1932).

Opposite: Scissor Sister. A pioneer of world animation and a legend of the form: Lotte Reiniger.

Right: *Aladdin* tells the story of how he was tricked by the evil sorcerer.

Below: As Achmed looks on, Peri Banu, the ruler of the magical island of Wak Wak, flies into frame to bathe in the lake.

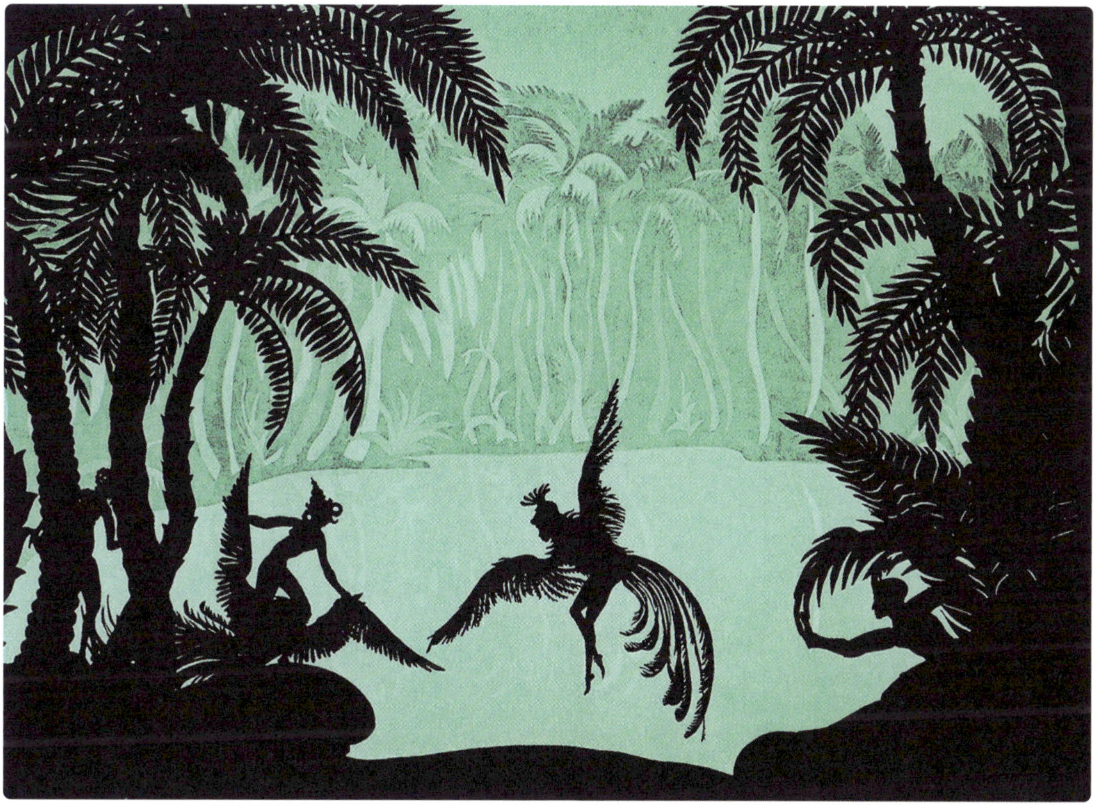

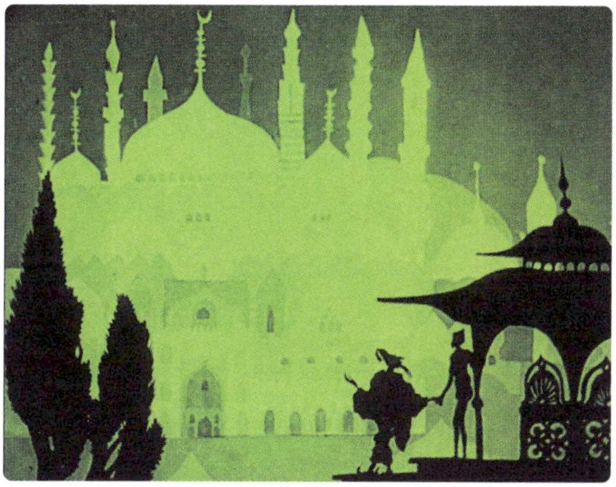

Reiniger's husband, Carl Koch, produced the film, with backing from patron Louis Hagen, a banker who first suggested the idea of giving Reiniger's silhouette technique a feature-length canvas. It was in their studio, in an attic above the garage in Hagen's garden in Potsdam, that Reiniger and company were given the time and space to experiment. There they tinkered

with innovations such as a precursor to the multiplane camera, which allowed figures and other elements in the foreground and background of a composition to be manipulated and shot on separate layers, giving a new sense of depth to the animated film image.

Reiniger had been introduced to the art of *scherenschnitte* – cutting intricate designs out of paper – at a young age. "I could cut out silhouettes almost as soon as I could manage to hold a pair of scissors," she wrote in an essay for *Sight and Sound* in 1936. "The silhouettes were very much praised, and I cut out silhouettes for all the birthdays in the family." As a young woman she discovered German Expressionist cinema and the films of director Paul Wegener, who gave Reiniger her first start in film.

To fill the feature-length runtime, *The Adventures of Prince Achmed* brings together a number of stories from the *One Thousand and One Nights*, including tales of Aladdin and the Ebony Horse, to create one rousing adventure filled with sorcerers, witches, demons, maidens, heroes and villains. As is to be expected, its characters are a hodgepodge of Orientalist caricatures, but there is an undeniable, timeless appeal to the film itself. Maybe it's the precision of Reiniger's skill, how sharply defined and lifelike her characters are, how intricately cut their robes, armour and headdresses, and how sprightly they are in movement.

Or perhaps it's the curious, ethereal quality of Reiniger's technique itself: how it stands apart from animation that is drawn, sculpted or modelled, using materials to create something fully formed before our eyes. This is, perhaps, the ultimate expression of the power of animation. Flying horses, dreadful monsters, fantastical transformations, tempestuous ocean odysseys and epic battles between spirits and heroes – all are suggested from mere silhouettes, shaped out of light and shadow. More than the familiar traditions of animated cinema, *The Adventures of Prince Achmed* is fundamentally connected to the pre-cinema era of the magic lantern, and the age-old traditions of shadow-puppetry and paper cutting – art forms so old and primal that their magic never fades.

"Those were the days," Reiniger recalled years later when reflecting on this fertile period of animation history. "With each new film we could make new discoveries. The whole field was virgin soil and we had all the joys of explorers in an unknown country."

Below: Errol Thin. Even though he's made out of cardboard, Prince Achmed is as dashing and daring as any big-screen action star.

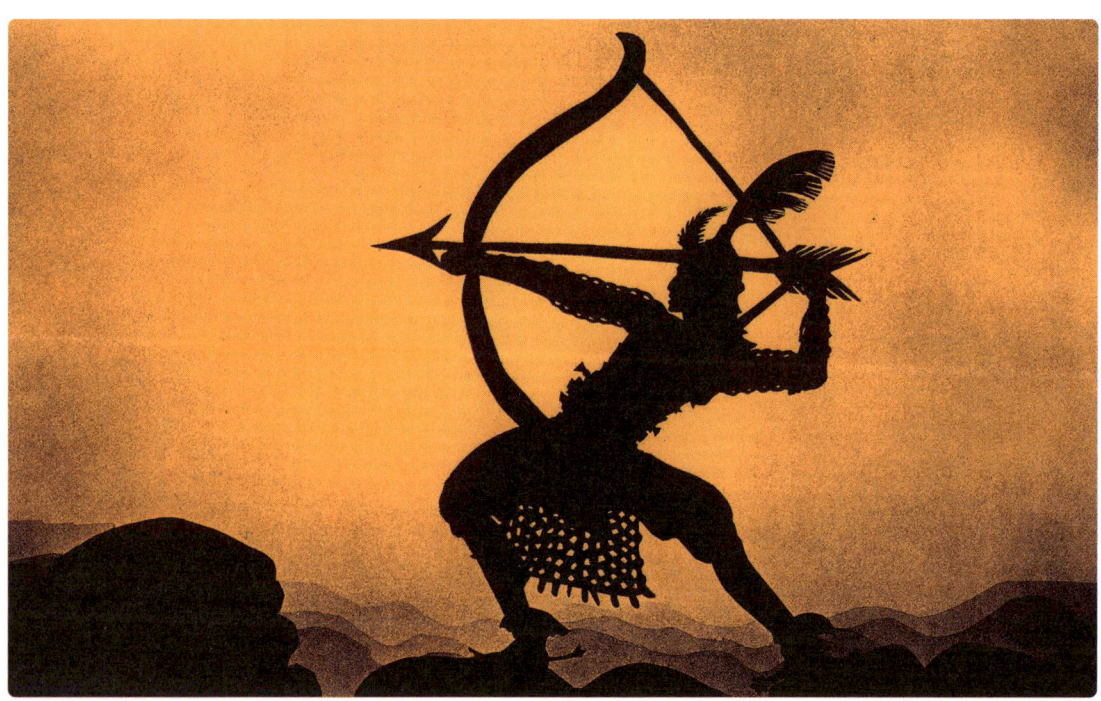

◉ Further Viewing

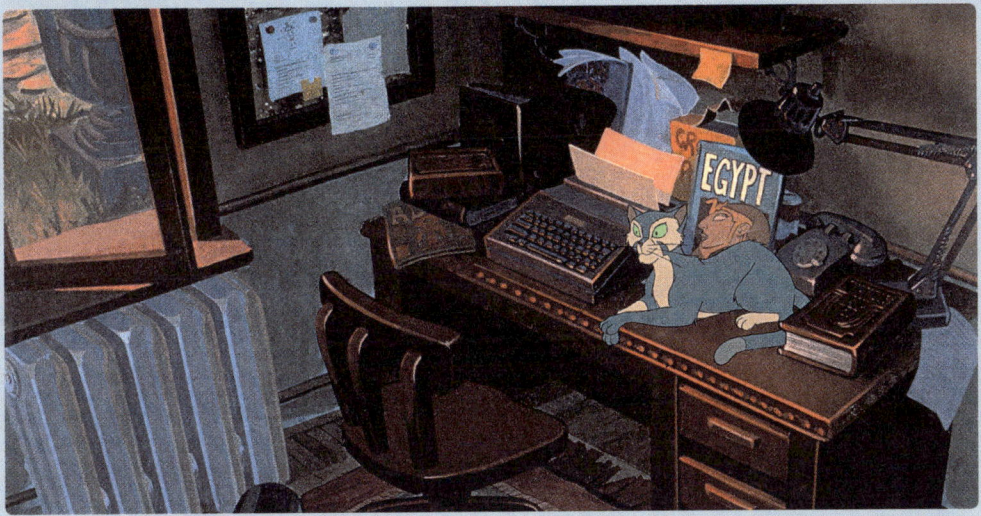

For a change of pace after Lotte Reiniger's magical children's fables, track down *Felidae* (1994), a self-described "Katzenthriller" adapted from German-Turkish author Akif Pirinçci's series of feline-fronted crime novels. It may look like a straight-to-video knock-off of *The Aristocats* (1970), but *Felidae* is a twisty murder-mystery thriller, all seen from the perspective of Francis, a new mog in town, who takes it upon himself to get to the bottom of a series of grisly deaths among the local cat community. While its overall look is rather conventional – all the better to subvert expectations, perhaps? – there's much to enjoy in its confident collision of cute animals and abject horror, as Francis's investigation exposes an undercurrent of sex, violence, animal testing, genetic experiments and extremist zealotry. A more serious-minded *chat noir* cousin to *Fritz the Cat* (1972), this curio should be filed next to *Watership Down* (1978) as a dense animal adventure that is more than what it may seem on the surface.

For more pioneering German animation, seek out the Diehl Brothers' stop-motion Grimm fairy-tale adaptation *The Seven Ravens* (1937), which arrived in German cinemas mere weeks before *Snow White and the Seven Dwarfs* (1937) was released on the other side of the Atlantic. On the more surreal and strange end of the scale, look for the trippy landscapes and experimental collage of East German artist Lutz Dammbeck's *Einmart* (1981), Wolfgang and Christoph Lauenstein's eerie, allegorical Oscar winner *Balance* (1989), and Steffen Schäffler's *Periwig Maker* (1999), a haunting stop-motion short drawn from the pages of Daniel Defoe's *A Journal of the Plague Year*. More recently, it's common to see German animators attached as co-producers to pan-European projects, such as the Austrian-German co-production *Tehran Taboo* (2017), an adult animated drama from German-Iranian animator Ali Soozandeh which explores hypocrisy around matters of sex and gender in contemporary Iranian society.

Above: Cat's Entertainment. 1994's *Felidae* brought the intrigue of detective fiction to the subgenre of feline animation.

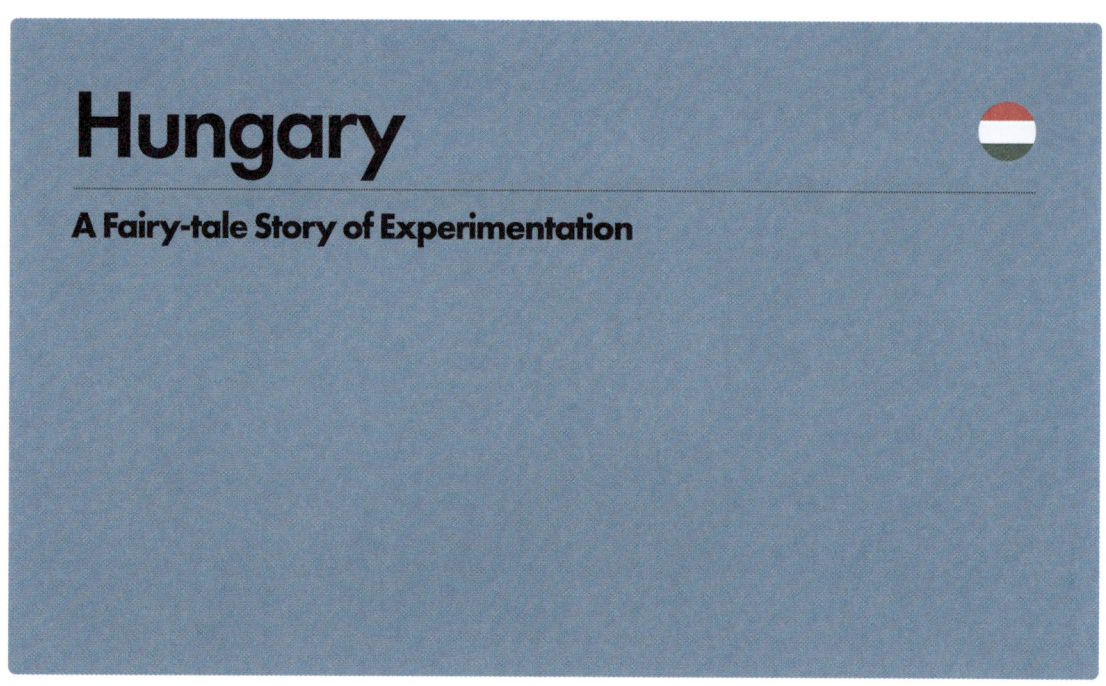

Hungary

A Fairy-tale Story of Experimentation

🎥 Son of the White Mare

Director: Marcell Jankovics
Released: 1981

Fairy tales have always been a playground for animators. *Snow White* (1937) was the pioneering princess, then more Grimm tales with the grim shaved off – and the growth of a giant corporate entity – followed in her footsteps.

Decades (and many more filmic fairy tales) later, the film to win 2002's inaugural Best Animated Feature Film, *Shrek*, offered an all-star deconstruction of fairy tale tropes, with its ogre turned hero, its princess eschewing transformative beauty standards and its surprising amount of toilet humour. But in between, in 1981, Hungarian director Marcell Jankovics offered up a different take on the animated fairy tale; one that can occupy equally the wide eyes of the mesmerized toddler and the pink-tinged ones of the herbal enthusiast.

Son of the White Mare, a psychedelic adaptation of a Hungarian fairy tale, is Jankovics' second feature. The first, *Johnny Corncob* (1973), is an adaptation of an epic poem about a soldier and the woman he yearns for, which takes a lot of visual cues from *Yellow Submarine*

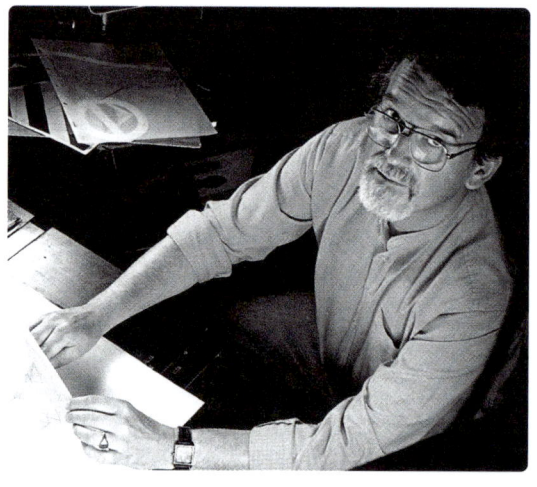

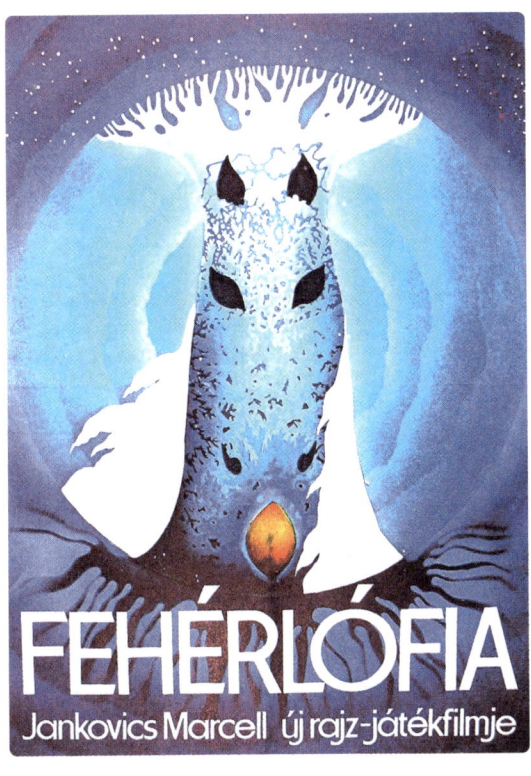

FEHÉRLÓFIA

Jankovics Marcell új rajz-játékfilmje

(1968, see page 120) and was Hungary's first ever feature animation. He followed it with two shorts: *Sisyphus* (1974), an elegant calligraphic telling of the ancient myth that would score him an Oscar nomination, and *The Struggle* (1977) which won the short film Palme d'Or at the Cannes Film Festival, and is one of the most striking and concise explorations of art, artist and legacy that one can discover.

1981 saw the release of *Son of the White Mare*, a film of simple, if nonsensical, narrative form and overwhelming beauty. In this film Jankovics shifts style from his earlier works, his outlines now thick, his textures flat and his curves and lines smooth and satisfying; they're filled with soft shades of bright colours, creating a warming radiance. It's like watching a stained-glass window form a pulse. There's a quasi-religious feeling to these images, something that extends to its lead

Opposite: Marcell Jankovics, the pioneering Hungarian writer and director behind *Son of the White Mare*.

Left: Just say neigh. If you need a dose of psychedelia, look no further than *Son of the White Mare*.

Below: Golden boy. Some of Jankovics' film feels like a stained-glass window entering Super Saiyan mode.

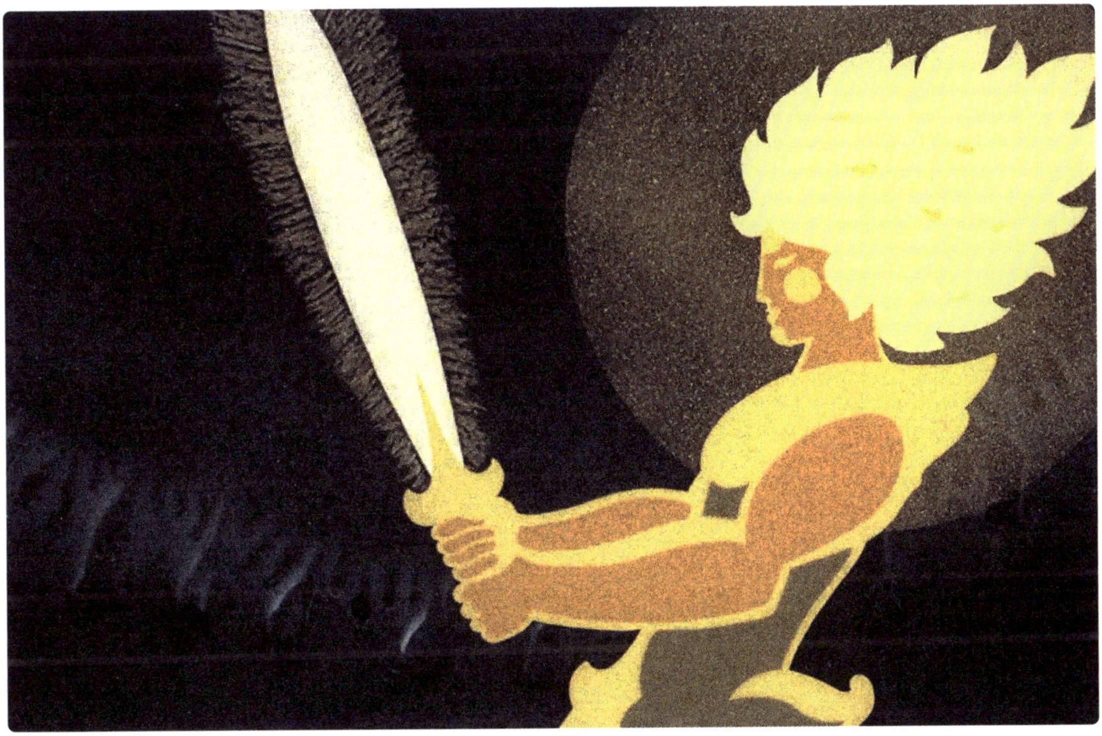

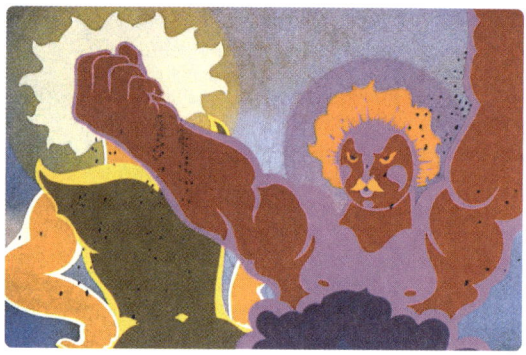

character's design; a mythic boy, raised on the milk of a horse, who's surrounded at all times by a halo. This is the titular Son, who becomes a brutishly strong man, meets his similarly masculine two brothers and then embarks with them on a quest to an underworld to rescue three princesses from three nefarious dragons.

The story itself isn't that gripping, and with its female characters reduced to either mothers or mistresses, it's not exactly modern; but on a frame-to-frame basis, it might be the best-looking film covered in this book. There's an overture of swirling shapes that undulate, morph and swallow each other by means of exposition; there's a gushing, volcanic birth scene; there are silhouettes that stutter with the precise rigidity and flow of a Saul Bass title sequence; there's flaming blonde hair like *Dragon Ball Z*; and there's a seven-headed dragon that looks like a tank dreamed up by a Soviet propagandist. Yet, somehow, there's complete fluidity between this diversity. Simple shapes like triangles and circles, which form the basis of so many characters and settings, act like a guide rope, pulling viewers through the madness via familiarity, while István Vajda's gorgeous, ambient synth score offers a soothing accompaniment.

When voting for the greatest films of all time, in the formidable poll conducted by *Sight and Sound* magazine once a decade, Cartoon Saloon director Tomm Moore (see page 80) ensured *Son of the White Mare* featured on his ballot. He's just one of many cinephiles and animators who have fallen for the film's potent spell over the last 40 years, turning this tale of legend into legend itself.

Above left: Fire arm. One of *Son of the White Mare's* trio of adventure-seeking brothers flexes his muscles.

Below: Dark horse. The white mare feeds her son right up until her death, after which his conquest begins.

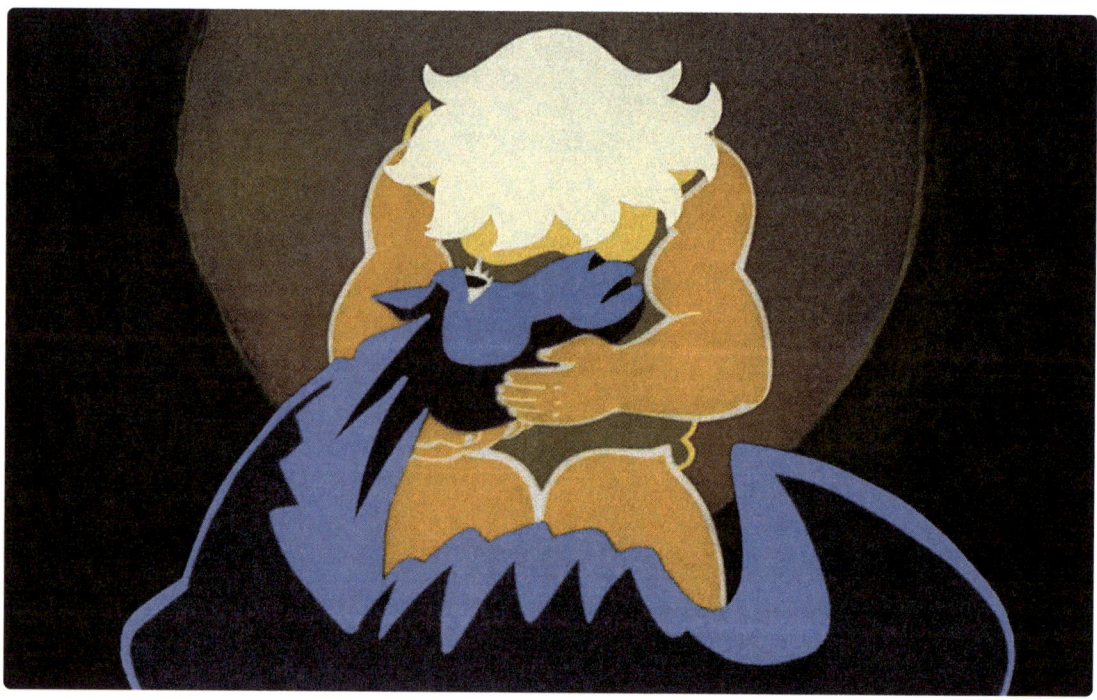

📽 Bubble Bath

Director: György Kovásznai
Release date: 1979

György Kovásznai didn't have a typical student life. Born in 1934, he survived the Second World War despite his family life and family home being destroyed, and then the artistically curious Kovásznai attended the Art Academy of Budapest.

But he wasn't a fan of the structured methodology of the institution, so he left; then he became a miner, then he worked in a factory, then eventually, he returned to the university. But, just before graduation he was kicked out for his commitment to two dual terrors: Marxism and abstract art. Radical and unpredictable, just like the artwork he would go on to create.

A painter who also worked in film, Kovásznai spent 20 years working at Pannonia Film Studio (which also made *Son of the White Mare*), where he made a compact and diverse collection of shorts and one feature: *Bubble Bath* (1979). Only the third animated feature to come out of Hungary, it's a postmodern collage of formal volatility and narrative flux. Introduced as "a musical animation

to the rhythm of a heartbeat", the tale features a love triangle between medical student Anikó and couple Zsolt and Klári – an artist and socialite, respectively – who jitteringly descend on Anikó's apartment on the day of their wedding.

Perpetually shifting in look and feel, Anikó's apartment may echo the thick lines and simple colouration of a comic panel, but then become more like an oil painting or snap into a cut-out collage. The liquidity of the interior

Below left: A poster for *Bubble Bath* displaying its original Hungarian title *Habfürdő*.

Below right: Director György Kovásznai, who ran the *Bubble Bath*, at work.

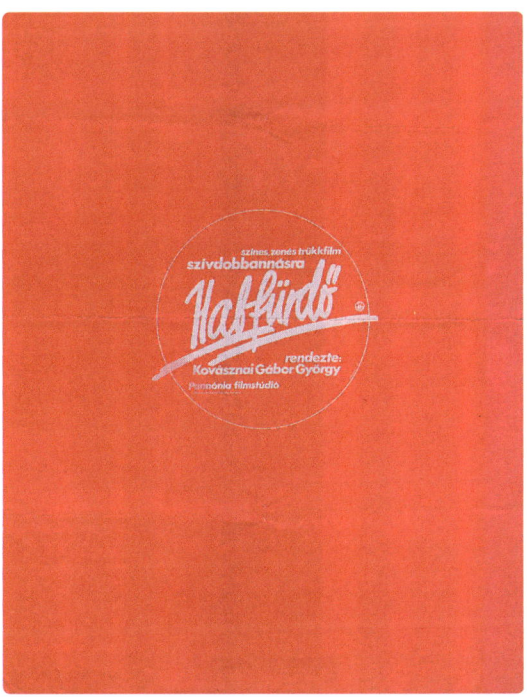

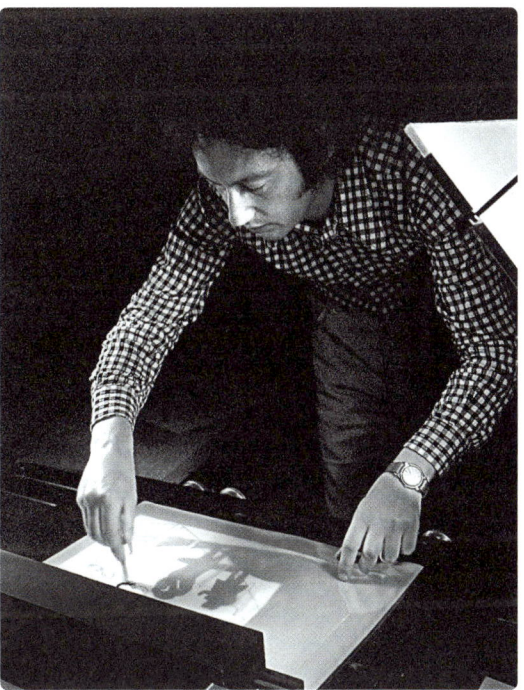

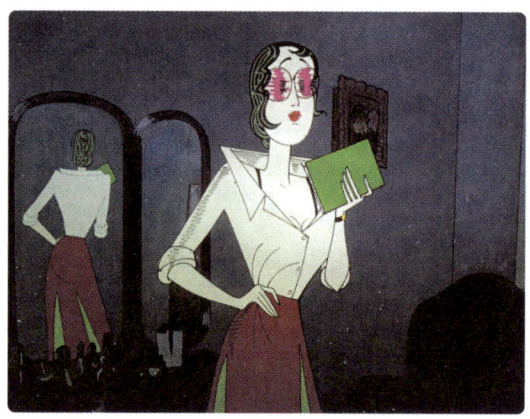

seconds. There is simply no set look to the film or the characters. They can go from being barely a complete outline to being uncannily detailed, to becoming vehicles to riff on the portraiture of art deco, pop art and cubism. The frames and cels they inhabit even get manipulated after they've been drawn, with lens distortion, light leaks and even real water droplets obscuring and refracting the day's various dramas. This variety appears in the film's music too, and composer János Másik's songs slide smoothly between slinky jazz, rollicking harmonica boogies and bombastic stage musical numbers.

Viewers may struggle with the film's diversity of aesthetic not being entirely matched by its story. Between vivid formal changes, debates about love, purpose and legacy are briefly latched on to, but the conversational

design extends to Anikó and her friends, and their own appearance. Walking, floating or just awkwardly bobbing through scenes, this trio can warp within frames, the lithe and moustachioed Zsolt being the most malleable, looking like Frank Zappa, then a mongoose, then a deep-sea diver and back again in a matter of

Above left: Rose tinted glasses. Whilst characters might have one style in one moment of *Bubble Bath*, their look (and their shades) might change in an instant...

Below: ... and become far more cubist in nature than they were before.

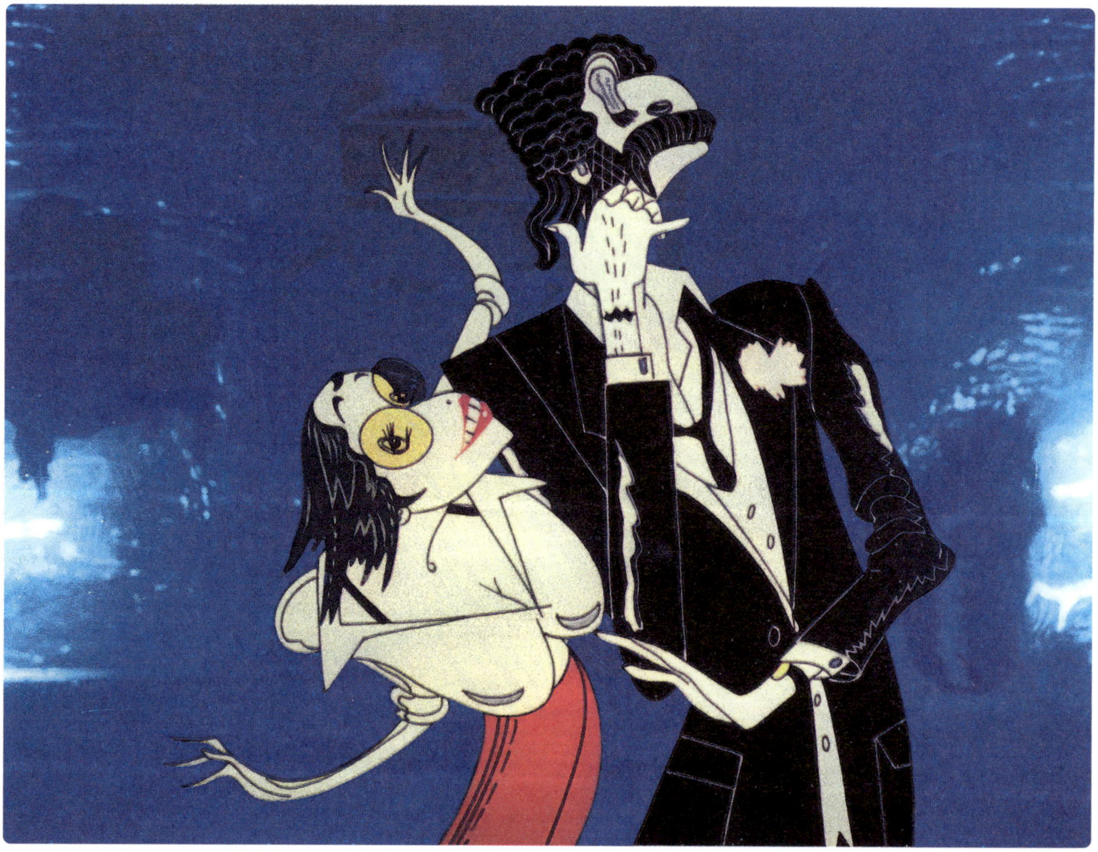

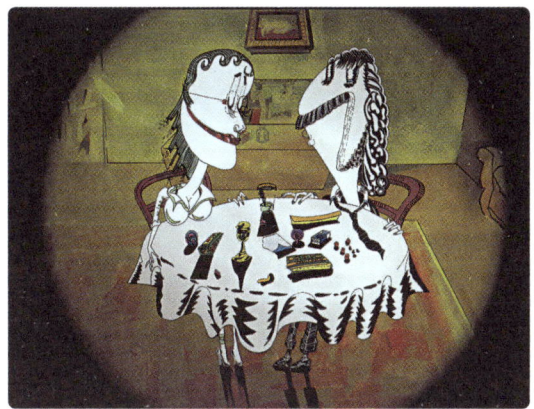

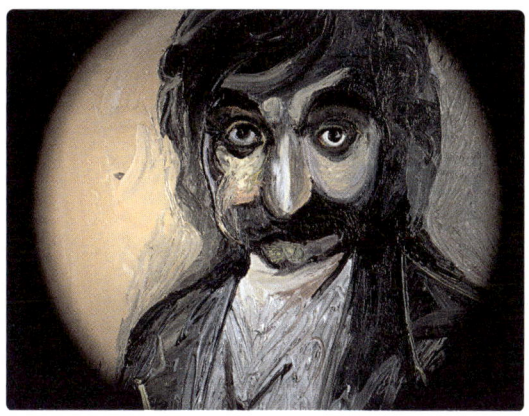

highlight (and go with us on this) is all about the role of the state within health and social care. Adapting an approach from one of his earlier works, in which he animated vox-pop interviews (see Aardman's *Creature Comforts* for a more zoological attempt at the technique), Kovásznai embraces the reality of documentary in this extremely surreal film – and the clashing styles of *Bubble Bath* create a perfect reflection of clashing political ideologies. The director saves one

flourish for the film's finale, when a live-action hand enters the frame, dispersing suds over a bathing Zsolt. Playful, political and surprising to the end, *Bubble Bath* is bursting with ideas.

Above left: Tableau for two. A dinner date in *Bubble Bath* doesn't necessarily scream romance.

Above right: Fish eye to eye. Transforming in style once more, the moustachioed Zsolt seems to peer at the film's viewers.

👁 Further Viewing

Another strong recommendation from us: seek out József Gémes' gorgeous, gory medieval saga *Heroic Times* (1983), which adapts the Toldi Trilogy, the nineteenth-century epic poem, with the rich style of an oil painting. Winner of the top prize at Annecy in 1985, the film was recently restored by Hungary's National Film Institute-Film Archive and can be appreciated anew, thanks to an international release on the Deaf Crocodile label.

To many, especially the millennials among us, the most prominent Hungarian-born animator is Gábor Csupó, who emigrated to the United States and founded the animation Klasky-Csupo with his then wife, Arlene Klasky. The studio served as the original animation team behind *The Simpsons*, both in their nascent form on *The Tracey Ullman Show* and during the first three seasons of the blockbuster spin-off series, while

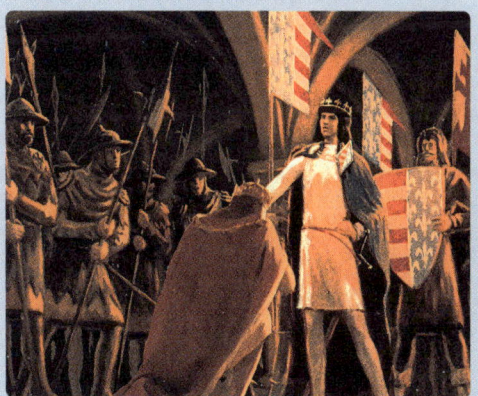

Csupó later co-created several era-defining shows for the Nickelodeon network, including *Rugrats* (1991–2004), *Aaahh!!! Real Monsters* (1994–1997) and *The Wild Thornberrys* (1998–2004).

Above: The Art of War. *Heroic Times* is a sumptuous, violent film that brings myth to life in a rich, painted style.

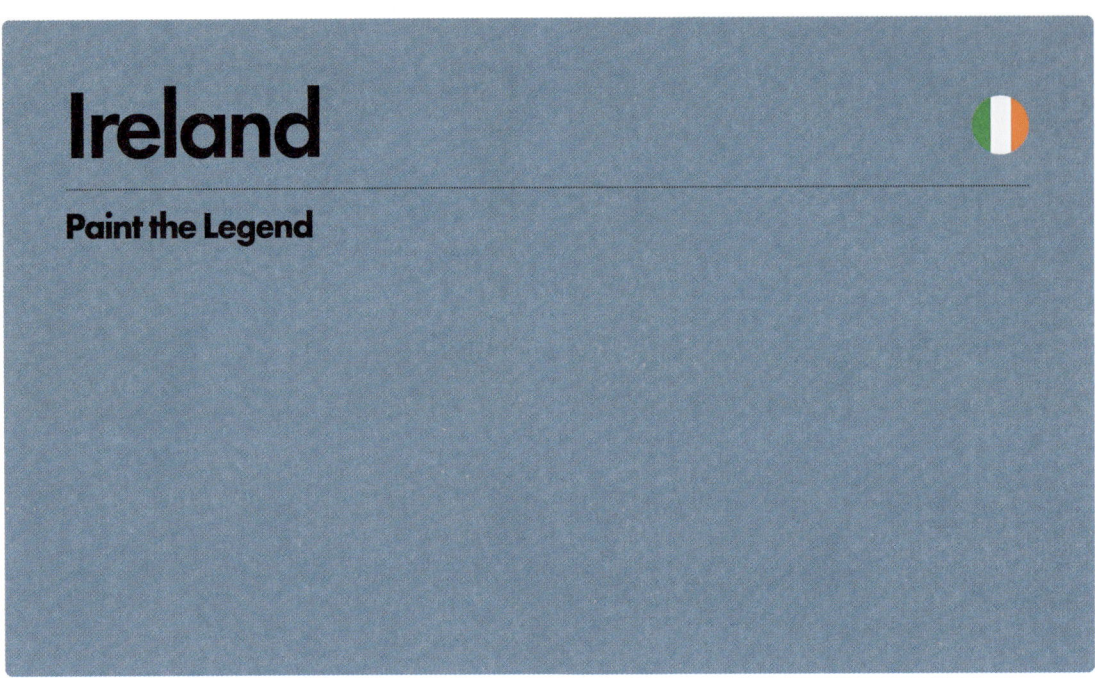

Ireland

Paint the Legend

🎬 The Folklore Trilogy

The Secret of Kells
Dir: Tomm Moore & Nora Twomey
Release date: 2009

Song of the Sea
Dir: Tomm Moore
Release date: 2014

Wolfwalkers
Dir: Tomm Moore & Ross Stewart
Release date: 2020

Just as the stories they tell bring legends to life and the ancient to the present, the rise of Irish animators Cartoon Saloon is itself the stuff of folklore. It begins with three intrepid art graduates, Tomm Moore, Nora Twomey and Paul Young, creating their own animation company in 1999, in the small town of Kilkenny.

A quarter of a century later, that company has five Oscar nominations, multiple hit TV shows and they've transformed Kilkenny too, turning it into a professional nucleus and essential pilgrimage for animation fans. At the heart of that story are three films: *The Secret of Kells*, *Song of the Sea* and *Wolfwalkers*.

Wanting to create something distinctly Irish for their first feature, they were inspired by the creation of the Book of Kells, a 9th-century illustrated, illuminated manuscript featuring the Gospels. They only found enough money to make it by 2005, and four years later (ten years since starting the studio), *The Secret of Kells* was released.

Written by Fabrice Ziolkowski (and directed by Moore with Twomey as co-director), this is a story full of mystery and magic, layered with deep historical and theological context and characters who navigate faith, modernity, nature and art with curiosity and caution in a refreshingly drawn world. *Kells'* hero Brendan, a scholar and painter of enlightened tales, leads a contained life within jagged city walls, until a quest into the woods for more ink opens up his worldview to a bright, rolling and rounded environment and the fantastical creatures within it. Eye-catching and empathetic, the characters' souls and shapes are expressively entwined; like the oppressive and devout Abbot Cellach, with his looming cathedral arch skeleton, or the wide-eyed and magical Aisling and her metamorphic plumes of white hair. Distinct and wise, *Kells* is about discovering the beauty in the fables of forebears and documenting them, but for Cartoon Saloon it was only the first chapter.

Released in 2014, the Moore-directed *Song of the Sea* embraced a tragedy-stricken, emotionally hefty, Spielbergian mode of family storytelling. Screenwriter Will Collins' tale, built from Moore's concept, begins with a selkie (part seal, part woman) who's torn between spirit and earthen realms, eventually disappearing after the birth of her daughter Saoirse. The following story builds around widower Conor (a crumbling cliff face of a man, with a voice like rubble, courtesy of Brendan Gleeson); his pained, hovering mother; his angry, renegade son Ben; and the curious and cherubic Saoirse. When the family is broken apart, a cross-country quest to reunite them begins, taking in musical fairies, evil owls, holy wells, giants and a witch who traps people's sadness in jars. Although absentee parents, magical companions and even a setting of Halloween seem familiar, this isn't *E.T. in Éire*. As reality and magic swirl together, the film becomes a frank but enchanting portrait

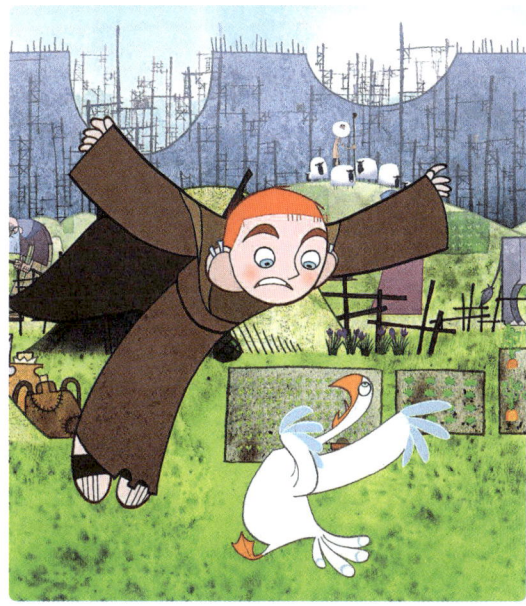

Above: Brendan grazer. As well as magical beings in the woods, Brendan finds drama with life in the fields closer to home too.

Below: Forest is history. Shapeshifting Aisling and Brendan uncover the beauty of nature, history and a bug or two in *The Secret of Kells*.

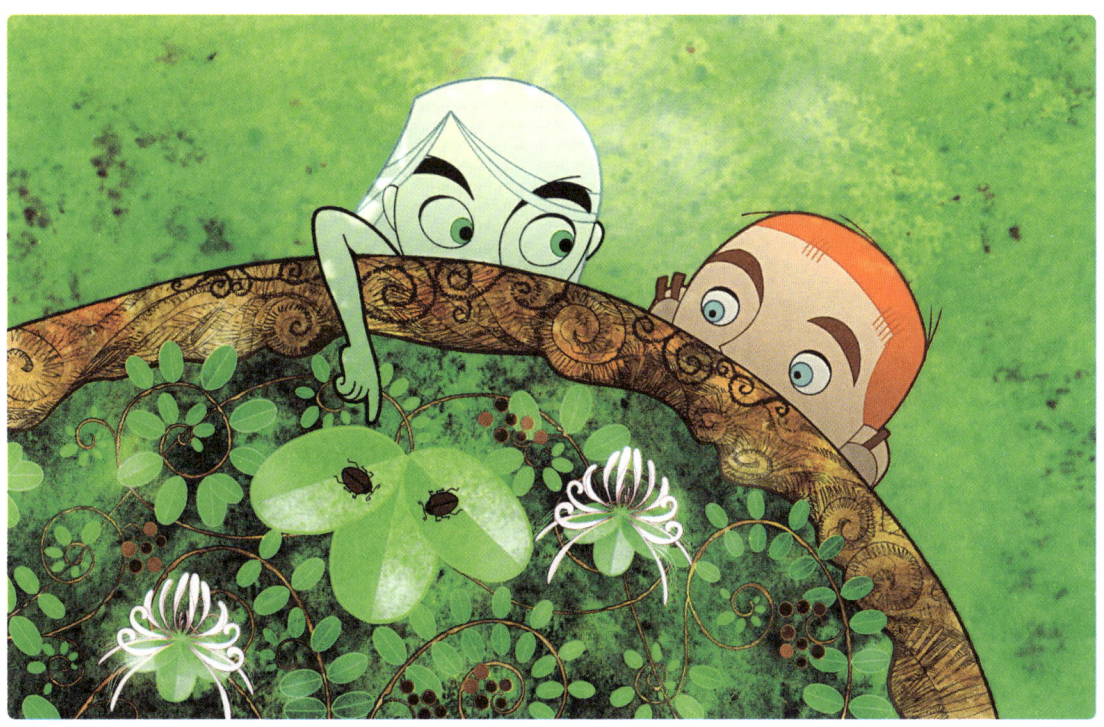

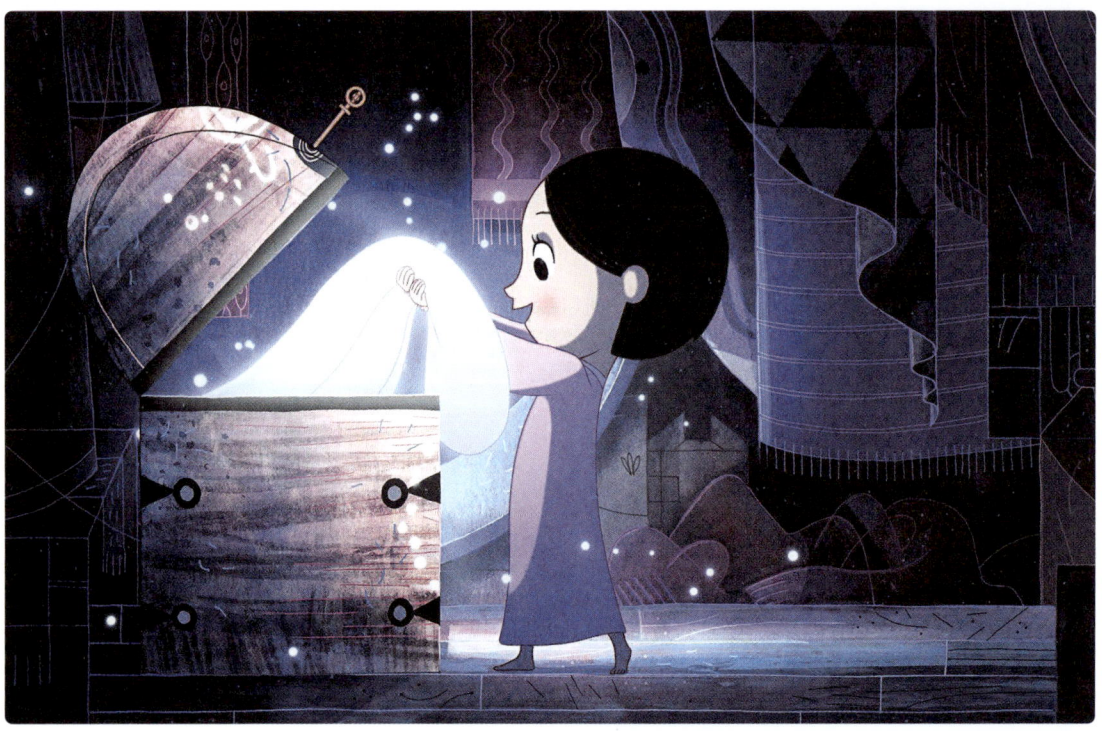

of grief that quite literally shows how fatal it can be to bottle up emotions; and tied to the family's quashed feelings are the memories of ancient Irish creatures and spirits who have become similarly constrained by time – and need to be released. It's when they are, in moments between fantasy and reality, that the film shines brightest, with glorious mandala-like swirling frames of celestial majesty in sync with humble, big-hearted humanity. A perfect family film, *Song of the Sea* is perhaps the studio's greatest hit.

Wolfwalkers, the trilogy-capping 2020 release which Moore directed with *Kells* art director Ross Stewart, saw a maturation in form and story. Focused on precocious English teen Robyn and her fierce, lupine-shifting Irish friend Mebh, it's a film interested in borders: the borders between nations, between industry and nature, between

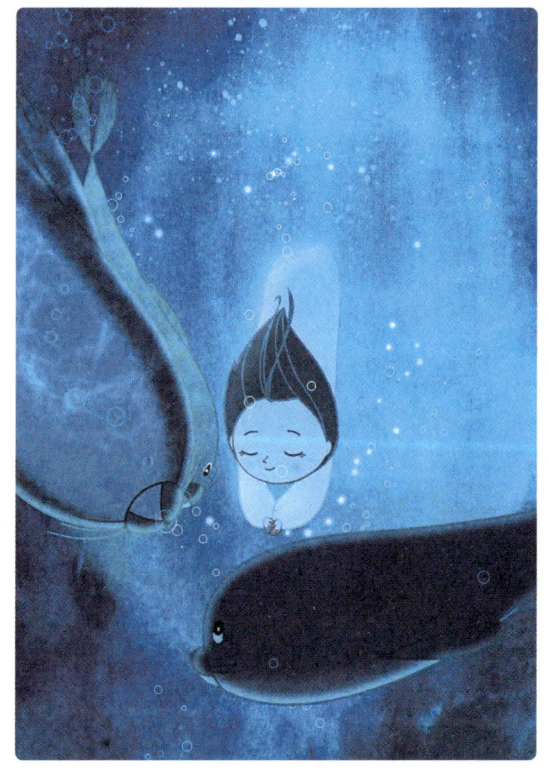

Above: Smooth as Selkie. Saoirse discovers the coat that will transform her into the mythical part seal part human creature.

Right: Sea the light. As Saoirse discovers her Selkie heritage, she must make a hard decision about mortality.

Opposite: Running with the wolves. *Wolfwalkers* marked a pivot into darker, more young-adult skewing storytelling for Cartoon Saloon.

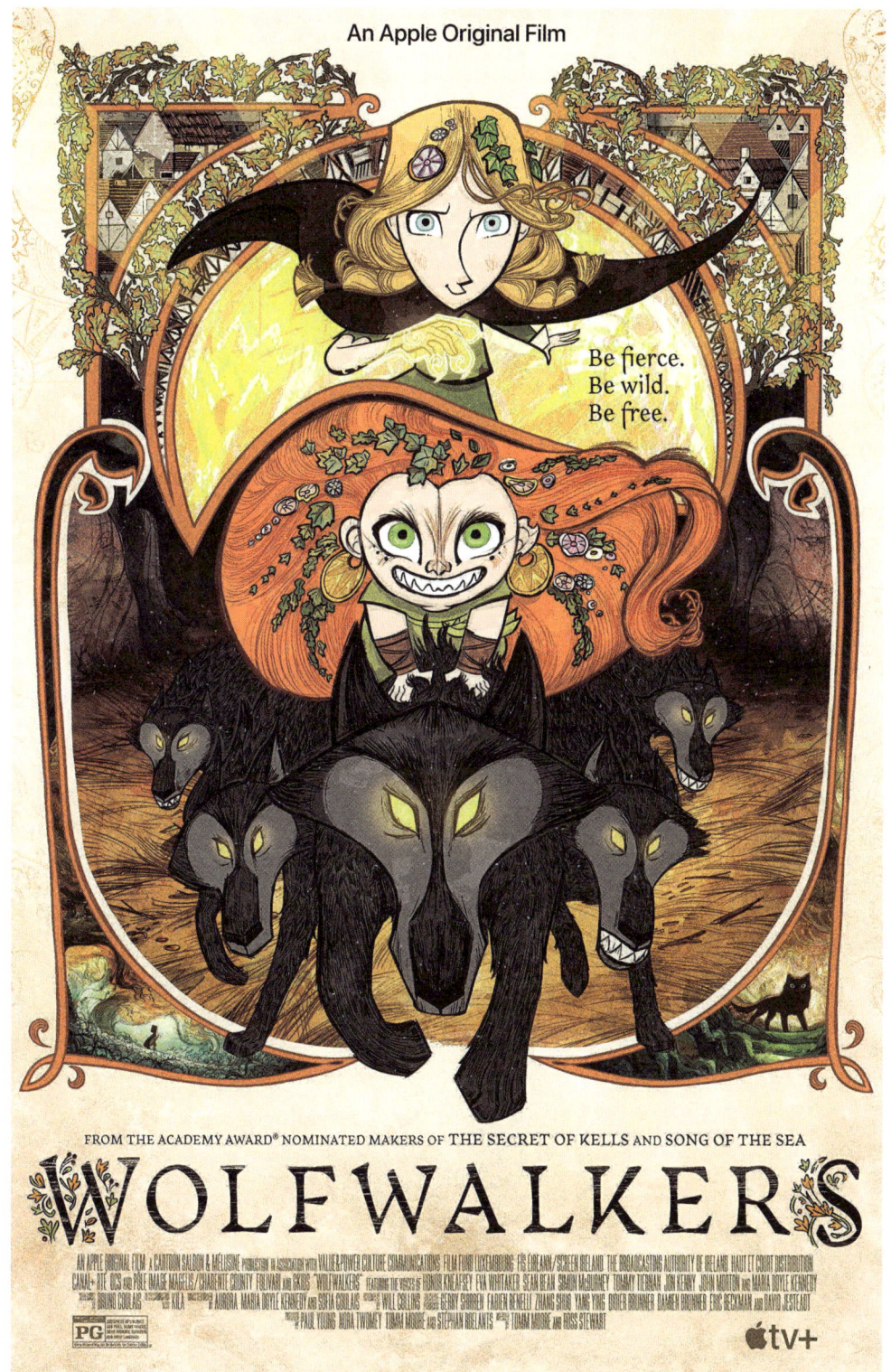

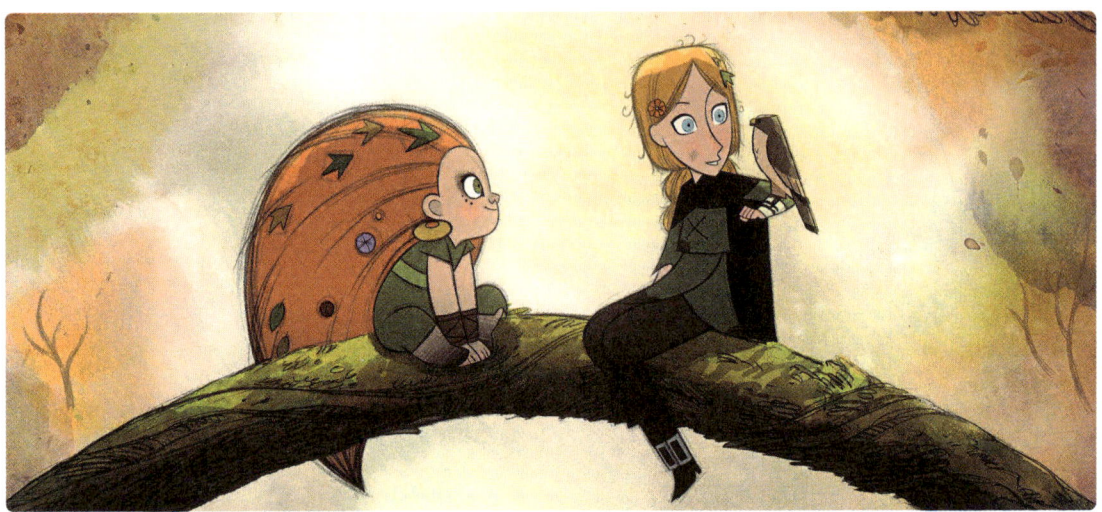

human and animal and even the borders of audiences' stylistic expectations, and how far and to where they can be stretched. Set within a walled community, led by the Cromwellian Lord Protector, which sits on the fringes of a mysterious woodland (very *Kells*), *Wolfwalkers* is the most political of the trilogy. Cartoon Saloon's debut had Vikings as a vague, faceless threat, but here English antagonism is present and poisonous, a fact that creeps up on Robyn, whose father emblematically hunts Irish

wolves. The diamond-headed Robyn and her set-square styled city are compact, strict and oppressively, thickly coloured; in contrast, Mebh and her forest are all curves, with grass, trunk, beast and river all harmoniously flowing

Above: An olive (green) branch. Despite their differences, Mebh and Robyn – and falcon Merlyn – begin to bond.

Below: 1988's prehistoric blockbuster *The Land Before Time* was the peak of Don Bluth's brief but impactful time producing films in Ireland.

◎ Sullivan Bluth Studios

At one point, it seemed that the future of Hollywood animation lay in Ireland. While Disney faltered through the 1980s, Don Bluth, formerly one of the studio's star animators, made a name for himself with lavishly animated adventures such as *The Secret of NIMH* (1982) and *An American Tail* (1986). He was then lured across the Atlantic by the promise of government incentives to form a new studio in Dublin. Fondly remembered flicks *The Land Before Time* (1988) and *All Dogs Go to Heaven* (1989) followed, before momentum slowed with critical and box-office failures such as *Rock-a-Doodle* (1991) and *Thumbelina* (1994). Bluth eventually returned to Hollywood, but the studio's impact was felt through the decades: its investment in the animation course at Ballyfermot College gave rise to a new generation of Irish talent, including the founding members of Cartoon Saloon and Brown Bag Films (the company behind such preschool hits as *Bing*, *Octonauts* and *Peter Rabbit*).

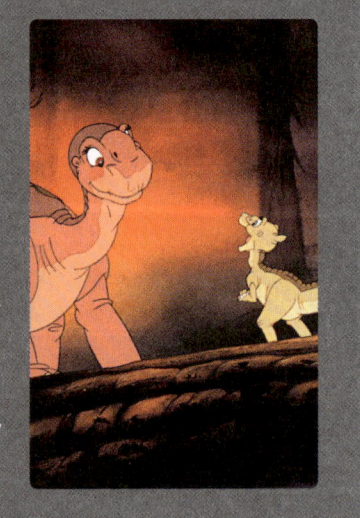

into each other. Robyn and Mebh's lives are complicated and challenging, as familial fracture, political violence, passionate friendship and self-identity must all be navigated, but the film is never weighed down by these journeys. *Wolfwalkers* is a darker film but it's full of glowing moments of joy, whether that's in reprieves of abandon – like stealing food, known to Mebh as "town tasties" – or in the ravishing, innovatively charcoal-lined perspective of "wolf vision". Here the studio is unafraid to push its style, but also unafraid to reveal it, as the wilder forest setting is full of the animator's own pencil outlines, unerased, haloing around each movement. These add dynamism to the film but they're also a beautiful reminder of how Cartoon Saloon clearly lives the environmental

and historical roots in its films, each line like a signature on a cultural manifesto.

In *Song of the Sea*, a character calls audiences to remember the spiritual and mythical "in your stories and in your songs", and with the Folklore Trilogy, Cartoon Saloon made something unforgettable.

Below left: Nora Twomey, Co-Director of *The Secret of Kells* and Director of *The Breadwinner* and *My Father's Dragon*.

Below right: Tomm Moore, Director of *The Secret of Kells* and *Song of the Sea* and, as well as Ross Stewart, Director of *Wolfwalkers*

Bottom: Set in Afghanistan, *The Breadwinner* is the first Cartoon Saloon feature film not set in Ireland, but it still has the craftsmanship and thematic richness we've come to expect from the studio.

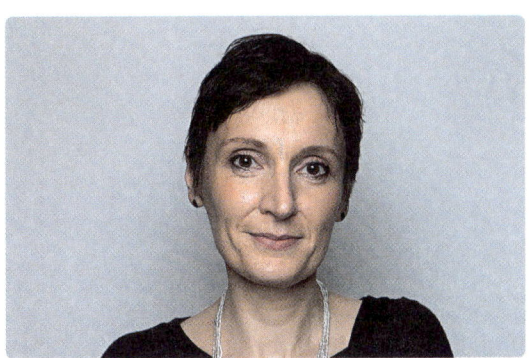

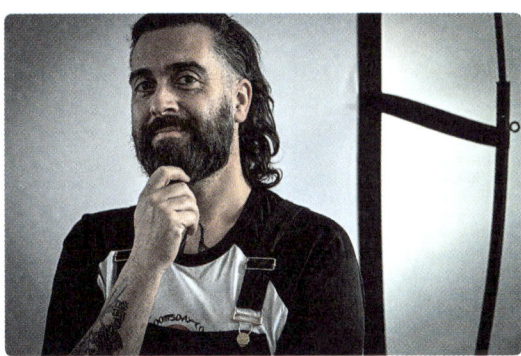

👁 Further Viewing

Cartoon Saloon's output reaches far beyond the Folklore Trilogy, and far beyond the shores of Ireland too. *The Breadwinner*, the 2017 solo directorial debut from Nora Twomey, further explores the power of myth and storytelling, this time set in Afghanistan during the War on Terror; 2017 also saw the release of *Late Afternoon*, a stunning short about an old woman's battle with dementia directed by Louise Bagnall. Both received Oscar nominations. Twomey's follow-up came in 2022, with *My Father's Dragon*, which offered a softer, more storybook quality compared to *The Breadwinner*'s wrenching authenticity. Set between a desaturated, suffocatingly realized New York-like city and a vibrant island and its mythical populace, it's a departure in setting and style but still a rewarding journey.

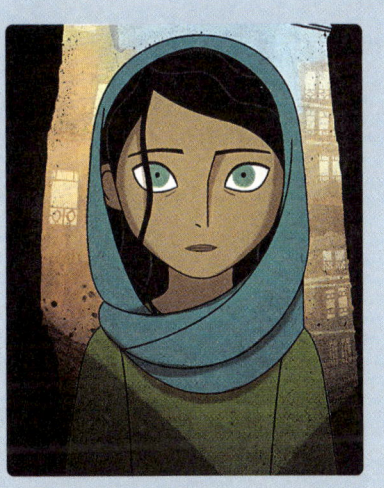

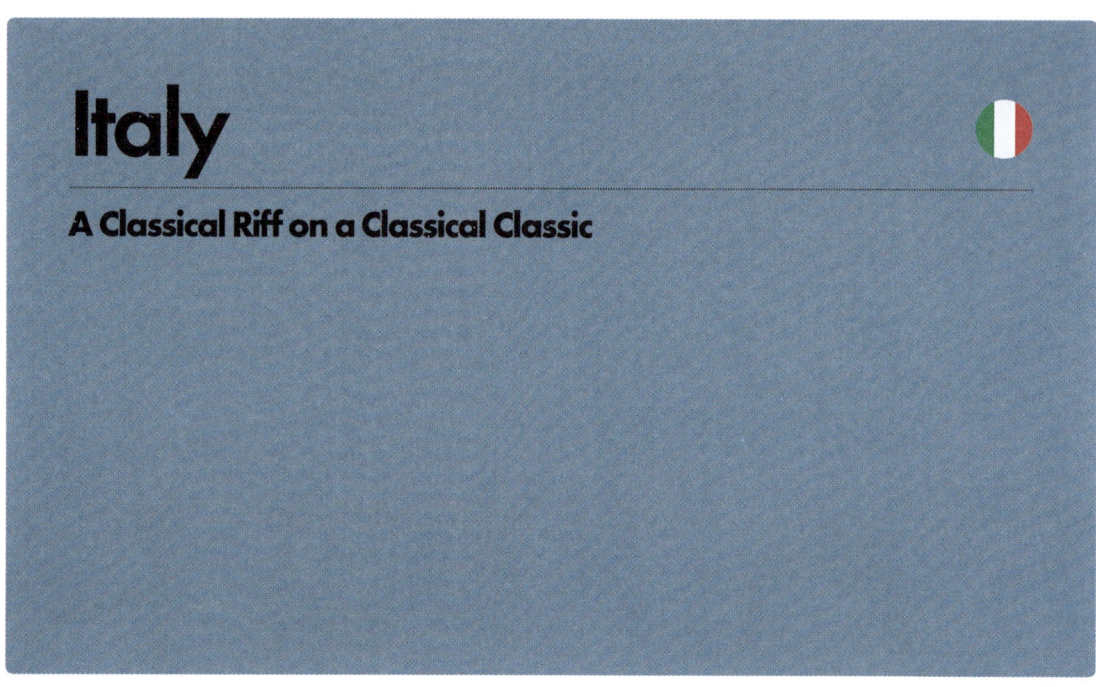

Italy

A Classical Riff on a Classical Classic

🎥 Allegro non Troppo

Director: Bruno Bozzetto
Released: 1976

Bruno Bozzetto has always loved cinema. In fact, he's said that he loves cinema more than animation. Of course, animation is cinema, but from a young age, Bozzetto, born in 1938, just loved the cinematic experience, in all its forms, and wanted to be a part of it.

But, after first corralling school friends into making something in live action, he realized he could have much more control over filmmaking if he just worked by himself. He had seen *Toot, Whistle, Plunk and Boom* (1953), a Disney short directed by Ward Kimball and Charles A. Nichols, and (according to the biography on his own website) had been "literally amazed"; so, knowing he didn't need a crew to rally, he started drawing his own animations, with his father converting the family ironing board so he could work from it.

After a diversion into studying law at university, Bozzetto returned to ironing out his animation skills, eventually creating the short film *Tapum! The History of Arms* (1958), a simplistic, comedic look at the evolution

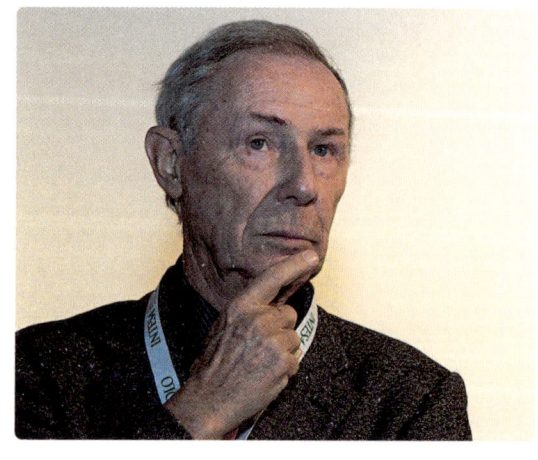

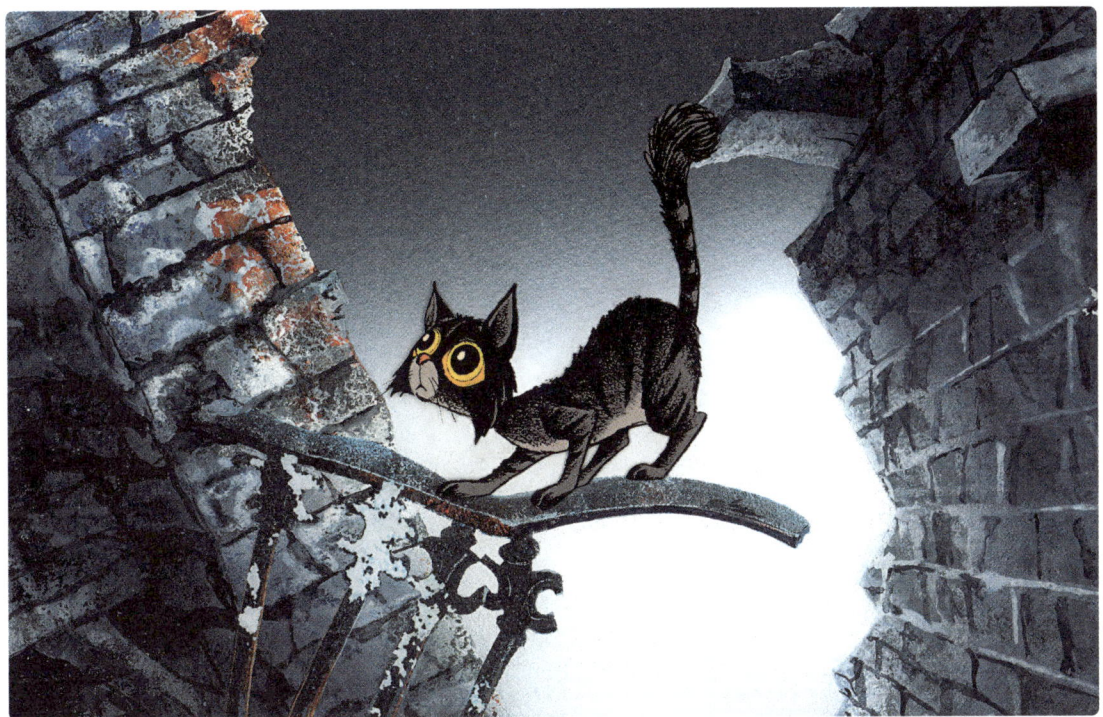

of weaponry that debuted at the Cannes Film Festival in a small, overlooked section of the programme. However, one Italian critic grew tired of a glitzy premiere and stumbled into Bozzetto's screening. Delighted by what he saw, he was soon declaring in the press that *Tapum!* was superior to the Sophia Loren film next door.

His feature film career that followed established both a cineliterate and sarcastic sensibility early on: 1968 saw the release of the superhero parody *VIP my Brother Superman* while earlier, in 1965, he had released *West and Soda*, an animated send-up of Westerns (which was, in Bozzetto's eyes, the invention of the spaghetti western, though his took longer to make than Sergio Leone's 1964 *A Fistful of Dollars*). In 1976 he completed his hat trick of American institutional satire, taking on Disney with *Allegro non Troppo*, a farcical, lewd and surprisingly deep parody of Mickey's maestro-piece, *Fantasia*.

The film begins with a live action introduction to the "fantasia" of classical music and animation that will follow, but a phone call then swiftly interrupts, providing the revelation that "Prisney or Grisney" has already made such a film. Unbothered, the emcee then releases a caged group of women from a pen to form his orchestra and unbuckles an animator from a cell wall – evidently

working standards for animators are not just a modern issue – to bring the project to life.

Featuring six sequences set to music – interspersed with live action – Bozzetto begins with an exploration of lust, set within a watercolour world bursting with feminine shapes set to tease an impish protagonist; this is followed by a scratchily drawn sketch involving a caveman's anger at escalating industrialism. These two whet the appetite, with raunchy dressing establishing the different flavour between Bruno and Walt, but as *Allegro* evolves, the cartoonishness transfers to the live action, which gradually becomes more slapstick as the animation becomes far more thoughtful, layered and on a par with *Fantasia* visually. A centrepiece set to Ravel's *Boléro* sees biological evolution through to its climactic, cataclysmic end via moodily hatched, constantly transforming life; while Sibelius's *Valse triste* uncovers a cat, reminiscing about its bulldozed home, swallowed by memories that leap from the screen in vivid

Opposite: Bruno Bozzetto, the maestro behind *Fantasia* parody *Allegro non Troppo*.

Above: So suite. Sibelius's *Valse triste* accompanies a cat on a heartbreaking homecoming in one of the film's standout sequences.

three-dimensional, luminescent colour. A reprieve from the pain and violence of mortality briefly arrives in the form of a bee, flying to Vivaldi, looking to have a romantic lunch with a flower and getting rudely disturbed by some humans; but an epic spin on the tale of Eden's Serpent follows, with the reptile sent into a nightmarish, fetid, neon-soaked, substance-addled landscape of twentieth-century temptation, set to Stravinsky's *The Firebird* – a piece that would go on to feature in *Fantasia 2000* (1999).

One might imagine the Disney family didn't take too kindly to this X-rated riff, but, perhaps surprisingly, they embraced it;.The Walt Disney Family Museum even put on an exhibition celebrating Bozzetto's work, with a focus on *Allegro*. And, like one of the evolving, almost circular narrative sequences contained within both this film and *Fantasia*, *Allegro* found its way to Disney's Ward Kimball, who reportedly called it "one of [his] favourite animated films of all time". Bravo!

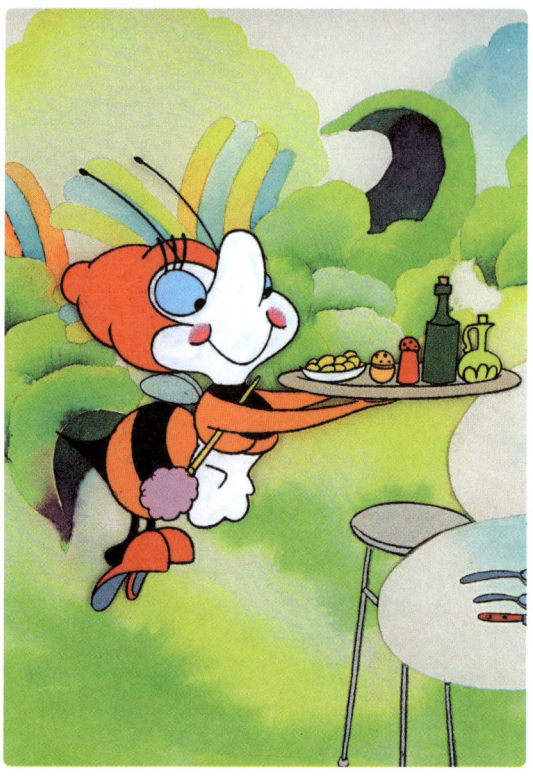

Right: Plight of the bumblebee. An insect faces a lunchtime interruption in one of the film's short and sweet sketches.

Below: Ravel-ution. In a remarkable scene set to Ravel's Boléro, the entire evolutionary life of a planet is constructed.

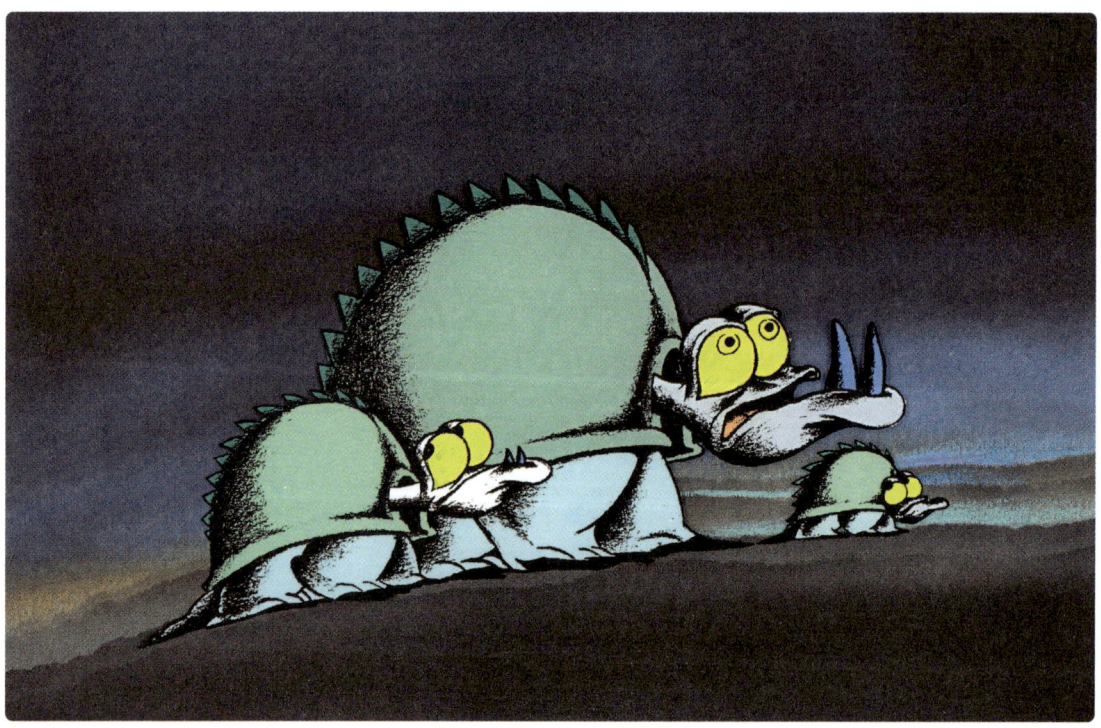

👁 Further Viewing

Italy's first all-colour animated feature was *The Dynamite Brothers* (1949), a chaotic knockabout comedy that bears the influence of both Disney and the Fleischer Brothers. Directors Toni and Nino Pagot had started their careers in comics before moving to animation, and their relatives Marco and Gi followed them a generation later – working on international co-productions including Hayao Miyazaki's *Sherlock Hound* series. (Miyazaki repaid the favour by naming the Italian flying ace hero of *Porco Rosso* after Marco Pagot.)

Check the credits for *The Dynamite Brothers* and you'll find an early credit for Osvaldo Cavandoli, the legendary cartoonist and creator of the long-running animation series *La Linea* (1971–1986), which moulds action, humour and a wit that breaks the fourth wall out of a simple white line drawn across the screen. More recently, we should salute Enzo d'Alò, a stalwart of European animation who is a familiar face at festivals, with films such as *How the Toys Saved Christmas* (1996), *Lucky and Zorba* (1998), *Momo* (2001) and the recent Roddy Doyle adaptation, *A Greyhound of a Girl* (2023).

And here's a final gem of a recommendation: *The War and the Dream of Momi* (1917). This inventive film from early cinema wizard Segundo de Chomón combines live action and spectacular stop-motion, as a young boy reads letters from his father sent from the front of the First World War, and later dreams of battles happening within his own household between his beloved toys – complete with artillery fire, chemical warfare, aerial dogfights and Zeppelin bombing raids.

Below: European Union. Italian director Enzo d'Alò's adaptation of the Irish children's book *A Greyhound of a Girl* was a co-production between seven European countries.

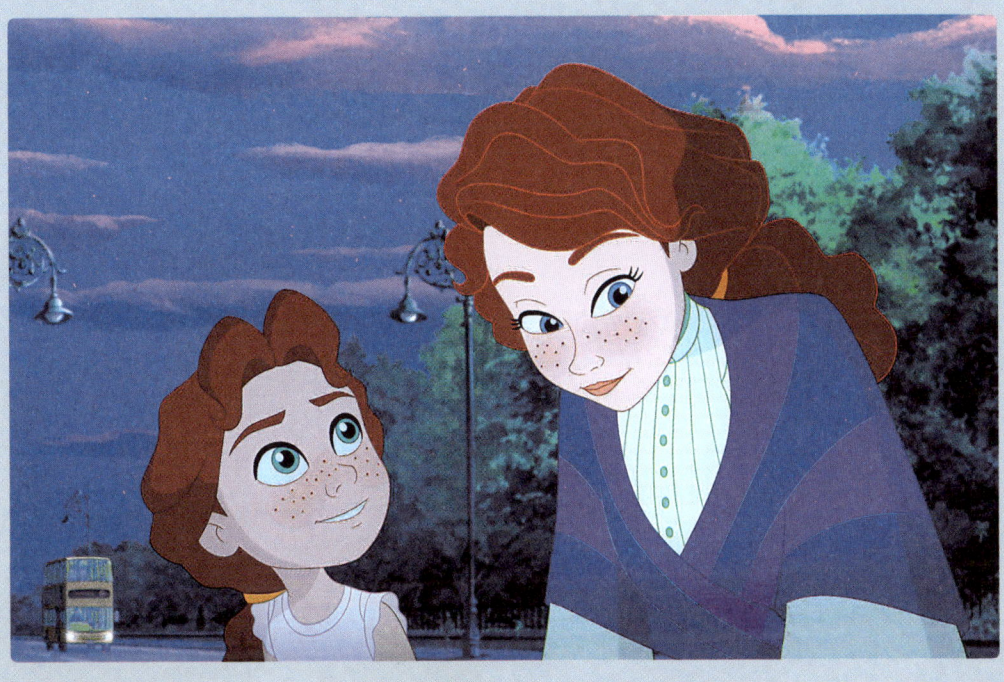

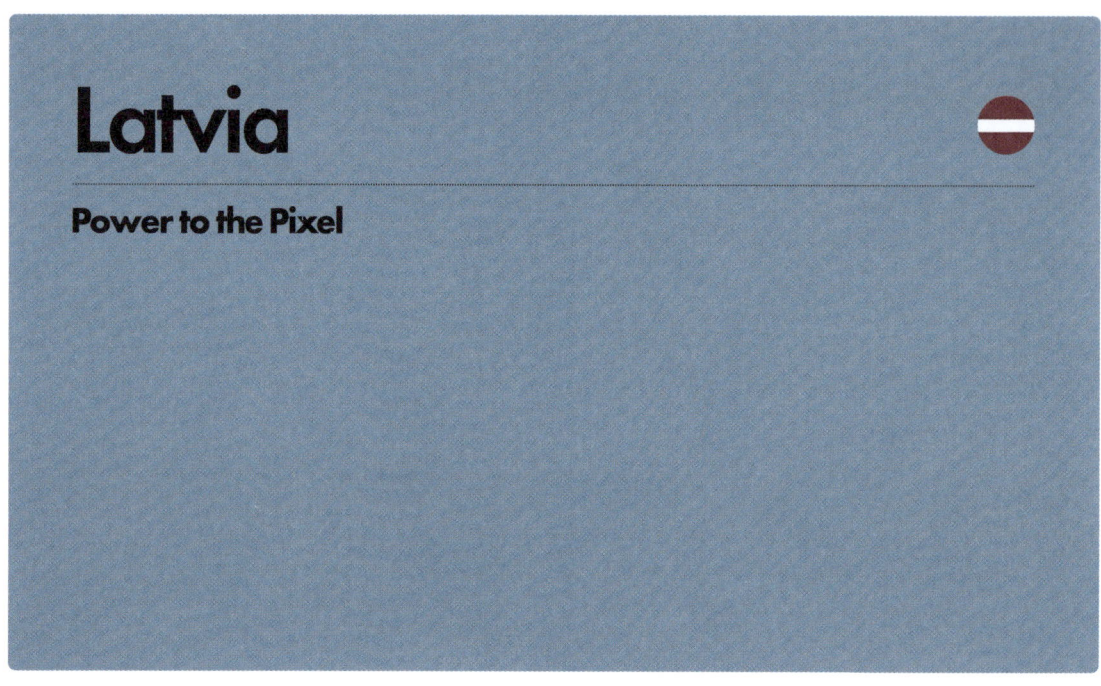

Latvia

Power to the Pixel

👤 Gints Zilbalodis

We haven't singled out a great deal of CG animation in this book. Perhaps that's because it is the style du jour, at least where the major studios and the box office are concerned. Just before the turn of the century, computer animation took over from the classic 2D style, and it has since become the de facto production process for big-budget projects.

And ever since, costs have ballooned into the hundreds of millions, and the crew lists have grown in step. Now, huge teams and entire render farms are employed, for instance, to animate every hair on Simba's body in the definitely-not-live-action, CGI remake of *The Lion King* (2019).

You can still find innovation within Western studio animation – simply look at the wildly imaginative, stylish spectacle of *Spider-Man: Into the Spider-Verse* (2018), *Arcane* (2021–2024) or *The Wild Robot* (2024) – but at a time of escalating budgets and diminishing creative returns, we have found our attentions drawn to Latvia and the work of Gints Zilbalodis. Zilbalodis started making animated shorts as a teenager and quickly hit upon a style that has served him well right up to 2024's *Flow*, which premiered to acclaim at the Cannes Film Festival and later won the Academy Award for Best Animated Feature.

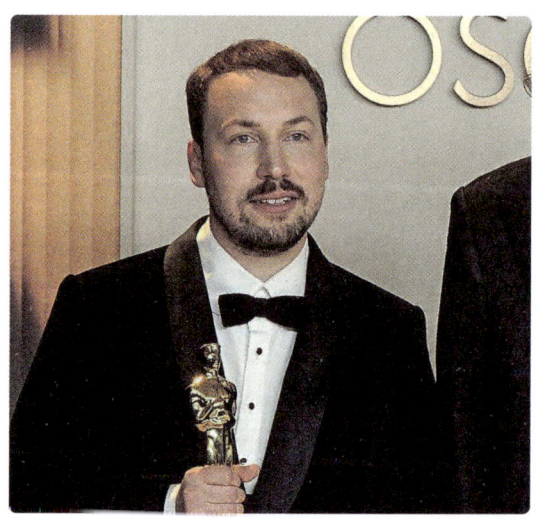

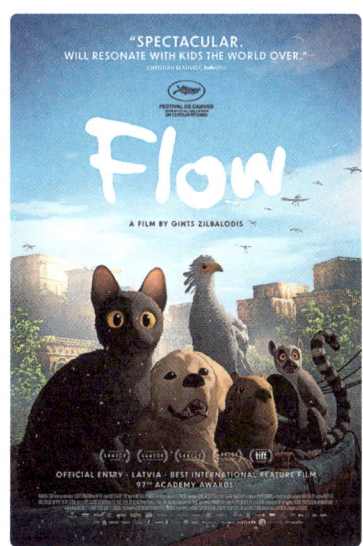

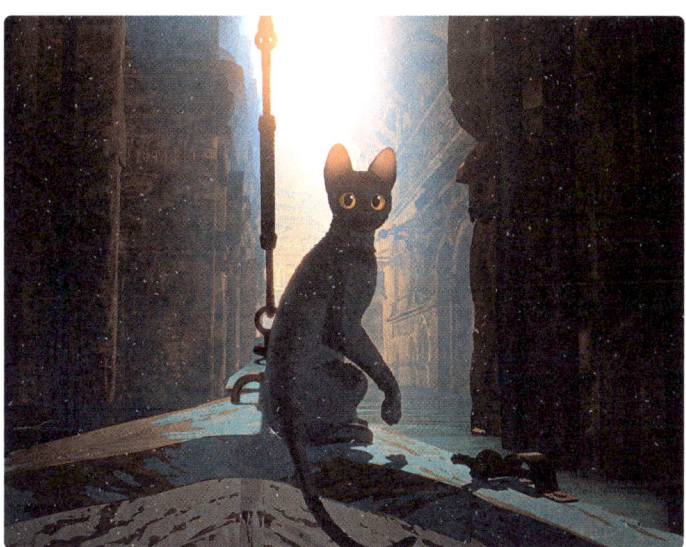

What unites his films to date is dialogue-free storytelling; character design and animation that is minimalist yet expressive and utterly engaging; a love of single-word titles (*Aqua, Followers, Inaudible*); and, in his features, a beguiling balance of mystery and momentum.

Zilbalodis's debut feature, the surreal adventure film *Away* (2019), was completely made by the director by himself on his computer. It is essentially a chase movie, with a young boy on a motorbike travelling through unknown landscapes, pursued by a giant, world-blighting monster. With his second feature, *Flow*, he consciously scaled up, and challenged himself to work with a larger team, albeit one that still numbered in the dozens, rather than the hundreds that is standard for a Disney or Pixar production.

But still, this stripped-back foundation remains: in *Flow*, it is a cat, and a loose alliance of fellow animals, who are adrift and fighting for survival when a devastating flood submerges their forest home.

"I think it's good to have limitations," Zilbalodis told us when *Flow* received its UK premiere in London. "With

Opposite: *Flow*'s Oscar win for Best Animated Feature was a historic achievement for animation, independent filmmaking, and Latvian cinema.

Above left: The English-language release poster for *Flow*.

Above right: Trick of the light. *Flow*'s dark-grey cat character set social media alight when fans disagreed over the colour of its fur.

Below: Motley Crew. The unlikely animal companions of *Flow* must learn to work together to fight for survival.

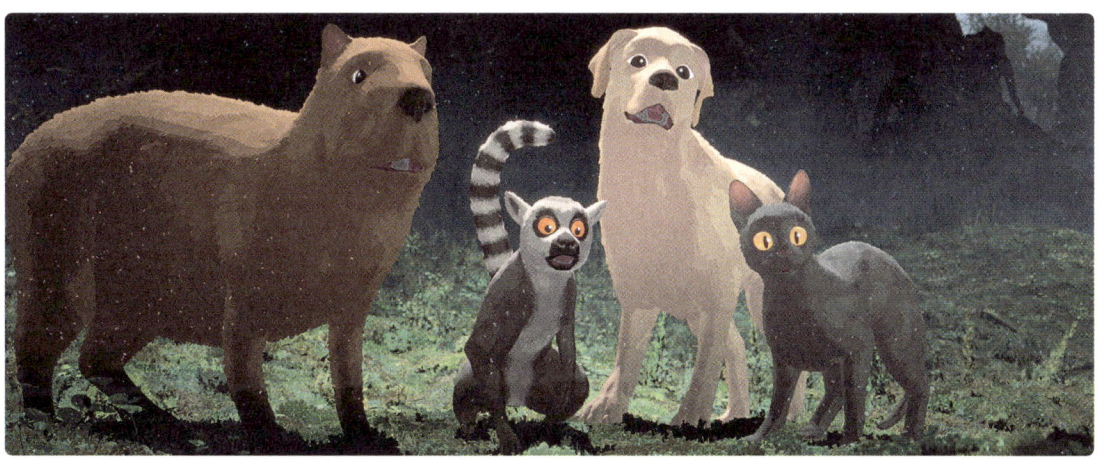

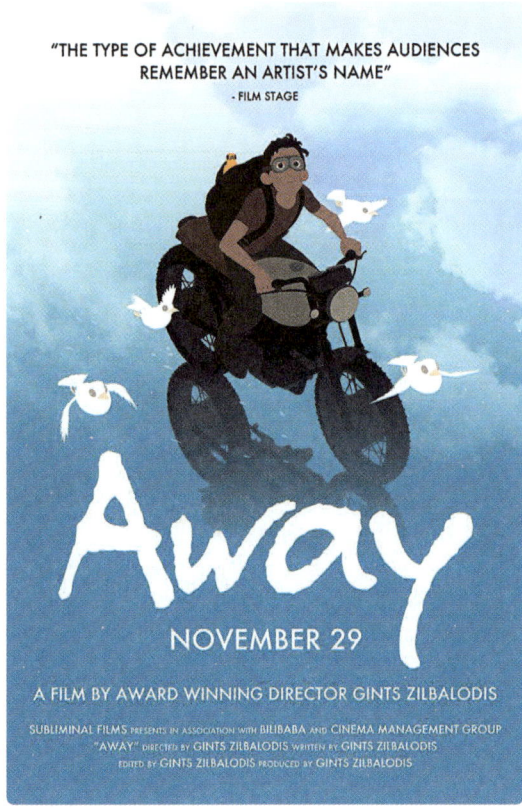

"THE TYPE OF ACHIEVEMENT THAT MAKES AUDIENCES
REMEMBER AN ARTIST'S NAME"
- FILM STAGE

Away

NOVEMBER 29

A FILM BY AWARD WINNING DIRECTOR GINTS ZILBALODIS

SUBLIMINAL FILMS PRESENTS IN ASSOCIATION WITH BILIBABA AND CINEMA MANAGEMENT GROUP
"AWAY" DIRECTED BY GINTS ZILBALODIS WRITTEN BY GINTS ZILBALODIS
EDITED BY GINTS ZILBALODIS PRODUCED BY GINTS ZILBALODIS

This idiosyncratic approach swims against the current of what constitutes contemporary mainstream animation. Economical yet epic, *Flow* is a beguiling piece of independent cinema that deserves to be seen big, and loud, on the largest possible screen. There is an insistent forward momentum to the animals' collective endeavours, which is only briefly broken by moments of breathtaking beauty and attention-grabbing curiosity. Flooded cities and abandoned workshops drift by, inviting the imagination to wonder what lies beyond the edges of Zilbalodis's chosen framing. It's at those times that these films feel almost akin to playing a video game, specifically those that hold something back while letting players pour their own emotion and meaning into the experience, such as the richly designed adventures *Shadow of the Colossus*, *Sable* and *Journey*. This is a mode of storytelling and world-building that leaves space for the untold, the unexplained, the unspoken.

The result makes us rethink the boundaries between the personal and the universal, the small-scale and the spectacular. Zilbalodis's wordless wonders travel around

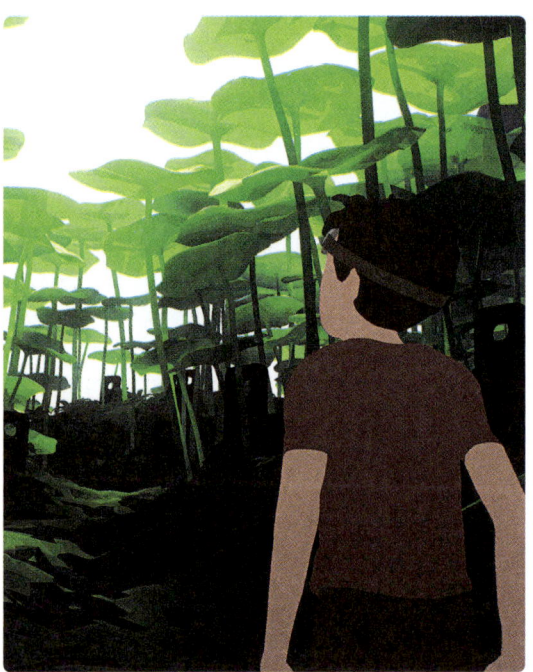

animation you can write whatever you want, and you have infinite possibilities, so you don't know where to begin. Having no dialogue and knowing that it's just animals, at least you have something to start with, and then you have to think about original ways of conveying these ideas. You can be more expressive with all the other tools you have."

A filmmaker's chosen tools often inform the qualities of their films. For someone like Hayao Miyazaki, it's the pencil; for Nick Park, it's a lump of coloured plasticine clay; for Satoshi Kon, it's the art of montage. By his own admission, Zilbalodis isn't particularly "good" at animation, and he isn't a compulsive doodler either: his tool of choice is the computer, and the possibilities of free, accessible software within which is he able to design shots and sequences from the ground up, exploring the space and positioning his invisible camera. More than any particular animator, Zilbalodis is inspired by the films of Paul Thomas Anderson, Alfonso Cuarón and Akira Kurosawa, and his work is defined by a freedom and fluidity of movement, and an eye for striking and meaningful composition.

Top left: The poster for Gints Zilbalodis's debut feature, *Away*, which he created entirely by himself.

Above: *Away* follows a young boy stranded on an island, as he explores his surroundings and evades a mysterious, shadowy giant.

the world and are enjoyed and embraced across language barriers. They couldn't be more digital, and yet they have an undeniable human element that is often hard to find in mega-budget CG animation. Elsewhere, we have grown used to seeing the literal fingerprints all over Aardman's claymation classics, or the flourish of a key animator's pen stroke in *The Tale of the Princess Kaguya*. Watching these films from Gints Zilbalodis, we wonder what the digital equivalent is – the clicks of a mouse, or swipes of a touchpad, that bear this personal trademark.

Right: Zilbalodis's films to date all have a shared love of natural landscape and subtle environmental themes – and animal characters, of course.

Below: Bracing, personal and often disarmingly hilarious, Signe Baumane's films are one of a kind.

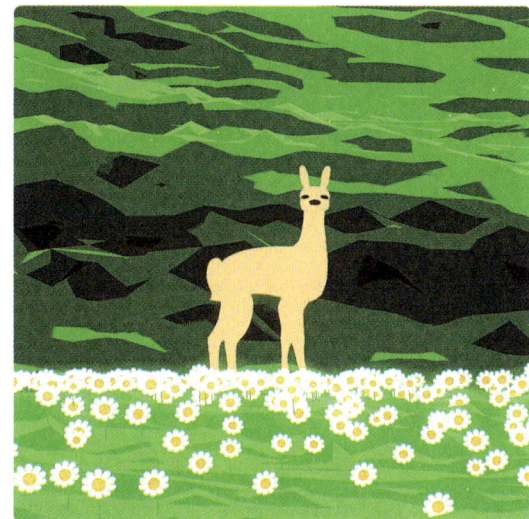

◉ Further Viewing

Another Latvian filmmaker to seek out is director Signe Baumane, whose work is the polar opposite of Gints Zilbalodis's wordless CG epics. Her independently produced animation explores autobiographical subjects, and is rendered in a distinctive hand-drawn style that recalls outsider art or alternative comix.

Born in the final decades of Soviet Latvia, Baumane studied in Russia and pursued a career in both animation and children's illustration, including working at Latvia's long-standing Dauka Animation Studio. In the mid-1990s, she relocated to the USA, where she struck up a creative relationship with the animator Bill Plympton, working on several of his projects in roles such as production manager, art supervisor and camera assistant.

Like Plympton, Baumane is a one-off, and her films could come from no one else: deeply personal, idiosyncratic, but vivid expressions of her life experience, often told in her own inimitable voice. Baumane's hilariously candid narration is a highlight in her "explicitly educational" short film series *Teat Beat of Sex* (2007–2009), which

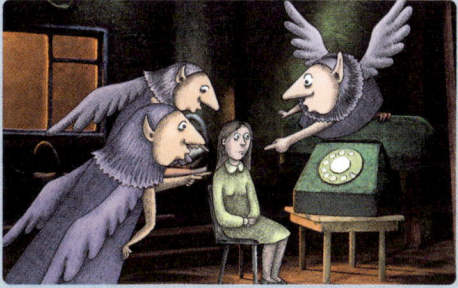

explores her point of view on everything from masturbation to penis envy.

That personal voice also drives the autobiographical feature *Rocks in My Pockets* (2014), which uses humour and visual metaphor to recount both Baumane's struggles with depression and suicidal thoughts, and those of several of her family members, too. This Kickstarter-backed breakthrough screened at festivals around the world and was followed in 2022 by another crowdfunded and critically acclaimed independent feature, *My Love Affair with Marriage*: an exuberant examination of romance and rebellion with a musical twist.

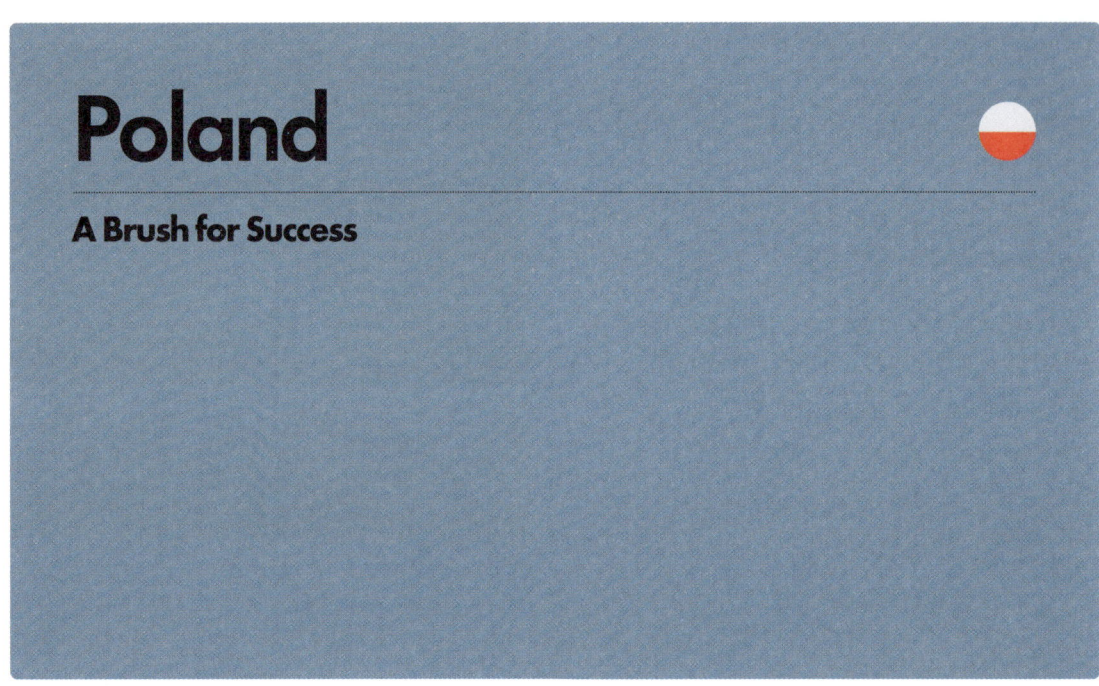

Poland

A Brush for Success

🎬 **Loving Vincent**

Director: Dorota Kobiela and Hugh Welchman
Released: 2017

As a concept, *Loving Vincent* makes perfect sense, but also none at all. Directed by Dorota Kobiela and Hugh Welchman, the 2017 film is over 65,000 frames long and made from handmade oil paintings, all created by a team of over a hundred artists, to tell a story of Vincent Van Gogh — in the painter's own style.

Van Gogh's paintings are some of the most famous and most beautiful in history, so immersing audiences into a world of their likeness, one outside of the exclusive bounds of a gallery's frame, is a strong pitch. And it's a pitch that worked: on a $5.5 million budget, the film made over $42 million. However, as powerful as that idea may be, and as intense and time-consuming as the process to create it was, *Loving Vincent* could also be seen as a gimmick, a film that takes the appearance of a great artist and uses it as a costume that undermines its subject's work.

After discovering a passion for animation during a course at London's National Film and Television School, Welchman started a production company that made a Norwegian, Polish and British co-produced stop-motion

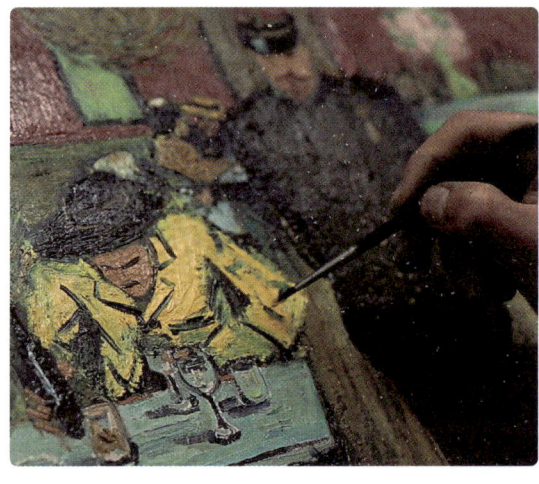

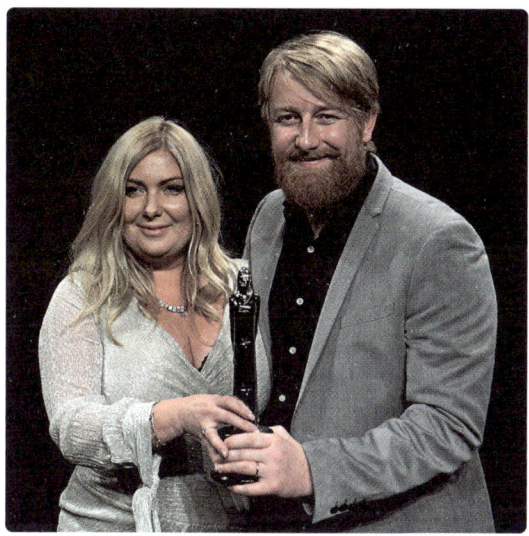

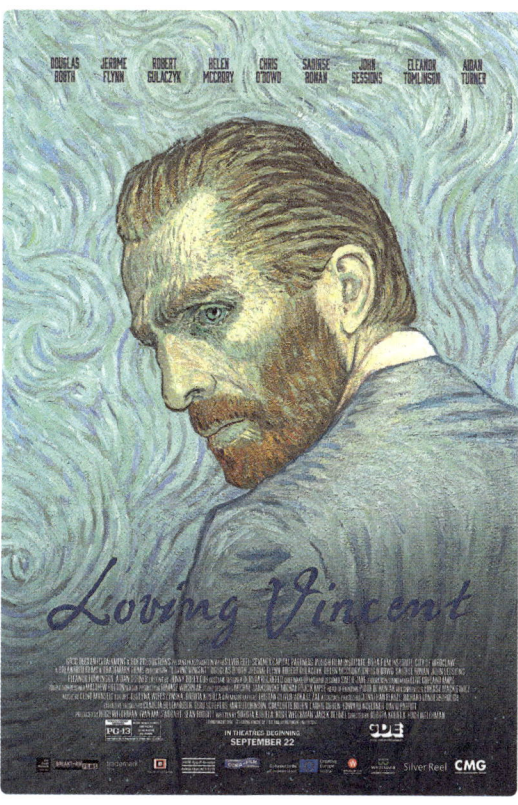

Opposite: Oil be back. An artist resurrects Vincent Van Gogh's style in the production of *Loving Vincent*.

Above: Dorota Kobiela and Hugh Welchman with the Best Animated Feature European Film Award, won by *Loving Vincent*.

Right: Although he only makes fleeting appearances in the film, Van Gogh is the star of *Loving Vincent*'s poster.

Below: Brushed aside. Booth's Armand Roulin paints a picture of conspiracy in the lead-up to Van Gogh's death.

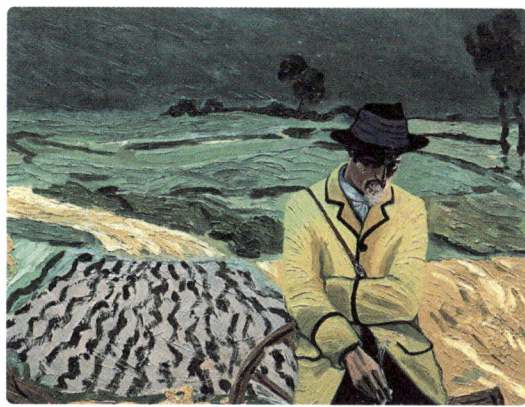

adaptation of *Peter & the Wolf* (2006), which won an Oscar. After that win, he was invited to produce another project in Poland, where he met – and fell in love with and later married – Kobiela. At the time, Kobiela, who had studied fine art, was working on a short film about Vincent Van Gogh. After discussing the idea with Welchman, *Loving Vincent* quickly grew, and rather than being her sixth animated short, painted solely by herself, it became her first feature (with Welchman as co-director) – and the first feature of its kind.

The story of *Loving Vincent*'s creation is perhaps more interesting than the film itself, which follows a young Frenchman's investigation into Van Gogh's death and his subsequent episodic jaunt through café, river and garden settings all populated with people who, if you squint, have some resemblance to those in the painter's own work. It's slight and repetitive and its promise of tabloid drama disintegrates into vague pontification, but its unfolding is a unique spectacle.

Each of the 898 individual shots that make up the film has an artist's hand very visibly at work which, compared to some anonymous CGI offerings, is a thing to be celebrated. The six-year process began with storyboards and an animatic, followed by actors being filmed on green screens or sets. These scenes were then used as reference as they were painted, frame by frame, in Van Gogh's style. The likes of Douglas Booth, Saoirse Ronan, Chris O'Dowd and Helen McCrory play figures adapted from Van Gogh's portraits, their likeness bringing star quality to the story, and in the case

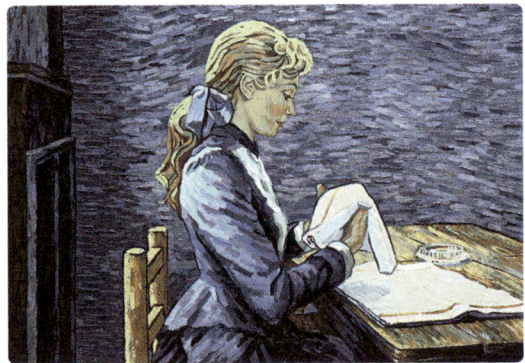

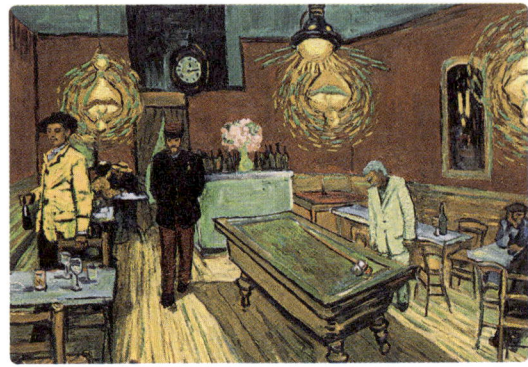

of Booth, a bizarre cockney accent too. The skill of the painters is undeniable: their thickly daubed oils and swirls of colour feel raised from the screen as they aim for an impression of the post-impressionist; always striking, occasionally breathtaking.

But, Van Gogh's ability to translate the movement of life into a static image is part of what makes his works so impressive, so by mutating them into motion, that aspect of his works becomes slightly flattened. Were *Jurassic Park*'s Dr Ian Malcolm (played by Jeff Goldblum) to pivot to humanities, *Loving Vincent* would certainly return him

to the debate around the difference between "could" and "should". The film's box office receipts and its Oscar nomination certainly argue one way, so if you haven't seen it, see how you go; you might end up loving Vincent too.

Above left: Adeline Ravoux, one of Van Gogh's most recognisable subjects, played by Eleanor Tomlinson.

Above right: The familiar sight of The Night Café, as recreated in *Loving Vincent*.

Below: Starry might. As well as Douglas Booth and Eleanor Tomlinson, *Loving Vincent* also had Saoirse Ronan, Chris O'Dowd and Helen McCrory in its impressive cast.

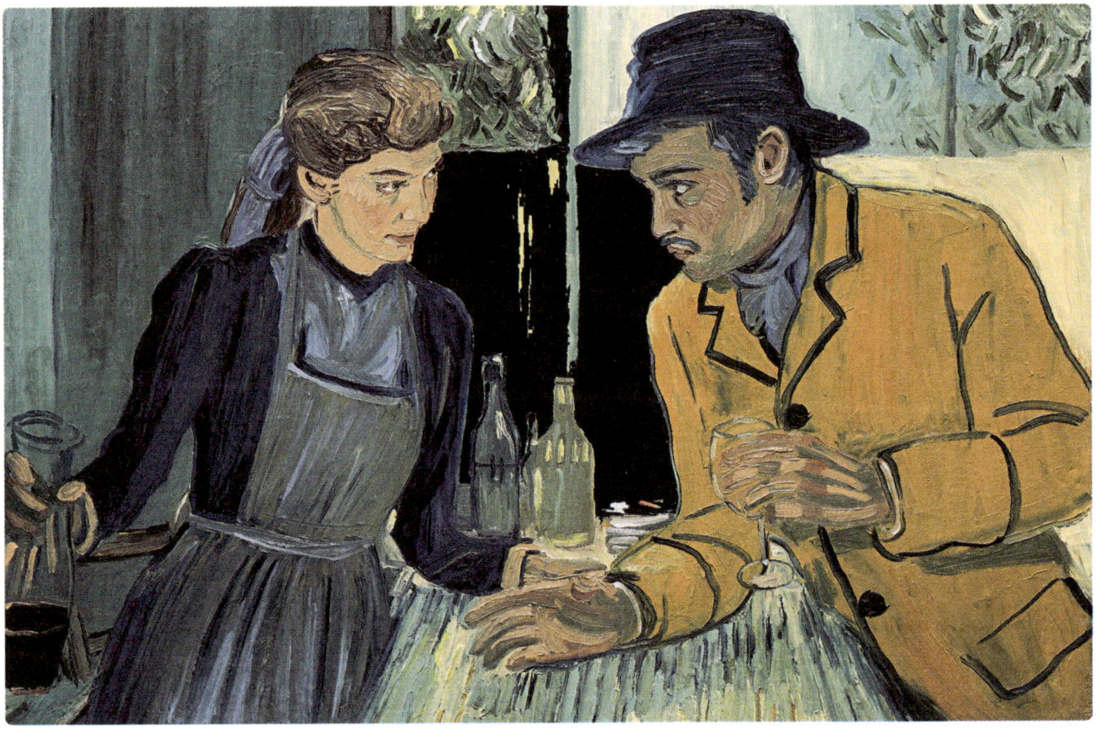

◉ Further Viewing

There's a long tradition of the experimental and the avant-garde running right through the history of Polish animation. We can't hope to cover it fully here, but let us present a few highlights. Before he moved to France and became a lurid live-action filmmaker renowned for exploring the overlap between genre, arthouse and erotic cinema, Walerian Borowczyk first made a name for himself as an animator, particularly in collaboration with graphic artist Jan Lenica on films such as the playful, perplexing, BAFTA-nominated film *Dom* (1958). Following their films together, Lenica continued to work solo, further developing his distinctive style of cut-out collage animation with the surrealist short film *Labyrinth* (1962). Like Borowczyk, Piotr Kamler emigrated to France, and created a canon of otherworldly stop-motion films that culminated in the moody, abstract sci-fi feature *Chronopolis* (1982), which features a musical score from musique concrète pioneer Luc Ferrari.

Julian Józef Antonisz developed his own idiosyncratic style of "non-camera" animation, directly painting, drawing and scratching onto strips of film, which he described in his Artistic Non-Camera Manifesto as the only true, authentic way of producing art. His short films *How a Sausage Dog Works* (1971) and *A Highly Committed Film* (1979) are an absolute riot: vibrant, strange, impassioned, unique. They're an assault on the senses, drawn in a primitive style and tackling eccentric subjects – one a parody of a scientific lecture focusing on, among other things, the humble dachshund; the other a polemic about the state of Polish visual culture, and the decline of the corner-shop kiosks that once acted as free public galleries for contemporary poster art.

In 1982, Zbigniew Rybczyński picked up an Oscar for *Tango* (1980), a remarkably complex animation that layers dozens of live-action characters acting out repeated cycles of action within the same, cramped room. *Tango* has been

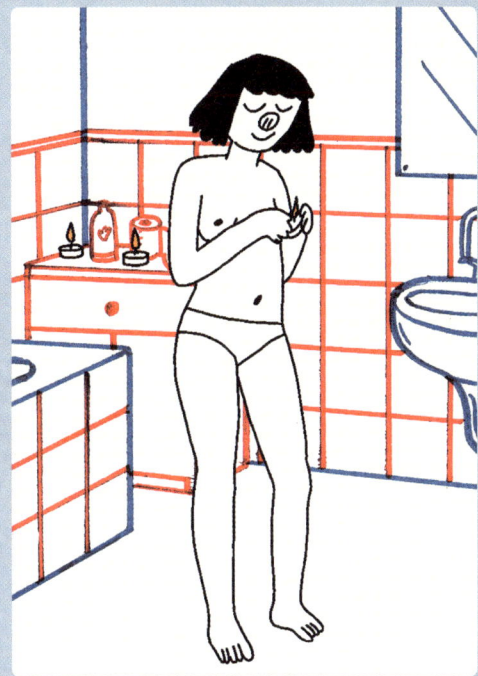

referenced, homaged and spoofed over the years, from the 1998 Green Day music video 'Redundant' to a 2020 episode of the Australian kids' cartoon series *Bluey*.

The simple linework of Renata Gasiorowska's *Pussy* (2016) may seem family-friendly, but its subject matter couldn't be more adult. An animated interaction between a woman and her anthropomorphized vagina, *Pussy* approaches the topics of masturbation and female desire with the frankness and humour of Signe Baumane (see page 93), before exploding into vibrant colour and free-form, abstract artwork that's reminiscent of the experimental films of Norman McLaren. An animated orgasm – now that's not something you see every day.

Above: Private Parts. Renata Gasiorowska's *Pussy* animates a hilarious and frank encounter between a woman and her vagina.

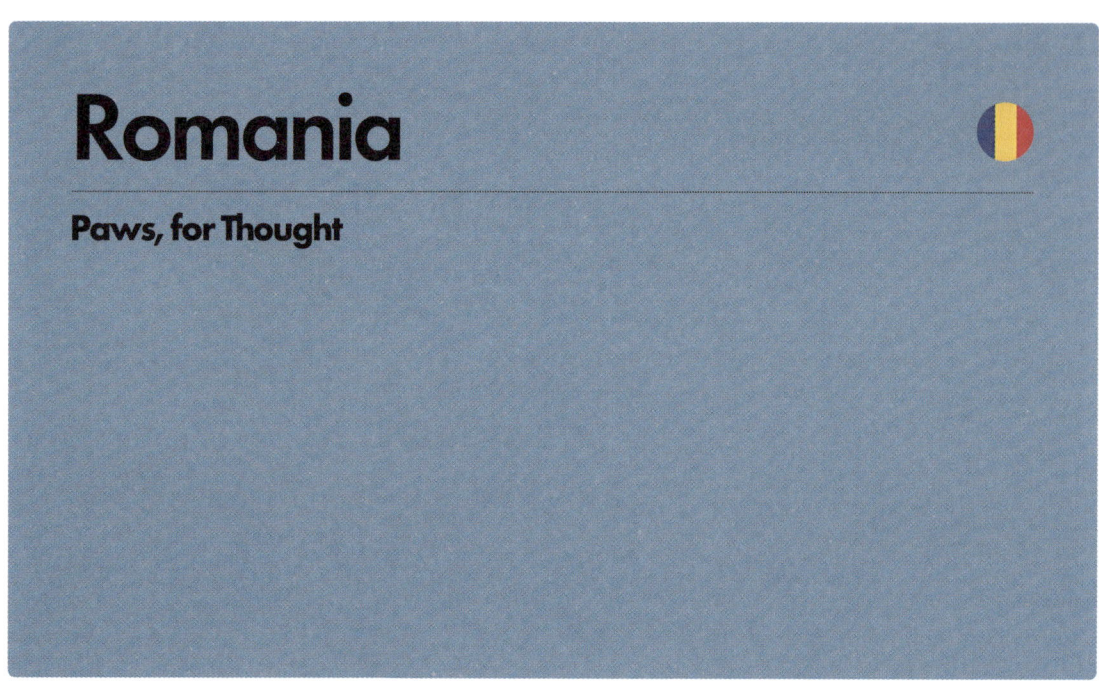

Romania

Paws, for Thought

📷 Marona's Fantastic Tale

Director: Anca Damian
Released: 2019

In any film about a dog, the primary concern looming over every viewer tends to be the mortality of the pooch protagonist. Romanian director Anca Damian's film removes that question in its first few seconds, beginning with the demise of its titular mastiff-mix hero, as she's struck in traffic and her body, illustrated here as the lightest dusting of chalk, gradually swirls away into the wind.

But, before the last speck drifts off, our canine narrator invites us to watch the film of her life, and despite this heartbreaking opener, what follows is a mesmeric, romantic and artistically unbound wonder.

Damian's previous works used animation within the documentary mode, but even though Marona's strange and wonderful tale does border on fantasy, it too contains many truths. Black and white and wide-eyed, with a heart-shaped nose and wing-tipped ears, Marona's striking, instantly sympathetic look is almost Mickey Mouse-esque in its simplicity. Her look is a pure and formal constant, while the world she enters is mercurially constructed in eye-popping fashion by

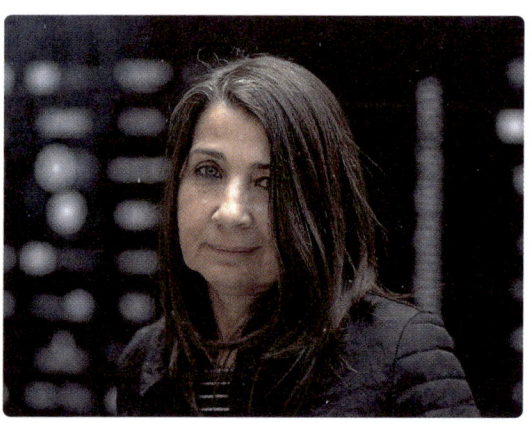

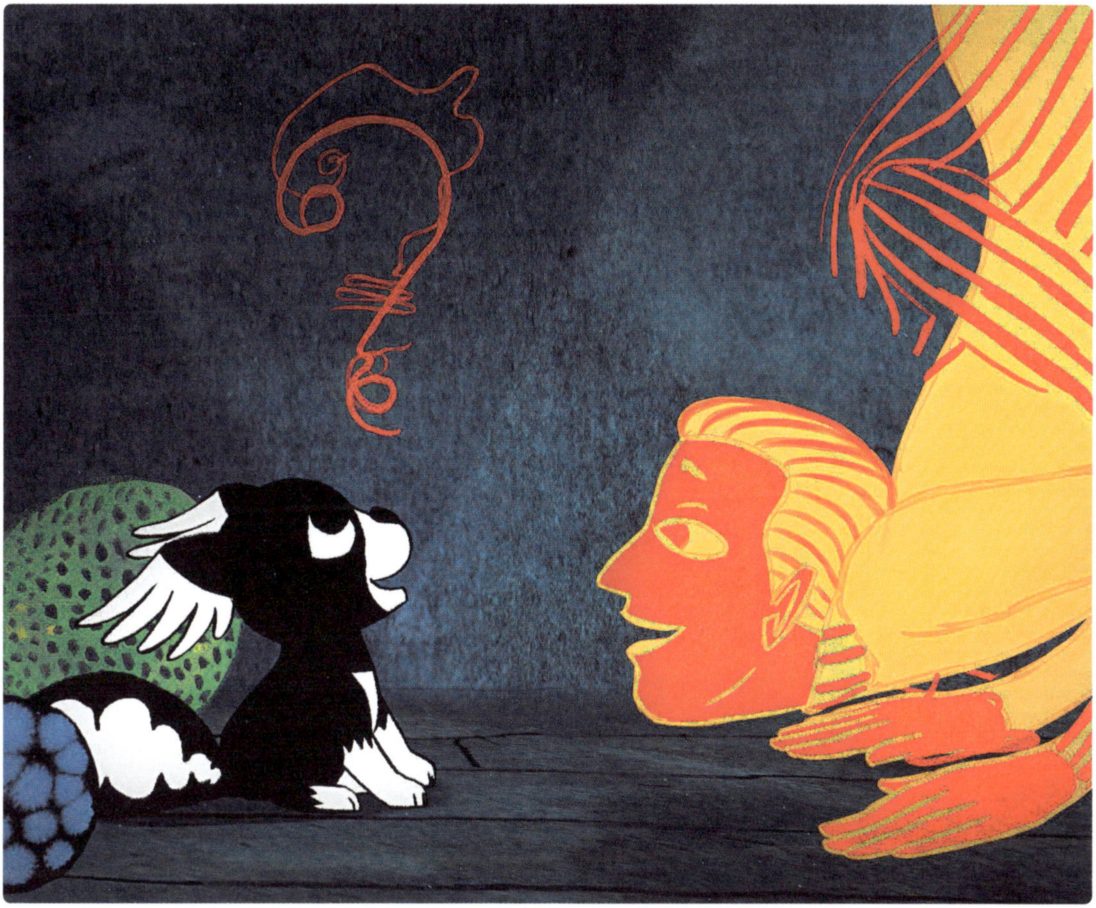

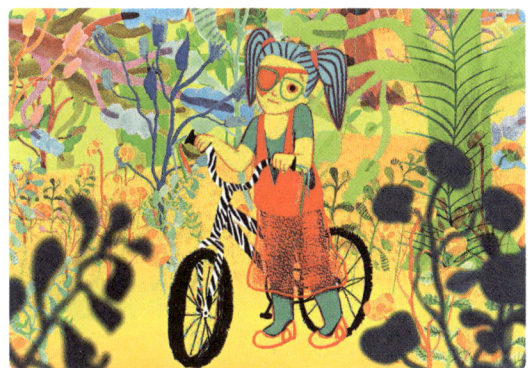

Damian's animators (she worked with three studios in France, two in Belgium and one in Romania), who embrace 2D, 3D, felt-tips, pencils and cut-outs.

After a brief origin story, scrappy ninth-born pup Marona meets her first true owner, Manole, an acrobat made of infinitely flexible red and orange licks of ribbon. He bounces, bulges and peels around Marona, filling their tiny flat and new life together with wonder; but it is not to be, as the selfless Marona leaves him so he can pursue his globe-trotting dreams. Her experience with Manole represents the possibilities of childhood, while the film's second chapter marks the confusion and darkness of adolescence, when Marona meets the colossal and kind construction worker Istvan, his ill mother and his vain wife. Characters and environments here are rich, expressive and precise – a building site laid out as blueprints, mixed with the jittering cubism of *Donkey Kong*; night-dwellers as just a brushstroke sitting on a pair of legs; and the crags of an

Opposite: Romanian director Anca Damian, who moved from using animation for documentary into fiction, with *Marona*.

Top: By the grace of dog. Marona and her first owner, the ribbon-limbed acrobat Manole.

Above: Girl's best friend. Solange, a brightly shaded young girl, is Marona's final owner.

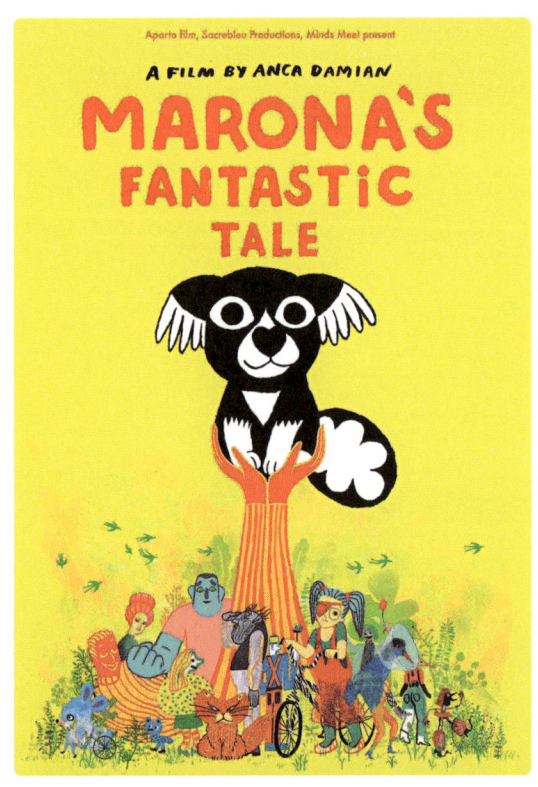

Aparte Film, Sacrebleu Productions, Minds Meet present

A FILM BY ANCA DAMIAN

MARONA'S FANTASTIC TALE

aged face forming, to Damian, an undulating "map of [a] life". Before circling back to the film's opening, Marona's final owner is introduced – a young girl, thickly sketched with crayons, called Solange. Here, a now emotionally weathered Marona enters adulthood, witnessing generational conflict from literal blockheaded elders, as well as the stresses of parenting via tidal waves of hair, belonging to Solange's mother, that swell into a drowning sea of admin.

These episodes form a remarkable eulogy, by turns bittersweet, reassuring and inspiring. Every padded step through Marona's world is joyously creative, and even in the darkest moments of hunger, abandonment or even death, her optimism can literally brighten up the screen. Abstractly reflecting a hyper-sensory approach to living, Damian's multiform scrapbooking draws viewers into a synaptically luminescent brain, one on a perpetually hopeful hunt for care – both for her and for herself to

Left: Tale of tails. Simple and sympathetic Marona, alongside some of the vibrantly coloured cast of characters from her life's ensemble.

Below: Embracing the abstract, Marona, with her wing-like ears, floats through a cosmic night-scape.

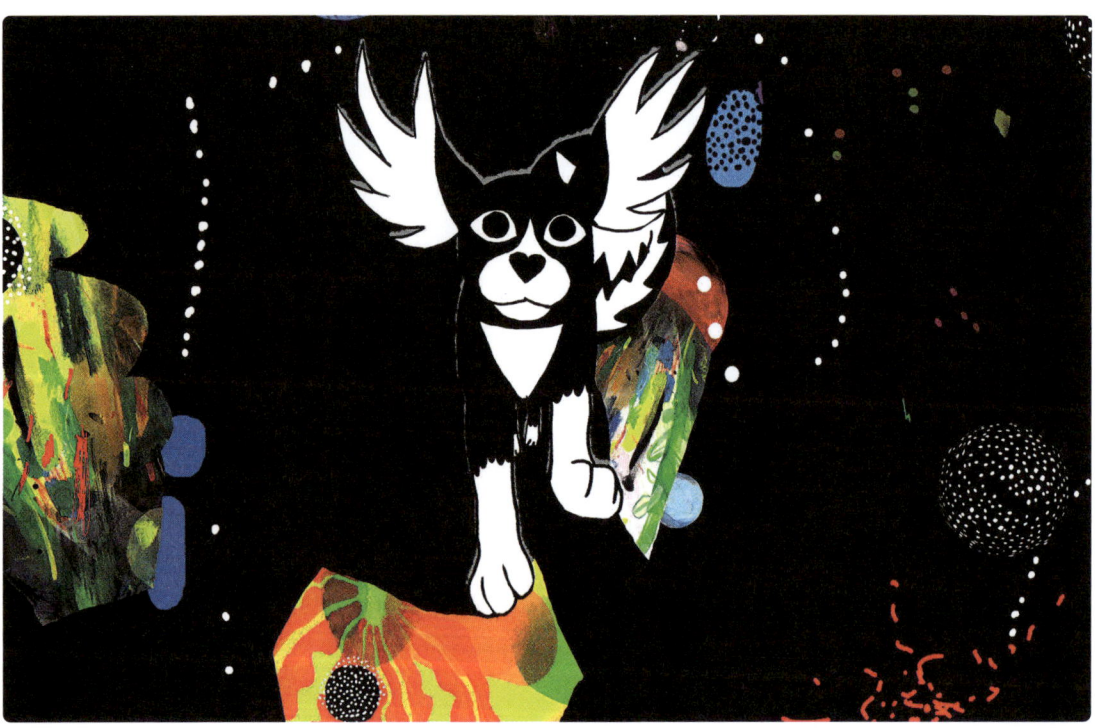

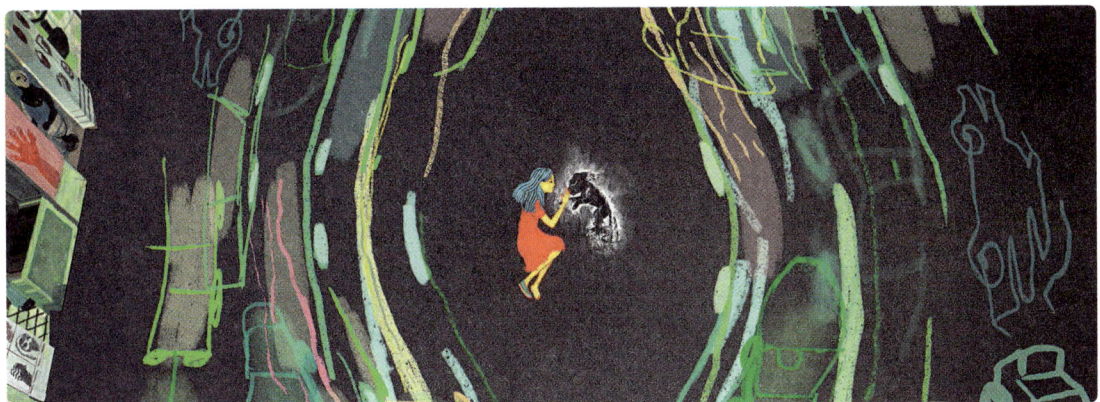

conduct. Through her kaleidoscopic lens on the world, Marona bounds through meditations on art, trust, care and responsibility, and in that delightfully doggy way, leaves only empathy for humans at all stages of life in her wake. She may have been the runt, but Marona's tale indisputably enters her into the canon of all-time filmic furry friends. It may begin with a notoriously wrenching narrative moment for any story, but once the chalk settles and the credits roll, the film proves the beautiful impact of a mighty mutt, even when their days are over.

Above: End of the road. Although bookended with sadness, *Marona's Fantastic Tale* is still a buoyant celebration of life.

Below: Writer in the Stars. The green-skinned journalist Alma is the protagonist of the pioneering Romanian sci-fi animation, *Delta Space Mission*.

👁 Further Viewing

For more of Anca Damian's formally diverse work, track down her Annecy prize-winning animated documentary *Crulic: The Path to Beyond* (2011), which tells the story of a Romanian man who goes on hunger strike after being wrongfully convicted and banged up in a Polish prison, or the more recent *The Island* (2021) – a vivid, surreal, musical spin on *Robinson Crusoe*. *Crulic* was hailed as Romania's first animated feature in two decades, but dig back further and you can find exemplary work from cartoonist-animator-director Ion Popescu-Gopo, whose *A Brief History* (1957) won the Cannes Palme d'Or for Short Film. Romania's answer to the Oscars, the Gopo Awards, are named in his memory. Also, seek out the haunting animated paintings of Sabin Bălașa, such as *The City* (1967) and *The Ode* (1975), which morph and transform between beguiling landscapes and arresting portraits like sci-fi or fantasy fiction cover artwork come to life. And speaking of sci-fi, we are grateful to Deaf Crocodile, home video label and archaeologists of world cinema, for shining a spotlight on two boldly coloured interstellar odysseys from Călin Cazan and Mircea Toia, *Delta Space Mission* (1984) and *The Son of the Stars* (1988).

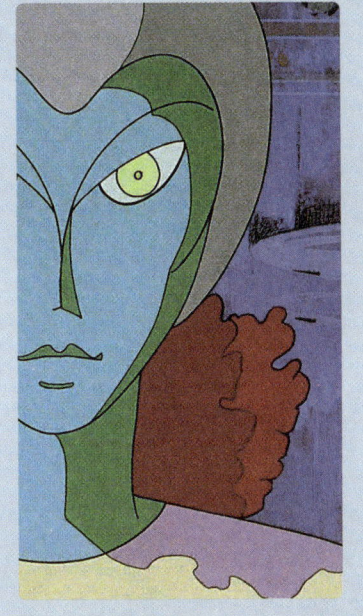

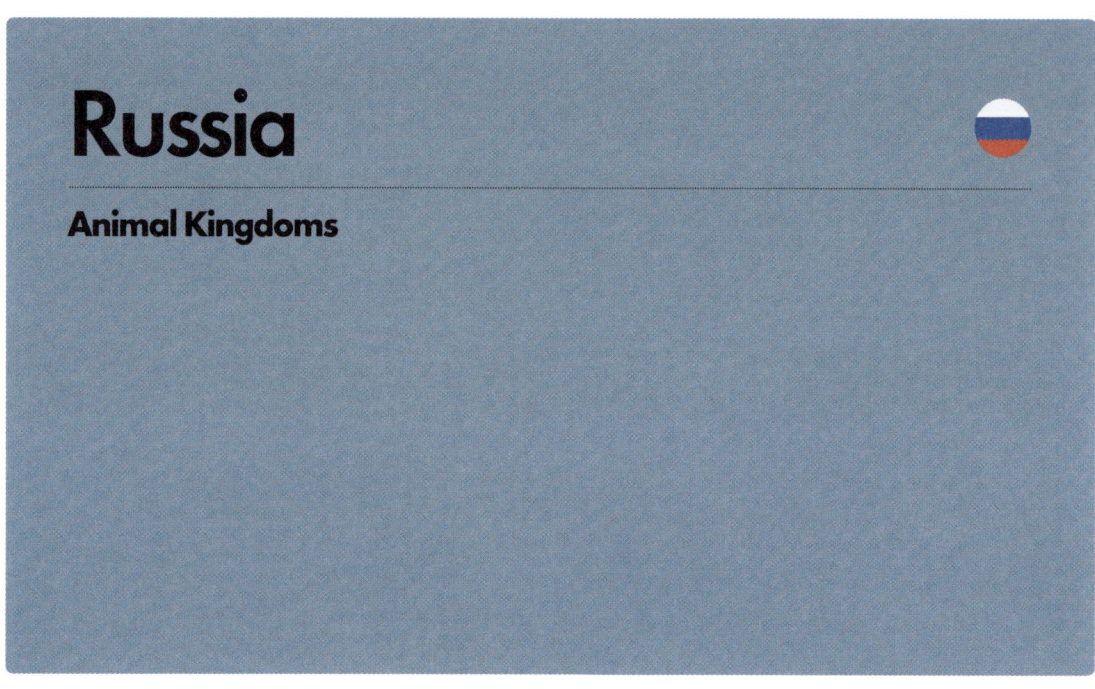

Russia

Animal Kingdoms

👤 Ladislas Starevich (1882–1965)

Several of the filmmakers that we discuss in this book make a mockery of our decision to divide up the world of animation by country, perhaps none more than Ladislas Starevich.

This pioneer of stop-motion animation was born Władysław Starewicz in Moscow to ethnically Polish parents from what is now Lithuania. In fact, he made his first steps as a filmmaker when living in the Lithuanian city of Kaunas (then part of the Russian Empire), where he worked for a museum of natural history making documentaries about stag beetles.

There is something macabre about stop-motion animation – a fact not helped by many of its popular practitioners having distinctive personal styles that tend towards the grim and grotesque – but that quality can be dated right back to Starevich's early experiments. The story goes that the stag beetles in Kaunas didn't cope well under hot stage lighting, so the director came up with a novel solution: why not animate them instead? For his first animated film, *Lucanus Cervus* (1910), Starevich made miniature puppets out of real, preserved beetles, gluing wire limbs to their abdomens and manipulating them one frame at a time in front of the camera: literally

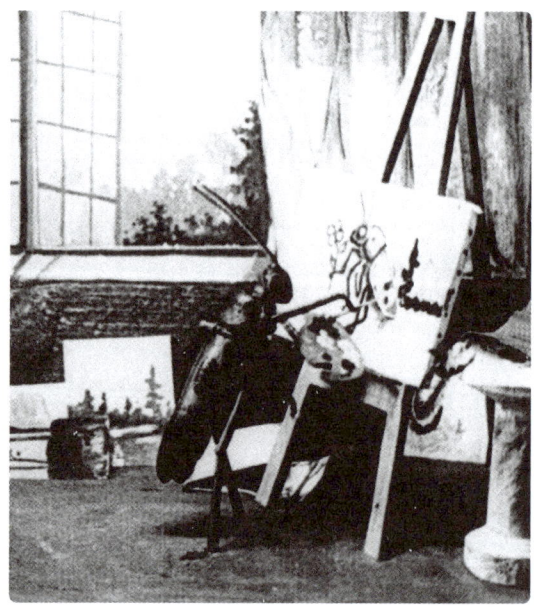

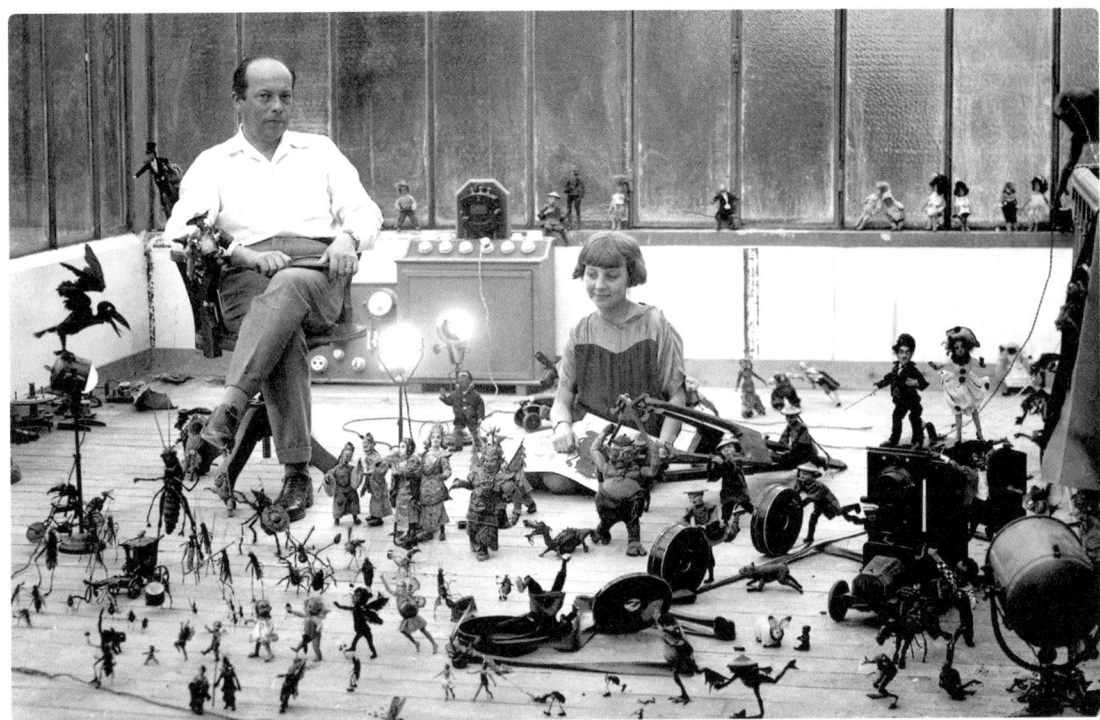

bringing the dead back to life through animation.

Starevich further developed this style with *The Beautiful Lukanida*, kitting out beetles with weapons and costumes and placing them in elaborate stage sets for a courtly tale of nobles duelling over the love of the queen. The film premiered in Moscow in 1912 to great success, and later travelled across Europe. When it reached London, the papers were astounded, and wondered if Starevich had actually trained a troupe of acting insects.

But the beetles were just the start. Starevich's company quickly grew to include grasshoppers, ants, dragonflies, frogs and other creatures that he cast in dozens of films, including *The Insects' Christmas* (1912) and *The Cameraman's Revenge* (1912) – an odd, melodramatic pastiche in which a cinema projectionist gets his own back on a cheating husband. This feverishly productive period also saw Starevich make scores of live-action films, until he left Russia following the October Revolution in 1917 and eventually settled in France, where he lived until his death in 1965.

In France, he returned to stop-motion, including a series of shorts about a child's stuffed toy come to life. The first of this character's adventures, *Fétiche* (1933, known as *The Mascot* on release in the UK), saw him venture

through dangerous city streets in search of an orange for his beloved owner. In one nightmarish sequence, he must contend with the dreadful creatures of the night, including the bones of discarded fish and chicken carcasses, reassembled into unholy monsters.

Where Starevich's early Russian films may now seem rudimentary and experimental, the films of this French period are directed with a panache that still impresses today, with the animator's hand imbuing his immaculately textured puppets with real personality. This culminated in Starevich's magnum opus, the feature-length swashbuckling caper *The Tale of the Fox* (1937), which he made with his daughter Irène. As the title card boldly claimed: "This film is not a cartoon... it is a revolution in the history of cinema."

Adapted from medieval fables of the wily fox and his schemes against a court of anthropomorphized animals, *The Tale of the Fox* is more of a menagerie than a movie. It is full to the brim with animal characters: wolves, bears,

Opposite: Meet the Beetles. Starevich's landmark film, *The Cameraman's Revenge*, is a comic tale of insect rivalry.

Above: Starevich sits alongside his daughter and close collaborator Irène in the middle of their menagerie of puppet creations.

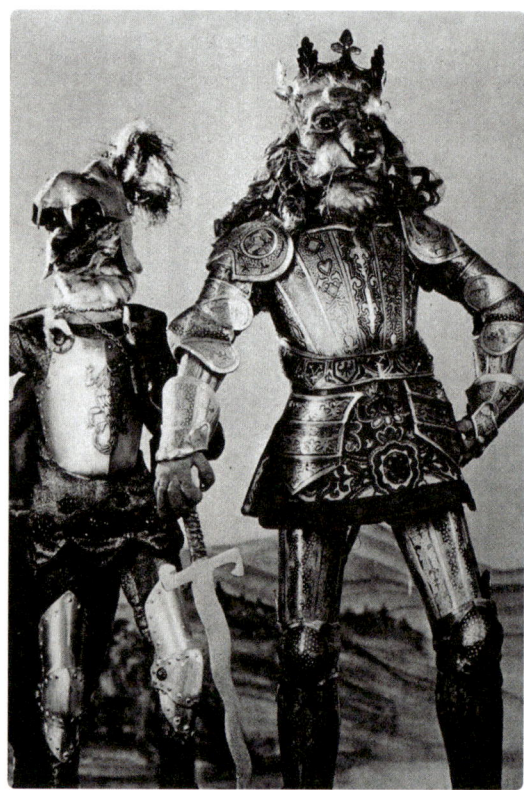

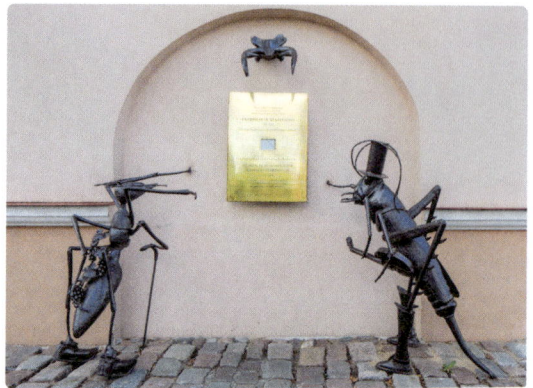

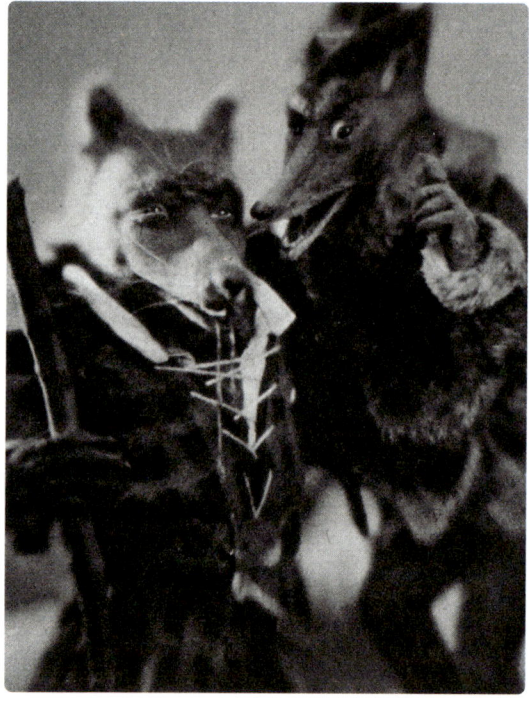

badgers, ravens, all with uncannily expressive features and perfectly articulating mouths, brows, snouts and eyes, which the Stareviches are unafraid of filming in tight close-up like they're screen idols. It's in these shots, and the sense of playful humour that pervades the film, that we can see a seed of inspiration which would grow, 70 years later, into Wes Anderson's *Fantastic Mr Fox* (2009).

The opening moments of *The Tale of the Fox* present us with a monkey cranking up the projector, spinning into action this heightened, animal world – one that is a playground for the Machiavellian Reynard the Fox. His plots and pranks come back to bite him, though, as the film builds up to a spectacular siege sequence where the aggrieved animals converge on his castle home, and the Fox and his child keep the attackers at bay with an arsenal of ingenious traps.

It's Buster Keaton, stop-motion style, yet while Starevich first planned to release *The Tale of the Fox* as a silent comedy, the rise of sound cinema changed everything. The animation had been finished in France in the early 1930s, but the addition of narration and dialogue took several years to crack. The film finally received its premiere

in 1937, months before the release of Disney's *Snow White* on the other side of the Atlantic – albeit in Berlin, in a German-language cut, adding yet another country to this wayward, international tale of Ladislas Starevich.

Top left: The Lion King. In the animal kingdom of *The Tale of the Fox*, the big cat is the top dog.

Top right: Stag Party. In Kaunas, Lithuania, a crowd of insect statues stand alongside a monument to Starevich and his groundbreaking work in animation.

Above: Telling Tales. The quick brown fox puts one over the dozy wolf.

👤 Yuri Norstein (b. 1941)

It's very likely that Yuri Norstein is your favourite animator's favourite animator. From Hayao Miyazaki to Nick Park, Norstein has fans and admirers around the world, and his films have been voted among the greatest of all time by filmmakers and critics alike.

Born in Soviet Russia in 1941, Norstein came of age in post-war Moscow and worked as an animator on projects for the Soyuzmultfilm studio, including many with the pioneering filmmaker Ivan Ivanov-Vano. It was with Ivanov-Vano that Norstein won prizes from the Karlovy Vary and Animafest Zagreb film festivals for co-directing *The Battle of Kerzhenets* (1971), which combined three pillars of Russian culture – old Slavic legends, the music of Nikolai Rimsky-Korsakov and the painted icons and frescoes from the fourteenth to sixteenth centuries – into one powerful work of cut-out, stop-motion animation.

Since *Kerzhenets*, Norstein has released only four finished films, all of them shorts, culminating in a body of work that doesn't exceed even an hour and a half. And yet, within this compact canon lie wonders as beloved by generations of Russian children as they are revered by the international animation community.

For a time, Norstein dedicated himself to animating whimsical fables such as *The Fox and the Hare* (1973) and *The Heron and the Crane* (1974), always in collaboration with his wife, and trusted art director, Francheska Yarbusova. It was across these two films that Yarbusova and Norstein started to experiment with assembling their cut-out characters and other elements from celluloid rather than just paper, which gave their films a rich graphic texture. Norstein also worked with cinematographer Alexander Zhukovsky to develop a process of layering sheets of glass in front of the camera, with characters and backgrounds lying on separate levels: their own version of the "multiplane" technique pioneered by the likes of Lotte Reiniger (see page 70), the Fleischer Brothers and Disney. But where others had used such a process to add the illusion of depth to a two-dimensional animated image, Norstein saw potential to infuse the image with a sense of space and atmosphere. As Norstein once described the effect to *Sight and Sound*, "The air is incarnated."

These techniques came to fruition in *Hedgehog in the Fog* (1975): a simple, yet quietly unsettling tale of a little Hedgehog traversing a field under a blanket of fog on

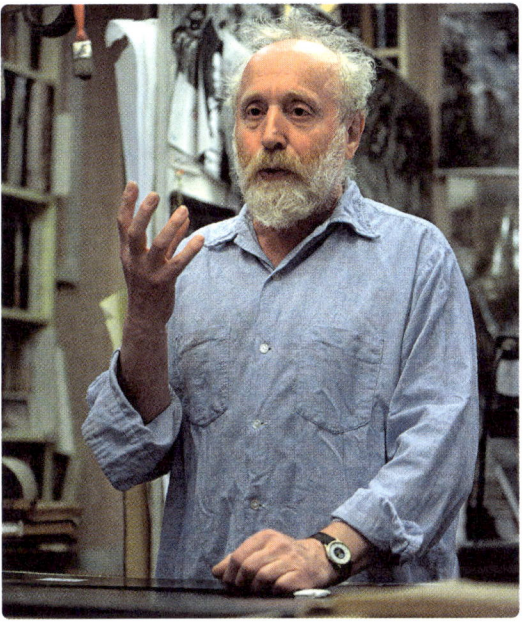

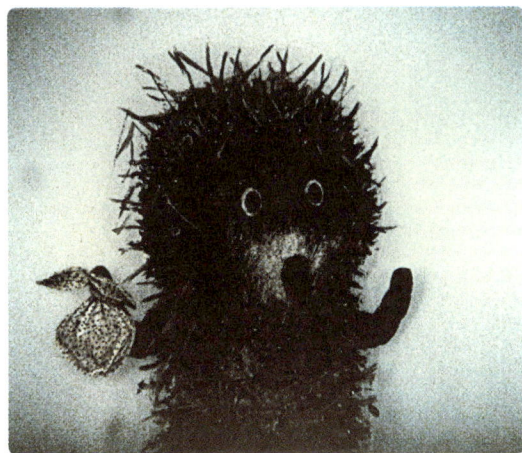

Top: Golden Snail. One of the animation world's most revered filmmakers – and one of our least prolific – Yuri Norstein.

Above: Fog Wild. Lost in the mist, the little Hedgehog is terrified by what he imagines is lurking just out of sight.

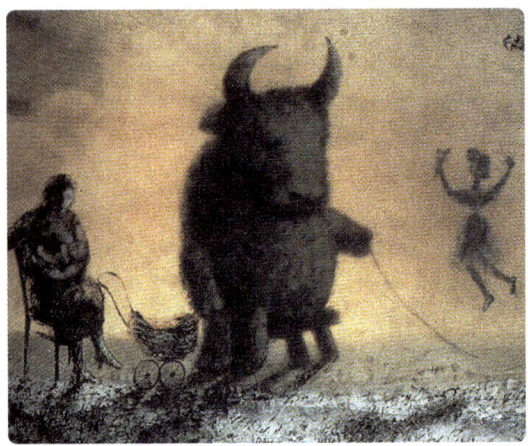

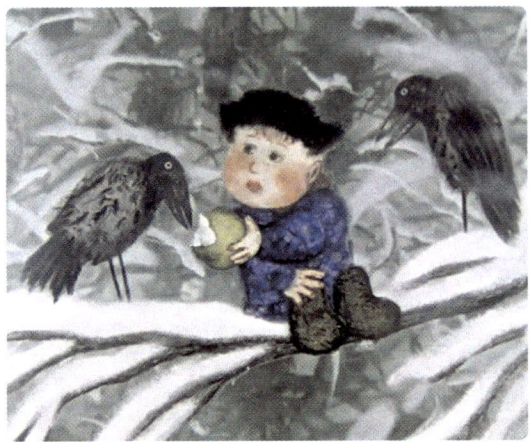

the way to an evening's stargazing with his pal, the Bear. Along the way, the Hedgehog is stalked by a persistent owl, assailed by bats and aided (to his terror) by a kind, floppy-eared hound. There are also creatures half-glimpsed, or merely imagined, that rise out of the murk: a hulking elephant that, on approach, turns out to be a huge tree trunk; and a magnificent white horse, which first tempts the Hedgehog to stray from the path and venture into the unknown.

Norstein used semi-transparent tracing paper in conjunction with his complex multiplane glass arrangements to make the mist that engulfs our poor protagonist all the more immersive. As the haze envelops the frame, it feels like we too could become lost – an effect which plays into a gnawing sense of melancholy that persists past the film's seemingly happy ending. Though the friends are united in the end, the thought still lingers: what really lies out there in the fog?

Compared to these children's fables, *Tale of Tales* (1979) was a leap into new territory. Inspired by Norstein's own childhood and what he described as "the horror of Russian life", *Tale of Tales* starts with a baby's lullaby and grows into an evocation of a nation torn apart by war, and of warm childhood experiences that have since faded into memory. A nursery-rhyme wolf acts as our guide through impressionistic scenes that shift through time and space, freely associating between overlapping themes, images and metaphors.

The film is often compared to Andrei Tarkovsky's loosely autobiographical visual poem *Mirror* (1975), and like that film, *Tale of Tales* is elusive on a narrative level, but ultimately powerful and profound on an emotional one. Here, Norstein and cinematographer Igor Skidan-Bosin

focus their experiments on the quality of light: the glowing embers of the hearth in Norstein's slum-like childhood apartment; a divine luminosity that saturates a family picnic tableau. Norstein explained to *Sight and Sound* that, to him, the essence of cinema is "light separated from darkness... The essential motif in *Tale of Tales* is that ray of light which draws you out of the darkness."

Norstein's reputation rests on these two miniature marvels, but another project casts a shadow over his entire filmography. At over 40 years and counting, Norstein's film adaptation of Nikolai Gogol's short story "The Overcoat" has the distinction of being the longest-gestating animation production on record. Unfinished excerpts have been shown at festivals over the years, and there was even a documentary about the production released in 2019, but we wonder if we'll ever get to see this film in full. His perfectionism has earned him the nickname "the Golden Snail": a fitting counterpart to the "descendant of a giant sloth" that was one of his most vocal champions, Isao Takahata.

Norstein has weathered all sorts of trials and setbacks during the making of *The Overcoat*, but he still stays committed. Way back in 1994, when the director seemed to be back on track after being unceremoniously evicted from his studio several years earlier, he was asked about the delays in production and the many wasted years in limbo. "It wasn't lost time," Norstein argued, "because I didn't stop living."

Above left: Remember Ember. One of the lush visual motifs of *Tale of Tales* is the warm glow of memory.

Above right: Core Memory. Another recurring motif is that of an apple – crisp, flavourful, Proustian – here enjoyed by a boy in winter.

👁 Further Viewing

Several years before Starevich first experimented with his insects, the ballet master Alexander Shiryaev used both hand-drawn and stop-motion puppet animation to choreograph intricate, miniature stage productions featuring harlequins and pierrots made of papier mâché and clay. His films were mostly forgotten for close to a century until they were restored in 2008, reaffirming Shiryaev's place as Russia's earliest-known animation pioneer.

Animation fell out of favour following the October Revolution, but later became one of the Soviet Union's strongest cultural pillars. Aleksandr Ptushko used dozens of stop-motion puppets to populate *The New Gulliver* (1935), one of the first feature-length films to use animation so extensively. Then, in 1936, the state authorities established an animation studio that was tasked with being the Soviet answer to Disney: Soyuzmultfilm, which would become one of the most important names in global animation history.

Production flourished at Soyuzmultfilm in the post-war years, with fairy tales and literary adaptations that were embraced by young audiences at home and lauded by international festivals and critics. On staff were some of the most celebrated animation directors of the period, such as Ivan Ivanov-Vano (*The Little Humpbacked Horse*, 1947), the Brumberg Sisters (*The Lost Letter*, 1945) and Lev Atamanov (*The Snow Queen*, 1957). *The Snow Queen* even had a theatrical release in the United States – no mean feat at the height of the Cold War. It also had a particular impact on a young Hayao Miyazaki in Japan, who said that watching the film made him feel glad that he had dedicated his life to animation. "How wonderful it would be," he once said, "if we could someday make something at the same high level as that."

Soyuzmultfilm's competition with Disney continued when both studios adapted A.A. Milne's Winnie-the-Pooh stories across the 1960s and 1970s. We'll

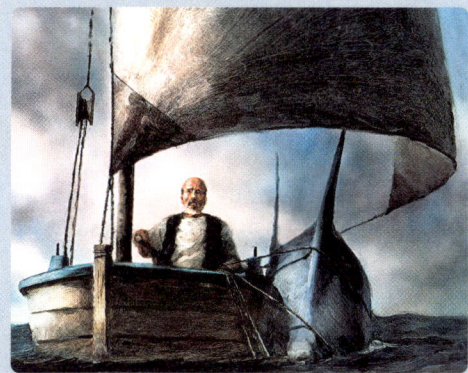

take Fyodor Khitruk's take on Hundred Acre Wood – with its textured pastel backgrounds and chatty eccentricities – over Disney's twee coziness any day. The Soviet Pooh is still beloved in Russia today, as is Soyuzmultfilm's other animated superstar, the adorable little creature Cherubashka – star of a clutch of charming stop-motion shorts from director Roman Kachanov.

Following the dissolution of the Soviet Union, the Russian animation industry faltered after losing its state backing. Today, the Russian animator with the greatest international renown is Aleksandr Petrov, a former student of Yuri Norstein who has adopted a breathtaking paint-on-glass technique for films such as *The Cow* (1989), *The Dream of a Ridiculous Man* (1992) and his Academy Award-winning adaptation of Ernest Hemingway's 1952 novella, *The Old Man and the Sea* (1999). However, going by sheer numbers, Russian animation's most successful contemporary export by far is the preschool animation juggernaut *Masha and the Bear* (2009 to present), which has been syndicated around the world and, at time of writing, has amassed over 30 billion views on YouTube alone.

Above One Man in a Boat. A vivid scene from Aleksandr Petrov's Oscar-winning *The Old Man and the Sea*.

Spain

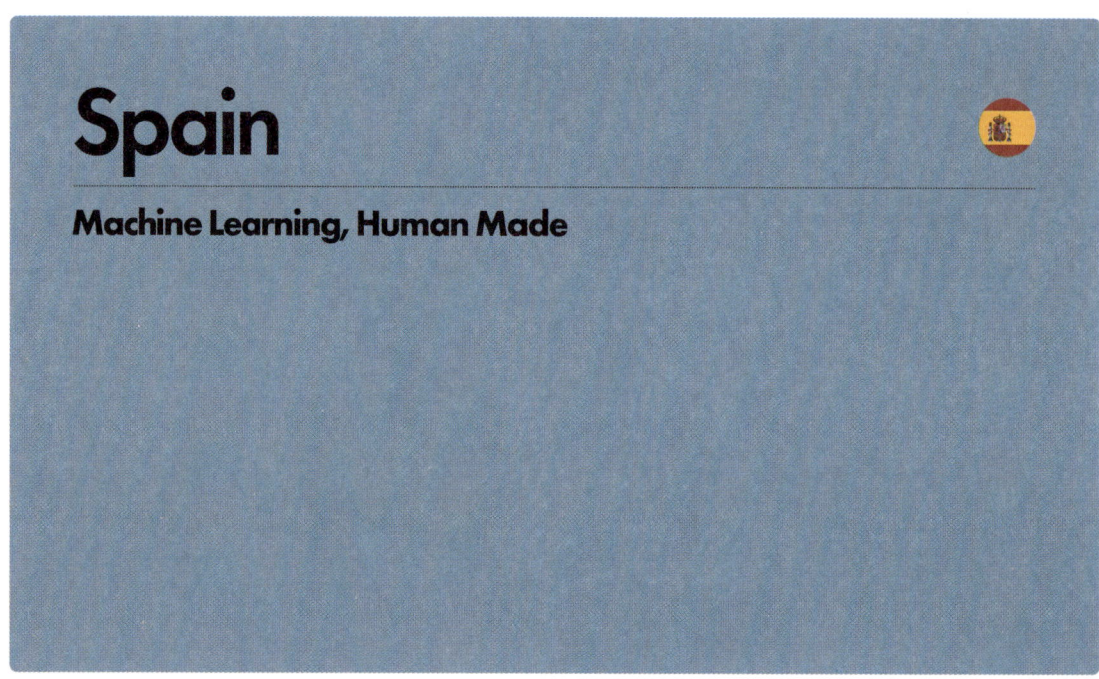

Machine Learning, Human Made

🎥 Robot Dreams

Director: Pablo Berger
Released: 2023

A few years ago, when Spanish director Pablo Berger was between projects, he pulled Sara Varon's dialogue-free, New York-set graphic novel from 2010 off his shelf. *Robot Dreams* was about a dog and its intimate and estranged relationship with a robot – and it left him in tears.

Varon's simple, evocative drawings were coming to life in Berger's head and at that moment he had decided on his next project. There was just one issue: he'd never made an animated film.

That didn't stop him though. Although his lewd comedy *Torremolinos 73* (2003), black-and-white fairy tale *Blancanieves* (2012) and magical realist tale *Abracadabra* (2017) had all been made in live action, Berger decided the pen was mightier than the camera and set to conquer his first animated frontier. He initially planned to work with Irish studio Cartoon Saloon on the project (read more about them on page 80), but the Covid-19 pandemic unfortunately led to that idea crumbling, forcing Berger to stay home to explore his new world. Setting up his own studio in Madrid, he

then joined forces with other native companies, and production on *Robot Dreams* began in 2021, with the film premiering two years later at the Cannes Film Festival before eventually finding its way to Los Angeles and the 2024 Academy Awards. It was nominated for the Best Animated feature award, but lost to Hayao Miyazaki's *The Boy and the Heron*. Berger told us in an interview: "Miyazaki is the master... there's no hard feelings."

Set in a full and fizzing anthropomorphized version of '80s New York (featuring 400 animal background characters), the story follows Dog, whose quiet, lonely, TV-dinner lifestyle needs a spark. After spending one too many nights alone in bed, with only their C-3PO and R2-D2 figures at the bedside for comfort, Dog stumbles serendipitously onto the shopping channel and swiftly

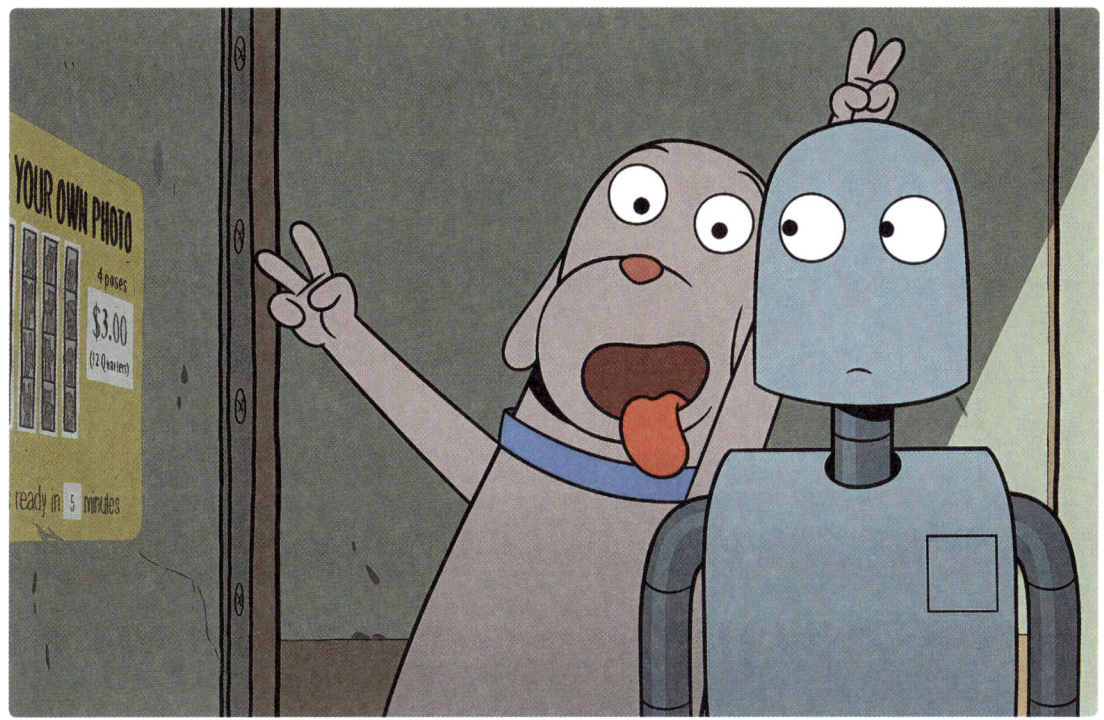

orders the Amica 2000, a robot built for friendship. Although almost childishly basic in design, Robot is remarkably animated, with most of their emotional cues coming from body language and a pencil stroke mouth with cavernous widening capabilities. Paired with Dog, whose restrained emotions are betrayed only occasionally by a wagging tail, the duo are not the most obviously expressive couple, but in being stripped back they become more relatable vessels, blank slates that allow the audience to "complete the film themselves". Dog and Robot's blossoming relationship forms the film's wonderful opening act. To a soundtrack from Earth, Wind & Fire, we see them strolling, dancing, even roller skating through their exquisitely designed city; all of the curiosity, humour and intimacy of a burgeoning friendship expertly constructed via looks and touches and heightening heart rates. Together, Dog and Robot are a joy to watch, but it's when they are broken apart that *Robot Dreams* pivots from its sunny romcom feel into something more interesting. Instead, it embraces melancholy and reveals a wiser and more inventive story.

Dog is forced to abandon a battery-drained Robot on a beach on the last day of the season before winter arrives, and the majority of Berger's film is about his attempt to try to build a life without Robot in it. And, like with any powerful relationship, truly removing the impact of that life is almost impossible. While Dog attempts to connect with other animals, and even a ten-pin bowling-loving snowman, the bricked Robot drifts into dreams, most of which lead them back to Dog; but

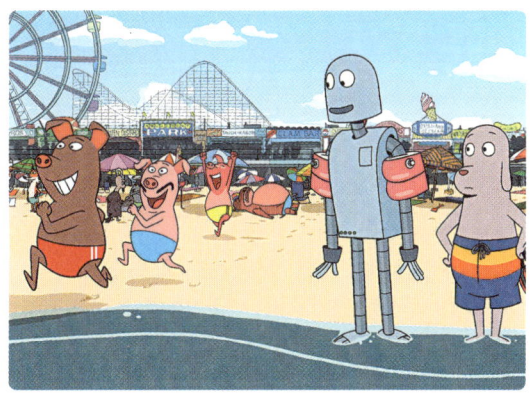

Top: Eye, robot. Despite being silent, Robot's face is full of expression.

Above: Life's a beach. After a day's fun by the sea, the beach soon becomes a place of isolation for Robot.

their journey remains similarly shaped around absence. Refreshingly and ultimately reassuringly, the story never resorts to saccharine reunions, instead acknowledging the importance of certain friends at certain times and the bittersweet power in forging new circuits. Although parted and bound by time and loss, there is another character who keeps Dog and Robot connected, a character with so much depth that they'll make you pause the film every few seconds, just to gawp at their detail. It is, of course, New York City.

In his book *Celluloid Skyline*, architect and filmmaker James Sanders wrote that there were two versions of New York: "one is a real city, an urban agglomeration of millions. The other is a mythic city, a dream city, born of that most pervasive of dream media, the movies." There is the city that is actually lived in and there is the city as we've seen it captured, cut, projected and explored though film. Animals fill Berger's take on these cinematic streets. They use their natural gifts to satisfying effect, like the octopus who's a dab hand (or tentacle) as a busking drummer, or the peacock whose tail is an ideal portable parasol. Created by an obvious film fanatic, the director captures these creatures and their sprawling habitat with live-action, cinephilic lensing, like hurtling toward Dog with a *Jaws*-style warping dolly-zoom effect while at the beach or swirling the frame to track ketchup down a plughole, *Psycho*-style. This formal fun is also used to add

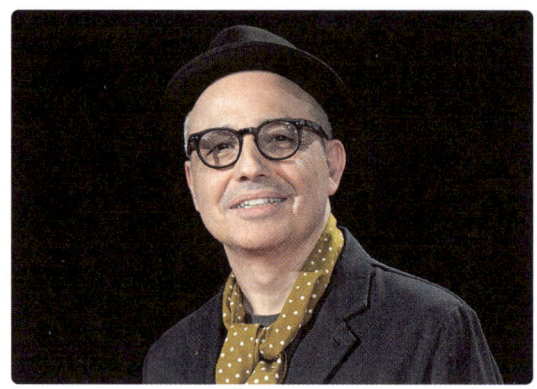

a superb existential edge to Robot's imaginings, with one standout sequence seeing them break the shape of, and escape from, the screen we're watching their story on, before literally flipping the story and jumping into a riff on *The Wizard of Oz*. Berger's New York – a place that in reality he once called home – is a perfect infinite loop of Sanders' second city. It's filled with references to stories and artists stamped in New York's cultural concrete – nods to *Manhattan*, *Midnight Cowboy* and *Taxi Driver*

Above: Pablo Berger, the director of *Robot Dreams*, had only made live-action features before embarking on this animated tale.

Below: Concrete jungle. In *Robot Dreams*, New York is transformed into a staggeringly detailed city inhabited by animals instead of humans.

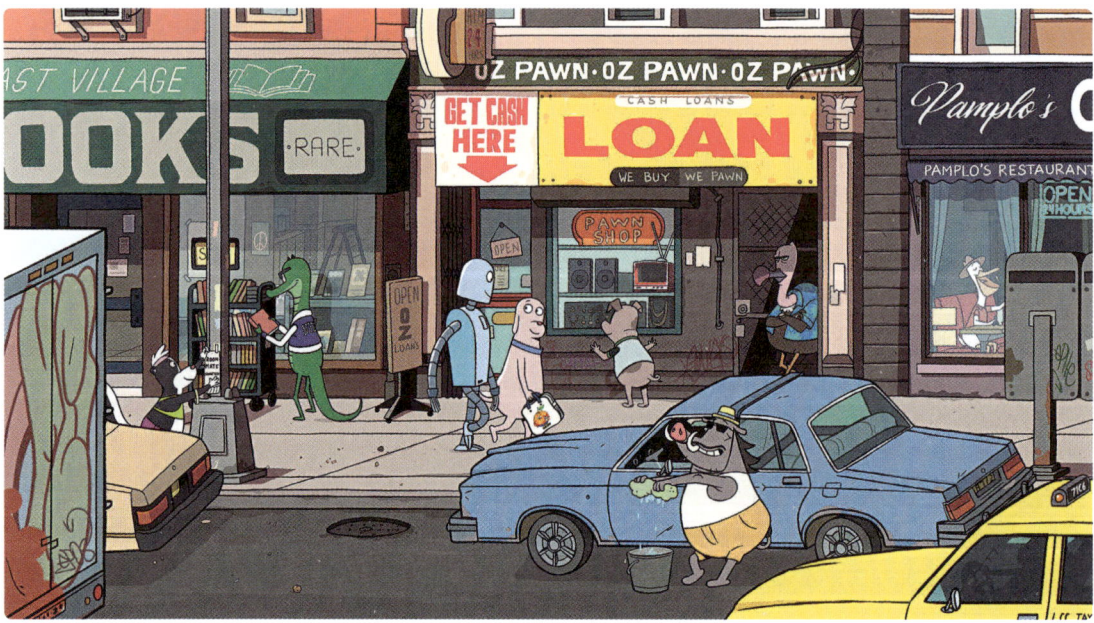

as well as Jean-Michel Basquiat, Keith Haring, Spike Lee and cult film retailer Kim's Video also appear – but it never loses itself within those visions. Rather, it only ever serves Robot and Dog, remaining a bespoke and unique delight in itself while cementing its own place within the mythic city. From its deep, foundational understanding of character and emotion, to its skyscrapingly ambitious formal highs, Berger's world is, for a first-time architect in animation, an astonishing exploration of emotional and urban geography.

Right: Paw things. Dog and Robot hold hands as they walk through the snowy streets of their city.

Below: For the Wing. Alberto Vázquez's Birdboy was acclaimed at festivals around the world, and picked up a Goya Award back home in Spain.

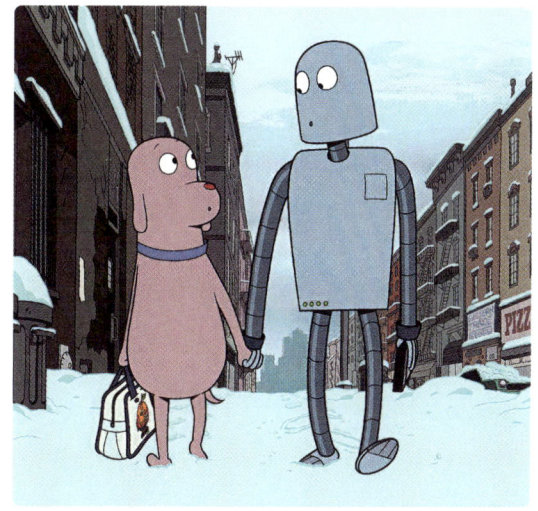

👁 Further Viewing

Robot Dreams may have been director Pablo Berger's first foray into the form, but Spanish animation has been enjoying something of a purple patch in recent years. Alongside more commercial fare such as director Enrique Gato's computer-animated *Tad, the Lost Explorer* franchise, Spain has produced several critically acclaimed and award-winning animated films that showcase a virtuosity of style, theme and genre while serving families and grown-up audiences alike. Fernando Trueba and Javier Mariscal's exuberant romantic drama *Chico*

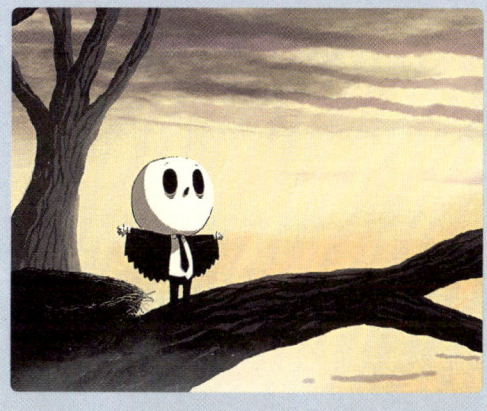

and Rita (2010) received an Oscar nomination for Best Animated Feature, as did *Klaus* (2019), the directorial debut of Madrid-born Disney veteran Sergio Pablos, which has rightly become part of the Christmas movie canon. Elsewhere, there's a strong vein of historical and biographical stories, including the surrealist biopic *Buñuel in the Labyrinth of the Turtles* (2018), the bossa nova docudrama *They Shot the Piano Player* (2023), the Angolan Civil War-set animation-documentary hybrid *Another Day of Life* (2018), and Isabel Herguera's Annecy prize-winning Indian odyssey, *Sultana's Dream* (2023). Some of these stories have been drawn from the pages of graphic novels, such as the poignant retirement home comedy-drama *Wrinkles* (2011), while comic book artists have also moved seamlessly from page to screen, such as Alberto Vázquez, who has produced two visually striking films to date: the Tim Burton-esque coming-of-age horror *Birdboy: The Forgotten Children* (2015) and the provocative *Unicorn Wars* (2022), which cross-pollinates *Bambi* and *Apocalypse Now* to tell a Technicolor tale of anthropomorphic animals radicalized and forced into cycles of senseless violence.

Switzerland

The Perfect (Found) Family Film

🎥 My Life as a Courgette

Director: Claude Barras
Released: 2016

Children and vegetables don't often mix, but in the hands of director Claude Barras and his astute animators, a group of kids and a Courgette (or Zucchini, depending on what territory you watch the film in) warm, enrich and sustain each other in their unification.

In this case the titular produce belongs to a little boy. It's his nickname, and it's one of the few things he inherited from his mother which he cautiously carries with him as he discovers a new chapter of life in a children's home.

Exquisitely adapted by Céline Sciamma (*Portrait of a Lady on Fire, Petite Maman*) from a 2002 novel by Gilles Paris (which was first adapted in 2007 for TV, in live action), the story of Courgette meeting his housemates gently begins to explore prejudice, abuse, addiction, suicide and murder. They're topics that shade the entire film, but don't overshadow it; instead, they fill in the backgrounds of a beautiful collection of characters, never defining them but giving them depth to glow with remarkable lightness.

Wide-eyed, heavy-headed and predominantly talc

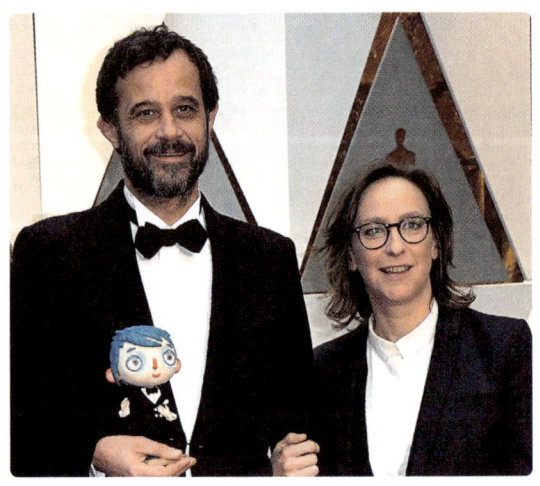

pale, the home's inhabitants look at first glance a bit like Tim Burton's attempt at making a Funko Pop, but there's a logic to their bobble-headed pastiness. In an interview with Cartoon Brew, Barras describes the faces in the film as "like emoticons" in their broad simplicity, but that doesn't mean these complexions can't be complex; in fact, "simplifying is not weakening, but going to what is essential". Unblinking, unwavering marble eyes translate huge hope, while an expertly timed intake of breath carries tightness and hesitancy. Even the characters' udon noodle arms (elbow-less, to avoid looking like orangutans, apparently) reveal so much in their limp hanging and tender gestures. Within the canvas of these bodies, Barras's animators sharply recreate delicate and hugely affecting action and detail. To the director, this emotionality is the result of the "creative magic" that comes from the "empathic intimacy between the animator and the puppet" – in feeling the puppets, they feel the story.

The story itself is perfectly scripted by Sciamma, who constantly finds surprising but entirely natural actions to access emotional truths and silently bridge relationship gaps. An early sign of this compassionate observation comes in a scene with the kindly police officer Raymond, who tries to raise the spirits of Courgette by letting him trail his beloved kite out of the car window, hitting the siren and the pedal just to give the boy's toy some airtime. It's an unspoken and incredibly thoughtful gesture, which Barras is smart enough not to linger on. The film's empathy is never signposted, but he and

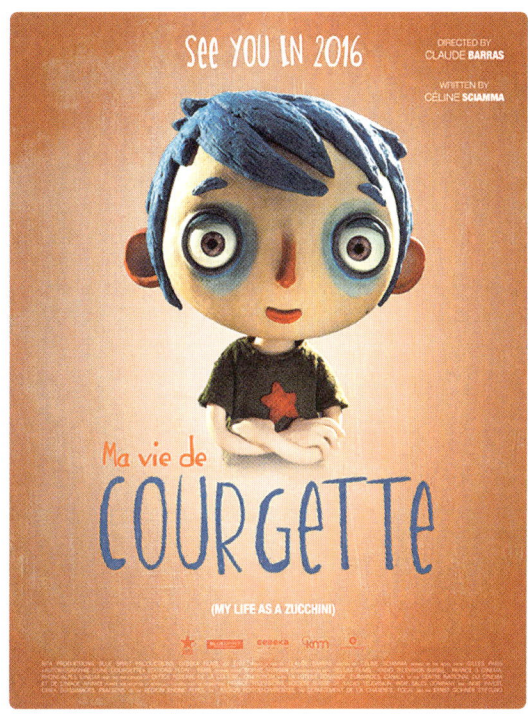

Opposite: Director Claude Barras and *Portrait of a Lady on Fire* writer/director Céline Sciamma, who co-wrote *Courgette.*

Above: You say Courgette, I say Zucchini. In America, the film was released under the name *My Life as a Zucchini,* to fit the territory's preferred moniker for the vegetable.

Below: Home is where the heart is. The fantastically varied inhabitants of Courgette's Children's Home wave for the camera.

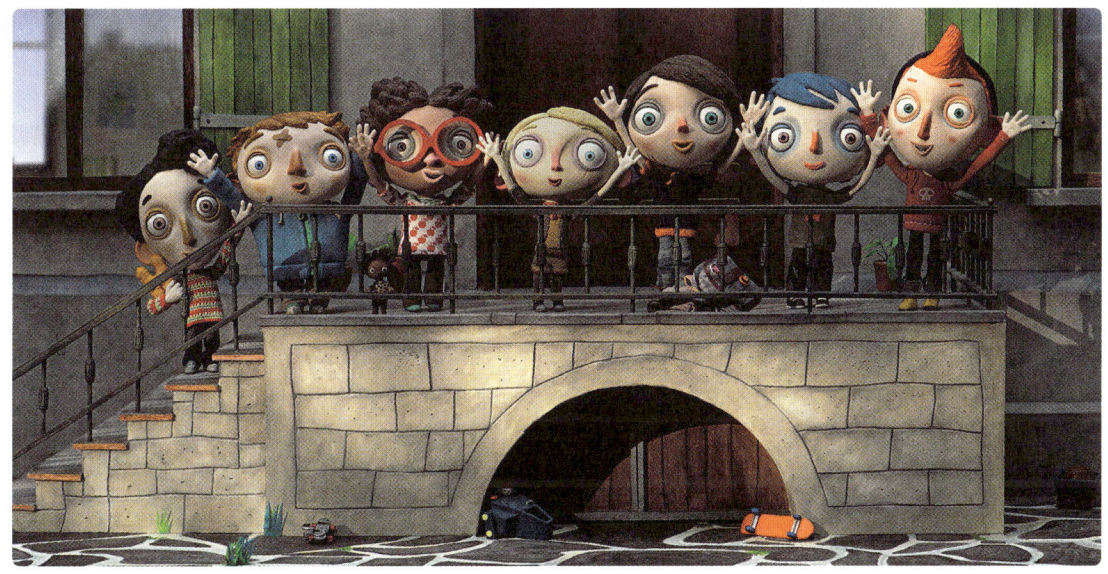

Sciamma make it a natural part of this world. Similarly, when Courgette bonds with new arrival Camille over an origami boat, the visual of it floating, stationary, in a tiny fissure of a frozen lake, cornered by snow and ice, feels immensely layered but entirely pure. Will life thaw out and let them explore it? Are they trapped by a system? Is the world only as big as the people you share it with, and is that okay? Is it just a beautiful image of an origami boat? Big questions and few straight answers fill Courgette's experience, but rather than make life's tragedies and ambiguities a source of terror, Sciamma uses them as opportunities for wisdom and support. She offers a compass for navigating a life rather than a textbook about living one.

Although it runs for only 67 minutes and is centred around one key location, *My Life as a Courgette* hums with vibrant life that fills out its characters' world, its frames and swiftly its viewers' hearts too. The film benefits from multiple rewatches – two viewings would be over in less time than most modern blockbusters take to finish – and little glimmers of magic continually appear in the film's minutiae, like the recurring visual of a bird's nest gradually being built and eventually flourishing with life; or the fact that the dry and devastating Camille carries a copy of Kafka's *Metamorphosis* with her; or even how

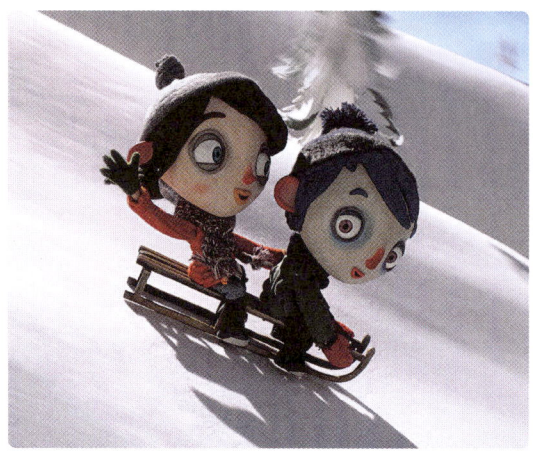

Simon, persecutor turned pal, receives a package and ignores the gift, searching in vain for a non-existent letter to go with it instead. He can't be bought but he can be cared for, something the families of these children can't or won't do, but which they can do for each other.

Above: Can friends who sleigh together stay together? Courgette and Camille enjoy the snow.

Below: This lingering shot, where the camera is perhaps perceived by the characters, is one of *Courgette's* most intriguing moments.

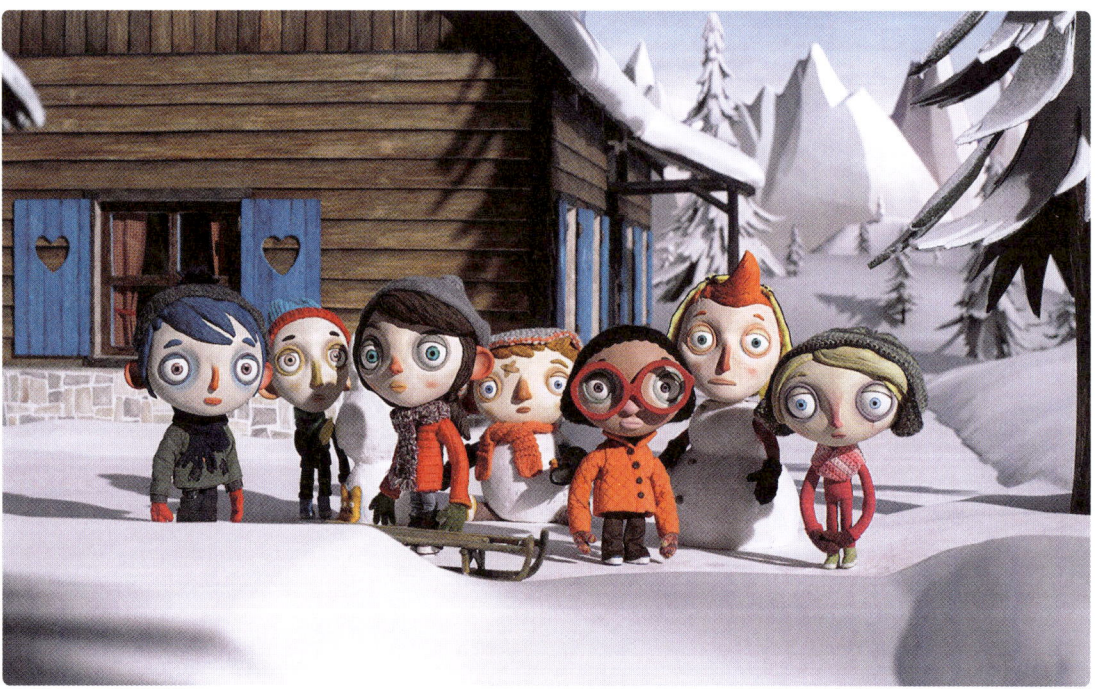

Claude Barras has lots of animation heroes. He loved the striking simplicity of the puppets in *Le Manège Enchanté* (1964, recycled and entirely rescripted into *The Magic Roundabout* in the English language) and Jiří Trnka's *The Hand* (1965, see page 48); he fell for the slight melodramas of Isao Takahata's *Heidi, Girl of the Alps* (1974); and he thought the unconventional angle on reality offered by Aardman's *Creature Comforts* (1989) was "immense".

When *Courgette* was released in the UK, Aardman's own co-founder Peter Lord recorded a video about Barras's film, describing it as having a "heart [that's] so clear and so compelling", and he's exactly right. It's an engrossing, tactile and refined work of great wisdom and quietly supreme power – and it is also, completely immense.

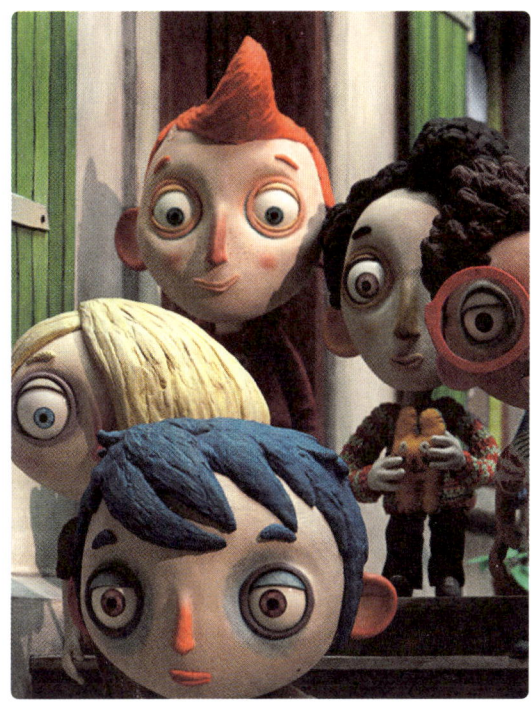

Right: Courgette (front) and some of his friends. Their faces were designed to look "like emoticons".

Below: Michaela Müller's short film *Miramare*, a Swiss-Croatian co-production, is a captivating example of paint-on-glass animation.

👁 Further Viewing

Swiss companies often appear in the credits of pan-European animated features, such as the Zurich-based Condor Films, which co-produced Jan Švankmajer's *Alice* (1988). Homegrown animation, on the other hand, tends to be short form, but it is rich and diverse in style. Seek out the supernatural short *Sabbat* (1991), an orgiastic tale of witches and devils rendered in sand animation by Gisèle and Ernest Ansorge, and the more recent festival favourite *Miramare* (2009), which follows a family holiday full of wistful seaside scenes, with real-world issues of immigration just out of sight, captured in an ethereal paint-on-glass technique by Michaela Müller. Georges Schwizgebel might be the Swiss animator with the most noteworthy international reputation, with his ingenious studies in shifting shapes and perspectives, such as the waltzing, dreamlike *78 Tours* (1985), the hypnotic cycles of *The Ravishing of Frank N. Stein* (1982), and *The Man With No Shadow* (2004), a prizewinner at Cannes and the Zagreb and Hiroshima animation festivals.

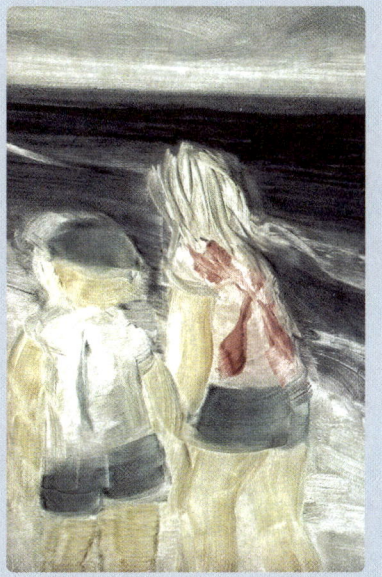

United Kingdom

Over the Moon, Under the Sea, to the End of the World

🎥 Wallace & Gromit

Director: Nick Park, Steve Box, Merlin Crossingham
Released: 1989-2024

In their most recent plasticine adventure, *Vengeance Most Fowl* (2024), eccentric inventor Wallace and his patient pooch Gromit battle rogue artificially intelligent garden gnomes, uninformed police and a notorious penguin thief (or is that chicken?) whose beady eyes are glinting over a precious diamond.

There's a lot at stake, but for Gromit the reward at the end of the day isn't about justice, fame or money, it's about getting a pat on the head from his old friend. He needs a human touch – something that's made this series so popular. Sculpted from everyday materials, pocked by thumbprints and thrown into outlandish, yet somehow entirely everyday, genre-bending antics, the Lancashire pair made their debut in 1989's *A Grand Day Out*, which sent them to the moon on a hunt for cheese, and the name Aardman across the world.

Established in 1972 by Peter Lord and David Sproxton, Aardman had built up a solid reputation in the animation industry, working on short films and TV, during which they created their first of many icons: the transformative,

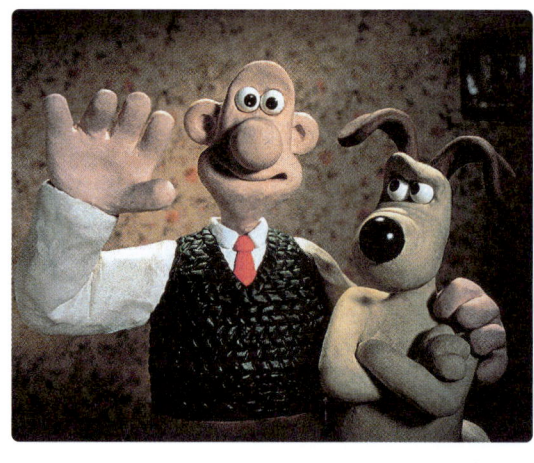

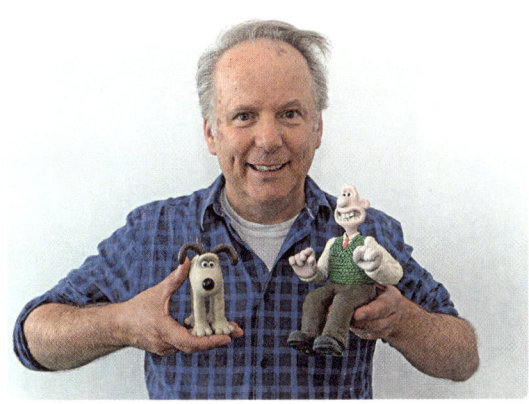

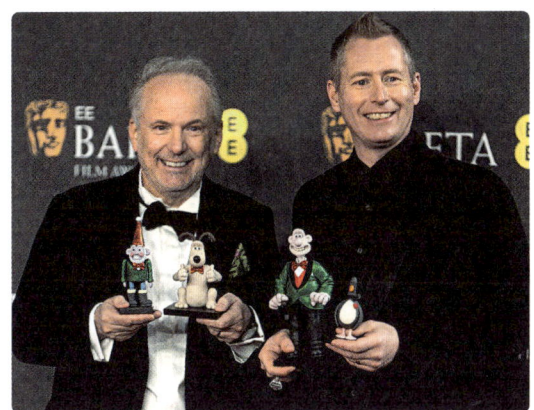

terracotta marvel Morph. An unintelligible, amorphous plasticine figure, Morph and his stop-motion endeavours caught the eye of a young animation fan called Nick Park. Born in 1958 in Preston in the north of England, Park loved not just *Morph* (1977 to present) but also *The Do-It-Yourself Film Animation Show* (1974), a self-explanatory show which saw artists like Richard Williams and Monty Python's Terry Gilliam give their insights on the form. Loaded with DIY inspiration and his dad's camera – which had a stop-motion function – Park made his own home movies and eventually enrolled at the National Film and Television School, where his final-year project would eventually become the debut of Wallace and Gromit.

The production took time, more time than Park's course, but he struck a deal with Aardman (after meeting them at a university event) and was able to finish it at their studio in Bristol while contributing to other projects. Amazingly, between the production and post-production period of the film, Park directed the short *Creature Comforts* (1989) for Aardman too. A mockumentary featuring plasticine animals regurgitating mundane human thoughts, it went on to win the Oscar for Animated Short Film, where it beat *A Grand Day Out* – but the latter won the equivalent BAFTA, so it was safe to say, Nick Park had arrived.

A Grand Day Out, at a spry 23 minutes, is as inventive as its human lead. Balancing intricate, patient craft with cheeky, left-field humour, its story of homespun astronauts on a quest for a snack lands just on the right side of the absurd, and its outlandish, illogical plot points (a wooden spaceship is just the start...) are easily brushed aside by sheer charm. Although instantly acclaimed, *A Grand Day Out* does lack narrative satisfaction, relying on surprise and delight to carry viewers home. In follow-up *The*

Wrong Trousers (1993), however, the recipe is perfected.

Elevating the series from quirky spectacle to something more character-driven and far more thrilling, *The Wrong Trousers* sees our heroes fall victim to the charms, and schemes, of bird-burglar Feathers McGraw. Naïve Wallace and frustrated Gromit become embroiled in a heist, in which Wallace's latest invention – a pair of superpowered trousers – is hijacked. The culmination of the cat and mouse game, or dog and penguin game, is a small-scale, high-speed sequence, with a model

Opposite: Give them a big hand. Wallace and Gromit, the plasticine odd couple who'd take over the world.

Above left: Nick Park, creator of *Wallace & Gromit*, with his cracking creations.

Above right: 2024 series entry *Vengeance Most Fowl* was directed by Nick Park and Merlin Crossingham, seen here at the BAFTA awards, where the film picked up two prizes.

Below: The Wrong Trousers themselves. Enduringly stylish and mightily powerful, they're the perfect choice for anyone plotting a diamond heist.

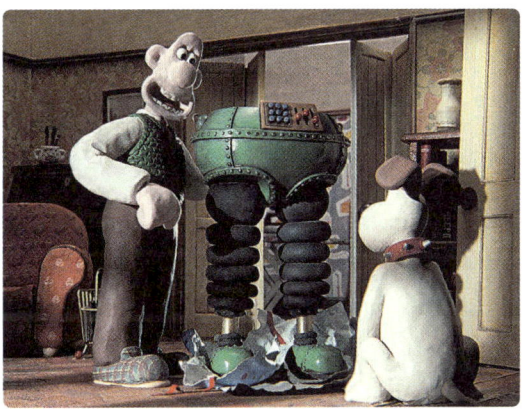

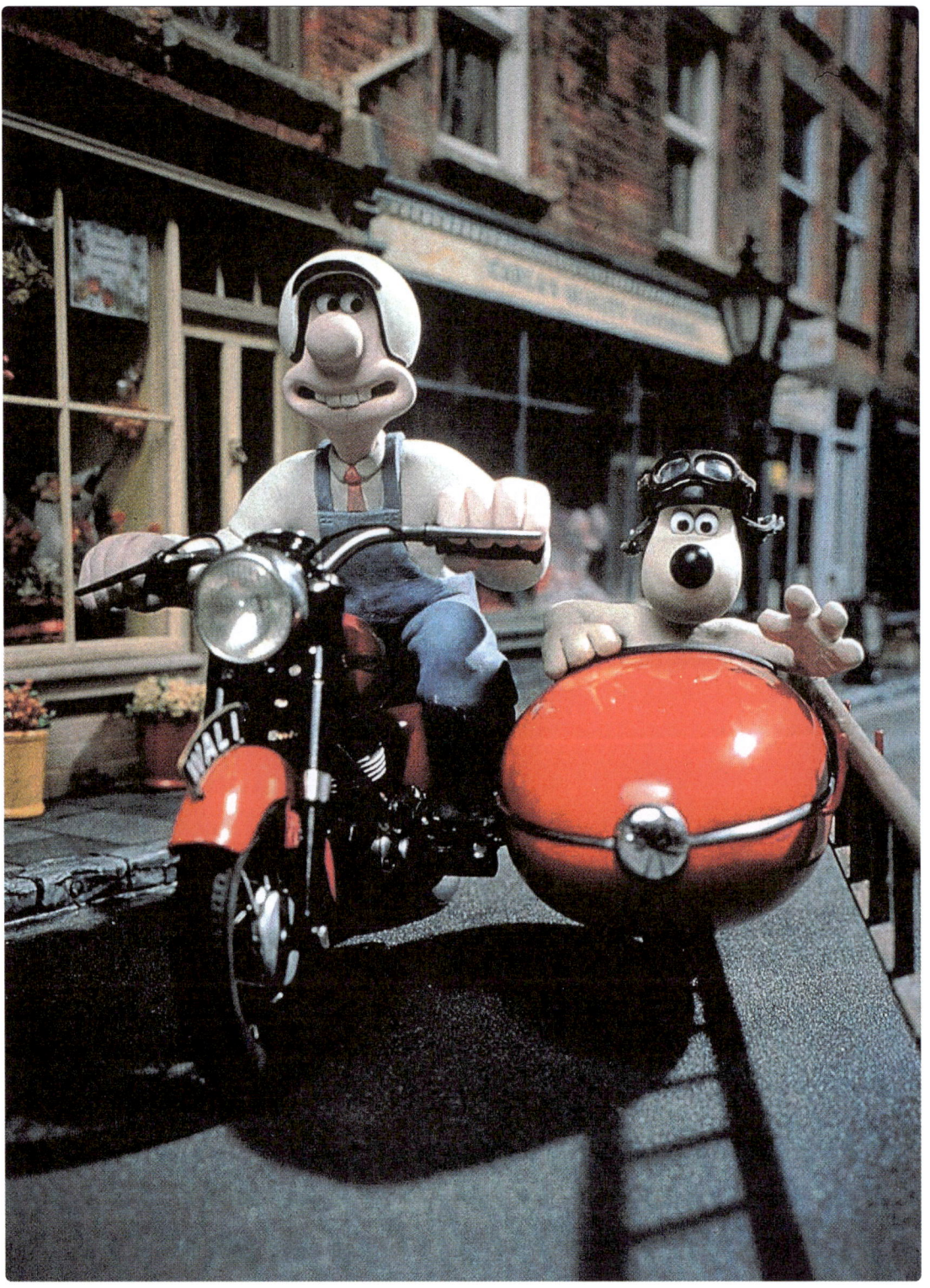

railway track providing the foundation for arguably the greatest chase scene in action film history; the relentless pace, hairpin surprises and pin-sharp comic timing contained within its few minutes revealing the skill of a master filmmaker.

1995's *A Close Shave* offers a slightly disappointing remix, most notably a high-stakes, high-flying third act aerial chase, feeling like recycled *Trousers*. It is still very entertaining, though its lingering impact is the introduction of woolly franchise-launcher Shaun the Sheep, who'd crow-baa himself into a TV series and spin-off films. Evolving the formula to greater success was 2005's *The Curse of the Were-Rabbit* (which Park co-directed with Aardman key animator Steve Box), Wallace and Gromit's feature debut, which packages classically destructive monster-movie tropes within the tightly wound, quaint and pristine realm of competitive vegetable growing. Mundanity and madness become wonderfully, at times horrifically, intertwined, the human-rabbit genetic experimentation allowing for some unforgettable visuals and gags.

Wallace and Gromit returned to their short-form roots with *A Matter of Loaf and Death*, a 2008 murder mystery with a body count almost as high as its gag count. Featuring Wallace being targeted by a serial killer, it counteracts a dark plot with a high turnover of set pieces and jokes, but unfortunately some of those are about a character's weight – a rare example of the series punching down for laughs. It's worth watching, but not one to savour.

Wallace & Gromit don't represent the whole Aardman story of course, or even the whole of Nick Park's – he made *Chicken Run* in 2000 with co-director Peter Lord and *Early Man* in 2018 – but for many viewers across the globe, the studio and their most famous creations are one and the same, presenting a plucky, inventive, distinctly British approach to animation. An approach that in 2024, with *Vengeance Most Fowl*, is still being discovered and applauded. Despite all the silliness within them, these are artworks where the touch of the artists behind them is visible in every frame, and that's why they've touched so many others. Cracking.

Opposite: Wallace with a side of Gromit. The duo in the motorcycle and sidecar that becomes key to the finale of *A Close Shave*.

Below: It takes a village. All the detail on Wallace and Gromit's neighbours shows just how much effort from Aardman's team goes into making these films.

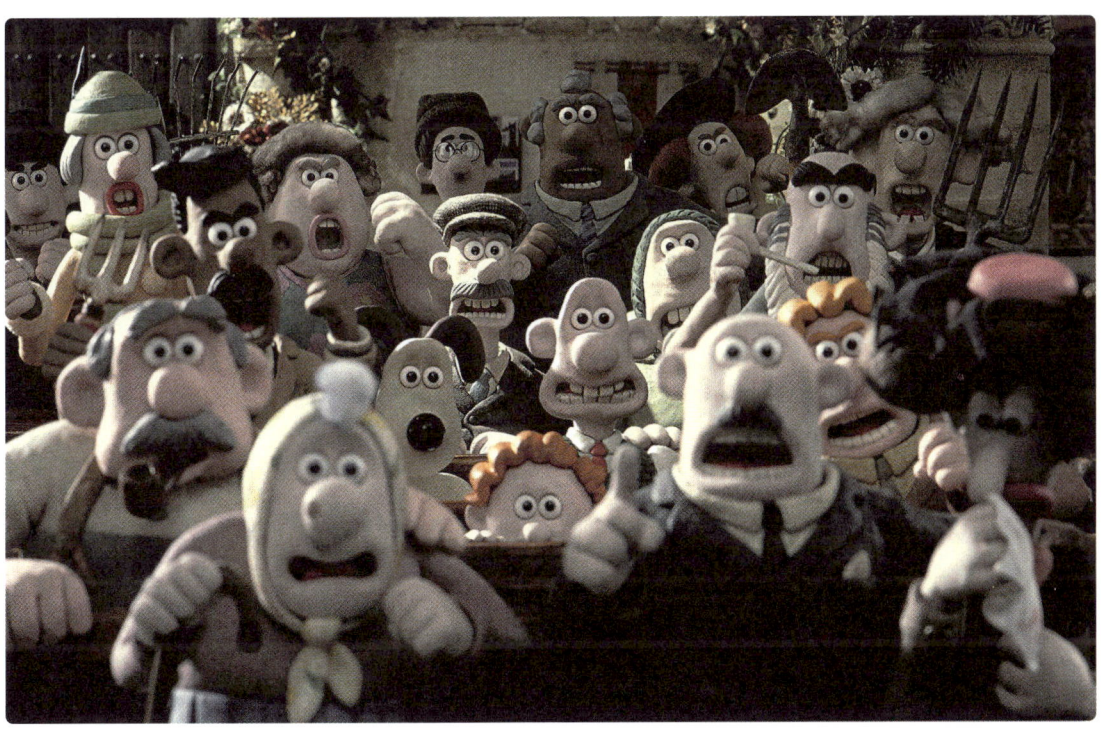

🎬 Yellow Submarine

Director: George Dunning
Release date: 1968

Across the four feature films and one TV movie released during the peak of their success, the Beatles revolutionized pop cinema as much as they did pop music.

They were a *bona fide* screen phenomenon, and wrote the rule book for pop stars stepping in front of the camera, from the exuberant, youthful energy of *A Hard Day's Night* (1964) to the rich colour photography and daft spoof comedy of *Help!* (1965), the insufferable indulgence of *Magical Mystery Tour* (1967) and the downbeat fly-on-the-wall documentary *Let It Be* (1970). And then there's *Yellow Submarine* (1968) – the transformative, mind-expanding, innovative animation that we'd argue is the pick of the bunch. (Well, we would, wouldn't we?)

While the Beatles themselves barely appear in *Yellow Submarine*, this glorious and groundbreaking film is true to the spirit of the band, using their songs as a launchpad for an overwhelming, psychedelic excursion into the imagination. When the Blue Meanie army invades the pastoral idyll of Pepperland, the animated avatars of John, Paul, George and Ringo have to leave Liverpool behind, board the Yellow Submarine, and traverse seas of monsters, holes, science and time before bringing the baddies to heel with a universal message of love and music. On page, it's undeniably daffy stuff: wilder still is that the screenplay has at least five pairs of hands on it, including "original story" writer Lee Minoff, producer Al Brodax (who successfully pitched the idea to manager Brian Epstein), cartoonist-screenwriter Jack Mendelsohn, *Love Story* author Erich Segal and poet Roger McGough, the "Mersey Sound" bard whose uncredited contribution reportedly consisted of punching up the script with dialogue that captured the Fab Four's droll, Northern wit.

Director George Dunning had cut his teeth at the National Film Board of Canada and worked at United Productions of America (UPA) before setting up his own studio, Television Cartoons (TVC), in London with producer John Coates. Alongside Dunning's own short films (such as *The Flying Man* and *The Apple*, both 1962), TVC churned out hundreds of commercials and

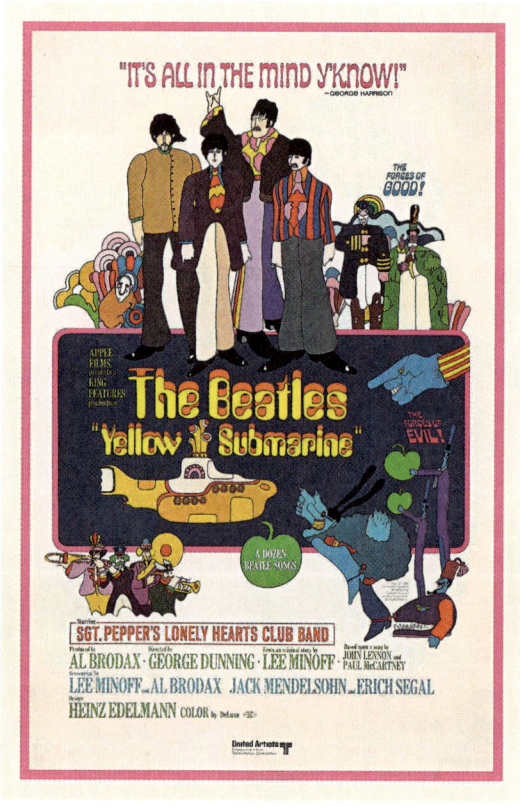

television episodes, including the cheap-and-cheerful, throwaway ABC cartoon series *The Beatles* (1965–1967). And so, it fell to Dunning and his studio to bring the animated Beatles to the big screen – with a tight budget, an unfinished script and less than a year until the scheduled release date.

And they threw everything at it. Burning through the meagre commission fee, Dunning and co went over budget, hiring hundreds of artists (including 40 animators) and promoting an eclectic, diverse approach to the film – one rooted in the psychedelic graphic

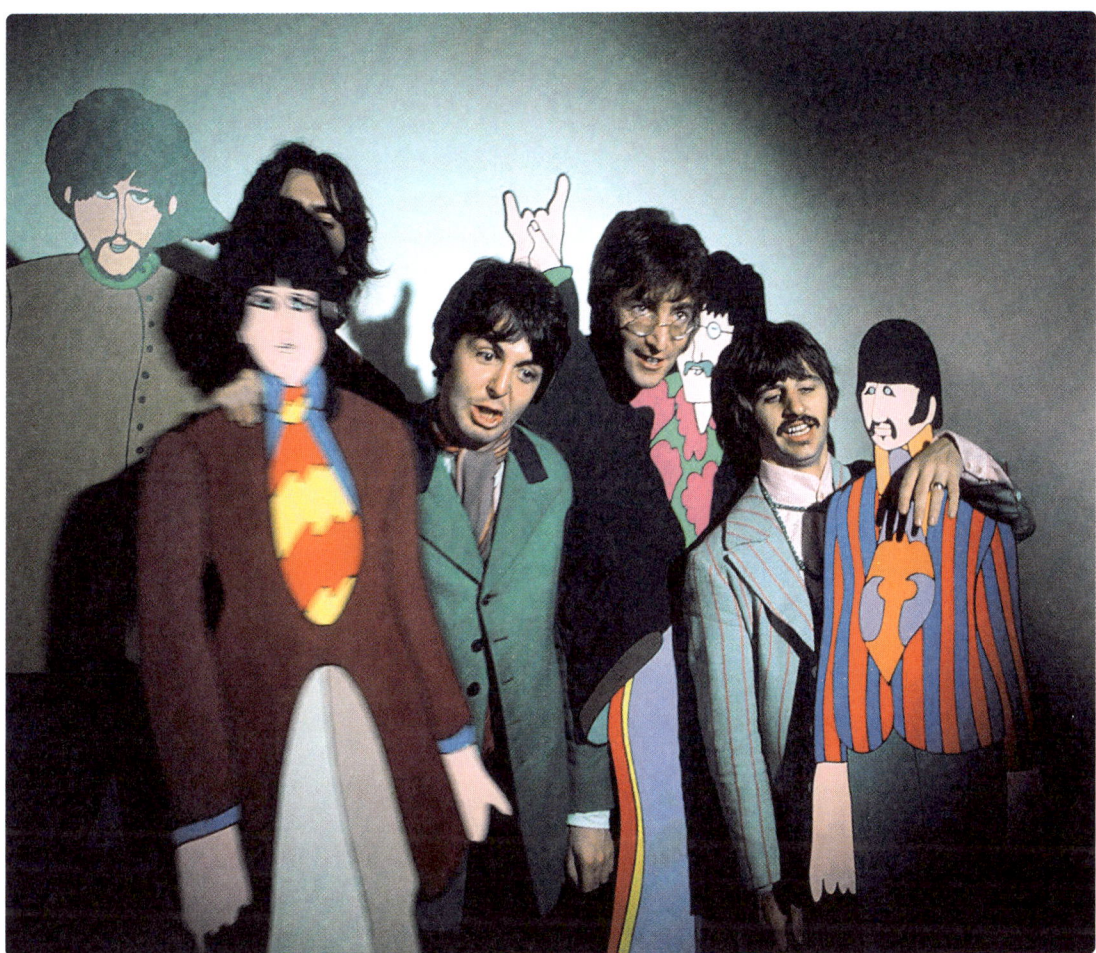

style of art director Heinz Edelmann, but with standout sequences that allowed individual artists their moments to shine.

"Special sequences" designer Charlie Jenkins led on the powerful 'Eleanor Rigby' scene, which creates a grim Liverpool landscape of slouching workers, gloomy graveyards and graffiti-strewn streets, peopled with gritty, Xeroxed characters multiplied and looped to fill the screen: lonely and bleak, with the only colour coming from the bold red and blue of pirouetting football teams, until we later enter the Beatles' mansion of wonder. Jenkins further remixes the everyday in the breathless sequence that sees the Yellow Submarine zoom across England's green and pleasant land to London, captured in a lightning-fast flurry of picture postcards of hills and glades, before colliding with a crash into Tower Bridge.

It has long been said that the Beatles brought intense colour to the drab, post-war milieu of Great Britain, and *Yellow Submarine* redraws that journey, from the grey chimney stacks of Liverpool to the kaleidoscopic fantasia of Pepperland, via a vibrant world of pop art, Americana, psychedelia and generous lashings of Lewis Carroll-style nonsense – all brought together under the utopian affirmations of KNOW, LOVE and YES ("the very best word for the whole world to use").

Yellow Submarine is a dizzying film, with so much creativity and inspiration crammed into an hour and a half: from the washes of rotoscoped colour splashed across dancing figures in Bill Sewell's dreamy 'Lucy in

Opposite: The poster for *Yellow Submarine* shows off its rich, colourful pop art style.

Above: The Fab Eight. The real-life Beatles pose with standees of their animated counterparts.

the Sky with Diamonds' sequence, to the sheer breadth of creative ideas on display within the Sea of Time, where the twee ditty 'When I'm Sixty-Four' is turned into a graphic design masterclass, counting from 0 to 60 and beyond with dozens of delightful drawings. For sheer imagination, Disney – who reportedly tried to court the Beatles for a cameo in their then most recent film, *The Jungle Book* (1967) – had been left in the dust.

Is there much beneath the surface? Entire books have been dedicated to exploring the film's unplumbed thematic depths (see the work of the excellently named Robert R Hieronimus, PhD). Ultimately, though, *Yellow Submarine* is a film best experienced with eyes open to the thrilling possibilities of animation. As the man once said: turn off your mind, relax and float downstream...

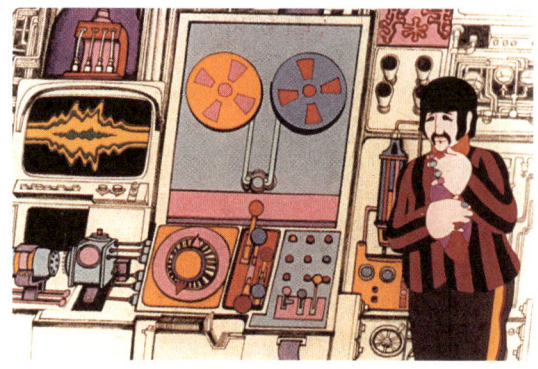

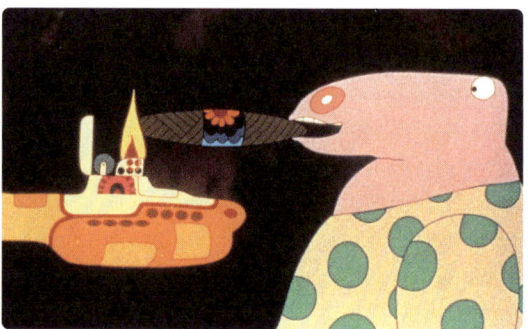

Above right: Press a Button. Ringo stands in front of the Submarine's console of controls: a source of colourful chaos during the band's adventure.

Right: Top Gear. Throughout the film, the Yellow Submarine is revealed to have countless gadgets and imaginative, if esoteric, uses.

Below: The Hole Story. The dazzling design of the Sea of Holes draws visual inspiration from the 'op art' style popularised in the 1960s.

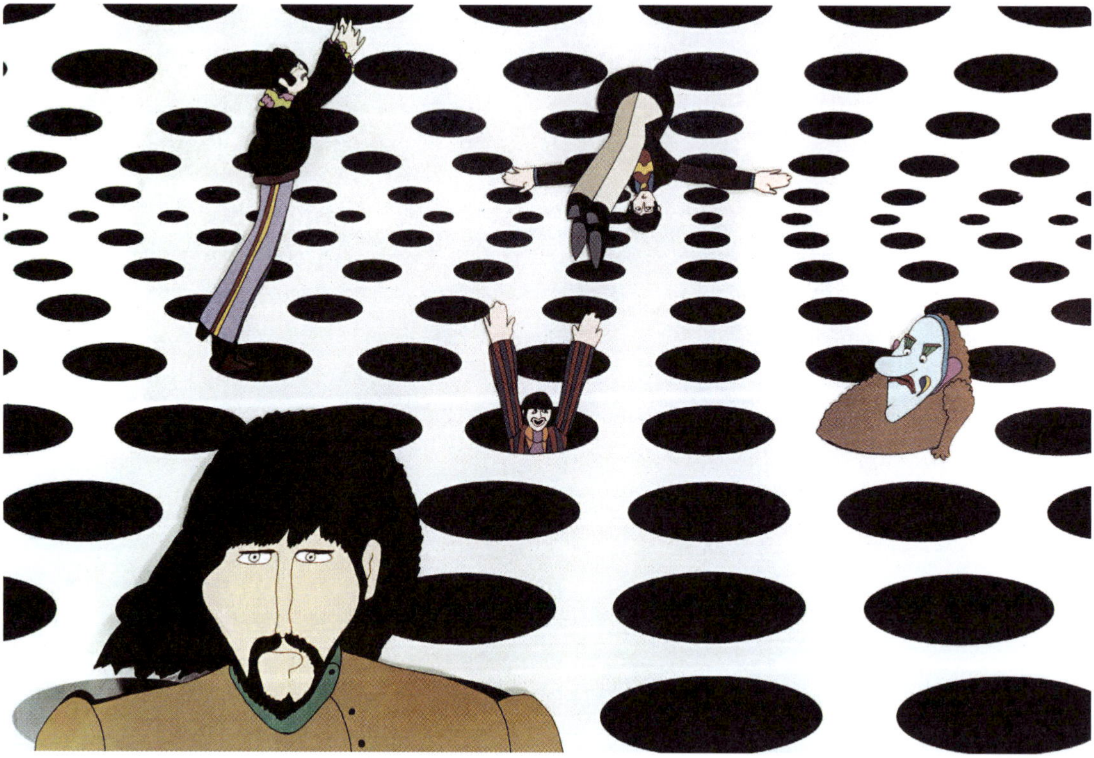

🎬 When the Wind Blows

Director: Jimmy T Murakami
Release date: 1986

In Britain, there's one animated film that arguably stands above all, an annual fixture in TV schedules and in family traditions across the country. That film is *The Snowman* (1982), the magical, Oscar-nominated animation based on Raymond Briggs' wordless picture book, masterfully adapted by director Dianne Jackson and the team at producer John Coates' TVC (TV Cartoons).

While the book was always more of a winter tale than a strictly festive one, the film and character have become integral icons of British Christmas celebrations, yielding a beloved hit single ('Walking in the Air'), featuring in seasonal advertising campaigns, and giving rise to a mountain of merchandise that still grows with each passing year. Even today, adaptations of kids' books are produced and premiered on television across the Christmas holidays, no doubt hoping to recapture a smidge of that *Snowman* magic.

In 1986, the same team of TVC and public broadcaster Channel 4 returned with another Raymond Briggs adaptation, this time a feature film destined for the big screen. But those hoping to see more flying snowmen and boy-soprano musical interludes were sorely disappointed. The only winter to be found in *When the Wind Blows* was a nuclear one.

The pairing of *The Snowman* and *When the Wind Blows* – one an adventure with an extraordinary creature that captures the wonder of childhood, the other a harrowing exploration of the devastation of war – recalls another diabolical double bill from the world of animation: Studio Ghibli's *My Neighbour Totoro* and *Grave of the Fireflies* (both 1988). But where *Fireflies* follows two children in the dying days of the Second World War, their youth and innocence bringing extra levels of tragedy to the tale, *When the Wind Blows* imagines a wholly fictional conflict – although one that felt all too likely in the 1980s – and focuses on two elderly characters as they weather a nuclear attack on Britain.

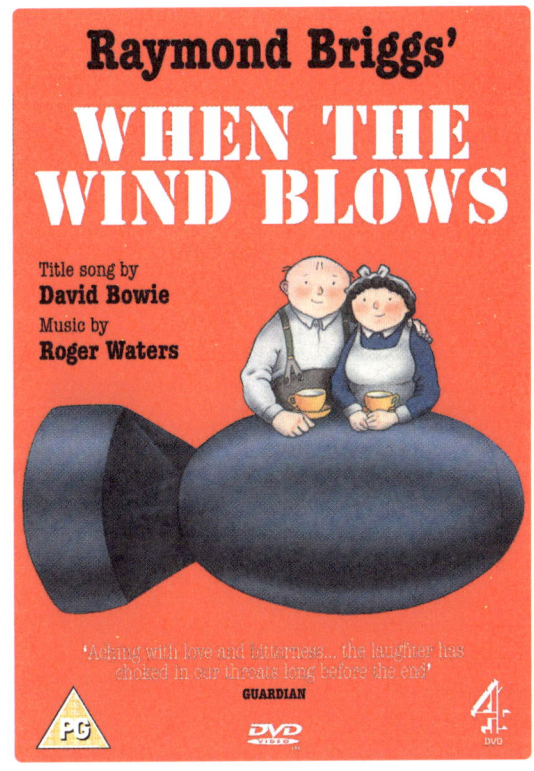

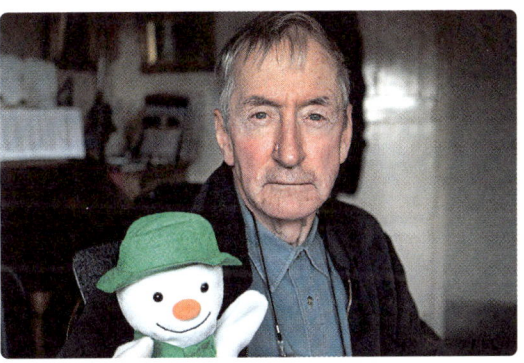

Above right: Nuclear Stars. A promotional graphic for *When the Wind Blows* prominently features its protagonists, Jim and Hilda Bloggs.

Right: Ray of Sunshine. The notoriously grumpy artist Raymond Briggs, pictured with his most enduring creation: the Snowman.

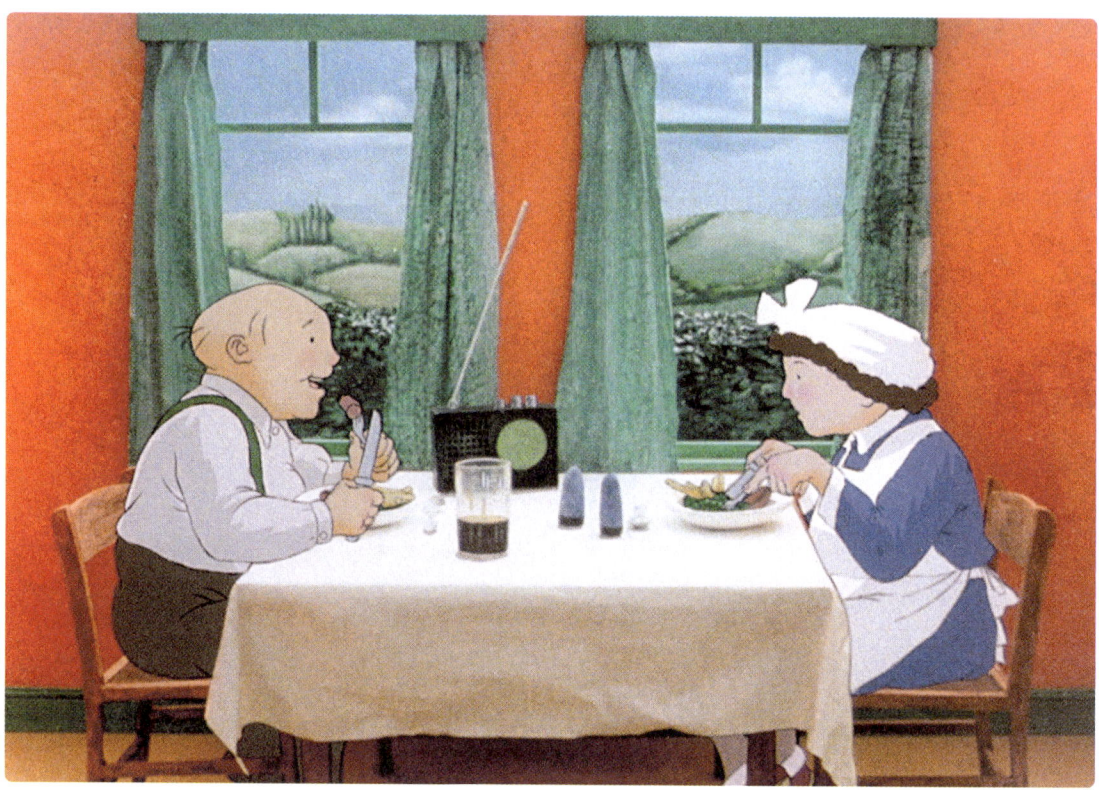

Director Jimmy T Murakami was already almost thirty years into a globe-trotting career in animation when he took on *When the Wind Blows*. Born in California, he worked for UPA in the States, Japan's Toei Animation studios and TVC in the UK, before directing a series of acclaimed shorts, including the BAFTA-winning *The Insects* (1964). He even crossed over into live-action filmmaking with the Star Wars knock-off *Battle Beyond the Stars* (1980), before returning to the UK and working with TVC on *The Snowman* and a segment of the anthology film *Heavy Metal* (1981). Murakami brought to *When the Wind Blows* a vision that combined hand-drawn characters and tangible, hand-crafted scale-model settings, inviting us into the warm domesticity of the Bloggs' rural routines before everything is violently interrupted by the blast – leaving behind silence and the promise of slow death by radiation poisoning.

Though he studied painting at the Slade School of Fine Art, Raymond Briggs dreamed of being a newspaper editorial cartoonist – but he was ultimately drawn into the world of children's book illustration. This gives his works a curious, utterly distinctive quality. In the case of *When the Wind Blows*, it's somehow equally painterly and caricatured, cozy and completely chilling. Briggs based the protagonists, Jim (John Mills) and Hilda (Peggy Ashcroft) Bloggs, on his own parents: a generation who implicitly trust their higher-ups and put their faith in public information pamphlets and films, such as the very real and widely lampooned Protect and Survive campaign. Both the film and book vividly illustrate how a make-do-and-mend Blitz spirit doesn't count for much against megaton-sized bombs.

Envisioned as a satirical broadside aimed squarely at the superpowers behind the Cold War, *When the Wind Blows* has a gut-wrenching emotional power that is undiminished today, largely due to Briggs and Murakami finding an unassuming, everyday angle on such unthinkable events. While Briggs himself would later look back on his depiction of Jim and Hilda's ignorance and naivety as perhaps a tad too exaggerated, there's an essential innocence and mundanity to their characterization that is often overlooked in films dealing with such weighty matters. It's there, too, in the other landmark British anti-nuclear film of the period, *Threads*

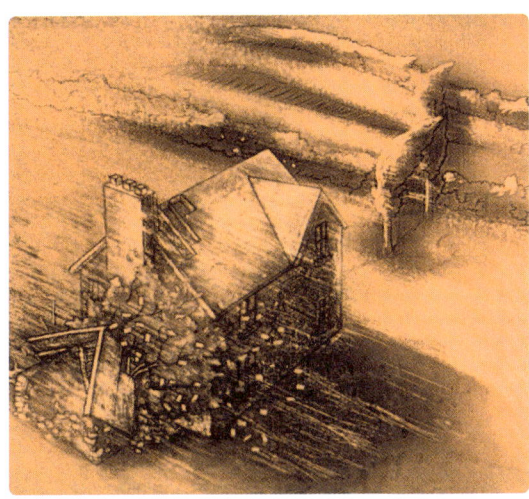

(1984) – another day-ruining, feel-bad film that, once watched, you won't return to in a hurry.

"The tragedy of nuclear war," Briggs once wrote in a column for the *Times Education Supplement* about picture books that attempt to grapple with the enormity of the atomic bomb, "is that something so primeval and elemental could occur while 'The Archers' are on the radio and the milkman is whistling up the garden path."

Opposite: The Home Front. *When the Wind Blows* used real, hand-crafted sets to immerse the viewer in the Bloggs household.

Left: Ground Zero. The film's central sequence of the bomb's shockwaves rolling across the rural landscape is captured in sickly, muddy monochrome.

Below: Our Clouded Hills. *When the Wind Blows* brings the realities of nuclear devastation to England's green and pleasant land.

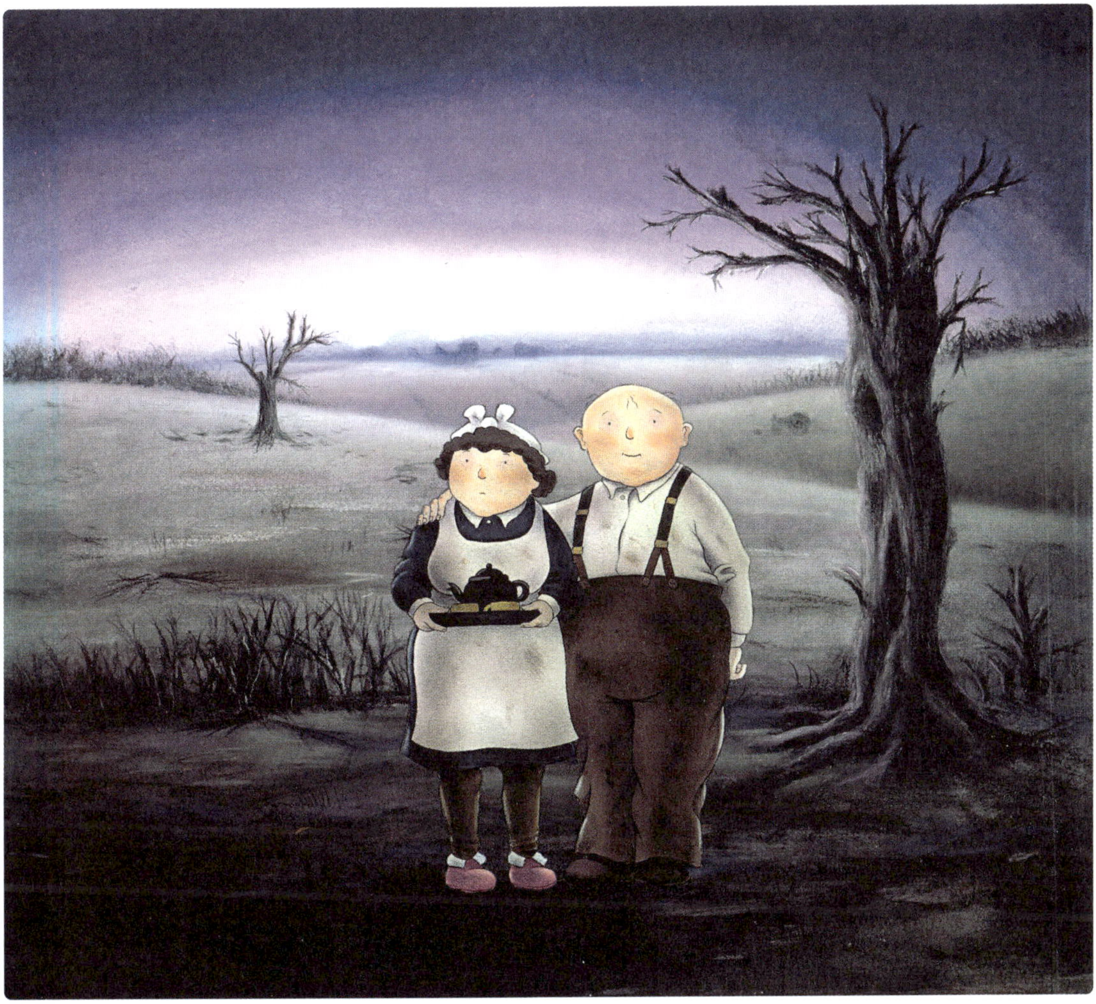

◉ Further Viewing

The United Kingdom has a long and rich history of animation, but you wouldn't necessarily think that if you looked solely for feature films. At the time of the release of *When the Wind Blows* in 1986, the press release trumpeted that the film was only the fifth feature-length British animation, presumably following John Halas and Joy Batchelor's *Animal Farm* (1954), *Yellow Submarine*, and director Martin Rosen's two adaptations of Richard Adams novels, the astonishing animated epic *Watership Down* (1979), which captures nature in all its majesty and horror, and its perhaps even bleaker follow-up, *The Plague Dogs* (1982).

Nitpicky film historians would point to John Halas's *Handling Ships* (1945), a training film commissioned by the British Admiralty, as the UK's first animated feature, albeit one not intended for public release – but that fact leads us to the vast history of animation created for the British government and its many public bodies, and more broadly in advertising. Pick up Jez Stewart's *The Story of British Animation* for a compact but comprehensive history of how animators such as Len Lye (*A Colour Box*, 1935), Richard Williams (*A Christmas Carol*, 1971), Bob Godfrey (*Do It Yourself Cartoon Kit*, 1961) and George Dunning were able to carve out eclectic and prolific careers, all while bouncing between commissioned projects and their own independent work.

Lye and Godfrey, like Dunning and Jimmy Murakami, came to Britain from abroad, and another international animator worth saluting here is Michaël Dudok de Wit (*Father & Daughter*, 2000), who was born in the Netherlands but has been based in Britain for decades. To be fair, you might not know it from his choice of animation studios and production partners, which included no less than Japan's Studio Ghibli on his absorbing, dialogue-free feature, *The Red Turtle* (2016).

Outside of Aardman, British animated features are currently in short supply, but that makes the sterling

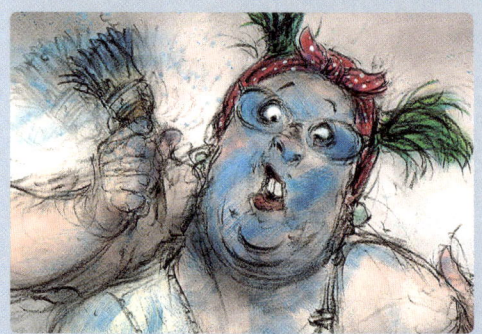

efforts of Lupus Films all the more noteworthy, with the sophisticated, understated charms of their adaptations of the work of Raymond Briggs (*Ethel and Ernest*, 2016) and Michael Morpurgo (*Kensuke's Kingdom*, 2023). Likewise, Locksmith Animation, formed by Aardman veterans Sarah Smith and Julie Lockhart, have also focused on feature projects, partnering with 20th Century Studios and Netflix respectively on *Ron's Gone Wrong* (2021) and *That Christmas* (2024).

The bulk of British animation, though, has flourished on the small screen and at shorter runtimes. There's the time-honoured tradition of British children's television, which ranges from the classic work of Smallfilms (*Clangers*, *Bagpuss*) and Cosgrove Hall (*Danger Mouse*, *The BFG*), to recent hits such as *Peppa Pig* (2004 to present), *The Amazing World of Gumball* (2011 to present) and *Hey Duggee* (2014 to present). For older audiences, the public service broadcaster Channel 4 funded innovative, artistic work for over two decades, backing acclaimed films from the likes of Alison de Vere (*The Black Dog*, 1987), Joanna Quinn (*Girls Night Out*, 1986), the Brothers Quay (*Street of Crocodiles*, 1986), Barry Purves (the frankly astounding *Screen Play*, 1993) and Suzie Templeton (the Oscar-winning *Peter & the Wolf*, 2006).

Above: Paint job. The eccentric Beryl, first seen in Joanna Quinn's *Girls Night Out*, finds her calling in the Oscar-nominated *Affairs of the Art*.

Elsewhere in Europe

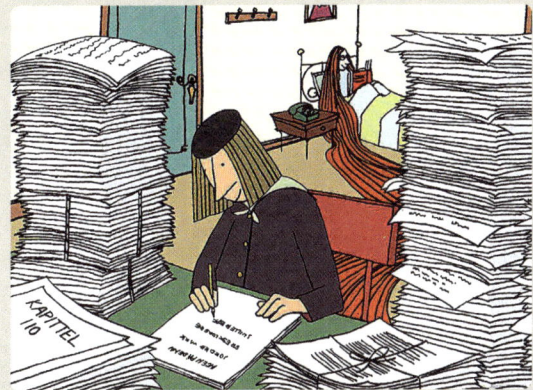

We had to draw the line somewhere. Honestly, we could have easily filled this book with just European countries; instead, though, we settled for just over a dozen, and we can only apologize to any of our European neighbours who feel snubbed if we left them out. Let's try to squeeze in a few more countries before we move on...

To start with the Nordic countries, Per Åhlin was a pioneer in Sweden, co-directing the country's first (almost) fully animated feature, *Out of an Old Man's Head* (1968). He built a reputation for children's animation, including the stalwart seasonal short *Christopher's Christmas Mission* (1975), in which a young postal worker turns Robin Hood, nicking presents addressed to rich families and instead distributing them to Stockholm's poor.

Next door in Norway, director Torill Kove has created several successful animations with the National Film Board of Canada, including the Oscar-winning *The Danish Poet* (2006) and the slice-of-life dramas that address childhood and parenthood, *Me and My Moulton* (2014) and *Threads* (2017), all captured in an inviting, minimal, clear-lined style.

Hop over the Baltic to Estonia, and dive into the playful, surreal, intentionally ugly world of maverick artist-animator Priit Pärn, starting with the hyper-active *Time Out* (1985), the freewheeling jazz animation of *Some Exercises in Preparation for an Independent Life* (1980) and the absurdist sketch of Soviet bureaucracy, *Breakfast on the Grass* (1987).

Dutch director Paul Driessen cut his teeth as an animator on *Yellow Submarine* and then worked both back home and in Canada, developing a wonky, off-kilter, sometimes consciously grating style with films such as *Cat's Cradle* (1974), *The Killing of an Egg* (1977) and *Oh What a Knight* (1982).

Brief mentions, too, to Portugal, which has recently enjoyed international acclaim with the Angolan Civil War drama *Nayola* (2022) and the stunning, affecting Oscar-nominated short *Ice Merchants* (2022), and to Ukraine, which has a long tradition of animation stretching from the pioneering work of Vyacheslav Levandovsky, all the way to *Mavka: The Forest Song* (2023) – a 3D-animated fantasy epic that was produced against the odds during both the Covid-19 crisis and the Russian invasion, and then released worldwide, breaking box office records.

But if we had space for a thirty-first chapter, we would probably dedicate it to the wildly creative body of work produced by artists in Zagreb, Croatia. Home to both the long-running Animafest Zagreb film festival and the Zagreb Film studio, the city has nurtured some of the most distinctive visionary artists in animation history. Helpfully, Zagreb Film recently launched a YouTube channel chock-full of restored films, allowing us to rediscover the stylized, experimental work of directors such as Dušan Vukotić (*Surogat*, 1961), Nedeljko Dragić (*Dnevnik – The Diary*, 1974) and Zdenko Gašparović (*Satiemania*, 1978).

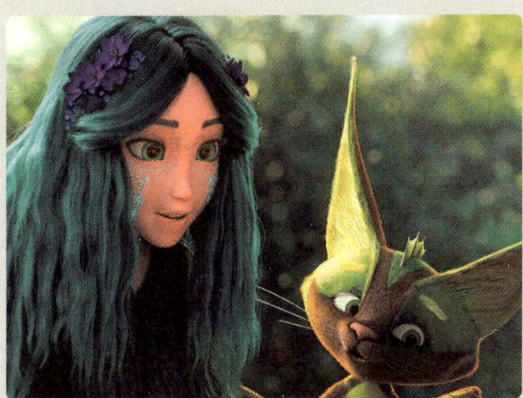

Top left: Pencil Pusher. Director Torill Kove won an Oscar for her short film *The Danish Poet*.

Above: A triumph of filmmaking through conflict and Covid, the Ukrainian animation *Mavka: The Forest Song* was released in over 80 countries worldwide.

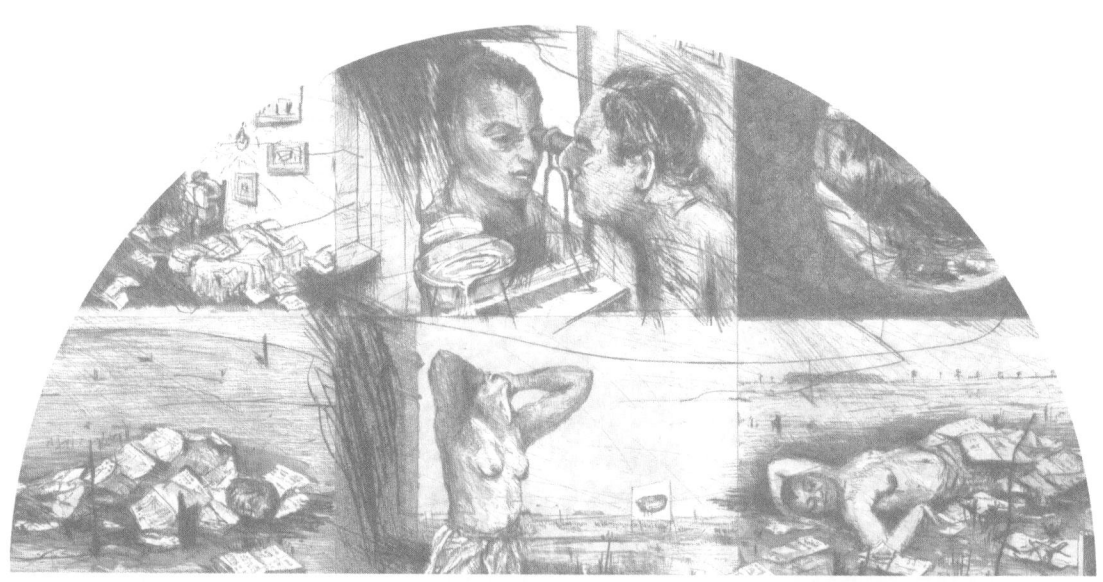
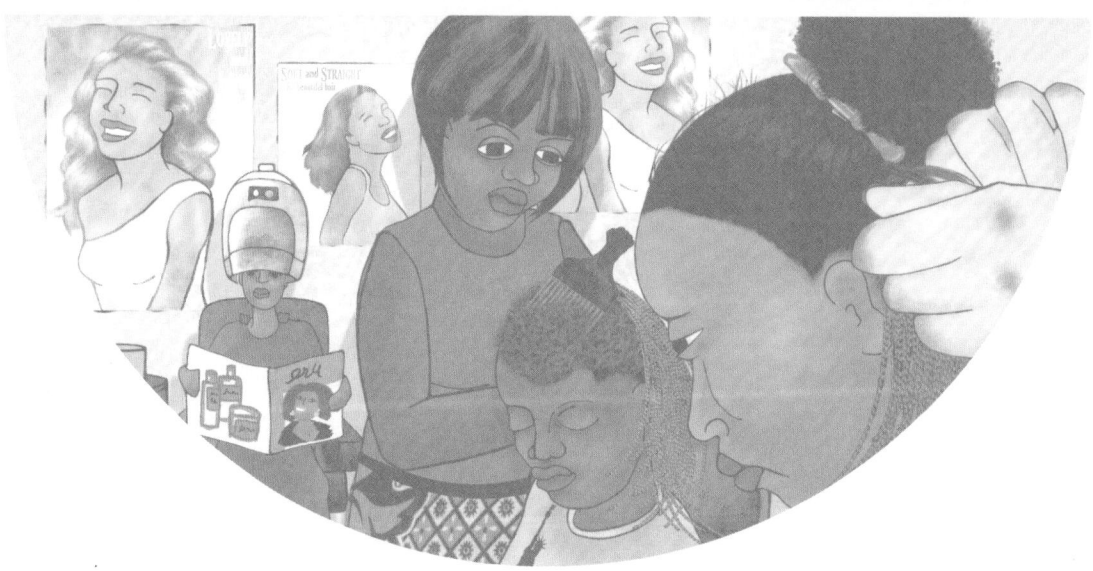

Africa

South Africa

Still Lives, Moving Pictures

✏ Drawings for Projection

Drawings by: William Kentridge
Released: 1989–2020

When most animation reaches its audience, it arrives fully formed.
The process of getting there is lengthy, tiresome, inventive and at times
illusory, and all of the errors – the spilled paint, the rough sketches, the
crashed computers – are nowhere to be seen.

William Kentridge's animations, however, are both
complete and works in progress because his progress
is his work. His animation utilizes an arresting technique,
enacted upon with no script or storyboard, in which
a single image is adapted over and over again on
the same piece of paper. Leaving behind a trail of
smudges and artefacts with each frame of movement,
the animation leaves scars on the page and a striking,
living timeline of its process. Released over three
decades, his *Drawings for Projection* series of short
films is a staggering example of this technique, and of
a maverick creative and thrillingly expressive artist who
erases, redraws and remixes the form he works in, while
maintaining and evolving his singular voice.

Kentridge still lives in Johannesburg, where he was

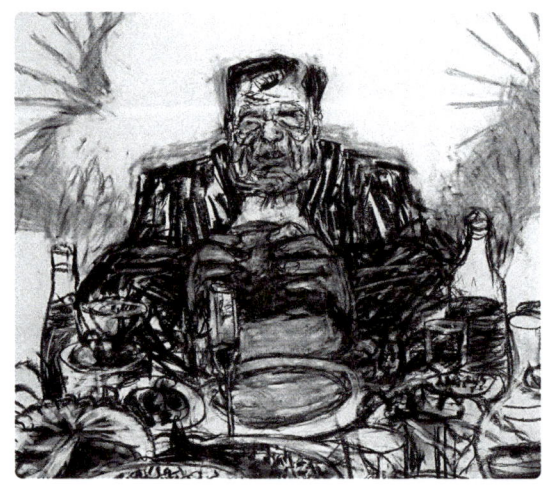

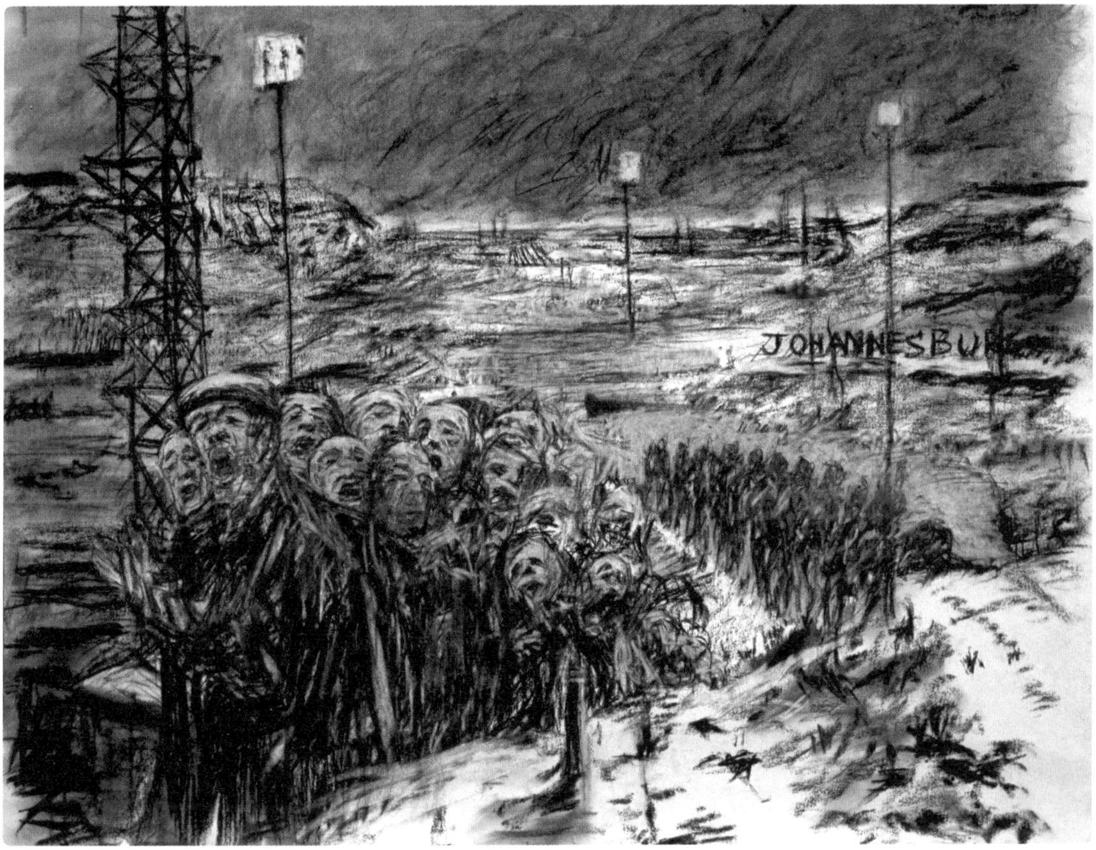

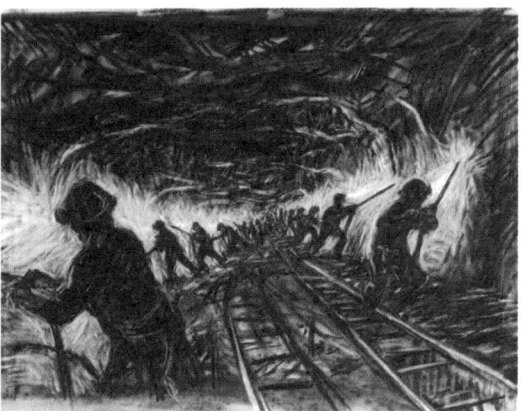

born in 1955, the child of two activist lawyers who both worked with victims of apartheid. A ferociously creative young mind, Kentridge followed his parents by studying politics but also explored art, acting and filmmaking throughout his twenties. He eventually found a thrilling medium at the intersection of all his interests and outlets with the first of his *Drawings* series in 1989, titled *Johannesburg, 2nd Greatest City After Paris.*

This first short introduces two proxies for Kentridge's psyche and fixture characters of the series: property developer Soho Eckstein and his sensitive, artistic love rival Felix Teitlebaum. Eckstein is a cinder block of a man, styled in thick pinstripe drags of charcoal, seated behind a desk from where he oversees his land, and crucially his gold mines and his Black miners; looming above them, like a mobster on the rail of his club. Teitlebaum, who cuts a softer figure, is more connected to the landscape and its people, and makes a cuckold of Eckstein, with images of frantic, amorphous sexual acts and flashes of blue colour against the primary black and white, sending

Opposite: Soho's house. Property developer and recurring character Soho Eckstein proves his wealth and excess at the dining table.

Top: Frozen in time. Works in *Drawings for Projection* are both films and individual paintings.

Above: Land of mine. Kentridge's series explores the exploitative work of Black miners in South Africa.

the fragile Eckstein into a violent, destructive rage with no care for anyone caught in the fallout. The film ends and the credit "Drawing: William Kentridge" comes up. A curious title, neither director nor animator, but it fits. It is both verb and noun, as the act of Kentridge's drawing – as seen in Eckstein's rigid, heaving body movement and the scuffs each frame leaves behind – is as much an active part of the film as the characters. Once the final frame of a scene has been completed, a process sometimes taking hundreds of tweaks, a single drawing is left, which in a gallery setting is often exhibited alongside the films.

One of the series' most powerful entries is 1991's *Mine*. A visceral examination of power and exploitation, it is built around the image of Soho luxuriously plunging a cafetière coffee, which metamorphosizes into a corkscrew that burrows through the beds, showers and even human remains of the Black workers residing, literally, beneath him. The scene that follows, featuring ribbons of receipts shifting into the shapes of discarded bodies, offers a brutal, shockingly current provocation.

As Kentridge revisits the characters, his own sociopolitical backdrop shifts, and therefore so too does the backdrop for Soho and Felix. Their story begins during apartheid and continues through its dissolution and into the "new South Africa" that followed, a journey which enhances the impact of Kentridge's established technique. Despite the legal ending of apartheid, its violent legacy and prejudices persist, with Kentridge stating in relation to his 1994 film *Felix in Exile* that "the very term 'new South Africa' has within it the idea of a painting over the old", further binding the practical and political. Each erasure of Kentridge's grimy frame creates shrapnel that flings forward into the image's future; memories, lives and pain that become foundational to the continuing story.

Although only a few specific titles in the series have been mentioned here, each entry in *Drawings for Projection* is worth seeking out, either viewed individually or in tandem with the others. Both in their form and the multifaceted nature of their exhibition, the drawings and their maker are entirely unique. If you are intrigued to learn more about his process and the philosophy behind

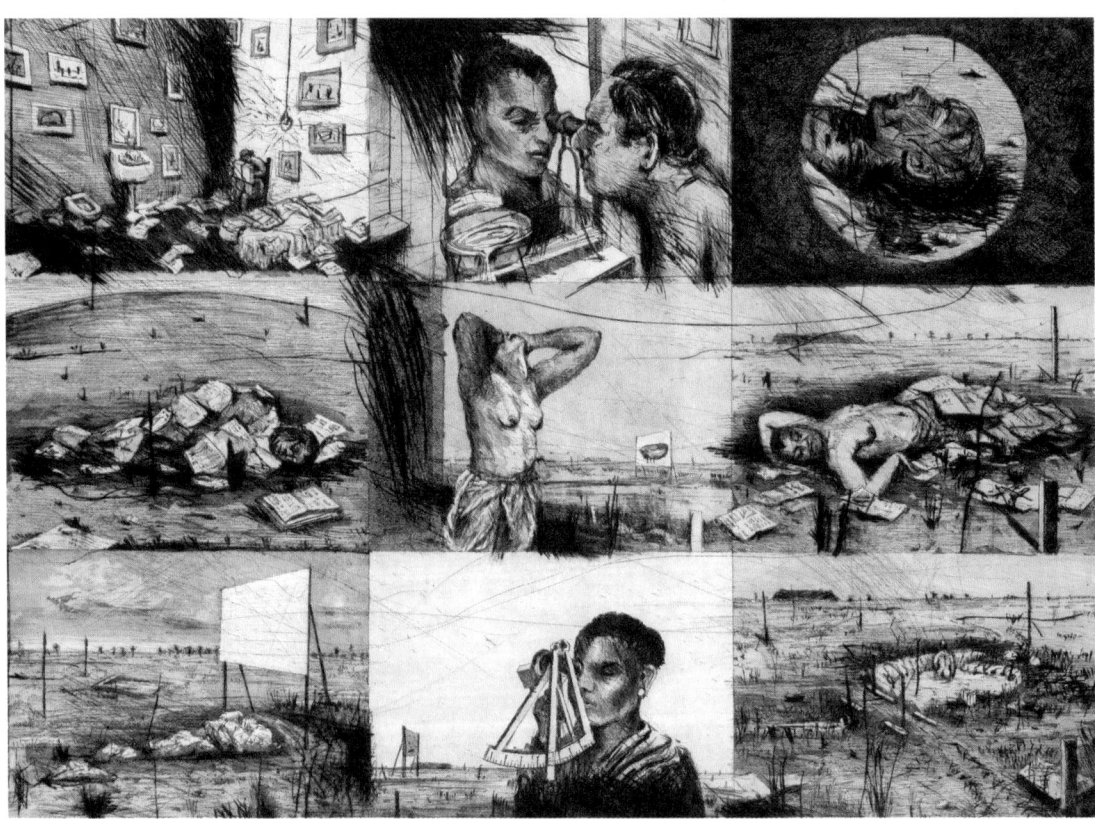

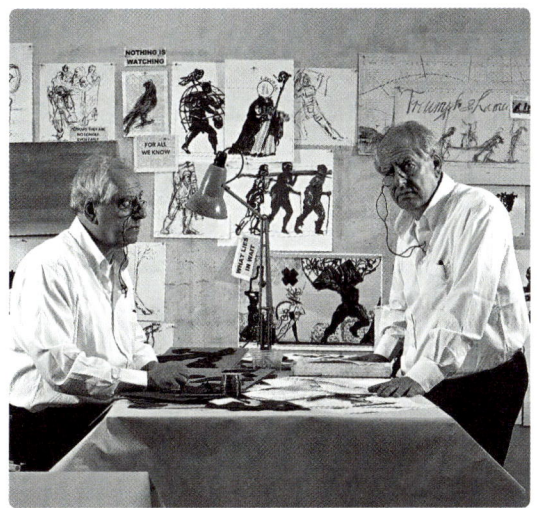

his work, you can't do better than *Self-Portrait as a Coffee-Pot* (2023). This is a self-reflexive TV series set inside Kentridge's studio, a location which doubles as an extension of his own brain and sees the artist (and many clones of him) hash out the great riddles of life and his work. It's mesmeric, meditative and feels wonderfully handmade, so take the chance to step inside his world – it doesn't look like anything else.

Opposite: Body talk. South African landscapes and human characters become entwined throughout *Drawings for Projection*.

Left: You're just projecting. In *Self-Portrait* as a *Coffee-Pot* a clone of Kentridge allows for a meta-textual analysis of the artist's work.

Below: Sea Shell. South Africa's Triggerfish Studios provided animation for the charming adaptation of the popular kids' picture book *The Snail and the Whale*.

👁 Further Viewing

On the opposite end of the scale to William Kentridge's gallery pieces is Triggerfish Animation Studios, which stands at the forefront of South Africa's mainstream animation industry. The studio has produced a clutch of features in the past, mainly talking-animal CG adventures such as *Adventures in Zambezia* (2012), *Khumba* (2013) and most recently, *Seal Team* (2021) – none of which have been terrifically successful at either the box office or with critics. Instead, Triggerfish's international reputation was built on its work for UK-based company Magic Light Pictures on a series of warmly received children's specials adapted from popular picture books, including *Stick Man* (2015), *Revolting Rhymes* (2016), *Zog* (2018) and *The Snail and the Whale* (2019). They also contributed the sublime short "Aau's Song" (2023) from first-time directors Nadia Darries and Daniel Clarke, to the *Star Wars: Visions* anthology series. The recent boom in streaming commissions has served South African animation well, with a bursting slate of series launching in 2023, including *Kiff*, and Triggerfish's own *Supa Team 4*, *Kiya & the Kimoja Heroes* and *Kizazi Moto: Generation Fire* (see "Elsewhere in Africa").

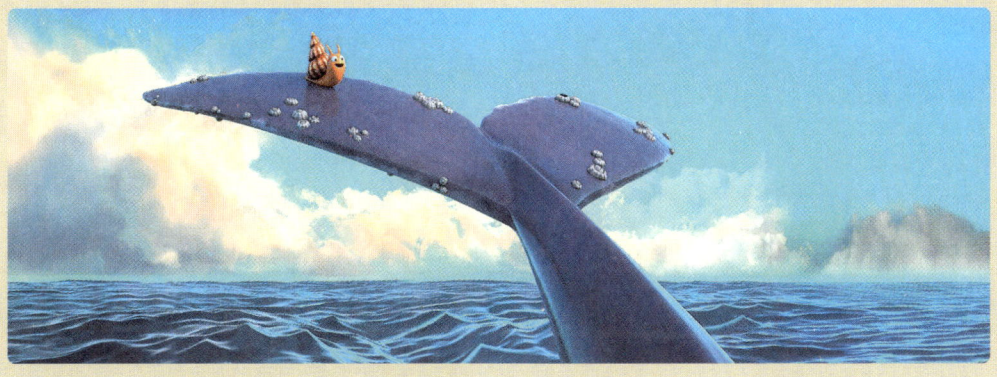

Niger

Toad Tales

👤 Moustapha Alassane (1942–2015)

With a career that started not long after the Republic of Niger gained its independence from France in 1960, Moustapha Alassane approached cinema with a restless curiosity.

This spirit of creativity and experimentation saw him make films in many forms and styles, from live-action films to animation that encompassed hand-drawn and stop-motion techniques.

Born in 1942, Alassane had the knack for drawing at a young age, and was clearly a storyteller too. He created amateur shadow theatre shows for his classmates in his village, playing with shapes and colours and animal characters. At that point, though, cinema was far from his mind. "Neither my friends nor me knew at the time about cinema," he said, "nor had we heard about it." Instead, he trained to be a mechanic, and it was only later, thanks in part to a mentorship from French filmmaker and cinéma-vérité pioneer Jean Rouch, that he changed direction towards filmmaking.

Four of Alassane's animated films are easily accessible, and they are delightfully distinctive, if rough around the edges. In the mid-1960s, Alassane had the opportunity to visit Canada and train with animator

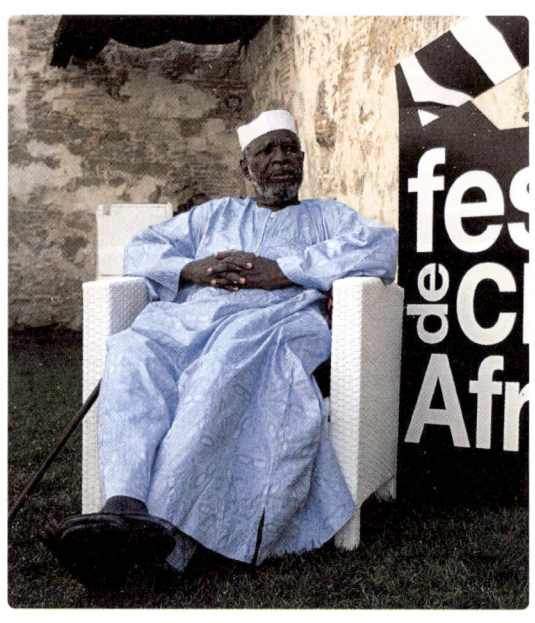

Norman McLaren at the National Film Board, where he produced the short film *The Death of Gandji* (1965) – a fable about a monster lurking in the bush outside a village of toads, and the crafty grasshopper that kills it. The thick-lined character designs and animation are rudimentary at best, but there is such joy in its narration, and exuberance in its caricatured forms and bold, colourful backgrounds.

Bon Voyage Sim (1966) returns to a land of frogs and toads, but with a more pointed satirical purpose, skewering the pomp and ceremony of an official visit from the Republic of Toads to a neighbouring state – a clear commentary on the diplomatic relations between the newly independent West African republics. Alassane's drawing style is once again clear-lined and childlike, but there's an inviting and playful quality to the film – especially its opening sequence featuring a frog cycling on a bike, backed by a jazz soundtrack.

Samba le Grand (1977) found Alassane experimenting with stop-motion puppets to tell the African folktale of Samba Gana, a hero who meets his match in a princess who demands he perform a series of trials before she'll deign to marry him. Compared to the intentionally rough hand-drawn features, *Samba le Grand* revels in the textures of the puppets' costumes and the colours of its painted backdrops. It's more stately in its storytelling, too – that is, until a vivid and thrilling, eight-year-long(!) scrap between Samba Gana and an evil serpent.

Alassane showed off his action chops again in *Kokoa* (2001, although some sources date it to 1985), a wild and wonderful film that dramatizes an evening's entertainment of West African wrestling (known as Kokowa, or Lutte). The toads are back, frantically banging drums and whipping up the crowd before the action begins, with fighters including turtles, birds and scorpions, and with a crab referee circling the action. Alassane meticulously choreographs the wrestling so there's real weight and suspense behind every grapple, and the film fizzes with humour and sparkling colour throughout, not least when the champion chameleon enters the ring, and changes hue mid-bout.

Moustapha Alassane's international recognition may not yet match that of the Senegalese master filmmaker Ousmane Sembène, whose work also flourished in the same post-colonial period and is now enshrined in canons such as the Criterion Collection, but his position in the annals of African Cinema is an important one.

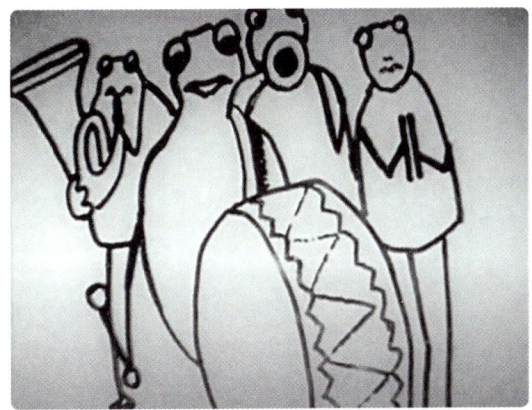

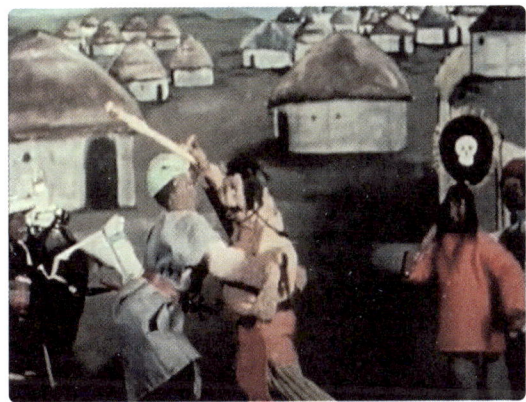

Retrospectives celebrating his eclectic, idiosyncratic work have been exhibited at the Il Cinema Ritrovato film festival in Bologna and the Museum of Modern Art in New York, and there are two documentaries tracing his career and influence. In time, maybe global audiences and film fans will come to appreciate him as the groundbreaking filmmaker he was – and see him, as the MoMA programme curator Amélie Garin-Davet once described him, as Africa's answer to Georges Méliès.

Opposite: Moustapha Alassane, pictured at the Festival de Cine Africano in Tarifa, Spain.

Top: Frog Chorus. Whether hand-drawn or in puppet form, frogs and toads appear all over Alassane's animated films.

Above: Across his animated films, Alassane worked in several different styles: *Samba le Grand* is a textured, tactile stop-motion folktale.

Kenya

Bodies, Landscapes and Legacies of Oppression

👤 Ng'endo Mukii

Born in Kenya, director, animator and artist Ng'endo Mukii studied at the Rhode Island School of Design and the Royal College of Art in London before turning her gaze as a filmmaker to matters closer to home.

Her father had encouraged her to draw from a young age, which led to a love of painting and drawing. "It truly soothed and satisfied me in a way that nothing else could," Mukii told the South Africa-based blog Design Indaba. A love of filmmaking and animation came later, during her time in Rhode Island, and these two journeys – one geographic, the other creative – have informed the hybrid styles of her films.

The 2012 short *Yellow Fever*, created while Mukii was studying in London, is a collision of forms: a mix of documentary, animation, dance and poetry is used to examine the cosmetic practice, common in Nairobi and elsewhere in Africa, of bleaching skin to appear more white. Interviews with Mukii's mother and niece, as well as her own reflective narration, are brought to life in a colourful illustrative style, starting from the teenage memory of seeing the disparity between a hairdresser's

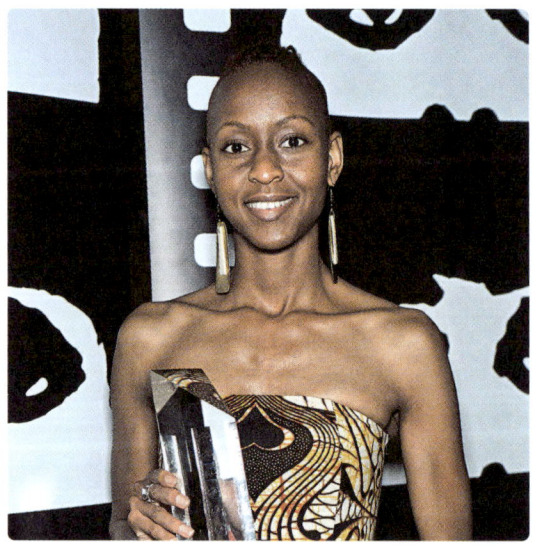

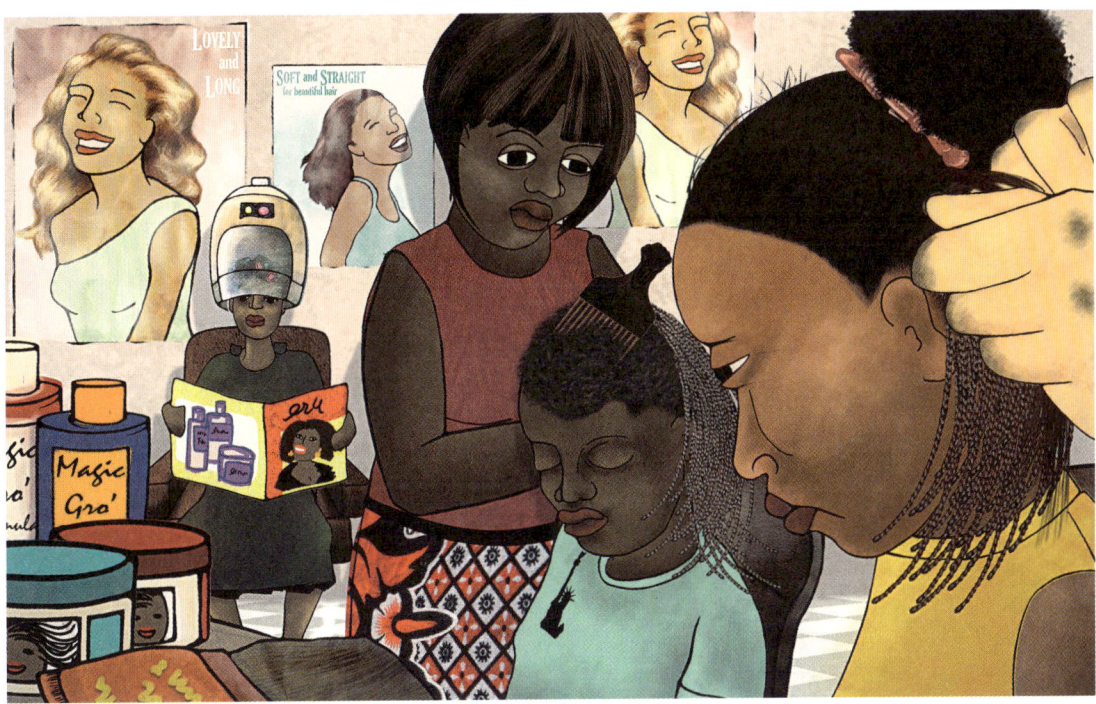

hands and face, both bleached pale, and her naturally dark arms, which are exposed as she braids the child's hair. "I see the West seeing us," Mukii's narration continues. "And in response this woman had worked hard to erase the element that marks her as truly African."

From this simple, yet striking image, which is contrasted with the beauty posters on the salon's wall and their slogans "Fair and Beautiful" and "Soft and Straight for Beautiful Hair", *Yellow Fever* unfolds into an incisive study of race, femininity, identity and cultural imperialism. Animated sequences are intercut with scenes of contorting dancers and the pointed use of racist colonialist caricatures and "medical" drawings, before landing on a heartbreaking conversation with Mukii's young niece, who says that her media-influenced dream of having white skin has made her feel "uncomfortable" in her own. All the while, Mukii trains her camera with a sensitivity to tactile details, homing in on the texture of hair and the contours of the torso. The narration describes "hierarchies of beauty cut into our skin", while these images cross-fade with shots of Kenyan landscapes, drawing a direct link between these two battlegrounds in a continuing post-colonial struggle.

There's a connection between the African landscape and the body, too, in "Enkai" (2023), Mukii's Annie

Award-winning episode of the Disney+ anthology series *Kizazi Moto: Generation Fire*, which was pitched as an Afrofuturist answer to the stylistically diverse animation series *Star Wars: Visions*, with writers and directors drawn from across the continent. Mukii's short presents a contrast

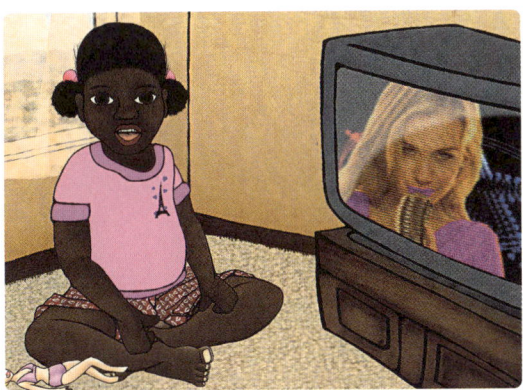

Opposite: Ng'endo Mukii at the 2013 Chicago International Film Festival, where *Yellow Fever* was awarded Best Animated Short Film.

Top: *Yellow Fever* uses the everyday setting of a hair salon to interrogate themes of identity, femininity and the lingering effects of colonialism.

Above: Recorded interviews with Mukii's young niece bring the film's issues into sharp relief.

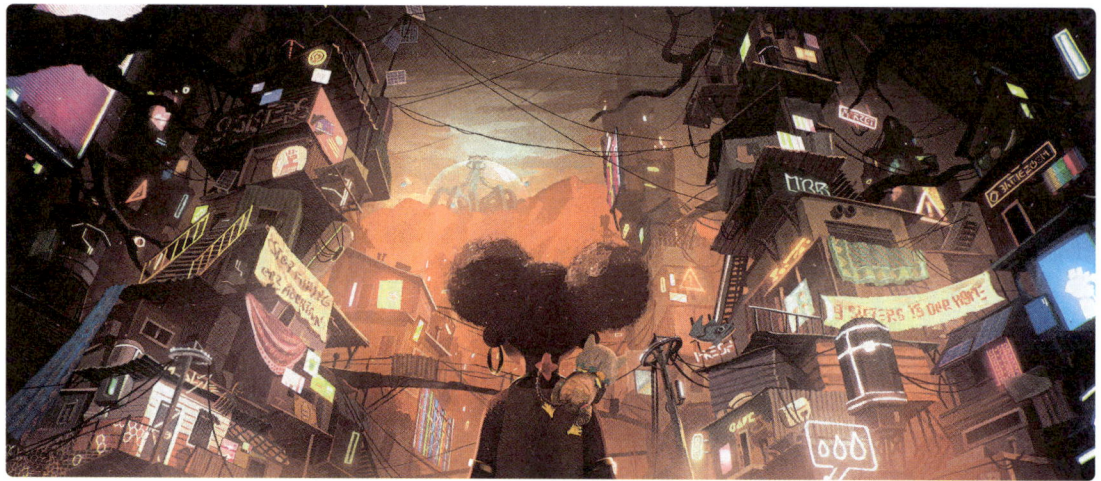

between the warm home life of a young girl, Enkai, and her mother, the divine magical being Shiro, and the outside world, where Shiro is always away working. When Enkai ventures outside of her family bubble, she discovers the dystopian slums of Kirinyaga Mega City, where a "Euro-Kenyan" corporation is violently displacing the local population and seeking to mine a sacred mountain that stands above the settlement. Shiro is their protector, but the struggle is proving to be too much for her – a fact that becomes apparent in Shiro's weathered features, greying hair and exhausted body.

Told in a gorgeous hybrid of stop-motion and CG animation in collaboration with the London-based studio Blink Industries, "Enkai" revisits themes that Mukii first explored a decade earlier in *Yellow Fever*, but reworks

them into accessible genre fiction. There's a focus here on family connections, bonds between mothers and daughters and the responsibilities that women shoulder – towards their families, their communities and the world. And yet, ultimately, there's a certain kind of hope that lies in the innocence of the young. Enkai herself learns to harness her powers of creation and starts a new world of her own, free from the cycles of violence, suppression and exploitation. A chance to start afresh, and dream of something new.

Above: "Enkai" envisions a dystopian future of natural landscapes and local communities ruined by capitalist greed.

Below: Maternal Light. Both *Yellow Fever* and *Enkai* are rooted in the bonds between mothers, daughters and family.

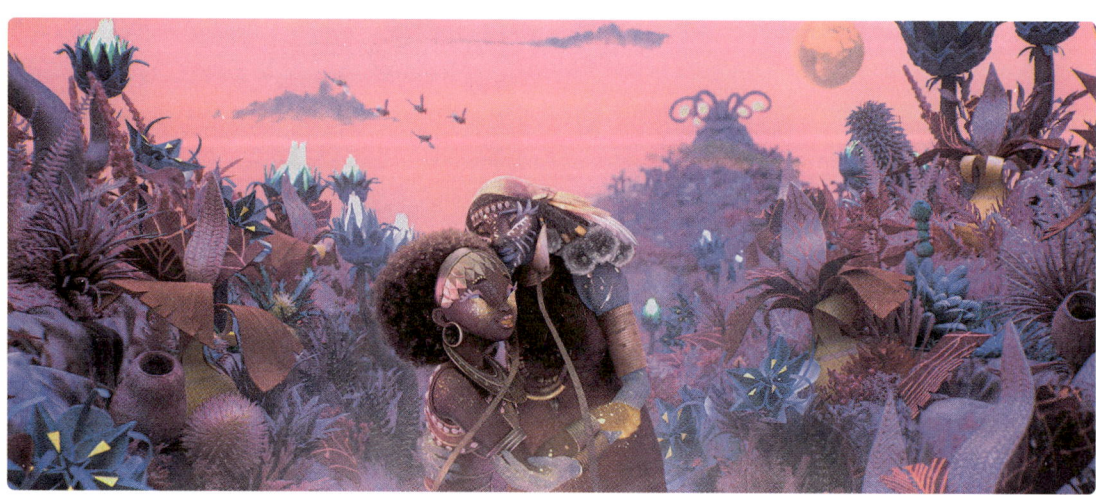

Elsewhere in Africa

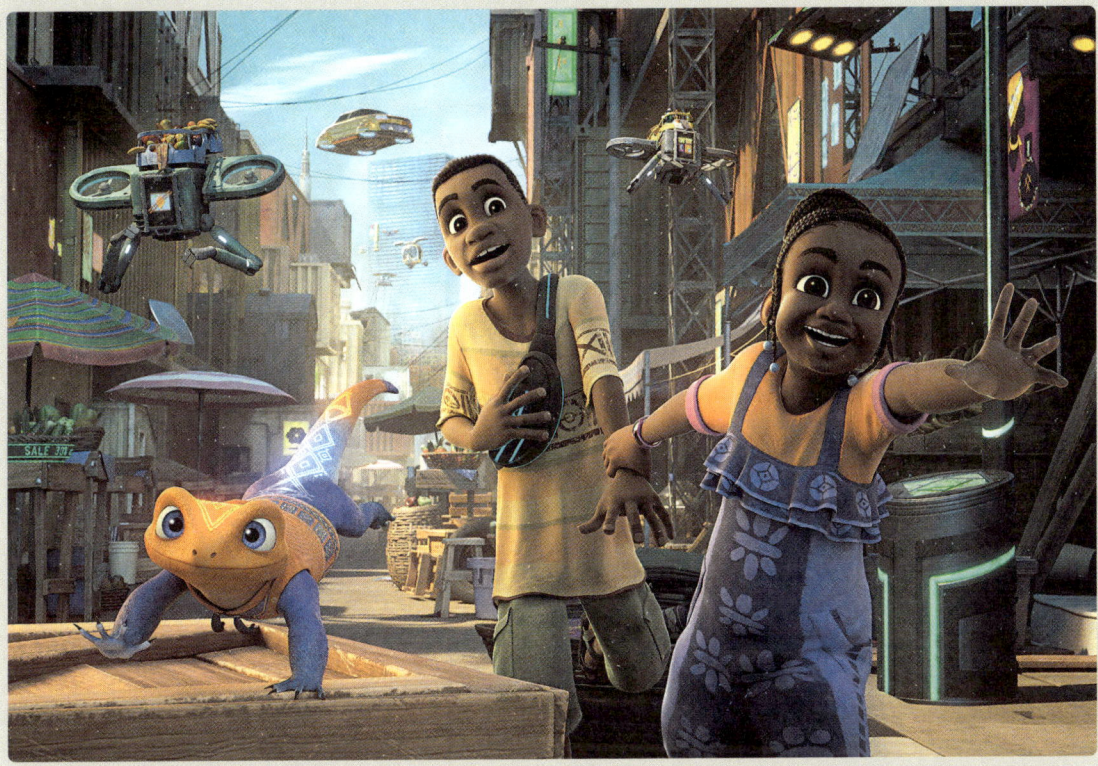

The history of African animation dates back to the films of Egypt's Frenkel Brothers, who worked in the 1930s in a style clearly influenced by Walt Disney and the Fleischer Brothers, and enjoyed success with their character Mish-Mish Effendi – described, after a recent rediscovery of their films, as "the Egyptian Mickey Mouse".

The ramshackle "junkmation" feature *The Legend of the Sky Kingdom* (2003), from Zimbabwean director Roger Hawkins, is commonly regarded to be the first feature-length African animation – although perhaps it's best left as a footnote. Better is *Aya of Yop City* (2019), a French animation inspired by the childhood memories of Ivorian writer Marguerite Abouet, directed by Abouet and her artist collaborator, Clément Oubrerie.

Stepping away from features, let's highlight two shorts from Malian filmmakers: Mambaye Coulibaly's *La geste de Ségou* (1989) is a richly designed stop-motion retelling of a story from the Bambara oral tradition with carved wooden puppets; and *On the Surface* (2021), a poetic musing from French-Malian artist Fan Sissoko

on new motherhood, identity and belonging among the mountains and lakes of Iceland, rendered with soft, impressionistic brush strokes.

Today, there are efforts to bring voices and visions from across the African continent to global audiences. That's the aim of British-based Kugali Media and their futuristic, Lagos-set sci-fi series *Iwájú* (2024), and the South African studio Triggerfish and their *Kizazi Moto: Generation Fire* (2023) anthology series, which both premiered on Disney+. The latter project truly delivered, with episodes directed by filmmakers from Zimbabwe, South Africa, Uganda, Nigeria, Kenya and Egypt, including Shofela Coker (*Iwa*, 2009) and Raymond Malinga (*A Kalabanda Ate My Homework*, 2017). African animation is catching up: if we revisit this chapter in a decade, we'll have a whole new story to tell.

Above: Although it was animated in London and Montreal, Kugali Media's Disney+ series *Iwájú* aims to bring 'Pan-African' storytelling to the global stage.

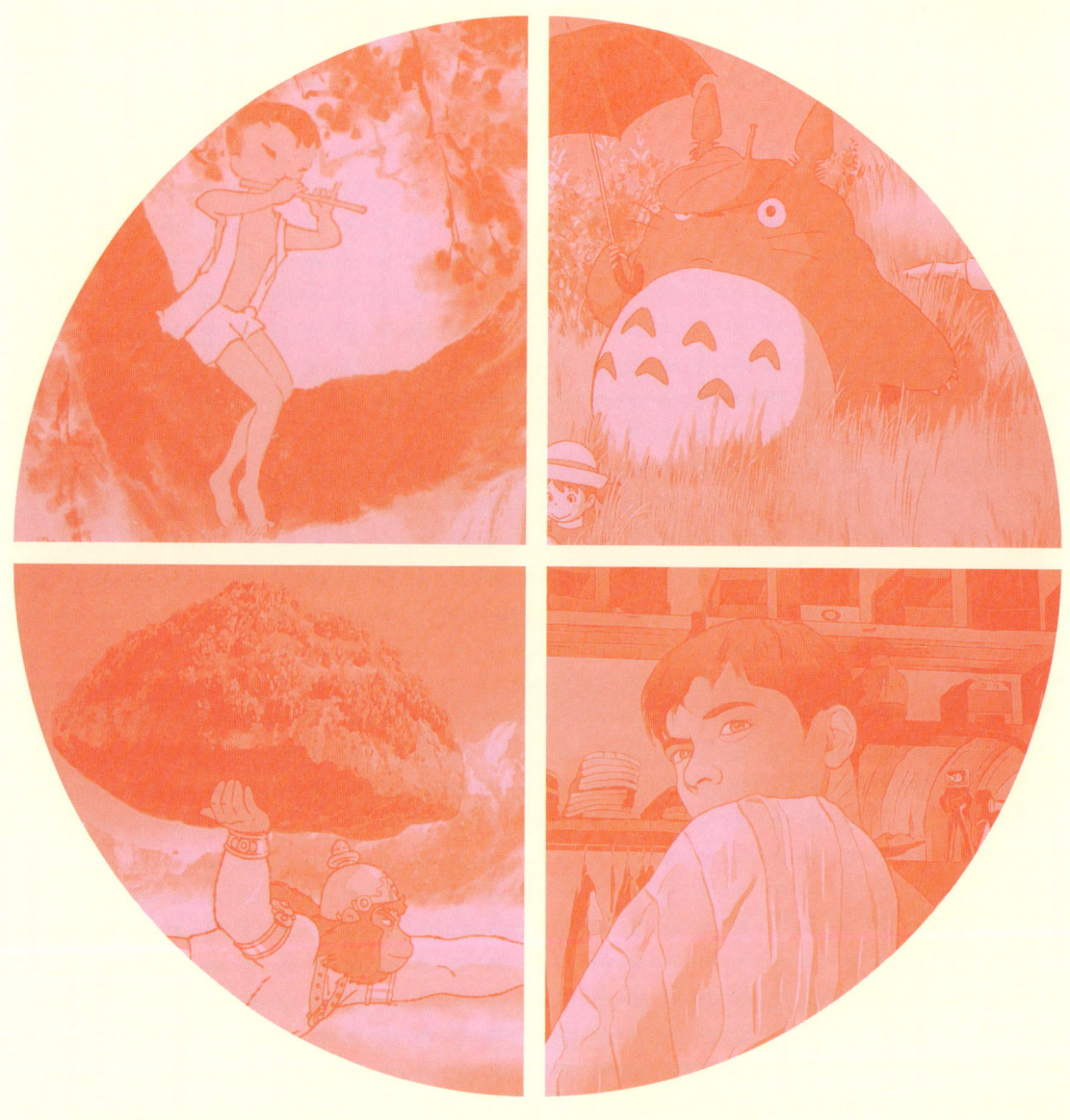

Asia

China

Myths and Legends of Animation

⊕ Shanghai Animation Film Studio

Like Soyuzmultfilm in the Soviet Union, Shanghai Animation Film Studio was a state-owned operation whose fortunes were governed by the whims and changing tastes of those in power.

Officially established in 1957, but with roots in prior studios, Shanghai Animation was intended to compete with Disney's cultural monopoly while finding a uniquely Chinese approach to the art form, one ready to educate and entertain children across the country.

In the mix from the start were the twin Wan brothers, Laiming and Guchan, pioneers of Chinese animation who had produced the country's first feature-length film, *Princess Iron Fan* (1941). A sweeping black-and-white adventure that drew its story from Wu Cheng'en's epic novel *Journey to the West*, *Princess Iron Fan* was initially released while Shanghai was under occupation from Japanese imperial forces. Consequently, the film was also shown in Japan, where it had an impact on young Osamu Tezuka (see page 152) and inspired the creation of the first feature-length Japanese animation, the propaganda film *Momotaro: Sacred Sailors* (1945).

After joining Shanghai Animation, the brothers pursued

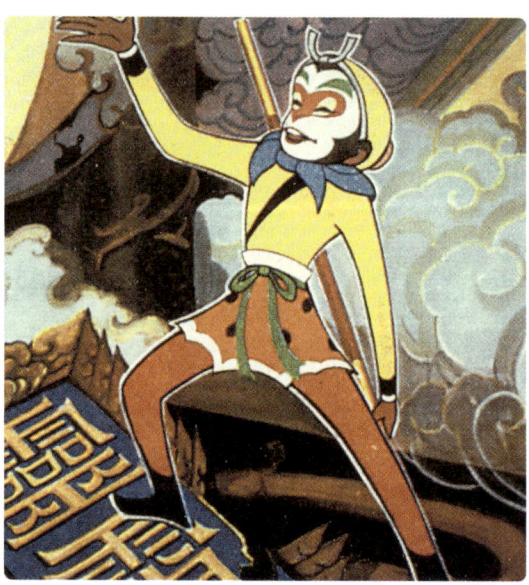

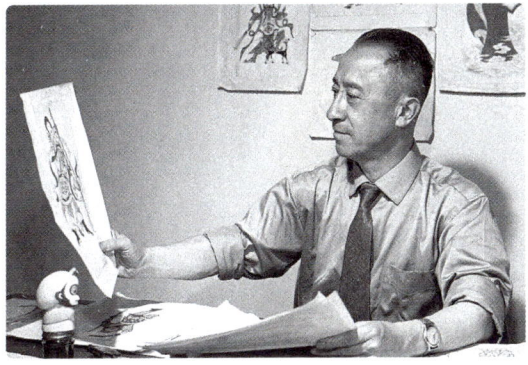

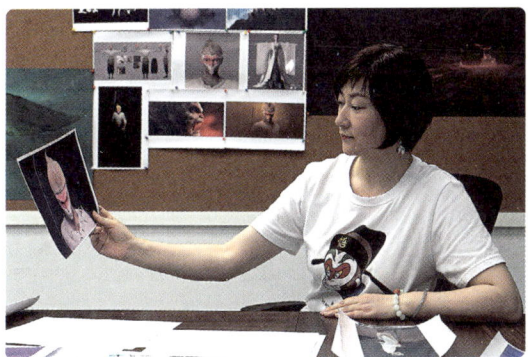

different techniques. Guchan directed short films in a paper cut-out style (*Pigsy Eats Watermelon*, 1958), while Laiming helmed *Havoc in Heaven* (1961–1964), an ambitious, all-colour hand-drawn feature that brought stories of Sun Wukong (The Monkey King) to vivid life, with music and balletic choreography reminiscent of the tradition of Beijing Opera. Released in two parts, the first instalment was a resounding hit in 1961, but by the release of the concluding part in 1964, the political tide was starting to turn against Shanghai Animation. In the latter half of the decade, Chairman Mao's Cultural Revolution sought to stamp out perceived anti-communist sentiment, and the animation industry wasn't spared.

One of Shanghai Animation's leading filmmakers, Te Wei, was imprisoned for a year and then exiled to the countryside. In Shanghai, he had directed the renowned satirical sketch *The Conceited General* (1956), and had

Above and left: Flashback. Shanghai Animation chief Su Da recreates a photograph of her predecessor, the pioneering animator Wan Laiming.

Opposite and below: Monkeying Around. Shanghai Animation's most enduring character, the acrobatic Sun Wukong.

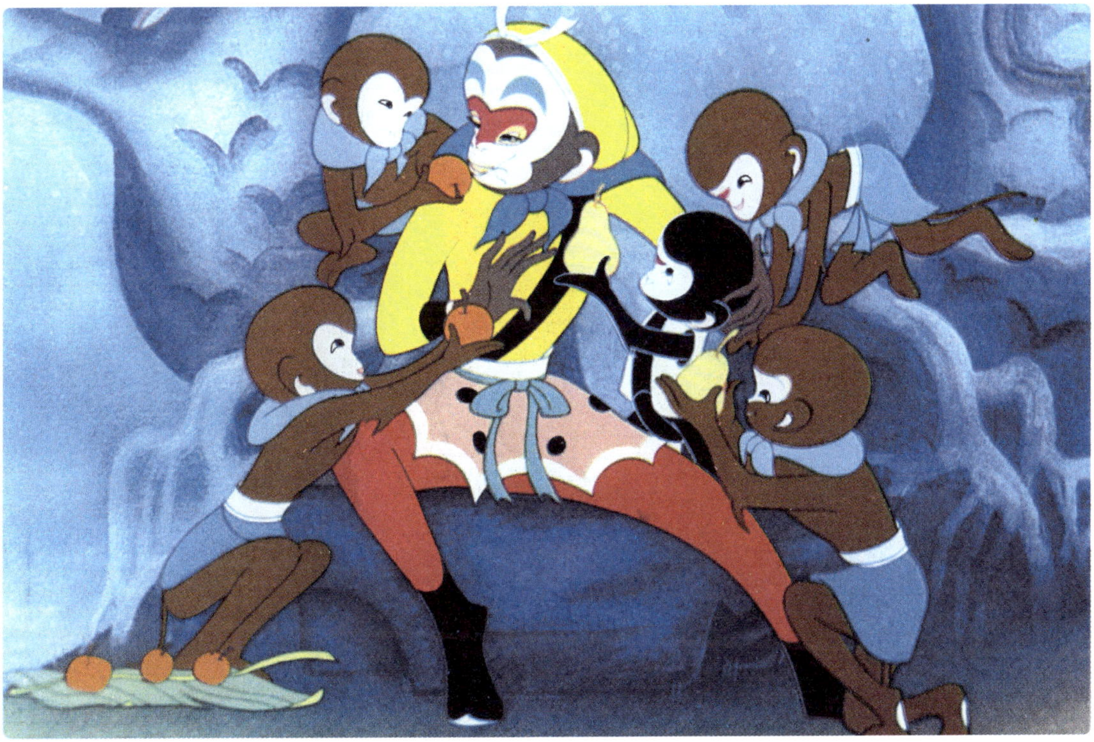

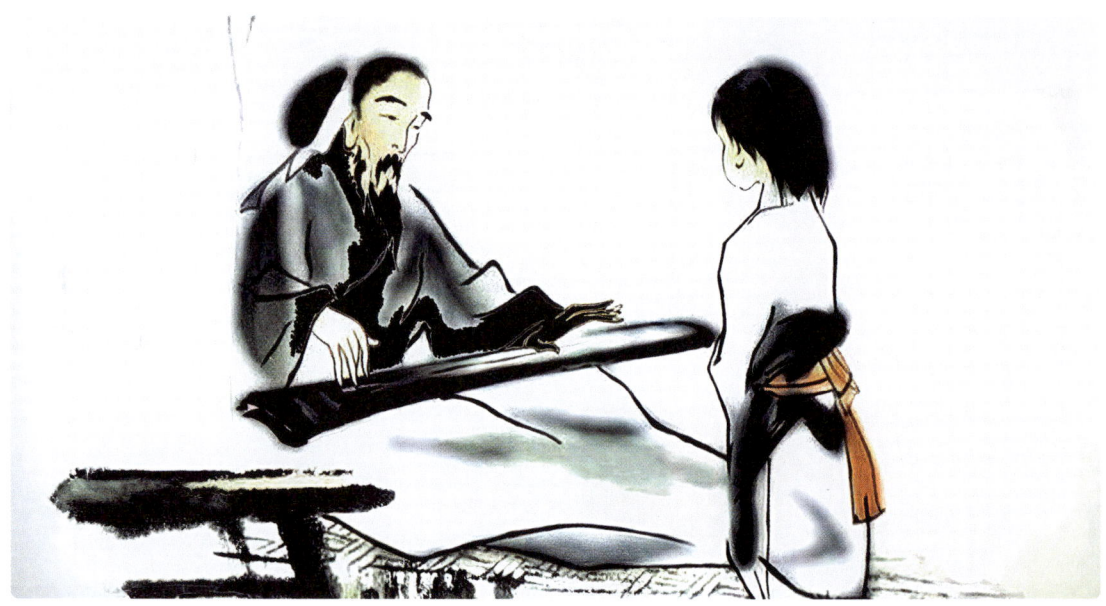

then explored a gorgeous, watercolour style influenced by the master Chinese painter Qi Baishi, in *Where is Mama* (1960) and *The Cowboy's Flute* (1963). Both films are replete with sumptuous background art and delicately painted animal characters, from the darting tadpoles searching for their mother in *Where is Mama*, to the butterflies, birds and water buffalo of *The Cowboy's Flute*. They are among the most purely beautiful pieces of animated art ever created.

And yet Te Wei was exiled from animation for a decade and a half, until the political situation eased and he was allowed to return to the studio at the tail end of the 1970s. By then, a new generation of younger animators were taking up the reins, such as A Da and Lin Wenxiao, who had both sharpened their skills on Te Wei's earlier films.

This new era of Shanghai Animation still traded in spectacular fantasy films drawing from Chinese myth and folklore, such as the features *Nezha Conquers the Dragon King* (1979) and *The Monkey King Conquers the Demon* (1985), but the real wonders are in their short-form work. A Da and Lin Wenxiao sent up the brutal and senseless violence of the Cultural Revolution in the pointed satire *One Night in the Art Gallery* (1978), in which a brutish pair of characters (an anthropomorphized top hat and spiked club) shut down and destroy an exhibition of children's paintings – but it's the children in the paintings themselves who leap off

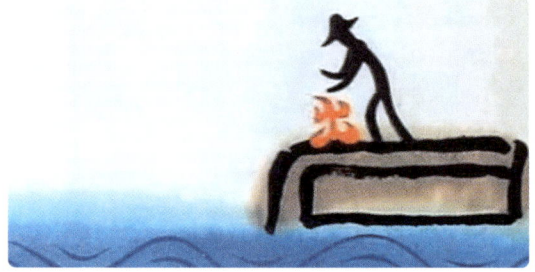

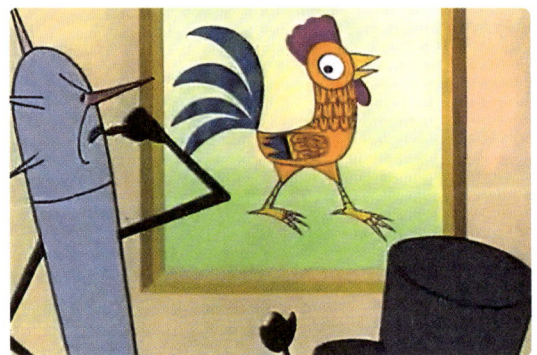

Top: Old Masters. Te Wei's final film, *Feeling from Mountain and Water*, is a breathtakingly beautiful, painted masterpiece.

Above middle: Drawn to Life. Pictographs become protagonists in A Da's ingenious late short, *36 Characters*.

Above: Private View. Shanghai Animation's *One Night in the Art Gallery* is a pointed broadside against bullying political forces who suppress artistic expression.

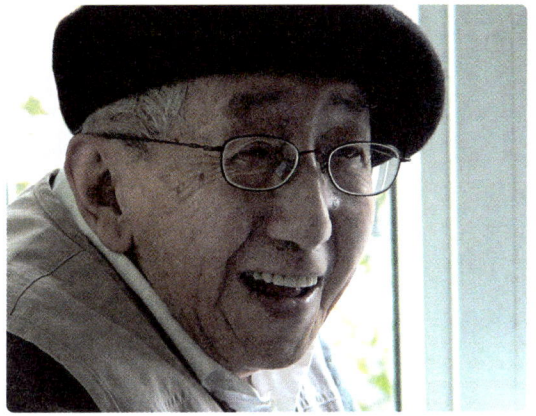

their canvases and fight back against the oppression. Then, directing on his own, A Da explored themes of disharmony, selfishness and collective responsibility in the playful, gently philosophical *Three Monks* (1980) – where the simple act of fetching water for a hilltop temple grows into a parable for society as a whole.

There's still much work to be done excavating and exploring Shanghai Animation's library of works, especially where the English-speaking world is concerned. Back in 2021, we were fortunate in the UK to enjoy a brief, online streaming season of 11 films curated by UK-China Film Collab, including many of the films discussed here – most receiving their first official release in Britain.

We still have far to go, but let's end on two late-period films from Shanghai Animation which deserve the spotlight, both fulfilling that initial aim of finding uniquely Chinese artistic expressions within animation. In A Da's delightful *36 Characters* (1984), a man teaches his young son about ancient Chinese pictographs (written characters that are derived from pictures of objects). He does this by making words such as fire, elephant, house and umbrella come to dynamic animated life, telling a story with these signs and symbols, and revealing a deep, age-old connection between art and language.

And then there's Te Wei's masterpiece, *Feeling from Mountain and Water* (1988). The pinnacle of his ink wash films, this immaculate study in space and silence among sighing breezes and flowing streams centres on an old musician and his young apprentice, and their quiet, daily habits living among the calm majesty of nature: an ageing master, passing on an ancient art form to the next generation.

Above left: Master of ink-wash animation, director Te Wei.

Below: Te Wei found this new, distinctive style for his films in the 1960s with *The Cowboy's Flute* (pictured) and *Where is Mama*.

Overleaf: This rich, vivid artwork for *The Cowboy's Flute* underscores the film's deep connection with the world of painting.

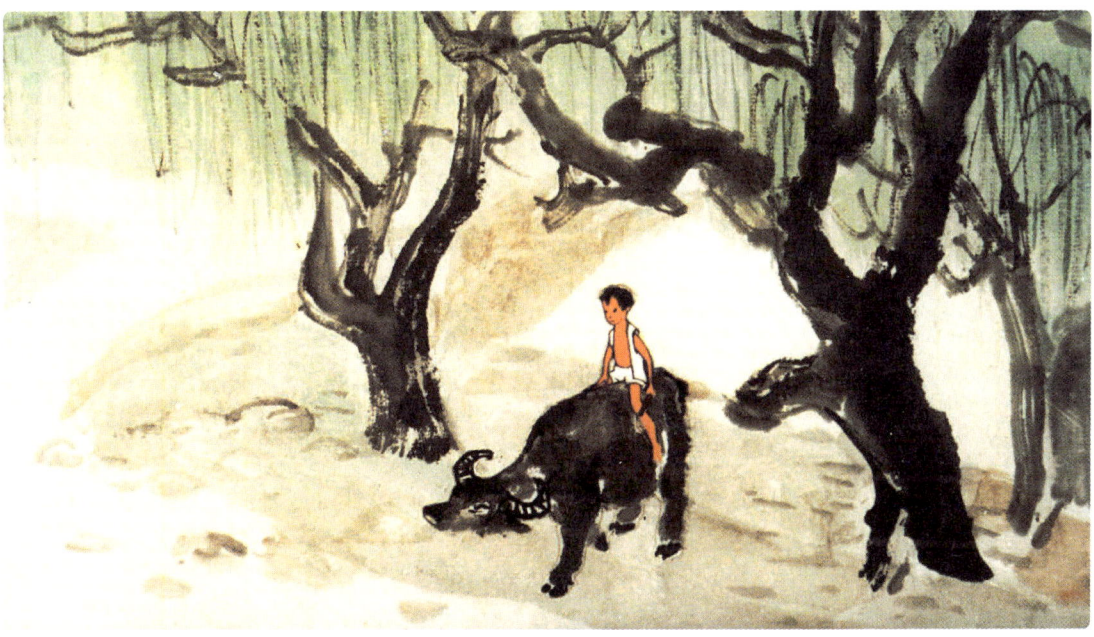

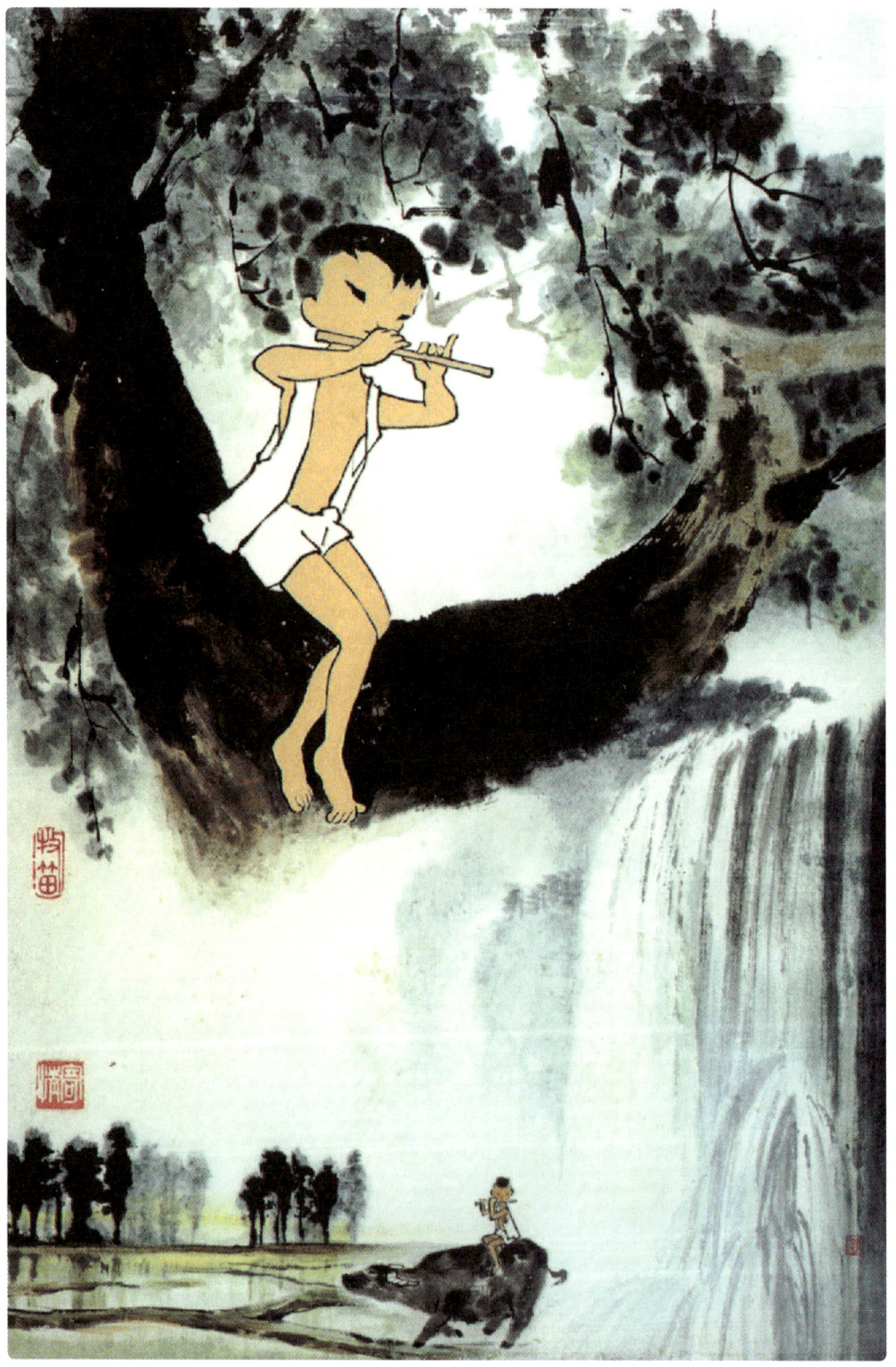

⊙ Further Viewing

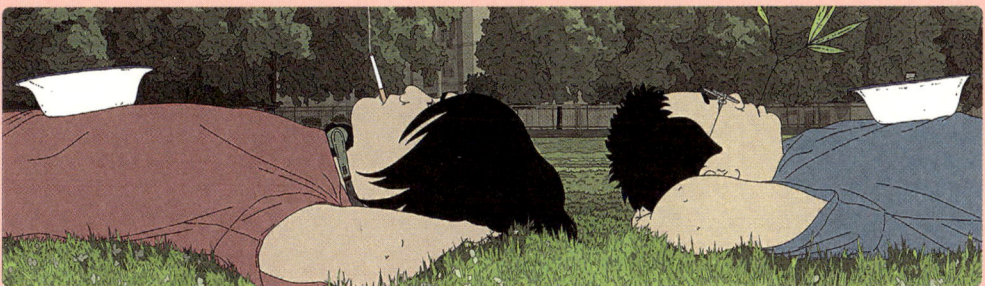

Chinese animated cinema is now a domestic powerhouse, and much like its live-action blockbusters, films are likely to gross hundreds of millions of dollars at home with only limited distribution elsewhere in the world. The most successful of these are spectacular, CG adventures drawing from Chinese history, folklore and mythology, such as *Monkey King: Hero Is Back* (2015), *Ne Zha* (2019) and *30,000 Miles from Chang'an* (2023), an epic nearly three hours long which stands as the longest animated feature ever released in cinemas. And then, as we were writing this book, came *Ne Zha 2* (2025), which stunned commentators around the world by becoming both the first film to take over a billion dollars in a single market and the highest grossing animated film of all time. And it achieved these feats in just under three weeks: such is the powerhouse potential of homegrown Chinese blockbuster cinema.

Away from the multiplexes, there is a growing canon of smaller-scale animated projects, encompassing the Studio Ghibli-esque fantasy of *Big Fish & Begonia* (2016), and the raw, rough-around-the-edges work of independent director Liu Jian. About as far as you can get from IMAX-sized spectacle, Liu's films are grounded at street level and are often laced with social commentary and sharp-edged humour, from the working-class drama *Piercing I* (2010), to the bleakly satirical gangster noir of *Have a Nice Day* (2017), to *Art College 1994* (2023), a coming-of-age drama set against a backdrop of political change.

Above: Quad Goals. Student life and turbulent politics collide in *Art College 1994*.

Below: Box Office Demon. *Ne Zha 2* was the talk of the industry in 2025 when it became the highest-grossing animated film of all time.

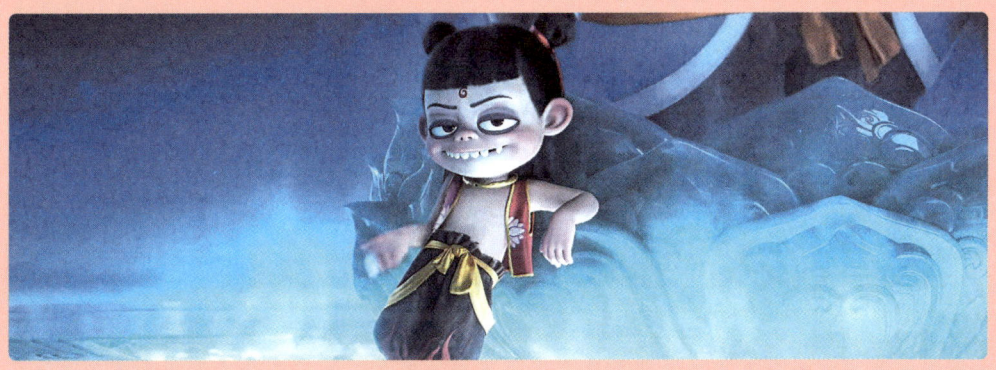

India

An Ancient Text Brought to Vivid Life

🎥 Ramayana: The Legend of Prince Rama

Director: Ram Mohan, Koichi Sasaki
Released: 1993

Although animated in Japan, this film was born in India.
***Ramayana* is, in many ways, epic.**

It's an epic in the tradition of epic poetry, being an adaptation of one of the most important Hindu stories; it's epic in a blockbuster sense, full of kings and demons and gruelling battles and great romance; it's an epic production too, one forged when the project's planner was only three years old.

At that age Japanese Yugo Sako was orphaned and raised to pursue Buddhist priesthood, but the lure of TV production stole him away from a monastic life and he became a documentarian instead. Attached to the Indian philosophy and spirituality that influenced his youth, he began travelling to India to make films and in 1983 documented an archaeological excavation of some relics that bore the *Ramayana* name; from there he plunged into a *Ramayana* rabbit hole, emerging with a passion for this ancient story about the life of an avatar of the Hindu deity Vishnu, and a desire to tell it in film.

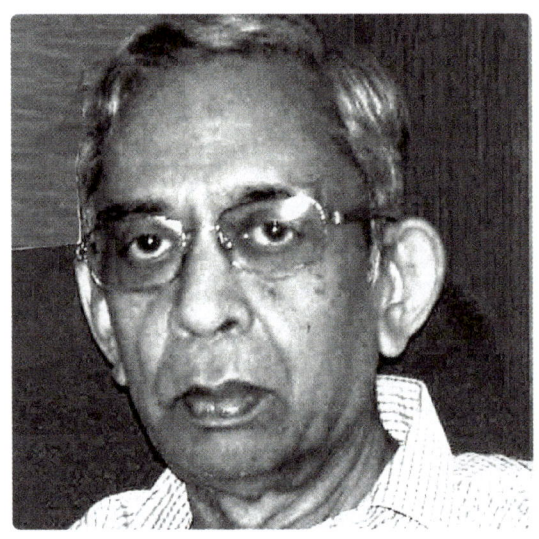

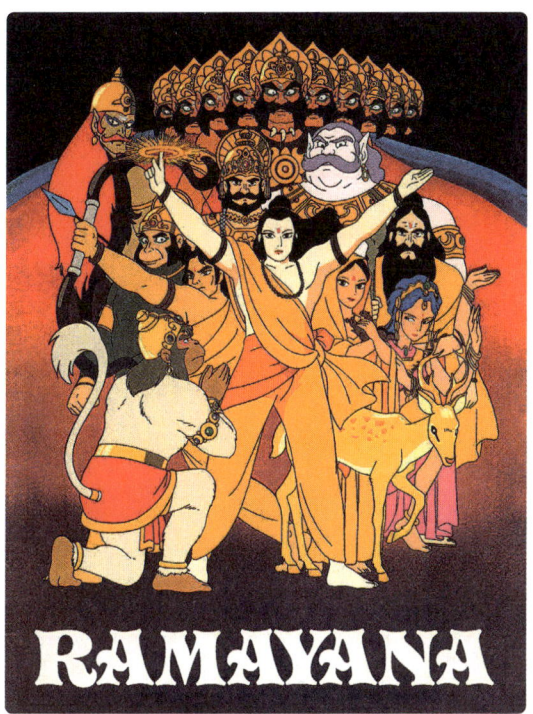

Controversy mired the early stages of production, with Sako's foreign status and the idea of portraying deific figures in animation both causing upset, but through collaboration, solutions were found: Sako convinced Ram Mohan, a pivotal figure in Indian animation, to join the project as a director.

Mohan had loved drawing cartoons as a child but went on to get a degree in science. After graduation, however, he was lured back to his passion, having met a Disney animator in 1956 called Clair Weeks (character animator on *Peter Pan*) who was setting up US government-supported animation training programmes in India. Weeks liked Mohan's stuff and got him on the programme, and from there Mohan worked on public information films. In 1967, after he spent time in Montreal with Norman McLaren, he set up his own company. Ram Mohan Biographics predominantly made adverts, the occasional title sequence (including for Satyajit Ray's *Shatranj Ke Khilari, 1977*) and after Yugo Sako called, they were in the feature film game too.

After the battle to animate *Ramayana* in India was lost, the process was moved to Japan, with Mohan going between the two countries to supervise and a TV anime director, Koichi Sasaki (who'd also worked on the 1977 animated adaptation of *The Hobbit*), joining him to direct alongside. Artistic direction, vocal performances and music were conducted in India, while a Japanese crew that expanded to 450 animators contributed to most of the film's visuals (including some animators who'd just worked

Opposite: Ram Mohan, a legendary figure in Indian animation and director of *Ramayana*.

Above: A flop on release in the early 90s, *Ramayana* has gained a following and a 4K restoration in the decades since.

Below: The big fight. One of many striking vistas in *Ramayana*, in this case the landscape for a memorable match-up.

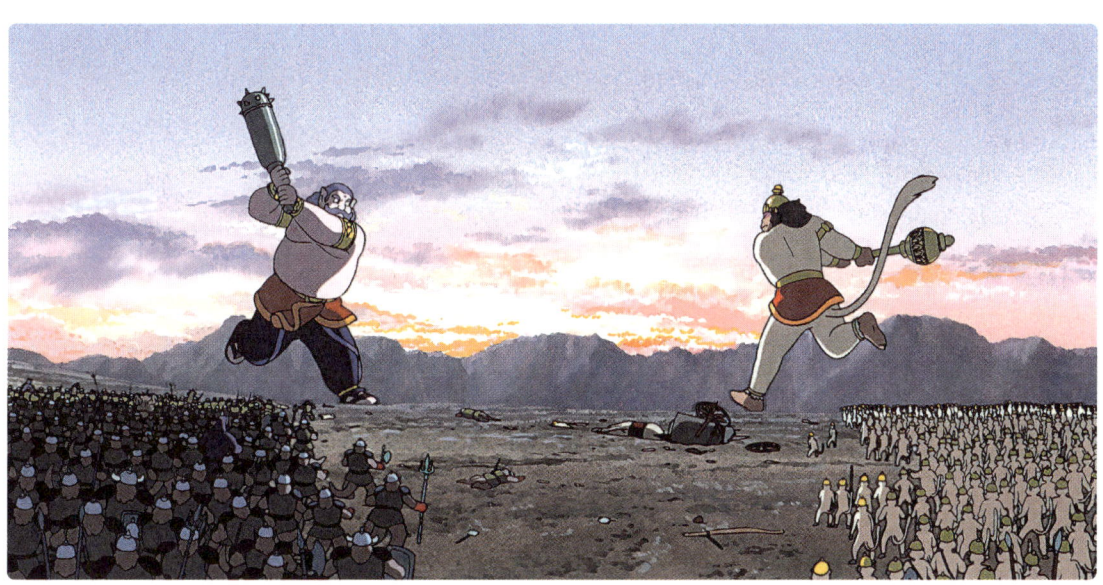

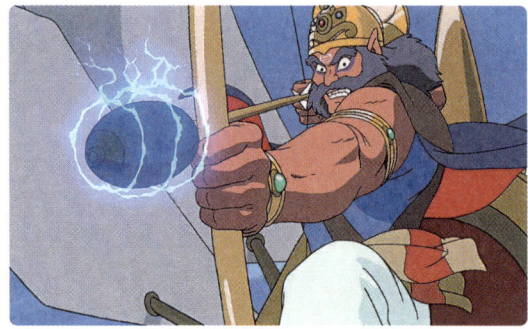

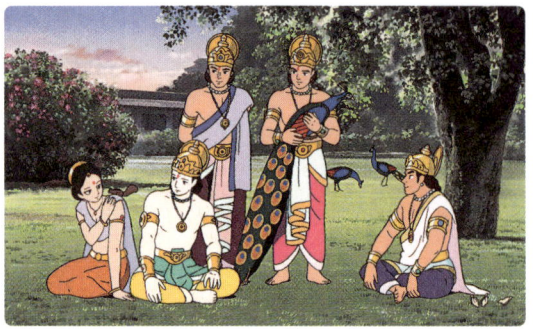

on Hayao Miyazaki's *Nausicaä of the Valley of the Wind* and *Laputa: Castle in the Sky*). Eventually, after more than 100,000 hand-drawn images, *Ramayana* finally premiered in 1993, a decade after Sako's journey began.

Given that the original poem runs to 24,000 verses, the adaptation has a lot to cover. The story (in very condensed fashion) follows young prince Rama, his 14-year royal exile, the kidnapping of his wife, the fight to get her back and their return home – with various creatures, villains and nefarious activities getting in their way. In the film the adventure feels sadly rushed, with expository dialogue explaining relationships, plotting and backstory, while there is no room for characters to develop before the next chapter begins. It's when the film takes occasional breathers that the spirituality of the tale comes through, like when some characters take a rest stop for water; we can drink in the rich and

layered natural forest backgrounds, joyously revel in the playfully choreographed Disney-esque animation of some magically communicative woodland creatures, and briefly consider the ideal of a harmonious relationship between humanity and nature. Recurring sequences of transformation, in which characters may instantly change attire, size or even number of heads, are prime examples of where Sako's insistence on animating the story proves most valuable, with the monstrous and magical forming with real physicality. Created in India, rather than Japan, the music of *Ramayana* is another highlight; courtesy of Indian film music legend Vanraj Bhatia, it enriches the story with percussive propulsion and plucked tranquillity.

Sadly, despite the level of craft and passion that went into the film there was no appetite for it, with Mohan telling one Indian arts website that it stayed "lying on the racks". Slowly audiences came to discover it, helped by

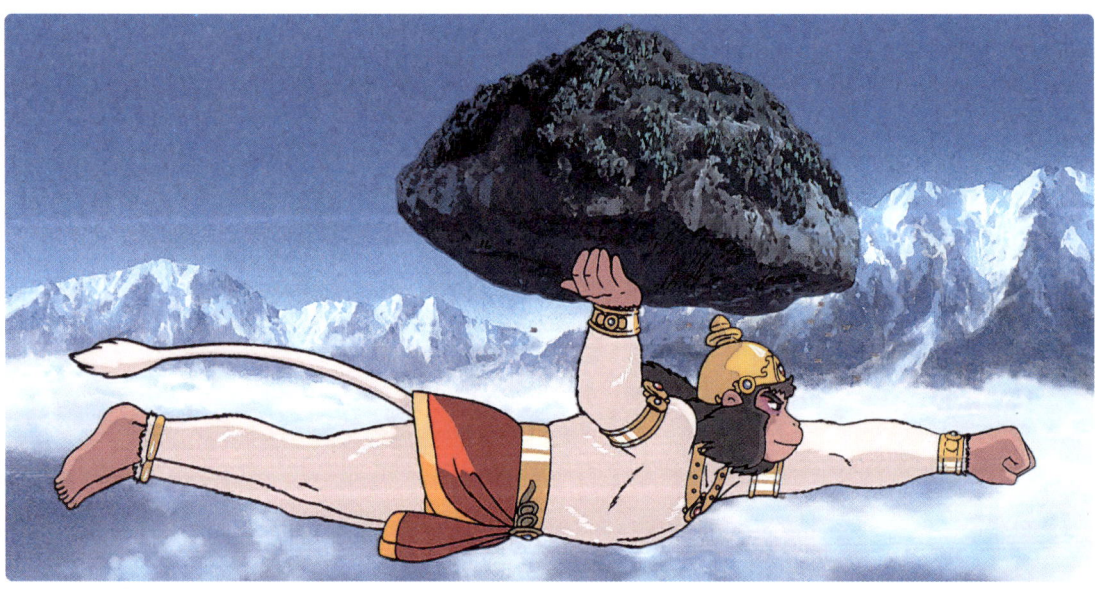

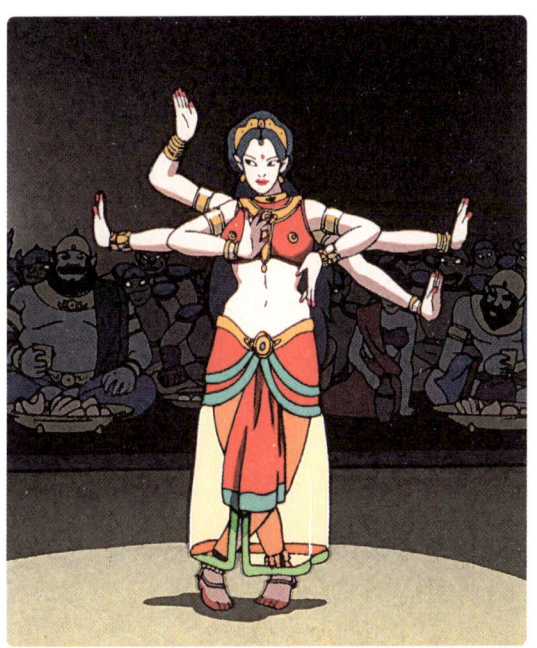

plays on Cartoon Network in the late '90s, and perhaps thanks also to an American recut and dubbed version called *The Prince of Light: The Legend of Ramayana* released in 2001 (featuring James Earl Jones and Bryan Cranston). It's in more recent years that *Ramayana's* following has really grown, with touring shows and film festival screenings reintroducing viewers to it, and a 4K restoration of the film being created. Eventually, in 2025, three decades after its failed first attempt – and with only Sasaki remaining from its core creative trio – *Ramayana* made a triumphant return to Indian cinemas, leaping off the racks to sell out screenings worldwide.

Opposite left: Bow before me. The evil demon king Ravana sets his target.

Opposite right: A moment of peace. Some of *Ramayana's* finest moments are the meditative beats it finds between action sequences.

Opposite below: Rock star. The super-powered Hanuman, a companion to Rama, is one of the film's standout characters.

Left: Transformative viewing. The form of animation is key to giving *Ramayana's* many bodily transformations their believability.

◉ Further Viewing

The story of the *Ramayana* was retold in 2010 in CG animation, to mixed reviews, as *Ramayana: The Epic.* Mainstream Indian animation hasn't yet experienced an international breakthrough and many of its pricier productions – such as the animal comedy *Roadside Romeo* (2008) and the Mahābhārata action epic *Arjun: the Warrior Prince* (2012), both backed by Disney – haven't made much of an impact back home, either. Faring much better is the independent filmmaker Gitanjali Rao, whose short films *Printed Rainbow* (2006) and *TrueLoveStory* (2014) were well received at Cannes. Her feature-length debut, *Bombay Rose* (2019), a sweeping, sumptuous, multifaceted romance set on the bustling streets of Mumbai, received high-profile premieres at the Venice and Toronto Film Festivals, ahead of worldwide distribution via Netflix.

Right: City Symphony. Gitanjali Rao's *Bombay Rose* is an urban romance that spans generations, anchored by its setting in India's biggest city.

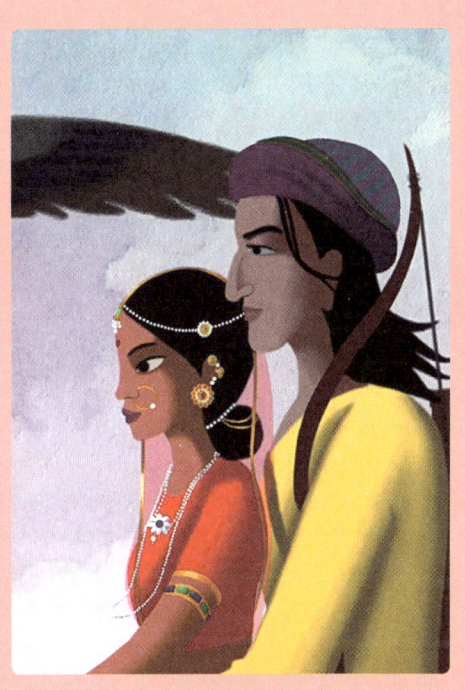

Japan

Asia's Animation Powerhouse

👤 Osamu Tezuka (1928–1989)

Like Walt Disney, Stan Lee or Shigeru Miyamoto, Osamu Tezuka stands as a figurehead at the forefront of an industry; but the tirelessly prolific "God of Manga" can be considered a major deity in the pantheon of Japanese animation, too.

Born in 1928, Tezuka was inspired as a youngster by the work of Disney (especially the 1942 feature *Bambi*) and China's Wan Brothers, but his earliest creative outlet was in comics: an art form he first pursued professionally as a teenager, and then came to dominate in the post-war period with popular manga series such as *New Treasure Island*, *Kimba the White Lion* and *Son Goku the Monkey*.

The latter series was a spin on the Chinese epic *Journey to the West* by Wu Cheng'en, and led to Tezuka's first taste of animation production, when he was brought on board for Toei Animation's fantasy feature *Saiyūki* (1960, also known as *Alakazam the Great*), which was loosely adapted from his manga. Nominally a co-director

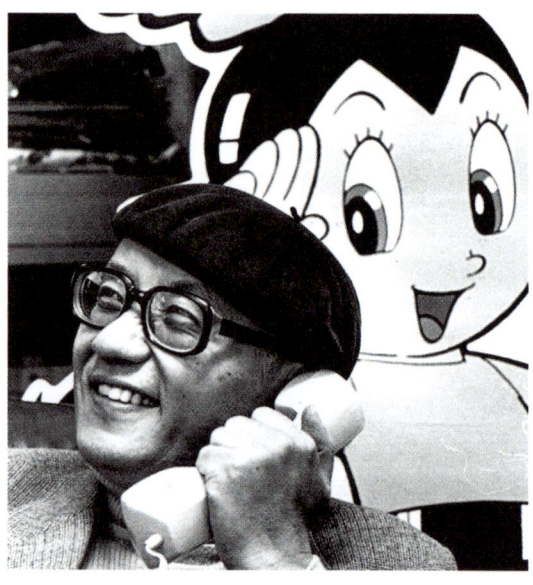

Right: Despite his sometimes controversial reputation, Osamu Tezuka was a fiercely productive and visionary pioneer in both manga and anime.

Opposite: Son of God. Tezuka's star creation, Astro Boy, was a groundbreaking global hit.

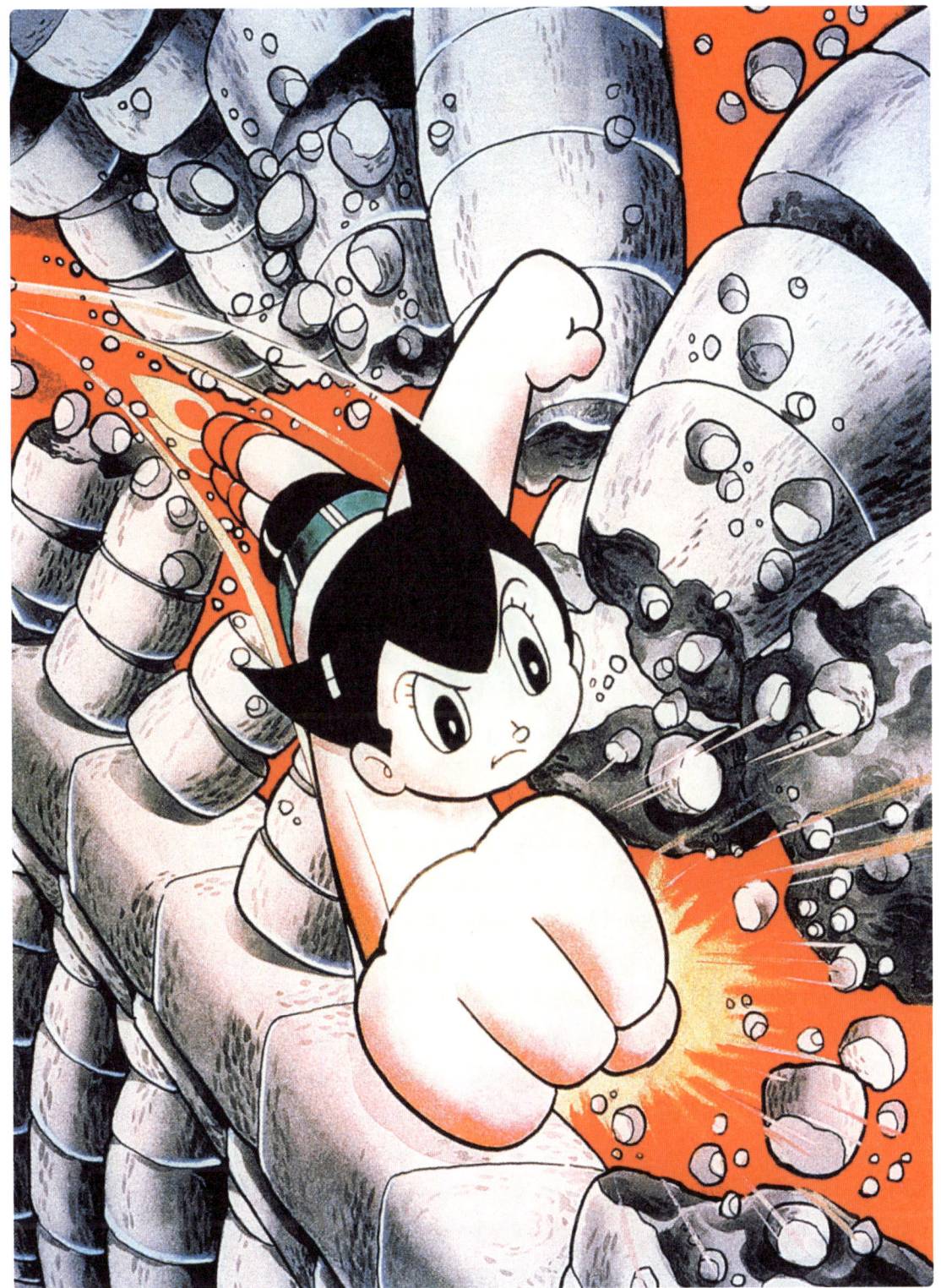

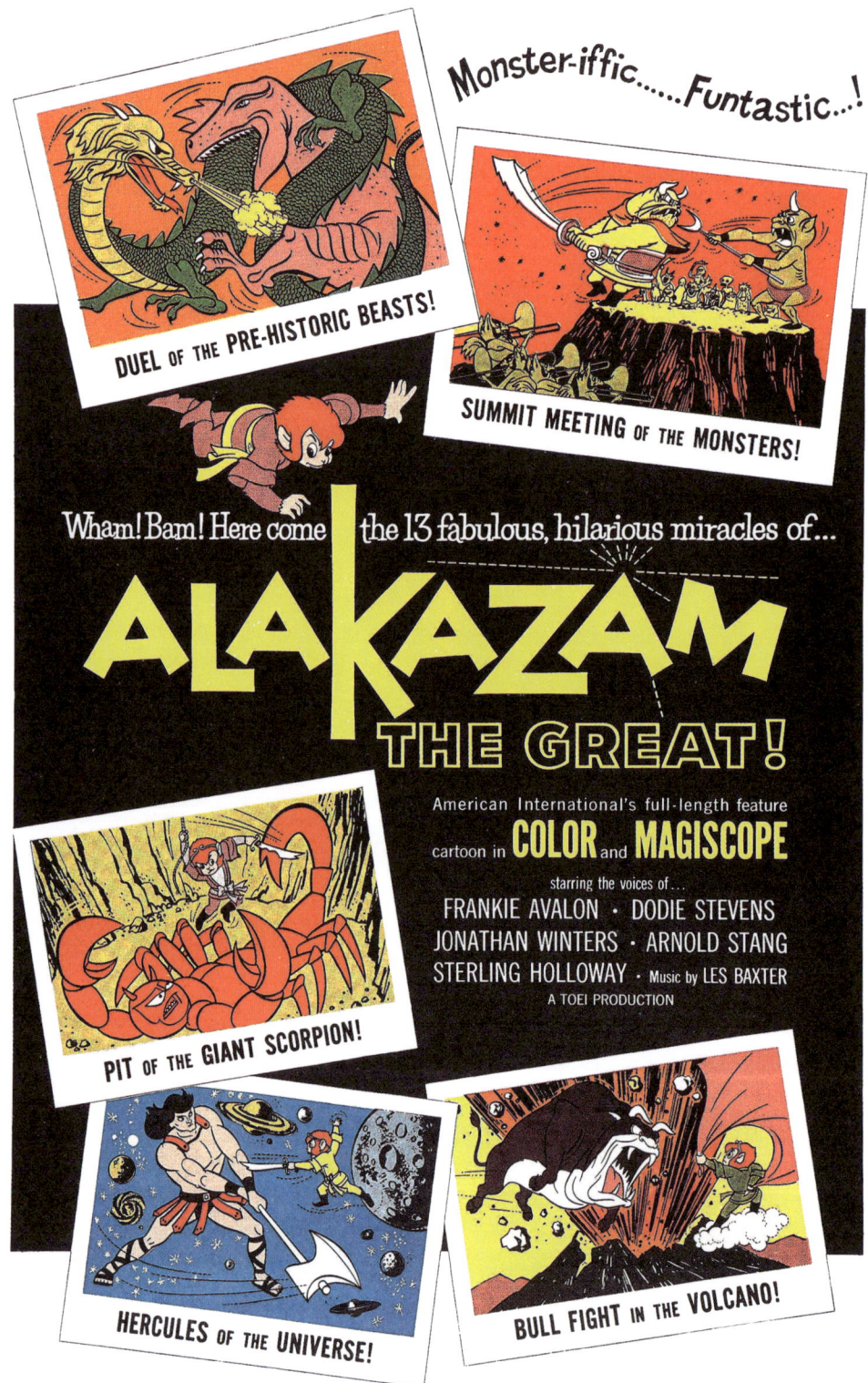

on the film alongside Daisaku Shirakawa and anime pioneer Taiji Yabushita (director of Japan's first full-colour animated feature, *Panda and the Magic Serpent*), Tezuka discovered that his role ultimately served more of a promotional purpose, but it sowed a seed that quickly sprouted.

In 1961 Tezuka founded his own studio, Mushi Production, with the ambition of creating animation in both artistic and commercial modes. The studio launched in 1962 with a slate of short works that acted as a statement of purpose: two innovative short films, *Osu* (often translated as *Male*) and *Tales of a Street Corner*, and the pilot episode for a series adaptation of Tezuka's sci-fi manga series *Astro Boy*.

Premiering on New Year's Day in 1963, *Astro Boy* is a historic series for many reasons, not least because it was Japan's first major anime series on television. It became Japan's first anime export, too, when it appeared on American screens later that year, with the title character becoming an international icon. *Astro Boy* also put into practice many aspects of what would come to define small-screen animation in Japan. Tezuka adopted a cost-saving "limited animation" technique for the series, cutting corners with fewer frames of movement per second, recycling certain drawings, and selectively animating only the essential elements of the frame like mouths and limbs. Furthermore, when negotiating with the network, Tezuka took a considerably lower budget than what was required, putting pressure on the production to recoup costs via sponsorship, merchandise and sales to other territories. This created a punishing precedent for the industry that has become known as "Tezuka's curse".

Tezuka's career as an animation mogul continued in a chaotic fashion. Several other television adaptations of his popular manga series followed in *Astro Boy*'s wake, but Mushi Production filed for bankruptcy in 1973. Tezuka had already jumped ship by then to form a new studio, Tezuka Productions, leaving his former staff to finish what is one of the studio's most enduring oddities: the minimalist, fully painted, psychedelic-erotic extravaganza *Belladonna of Sadness* (1973), the third part of Tezuka's ambitious *Animerama* series of more overtly adult-oriented animated features, following *A Thousand and One Nights* (1969) and *Cleopatra* (1970).

During its heyday, Mushi Production's output was phenomenally successful, but, ultimately, its production model was not commercially viable. However, many of the studio's staffers would go on to create innovative and impactful work of their own throughout the 1970s and '80s, including Yoshiyuki Tomino (creator of the *Gundam* franchise), Rintaro (*Galaxy Express 999*), Gisaburo Sugii (*Night on the Galactic Railroad*), and Eiichi Yamamoto (*Space Battleship Yamato*), as well as Masao Maruyama, Osamu Dezaki and Yoshiaki Kawajiri, who founded the legendary studio Madhouse.

Tezuka's reputation may be complicated by his shoddy business practices, but his consistent sideline in more "artistic" animation is worthy of note and reappraisal. While his storytelling has a tendency towards the simplistic and the didactic – you're never far from a bluntly pacifist, anti-fascist moral – these films show a creator who is fascinated by both the potential of the medium and the inner workings of the art form.

This is especially true in the 1980s, a full two decades after *Astro Boy*'s historic television debut. In these final years before his death in 1989, Tezuka still approached his experimental projects with imagination and flair, such as the puckish *Broken Down Film* (1985), a deceptively simple comic cowboy sketch, drawn in the style of a Fleischer Brothers toon, where the very wear and tear of an ancient, deteriorating film print almost becomes a character in the action itself. And then there's the ingenious *Jumping* (1984), a wild journey through the eyes of a child character as they leap progressively higher through landscapes that turn from rural to urban, industrial to war-torn, told in one consistent, visually dazzling shot.

Opposite: The feature *Saiyuki* was released in American cinemas under the English language title *Alakazam the Great*.

Below: After Tezuka left his own studio, his staff created a cult classic: the erotic art film, *Belladonna of Sadness*.

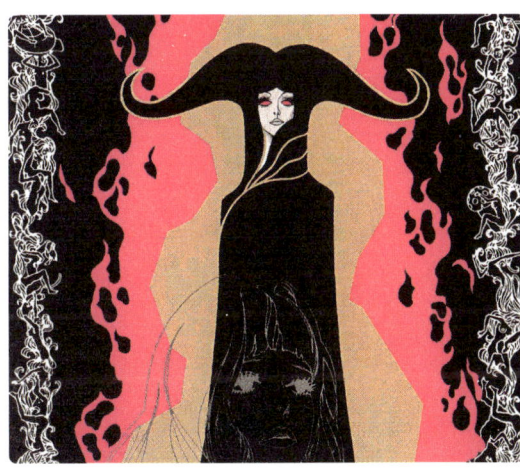

🎬 My Neighbour Totoro

Dir. Hayao Miyazaki
Release date: 1988

In April 1988 the legendary Japanese animation house Studio Ghibli released one of the most notorious double bills ever unleashed upon cinema audiences.

There is no right way to watch the pair of them. Do you begin with *Fireflies*, one of the most heart-wrenching but soulful wartime stories ever put to film, in the hope that *Totoro*'s lighter family adventure will mop your tears? Or do you start with the joyous and inventive modern fable for an oxytocin rush, only for the tragedy of suffering children to crash you back down? When the authors of this book spoke to some Japanese viewers of this diabolical pairing, they revealed that despite *Totoro*'s endless charms, the impact of Takahata's film was so great it made them never want to watch Miyazaki's film ever again. Don't make the same mistake. Ensure you leave plenty of space between screenings: the sheer pain of it may ensure you never watch *Grave of the Fireflies* again, but once you discover *Totoro*, you'll want to revisit it endlessly.

Like the films that would follow in *Spirited Away* (2001) and *The Boy and the Heron* (2023), Miyazaki's first true masterpiece begins with a family in transit, moving from the city out to the country. These are the Kusakabes: father Tatsuo, who has taken his eldest daughter Satsuki and his youngest Mei to the rural air to be closer to their mother Yasuko, who is ill and convalescing at a nearby hospital. Pitched next to an enormous camphor tree, the young siblings bounce and shriek through their dilapidated, and potentially haunted, new home, eventually discovering a collection of creatures in the nearby woodland – led by the oh so cute and oh so merchandisable King Totoro.

An uncategorizable medley of feline whiskers, grizzly fur and blue whale tongue, this enormous and sleepy being offers comfort, charm and escape to the Kusakabe family. He transports the family through dreamy encounters with buses shaped like cats, forests that grow in seconds and even brushes with parental mortality, all while tinkling away at a soothing ocarina that blows in step with the wind. His far-reaching, all-welcoming embrace is one that audiences felt too. Big-bellied,

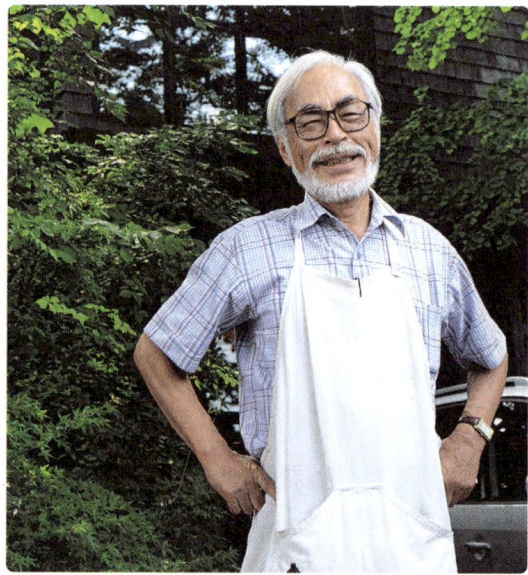

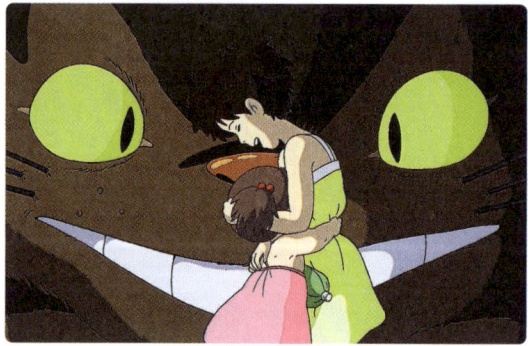

Above top: Rarely seen at the studio without his signature apron, notoriously grumpy Hayao Miyazaki offers a Totoro-sized smile.

Above: Grin and bus it. The loveable and frightening Catbus reveals its Cheshire Cat smile.

Opposite above: Toto-Go! Mei pursues the smaller Totoros through the undergrowth.

Opposite below: Accompanying Mei and Satsuki, umbrella in hand, Totoro is prepared for any conditions.

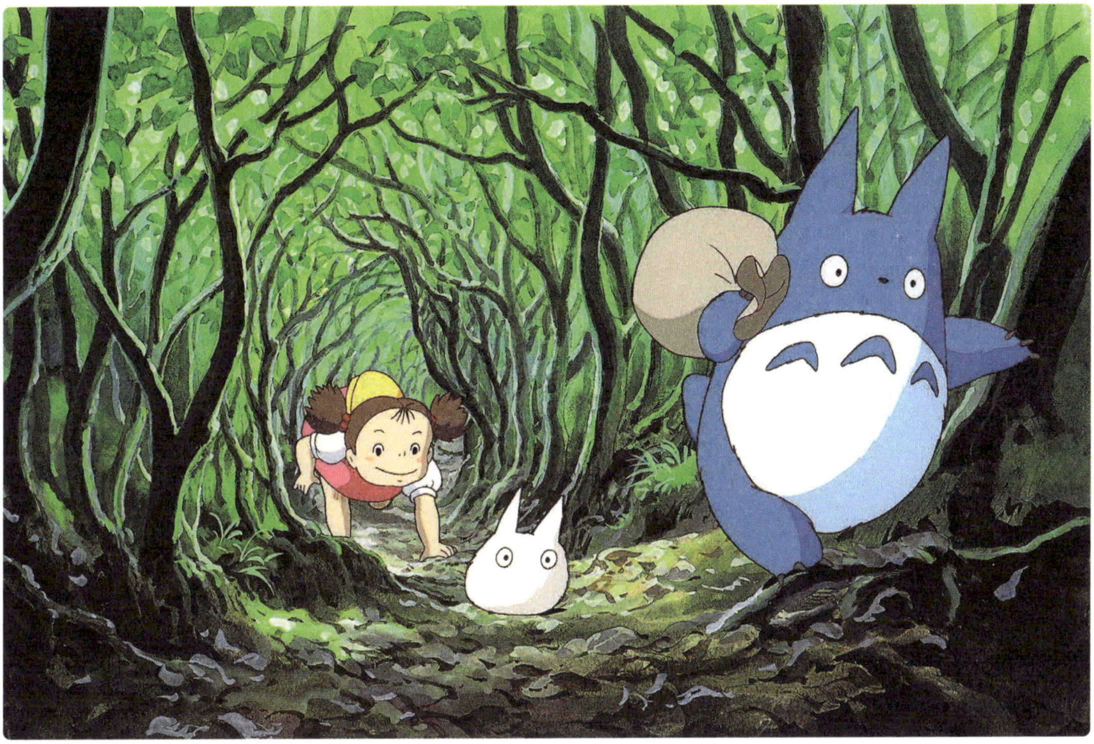

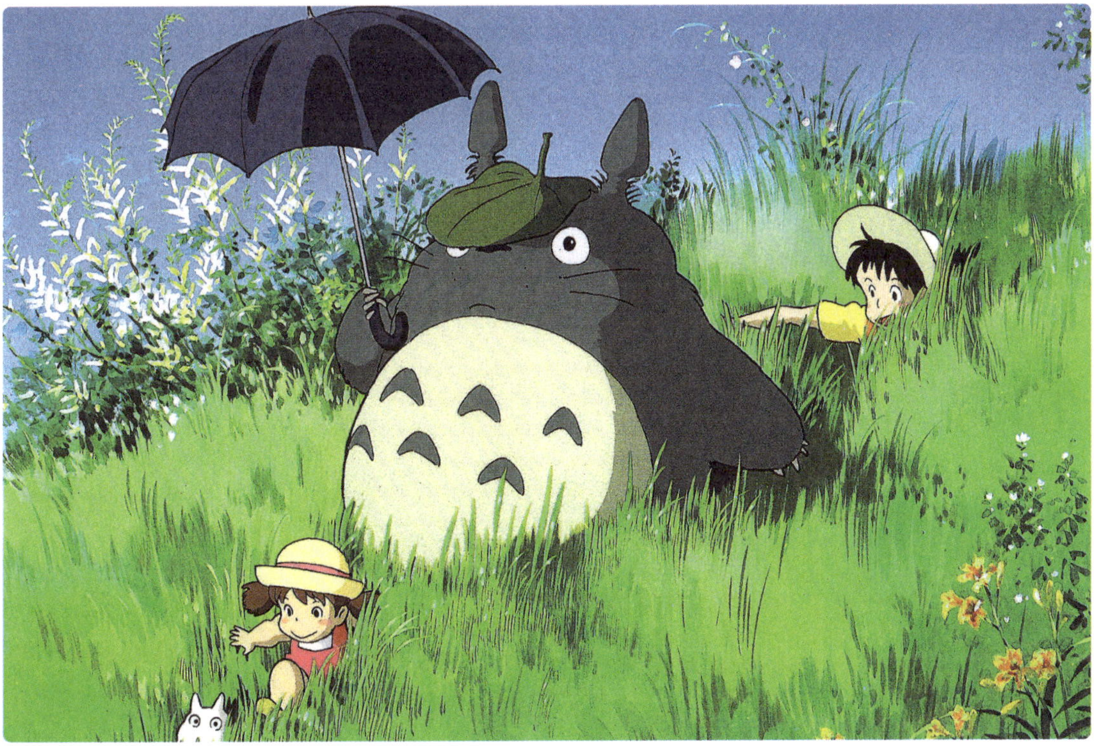

pointy-eared and roundly snouted, the silhouette of Totoro marked an expert piece of character design, and became a studio icon: his outline was quickly adopted as Ghibli's logo, appearing in front of all of their films and becoming a fixture of Ghibli's memorabilia, helping to turn a disastrous double bill into a long-term success.

Since the release of the film, the power of the story seems to be unstoppable. Having made a cameo in *Toy Story 3* (2010) – as well as references to him appearing in the *X-Men* comics, *Samurai Jack* and *Bob's Burgers* among many other pop culture tributes – Totoro's star has continued to rise, with notebooks, backpacks and badges adorned with him selling across the globe. An acclaimed London-based stage adaptation of the film eventually premiered in 2022, followed by continuing season-long sell-out runs and awards.

It's now been almost four decades since *Totoro* debuted, but what's the secret to its longevity? It's light in plot, but rich in openly interpretable emotion, and its continued popularity can perhaps be attributed to this, as the universal Totoro can mean anything to any viewer. In one drizzly scene Satsuki says to Mei: "Daddy's forgotten his umbrella?" and instead of any debate between the sisters about a plan to return the item to their father, Mei quickly responds: "I'm going too." It's a minor interaction, but it shows the understanding and harmony between the siblings, revealing their intuitive closeness. The entire film is built around similar gaps in dialogue, explanation and logic; whether that might be Yasuko's illness, a dance routine based on agriculture or Totoro's flying skills, nothing is explained and nothing needs to be. After making *Nausicaä* and *Laputa*, and looking at the wider industry's similarly fantastical and otherworldly output, Miyazaki began to lament "animation films that avoid depicting Japan", so he wanted to make something that felt closer to home. To his surprise and to the delight of millions of fans, it was this intimate, local approach that eventually connected with the entire world.

Right: Bearing gifts. This scene, with the girls and Totoro huddled at a bus stop during a downpour, is one of the most recognizable in animated cinema.

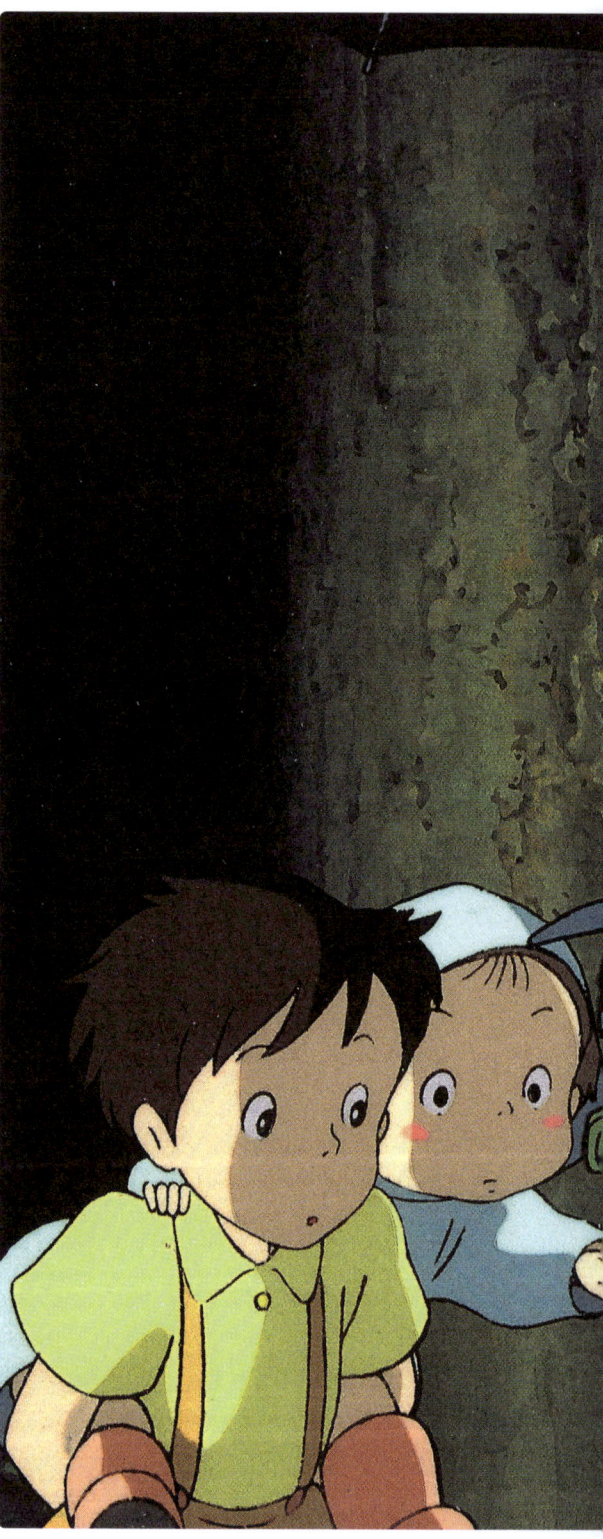

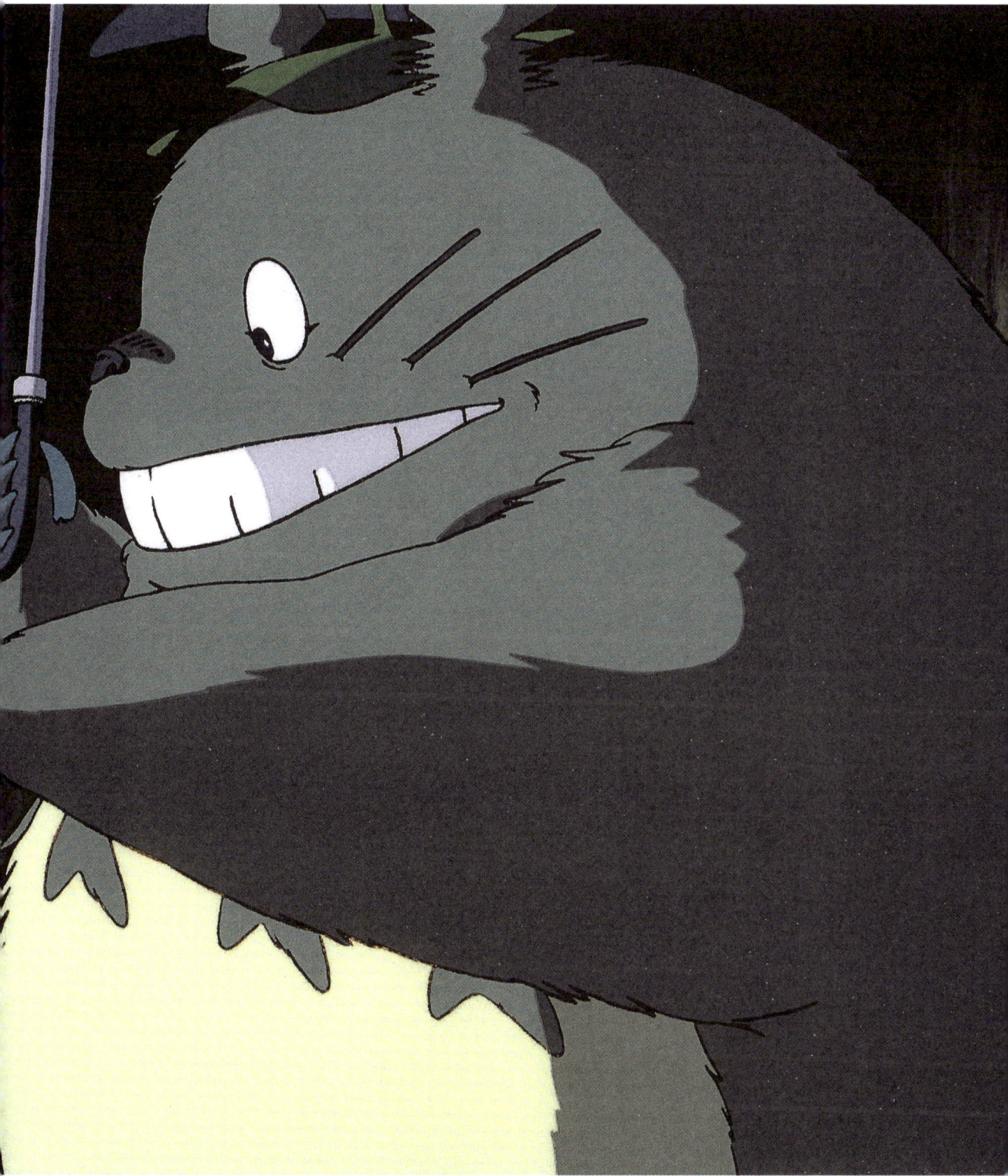

👤 Kōji Yamamura (born 1964)

When it comes to Japanese animation, the mainstream commercial industry known as "anime" tends to hog the limelight. Outside of that system, though, there have always been scores of accomplished animators creating works in their own distinctive styles and exhibiting their work at festivals to great acclaim.

Kōji Yamamura is one of the leading filmmakers working in this more independent, experimental space, and he came to a new level of international attention when his ten-minute short film *Mt. Head* (2002) was nominated for Best Animated Short at the same Academy Awards ceremony where Hayao Miyazaki's *Spirited Away* (2001) picked up Best Animated Feature. That night, the Oscar went to the Sony-produced CG short *The ChubbChubbs!* (2002), but *Mt. Head* proved to be a pivotal film, not just for Japanese animation but for Yamamura himself.

Self-funded and designed and animated by Yamamura himself over a period of six years, *Mt. Head* acts as the perfect entry point into the director's weird and wonderful body of work, which encompasses shorts, commercials, music videos, picture books, children's TV series and even a feature film, *Dozens of Norths* (2021). Drawing inspiration from a work in the *rakugo* tradition

of Japanese theatrical storytelling, *Mt. Head* is a tall tale equal parts comic and surreal, in which a miserly loner finds a sprout growing from the centre of his bald head. Attempts to prune the shoot prove fruitless – and then it starts to attract unwanted attention from neighbours and fellow commuters.

Effortlessly treading the line between the darkly humorous and vaguely unsettling, *Mt. Head* is never less than completely captivating, even when it takes its more outlandish turns. Yamamura's approach to animation is visually vibrant, constantly moving and shifting with every frame: his grotesque characters dance and warp with each move of the camera, and each flourish of the artist's hand. You expect the unexpected, and all givens are thrown out of the window, such as when a gaggle

Below: Art Animation. Koji Yamamura visits a decades-spanning exhibition of his artwork in a gallery in Liberec, Czechia.

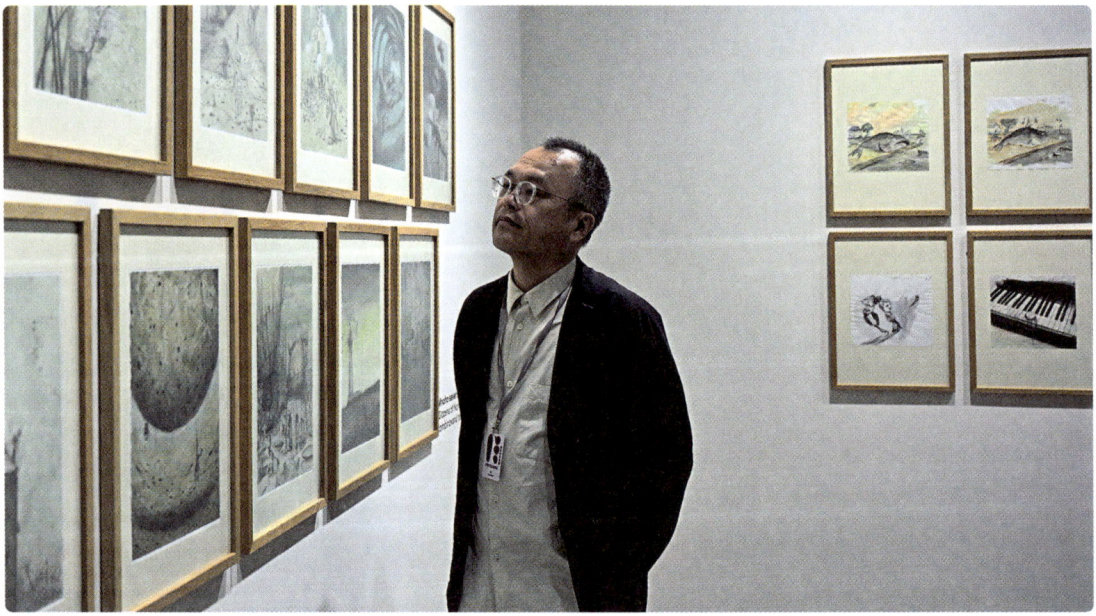

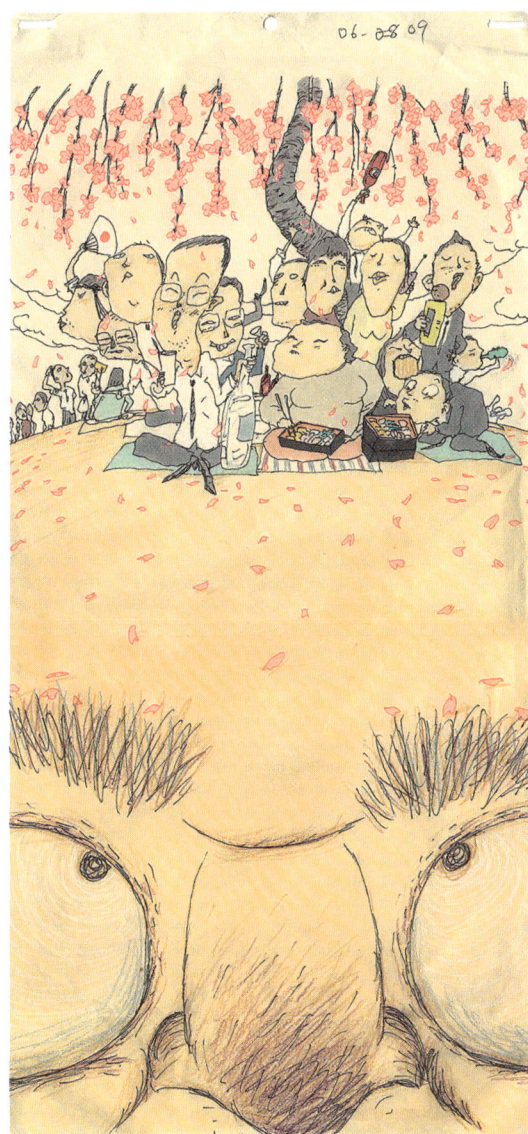

06-28 09

Left: Head Boy. In this original pencil drawing from the film, the protagonist of *Mt. Head* strains to see what's growing up there.

Below: Scissor Cut. At first, he tries to trim the plant to stop its growth...

Below middle: Fête on the Pate. Soon, the tree grows back with a vengeance, and groups of tiny people start to gather around it for raucous picnics.

Bottom: Man Hole. Plucked out like a weed, the tree leaves a strange, small cavity in the man's head.

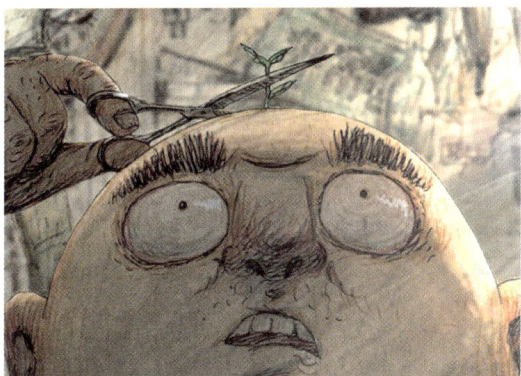

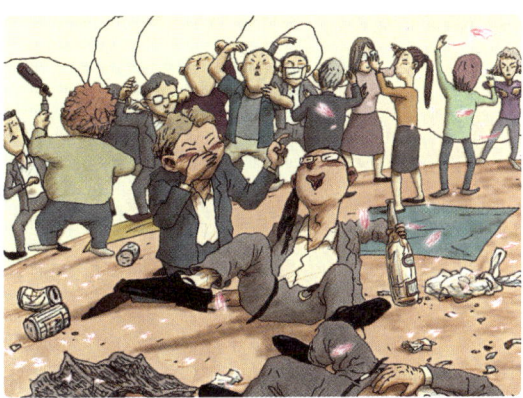

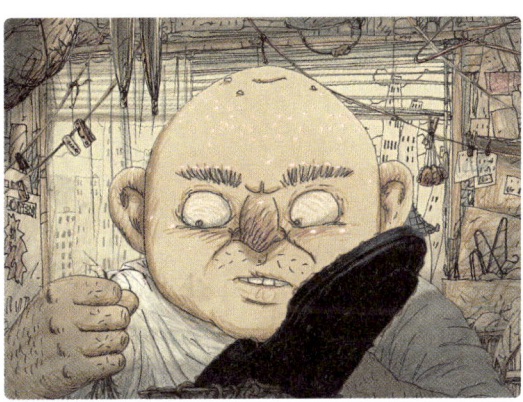

of boozy office workers are revealed to be partying, in miniature, on the man's head, in the shadow of his now-blooming cranial tree. They litter, cavort and defile their surroundings, all while the man himself is trying to stick to his humble daily routine and chow down on his instant ramen. In a moment that defies all sense of scale, a shoe tossed by a sozzled salaryman lands, life-size, in his Cup Noodle pot.

Mt. Head's most striking sequence is saved for last. After the man pulls the tree, root and all, from his head, a small pool grows in the hole left behind, which becomes

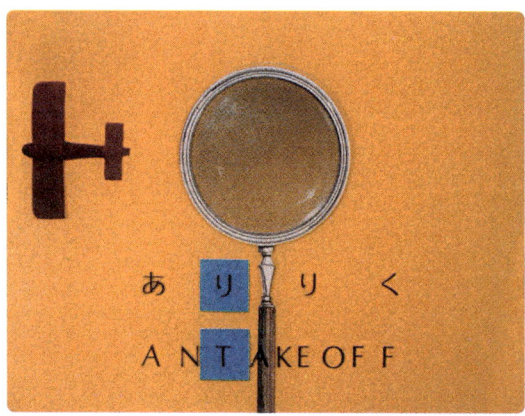

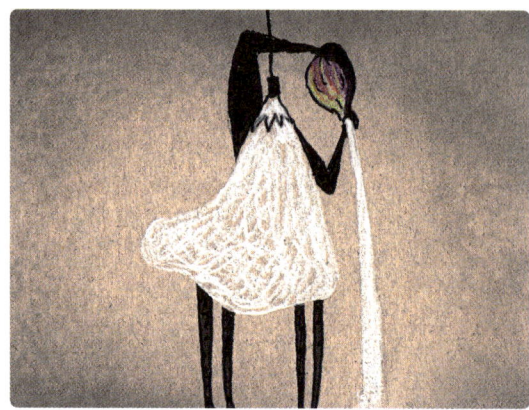

a whole new attraction for small-scale sojourners. At his wits' end, he races through the city at night, happening upon a pond, or a stream, where he gazes at his own reflection – and is consumed, quite literally, by the hole. The film becomes a roller coaster, or a perpetual motion machine, as the dizzying cycle of reflection and consumption repeats, over and over. "Finally, the man threw himself into his own head pond," the playful narrator explains. "And he died." The ultimate head trip film, *Mt. Head* might leave you scratching yours. Its bundle of themes runs the gamut from the destruction of the environment to the paradox of the big city: where you're alone in a crowd, anonymous until recognized.

Yamamura's films can often enthral on a deeper level, while remaining utterly elusive. You follow the flow of the images, like in *Fig* (2006), which bends and twists the Tokyo skyline into a procession of uncanny characters and visual associations. The same is true in earlier phases of his career, too, such as in the acrobatic mixed-media wordplay game *Japanese-English Pictionary* (1989), which passes the baton both visually and verbally between words that end and then start with the same syllable in Japanese (or letter in English): "triangle... eat... turtle... eye... eyeball...". Or in the strange and sinister *Your Choice!* (1999), a collaboration with "junior directors" from children's workshops in Japan and America, in which a cast of wonkily designed characters face increasingly bizarre dilemmas.

Elsewhere, Yamamura turns to literary, theatrical and historical sources to provide foundations for his animated odysseys, such as the dark and ominous folktale *The Old Crocodile* (2005), the nightmarish *Franz Kafka's A Country Doctor* (2007), and the ultimately quite poignant *Muybridge's Strings* (2011), which uses the life and work of the motion-picture pioneer

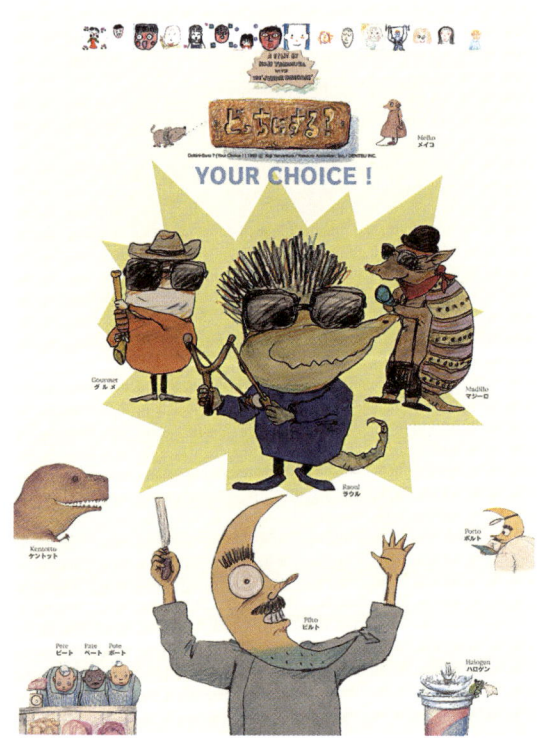

Above left: Word Play. *Japanese-English Pictionary* is a feat of language as well as animation.

Above right: Pore Over. The playful and inventive *Fig* is filled with visual puns and wildly imaginative, associative animation.

Right: While his films tend to be surreal and strange, Kōji Yamamura has also created many offbeat works for and with children, such as *Your Choice!*

Eadweard Muybridge to weave a meditation on the forward march of time, and one man's desire to use still photography to master it. But throughout, there's always the thrill of animation as a playground for expression, experimentation and imagination. In these films, our eyes are opened to a spirit of independence, invention and creativity that can only lie outside of the mainstream of Japanese animation.

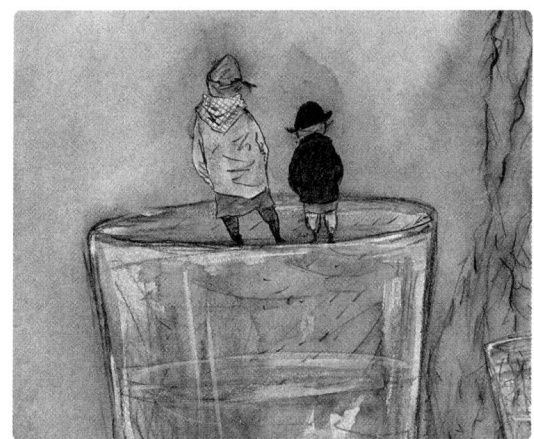

Right: Long Form. After decades of making short films, Yamamura finally created the feature-length *Dozens of Norths* in 2021.

Below: Junk Modelling. The idiosyncratic, crowdfunded stop-motion sci-fi *Junk Head* subverted all expectations for Japanese animation.

👁 Further Viewing

This chapter was a tough one. The three picks we landed on reflect some of the diversity and breadth that you'll find in Japanese animation, but they barely scratch the surface. Dig deeper, and there is so much to discover, in a dazzling array of styles that lie beyond the anime model. Start with the pioneering and eclectic work of Noburō Ōfuji, whose work ranged from live-action/animation hybrid experiments (*A Story of Tobacco*, 1926) to haunting cut-out epics (*The Phantom Ship*, 1956), then follow the careers of Kihachirō Kawamoto (*The Demon*, 1972) and Tadanari Okamoto (*The Magic Ballad*, 1982), masters of stop-motion puppetry. Independent filmmaking persists today in the work of animators such as Mirai Mizue (*Wonder*, 2014) and Takehide Hori, the self-taught fan turned filmmaker who impressed the international community with his spectacular and strange stop-motion sci-fi feature, *Junk Head* (2021).

And then there's anime, a world full to the brim with creativity and expression, from bold visionaries such as Katsuhiro Otomo (*Akira*, 1988), Mamoru Oshii (*Ghost in the Shell*, 1995) and Satoshi Kon (*Paprika*, 2006) to virtuosic stylists such as Osamu Dezaki (*Tomorrow's Joe*), Yoshiaki Kawajiri (*Ninja Scroll*, 1993) and Masaaki Yuasa (*The Night Is Short, Walk on Girl*, 2017), to rising stars such as

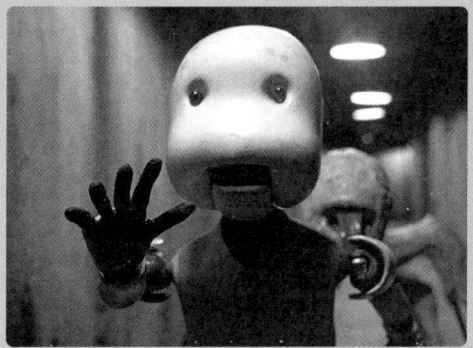

Naoko Yamada (*Liz and the Blue Bird*, 2018) and Mari Okada (*Maquia: When the Promised Flower Blooms*, 2018).

Before we embarked on this round-the-world trip for the *Animation Atlas*, we delved into this vibrant corner of animation history in our *Anime Movie Guide*, showcasing 30 films and filmmakers from the groundbreaking Disney-style fantasy *Panda and the Magic Serpent* (1958) to Makoto Shinkai's box-office smash *Your Name* (2016). Where *My Neighbour Totoro* and the films of Studio Ghibli are concerned, we covered their entire output in our books *Ghibliotheque: The Unofficial Guide to the Films of Studio Ghibli* and *Ghibliverse: Studio Ghibli Beyond the Movies*.

Korea

A Royally Disturbing Coming of Rage

🎥 The King of Pigs

Director: Yeon Sang-ho
Released: 2016

If the name of director Yeon Sang-ho sounds familiar, it might be because you've seen his 2016 first-class zombie hit *Train to Busan*, maybe its (slightly disappointing) 2020 sequel *Peninsula* or even his 2023 big-budget Netflix effort *Jung_E*. But, before those live action blockbuster efforts, Yeon made animated films, with his feature debut, *The King of Pigs*, being unleashed from its grippingly gnarled and noisome pen in 2011.

Having spent the late '90s and '00s making animated shorts, gradually receiving more acclaim from international film festivals, Yeon rifled through his school memories for his first feature. Initially, it's not exactly child's play. The film opens with the shocking sight of a strangled woman's corpse, before resting on the murderer – the woman's husband and the film's co-leading protagonist, Kyung-min. He eventually reunites with his old school friend, the pathetic, violent ghostwriter Jong-suk, to reminisce (for the bulk of the film) about their experiences of adolescent bullying. Awkward, poor outsiders, they see themselves as pigs, while the polo-wearing, brown-nosing boys across the class hunt

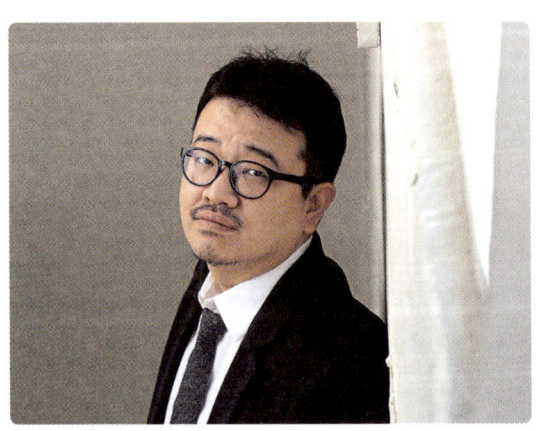

them like dogs. It's only with the emergence of uprising vigilante Chul, who soon ascends to the titular porcine crown, that the societal food chain gets chewed at.

Yeon cites Hayao Miyazaki and Satoshi Kon as two of his biggest inspirations. While it might be a challenge to see much of the former's adventurous, environmentalist spirit in *The King of Pigs*, the latter's more psychological, unsettling works can clearly be traced. Kon's TV series *Paranoia Agent* (2004), and its escalating, unflinching violence and murky morality built around a youthful setting is certainly visible here; but more obviously, Yeon's therianthropic character designs make beastly desires skin-deep, something Kon similarly deployed with a minotaur-headed stalker in his modern classic *Perfect Blue* (1997). Unfortunately, while his designs are instantly perturbing, the weight of their appearance is regretfully undone by, well, weightlessness. Operating at a low budget, Yeon maintains a lot of the film in static mid-shots and close-ups, meaning fewer full bodies

Opposite: The king of *The King of Pigs*, director Yeon Sang-ho.

Right: Shattered class. Yeon Sang-ho's film is a sharp analysis of societal class, as well as the classroom.

Below: Snout of place. Not since *Animal Farm* have animated pigs been as unsettling as they are here.

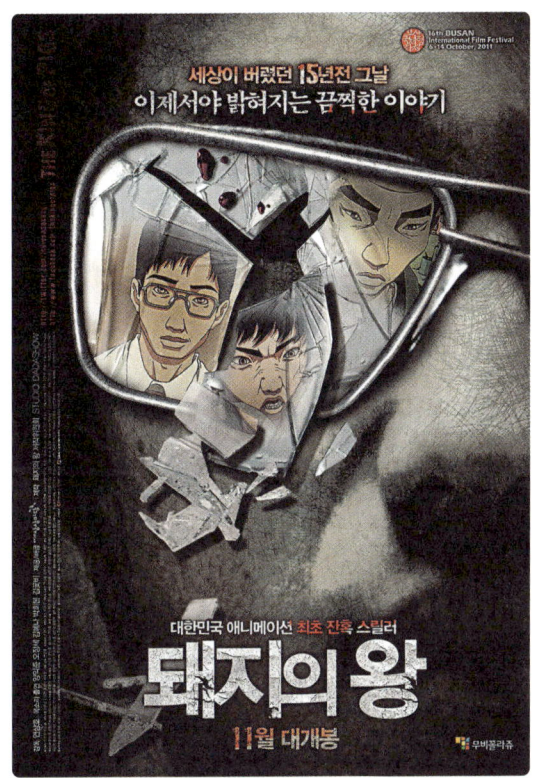

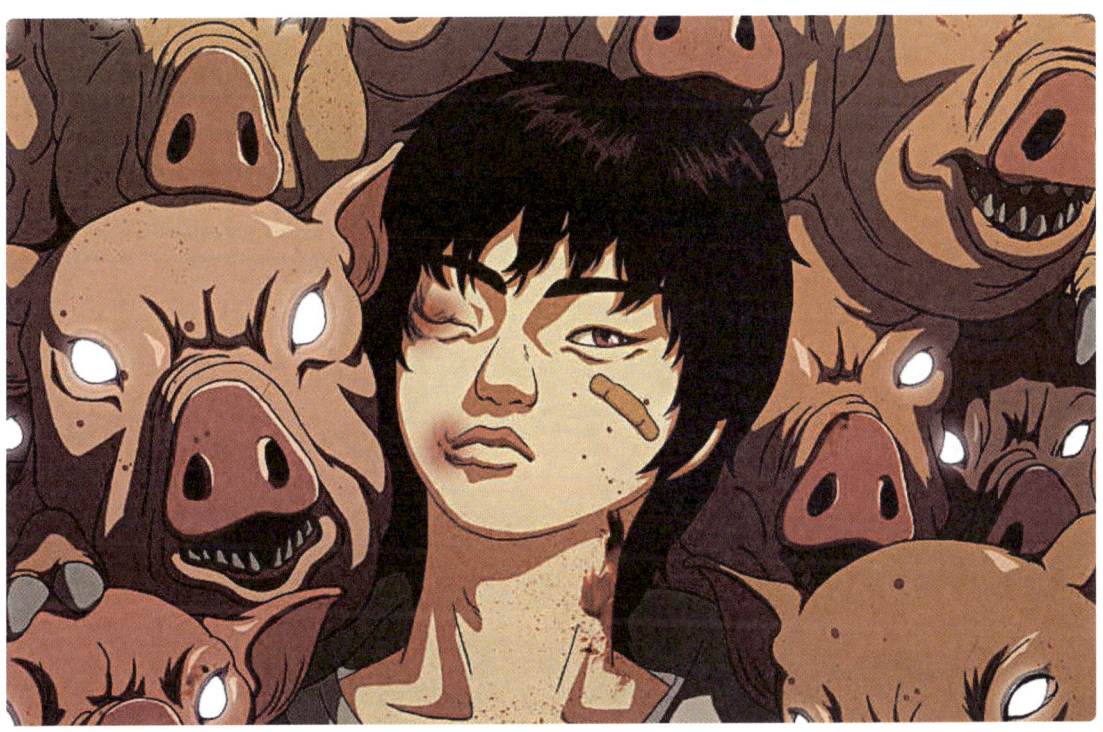

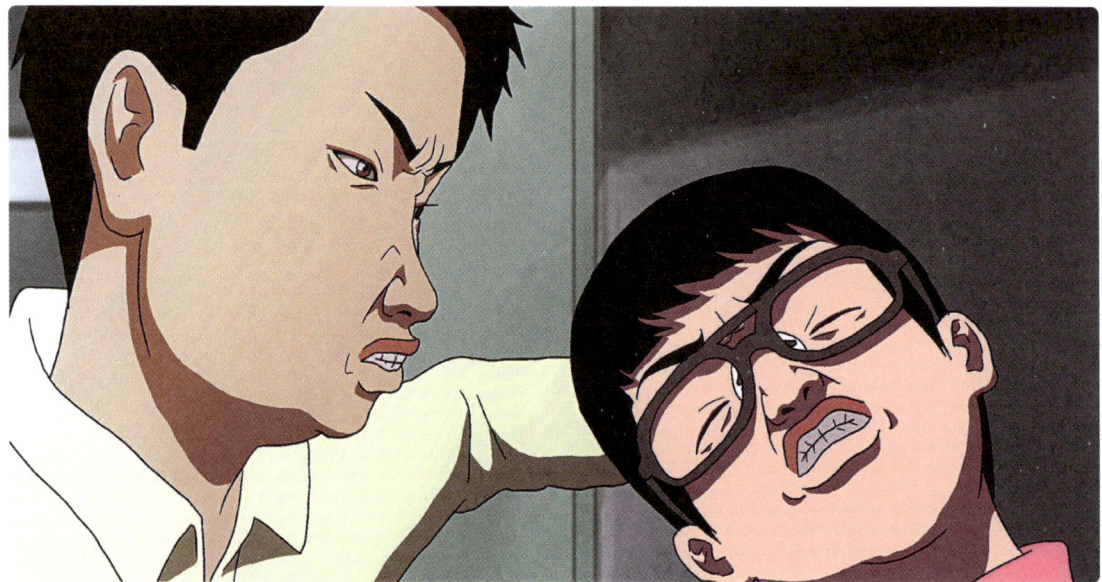

to animate. But, when movement around the school is required, figures move with an awkward lightness and jagged movement, like NPC characters in a video game searching for a mission.

Much like *Train to Busan*, class warfare (excuse the pun) gradually consumes the school and the characters (Yeon himself makes a cameo as one of many forgotten students placed in the backgrounds), with materialism, money, status and structure all weaving between home, school,

private and public. While the acts of Kyung-min, Jong-suk and Chul escalate in troubling, unjustifiable fashion, Yeon carefully details the societal and domestic issues that can cause such continued, cyclical violence. The boys

Above: Stuck pigs. In *The King of Pigs* acts of violence escalate to the point where there's no escape.

Below: Pig-headed. Chul, the leader of the film's outsider revolution, who here has been beaten, and at other times appears with a pig-like head.

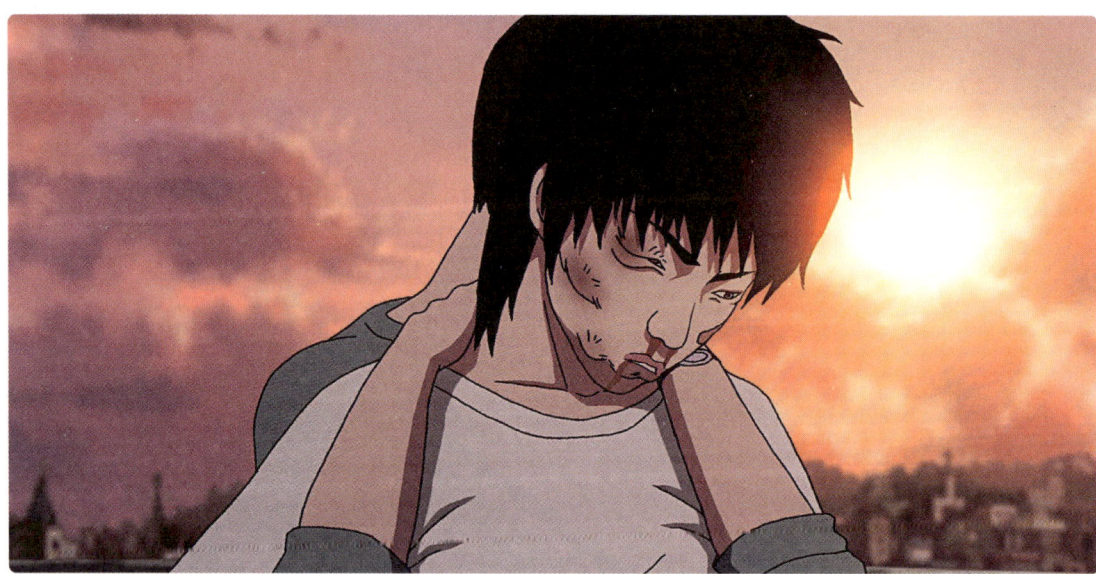

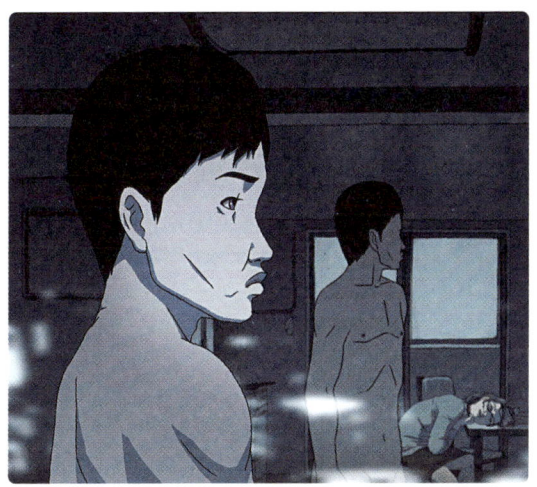

are victims and villains and the dark heart of a fiercely fascinating story – one that became the first South Korean animated film to appear at the Cannes Film Festival.

After *The Kings of Pigs*, Yeon continued in animation, with religious drama *The Fake* in 2013, as well as 2016 animated *Train to Busan* prequel *Seoul Station*. However, *The King of Pigs* (which had a 2022 live action remake, going the whole hog and splitting the drama into 12 episodes) will always be the first stop on his feature film journey, and is still the most thought-provoking. All hail!

Left: Although at times hard to look at, *The King of Pigs* is a valuable and grizzly reflection of society.

Below: Mecha Bongzilla. A Korean spin on the anime franchise *Mazinger Z*, *Robot Taekwon V* inspired one of the country's great directors: Bong Joon-ho.

◉ Further Viewing

Unlike the phenomenally popular worlds of K-Drama, K-Pop and K-Cinema, Korean animation has not yet had its international breakthrough moment – at least, not in the English-speaking world. That's not to say it's an underdeveloped industry: wind back the clock and search through the Korean Film Archive's animation-only YouTube channel and you'll find noteworthy feature-length adventures (*A Story of Hong Gil-dong*, 1967) and stop-motion puppet fairy tales (*Kongjwi and Patjwi*, 1978). It's not a matter of talent, either: for decades, studios in America, Japan and Europe have outsourced work to Korean teams when their productions have been in a pinch. Features such as *My Beautiful Girl, Mari* (2002) and *Oseam* (2003) have picked up top prizes at the Annecy International Animation Film Festival, and there are young filmmakers today producing distinctive work that tours the festival circuit, such as Nari Jang (*My Father's Room*, 2017), Lee Jong-hoon (*The Starry Night*, 2017) and Han Ji-won (*The Summer*, 2023). Things might change in the near future, though. Director Bong Joon-ho, Korea's most successful filmmaker on the international stage, has always been vocal about his love of animation, citing the Korean mecha anime *Robot Taekwon V* (1976)

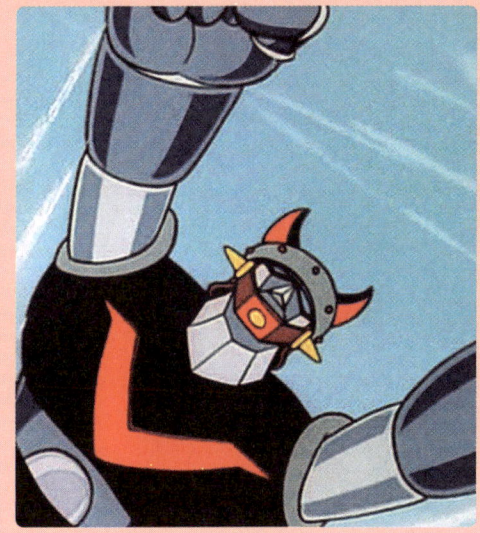

as a film that had a huge impact on him when he was a young cinemagoer. And in 2024, he put his money where his mouth is, bringing investment back to Korea to mount the country's most ambitious animated project yet – a CG feature that he will direct himself, with international distribution reportedly secured. Has Korean animation's time come?

Pakistan

The Young Ones

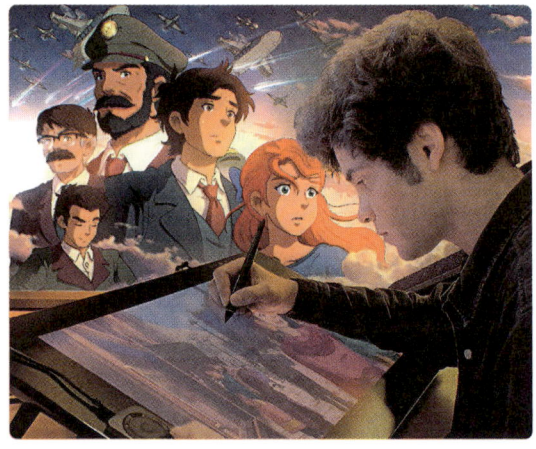 The Glassworker

Director: Usman Riaz
Released: 2024

Every film is a miracle. A perfect storm of imagination, craft and talent
– plus a bit of luck and a barrel load of cash. But some films are more
miraculous than others, and *The Glassworker* is one of them: a project
undertaken by young friends passionate about animation, which
resulted in Pakistan's first hand-drawn animated feature film.

Director Usman Riaz, a phenomenally industrious
young man based in Karachi, Pakistan, was already
a prodigiously talented musician, Berklee College
graduate and TED Fellow before he decided to
undertake a decade-long project to bring *The
Glassworker* to the screen. Along for the journey were his
wife, Mariam Riaz Paracha, and cousin, Khizer Riaz, as
they founded their company, Mano Animation Studios,
built connections, pulled off a successful Kickstarter
campaign, and crewed up the project in a country with
no prior infrastructure for creating animation in this style
or at this scale.

Youthful passion drives *The Glassworker*. It tells the
story of Vincent and Alliz, youngsters in love united by

their creative obsessions: Vincent, a budding blower of glass artefacts, and Alliz, a promising violinist. But their romantic idyll is thrown into jeopardy when war arrives on their doorstep, and their town is swarmed by the military. The deep influence drawn from the films of Hayao Miyazaki is unmistakable: the dreams of young people, the joy of craft and expression, the spectre of war and mistrust of military might.

By his own admission, Riaz wears his inspirations on his sleeve. There's a strong impression of *The Wind Rises* (2013), Miyazaki's musing on creativity and the machinery of war, when Vincent and his father are pressured to provide glass bulbs for the war effort to help power gigantic, Steampunk-style amphibian airships. The art of glass blowing and moulding is initially framed as pure magic, with sand being turned into shimmering, gleaming baubles that refract light into beams of colour; but its purity is blackened by harsh, pragmatic reality.

Even the pan-European architecture of Waterfront Town will seem familiar to fans of *Kiki's Delivery Service* (1989) or *Howl's Moving Castle* (2004), but Riaz often uses these touchstones to his own ends. For example, look at the scene of Vincent and Alliz tumbling on green, grassy hills and beaming up at the sky – until airships start to block out the blue horizons. Vincent, the son of a fierce pacifist, fears the encroaching fleet; Alliz, the daughter of a colonel, waves to greet them.

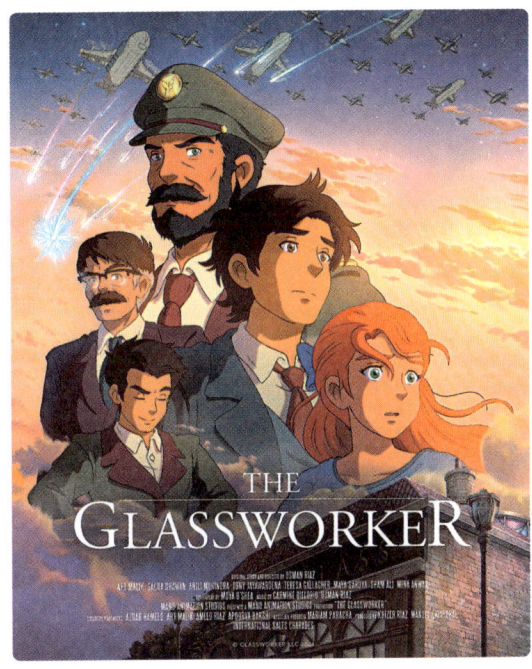

Opposite: Fellow kid. Director Usman Riaz spent ten years realising his dream of making a feature-length animation in Pakistan.

Above: The poster for *The Glassworker*, complete with its cast of characters that bear the undeniable influence of Studio Ghibli.

Below: Mano Made. This production artwork showcases Mano Animation Studio's commitment to the tradition of hand-drawn animation.

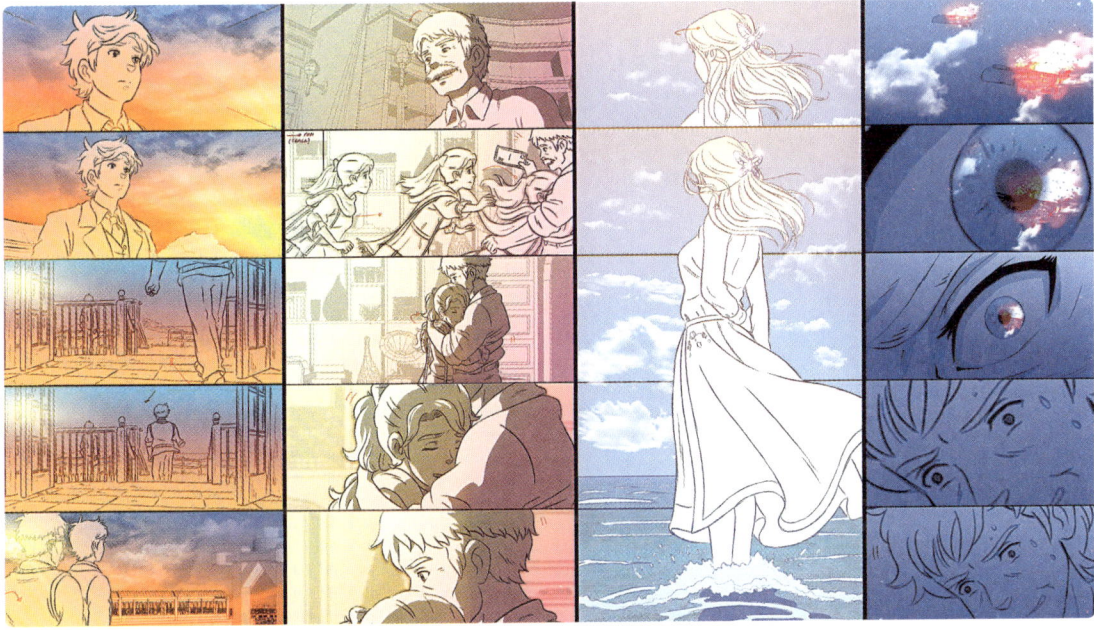

Elsewhere, there are textures that tie the film directly to its origins in Pakistan: food stalls selling gulab jamun, characters drinking chai and playing games of carrom, and the mystical presence of djinn spirits from Pakistani folklore. Dig deeper, and there's an undeniably personal thread running throughout: one of living, loving and creating in a region subject to the jostling of military powers. "Without art and music," Alliz wonders, "what do we have in this world full of conflict and war?"

Riaz also points to the influence of Makoto Shinkai's stories of young people striving against the odds, such as *Voices of a Distant Star* (2002) and *The Place Promised in Our Early Days* (2004), and it's hard not to see that struggle reflected in the production itself. Riaz himself acted as co-writer and co-composer, in addition to drawing the film's meticulous storyboards. Paracha is credited as art director, assistant director, associate producer and background artist. Another husband and wife, Sofia Abdullah and Aamir Riffat, served as character designer and lead animator respectively. At *The Glassworker's* premiere in Annecy, Riaz revealed that the average age of the animation team was 25. At the time, the director himself was only 33.

Their triumph in producing this miracle of a film is as endearing as it is impressive. "Everyone loves watching animation," Riaz told Claire Knight of the Animation Obsessive newsletter. "Making animation is a whole other story. That we found out the hard way." Here's hoping more studios and aspiring filmmakers follow their lead.

Opposite: Beautiful, Cursed Dreams. Vincent's father, a humble glass blower, becomes coerced into aiding the war effort.

Below: Local Markets. *The Glassworker* adapts a familiar anime style to suit a Pakistani worldview: complete with local food, flavours and fashions.

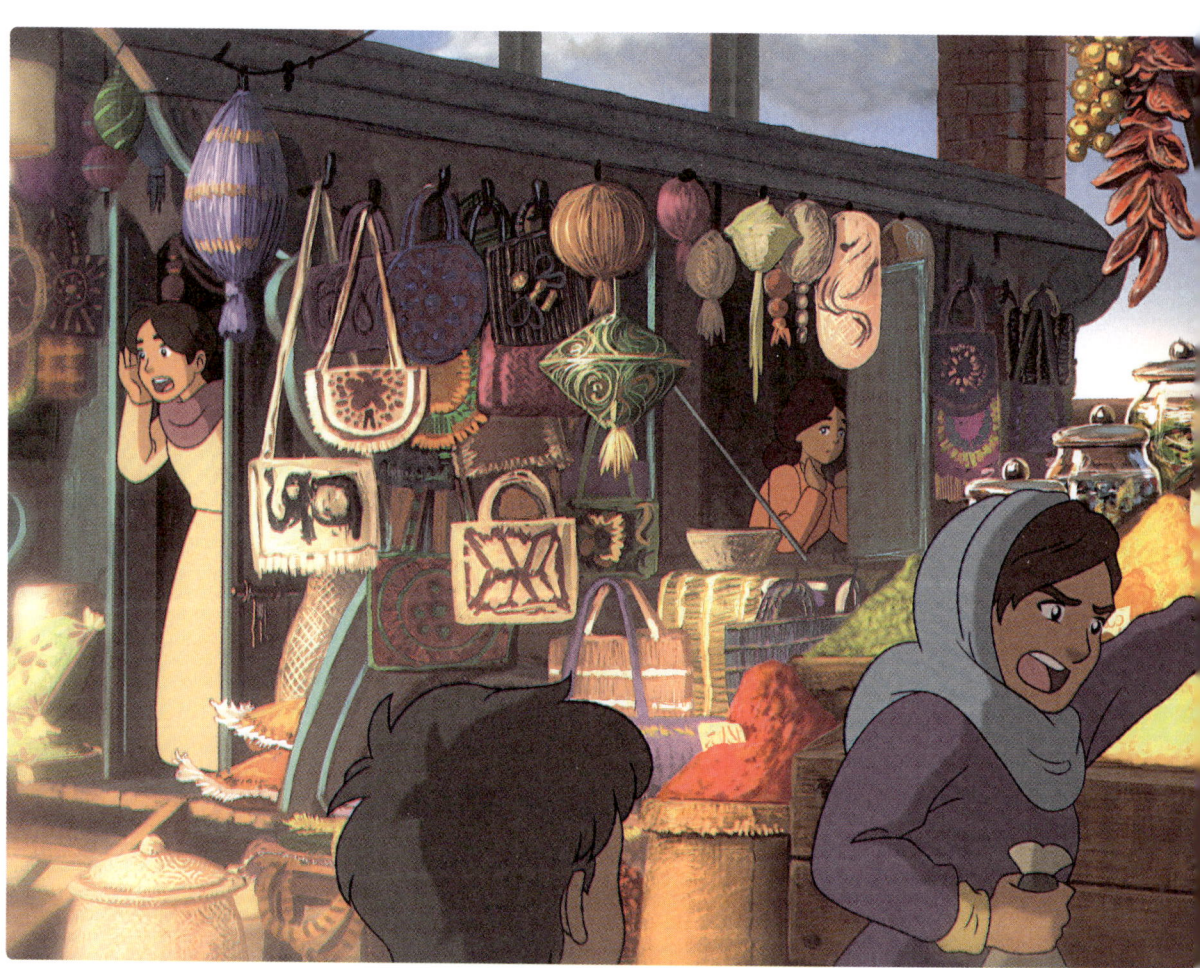

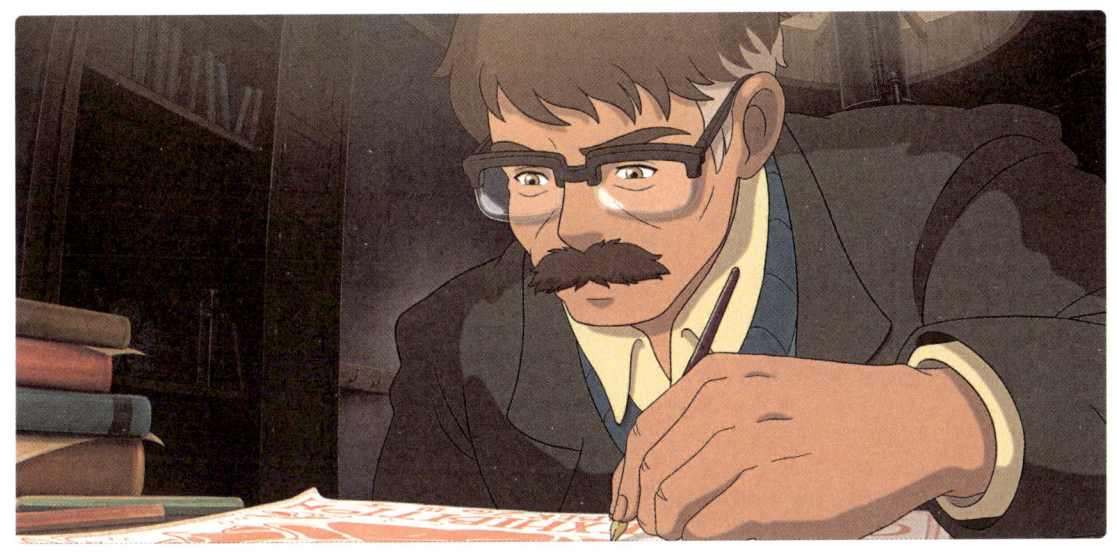

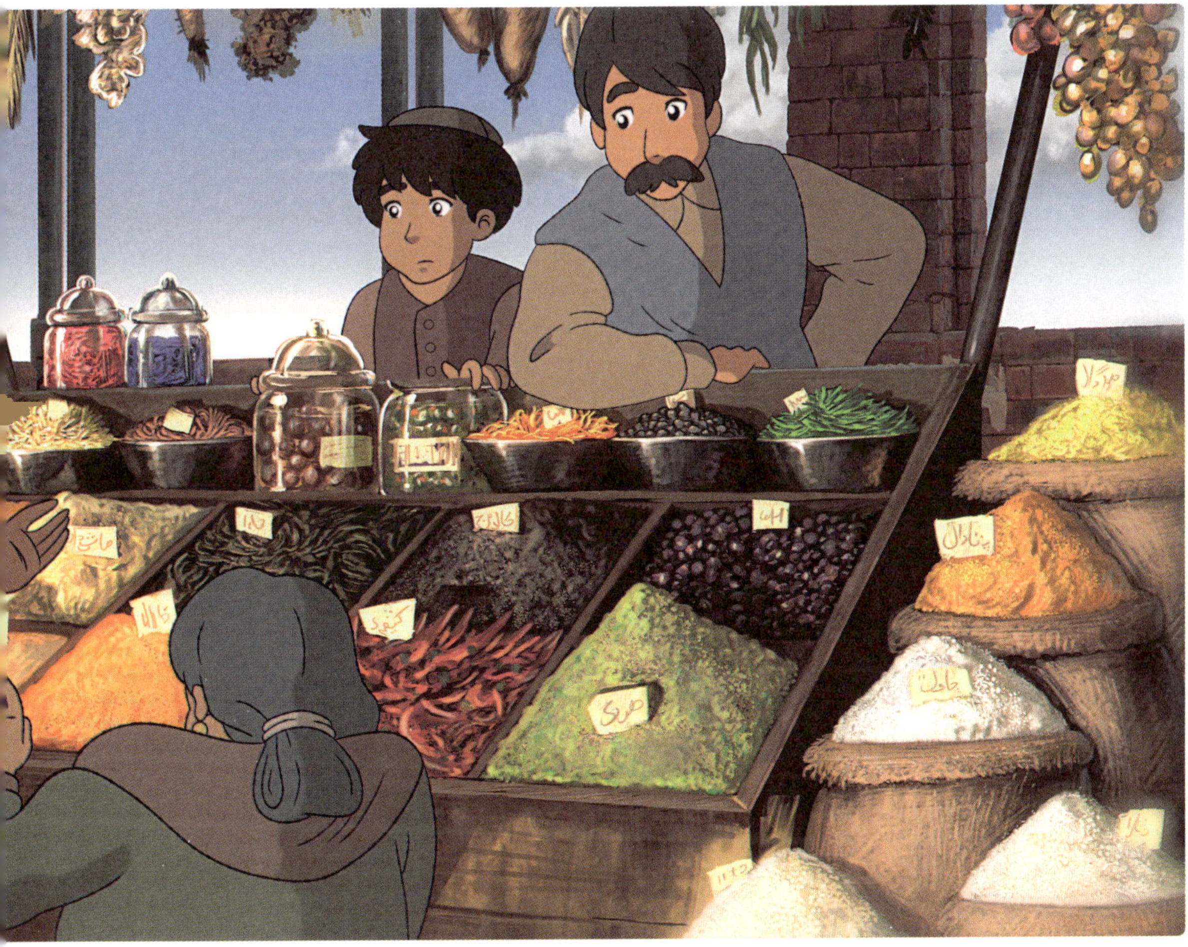

Tracing Memories with Rotoscope Technique

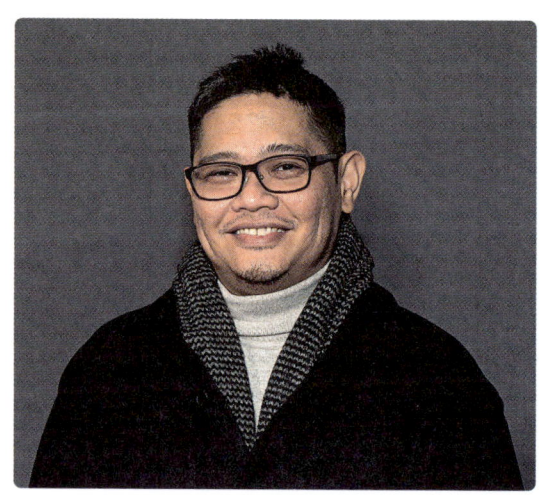 The Missing

Director: Carl Joseph Papa
Released: 2023

Eric (Carlo Aquino), the main character in Carl Joseph Papa's *The Missing*, is an animator. He stays late at his office, hunched over his desk in the dark, painstakingly moving his characters through their stories – but his own story finds him painfully inert.

As the majority of Filipino animation is work outsourced from international territories, there's a good chance Eric's project isn't an original feature film like the one in which his own story is told. In fact, the first animated feature made in the Philippines wasn't released until 1997 and it's sadly already been lost (*Adarna: The Mythical Bird*, directed by Gerry Garcia), with only a handful more made since. But *The Missing* is one of the country's best, becoming the first animated film to be the Philippines' submission for the Best International Feature category at the Academy Awards; and at its centre is Eric, a mute artist, who gets drawn into and draws *himself* into a troubling, yet vivifying mystery.

The Missing, like Papa's previous two films, is told predominantly in a rotoscoped style, its animators

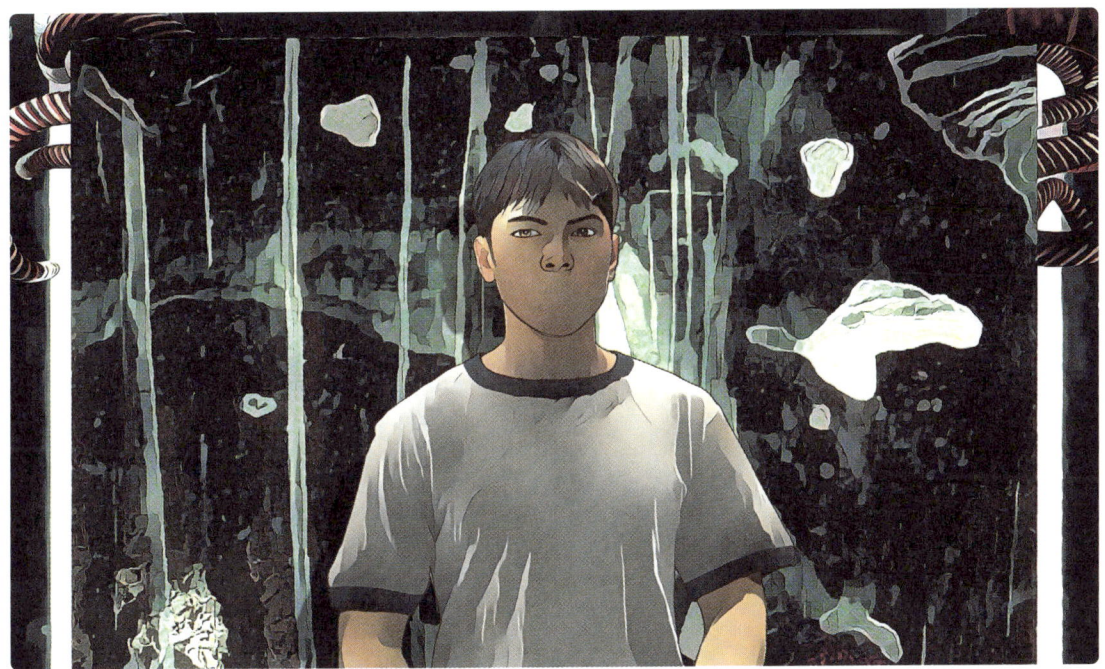

digitally drawing characters and settings over footage of the actors, who were filmed on camera in front of a green screen over a four-day shoot. (To see more of the technique at its best, try Richard Linklater's trilogy of rotoscoped films: *Waking Life*, *A Scanner Darkly* and *Apollo 10½: A Space Age Childhood*.) The look is slippery and uncomfortable, with hyper-real details and sludgy blurs existing within the same textural spaces, the most arresting example being right on Eric's face: he has no mouth.

The film's central visual metaphor, which sees Eric communicate via a whiteboard and pen hung around his neck, reflects a mute state he entered after a childhood trauma, the details of which are parsed out over the course of the film. Unspeakable acts are forced upon Eric, and his mouth has vanished, and as more memories of the sights and sounds of this trauma flash back to him, his eyes and ears start to fall from his face too. The uncannily human rotoscoped style gives these moments a visceral edge, pushing the film from something like the stylized YA mystery of *Brick* (2005) into more of the body horror realm of David Cronenberg. His memories, however, are crudely drawn and rigidly animated, the scrawled style of a mind frozen in perpetual innocent youth, featuring *Frankenstein*-esque operating tables, disconcerting devices and upsettingly sexual aliens.

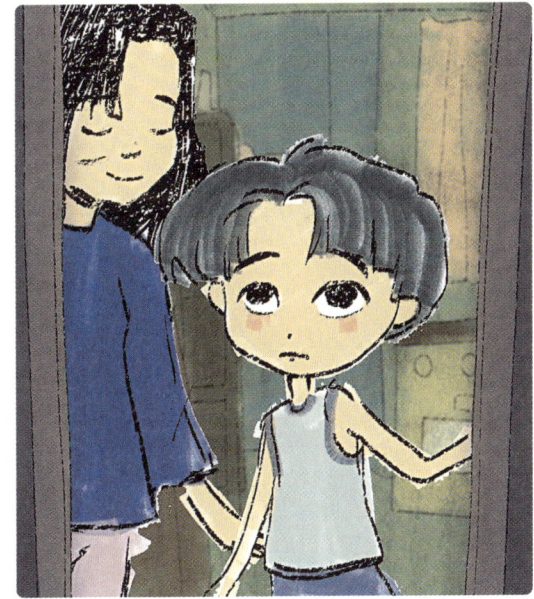

Opposite: Carl Joseph Papa, director of *The Missing*, is found here.

Top: Mouthing off. Despite being mute, through expressive performance and animation *The Missing*'s Eric still manages to say a lot.

Above: Dawn from memory. Flashbacks in the film appear in a more childish sketch style, highlighting Eric's innocence (and the destruction of it) at that age.

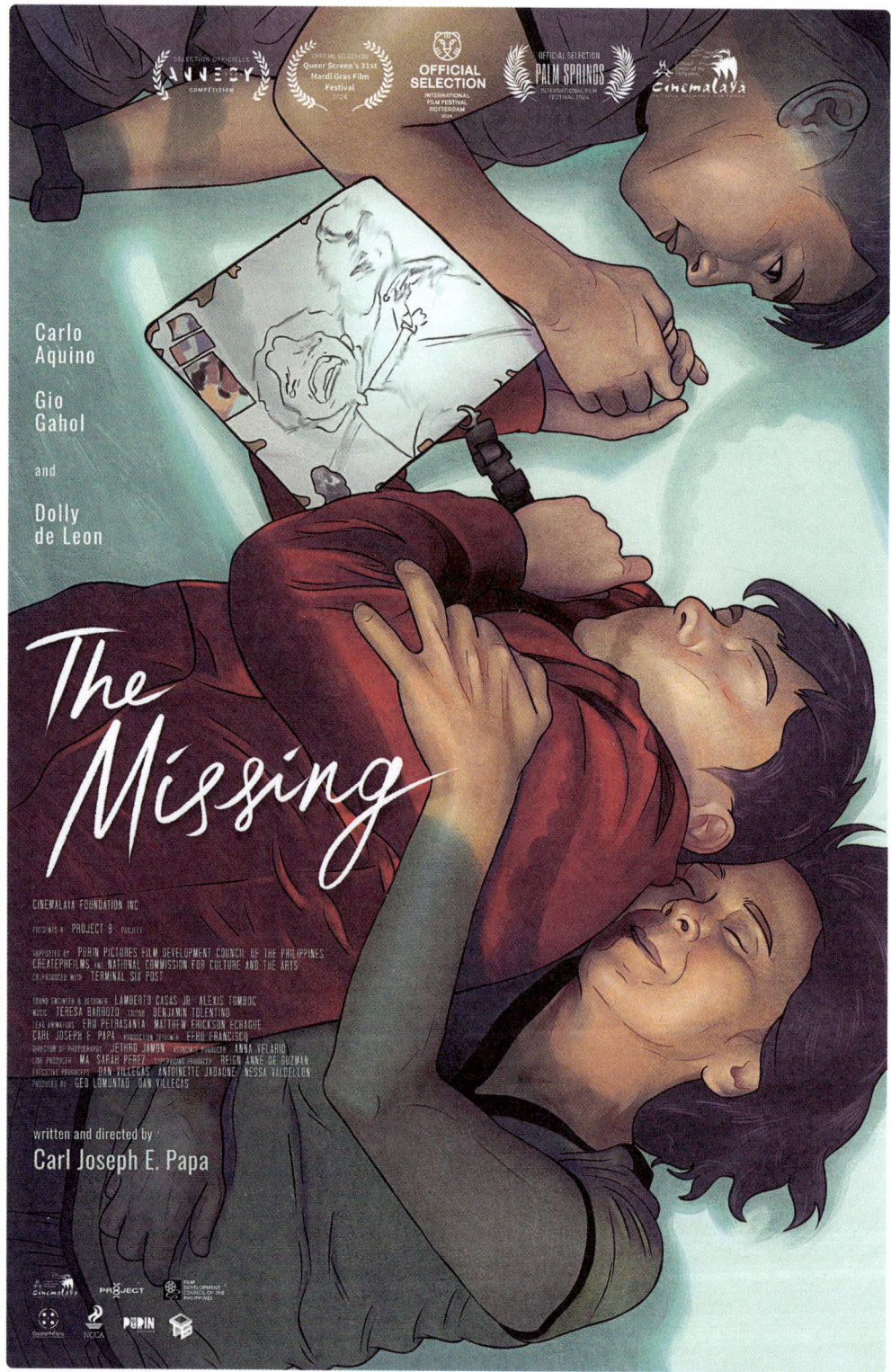

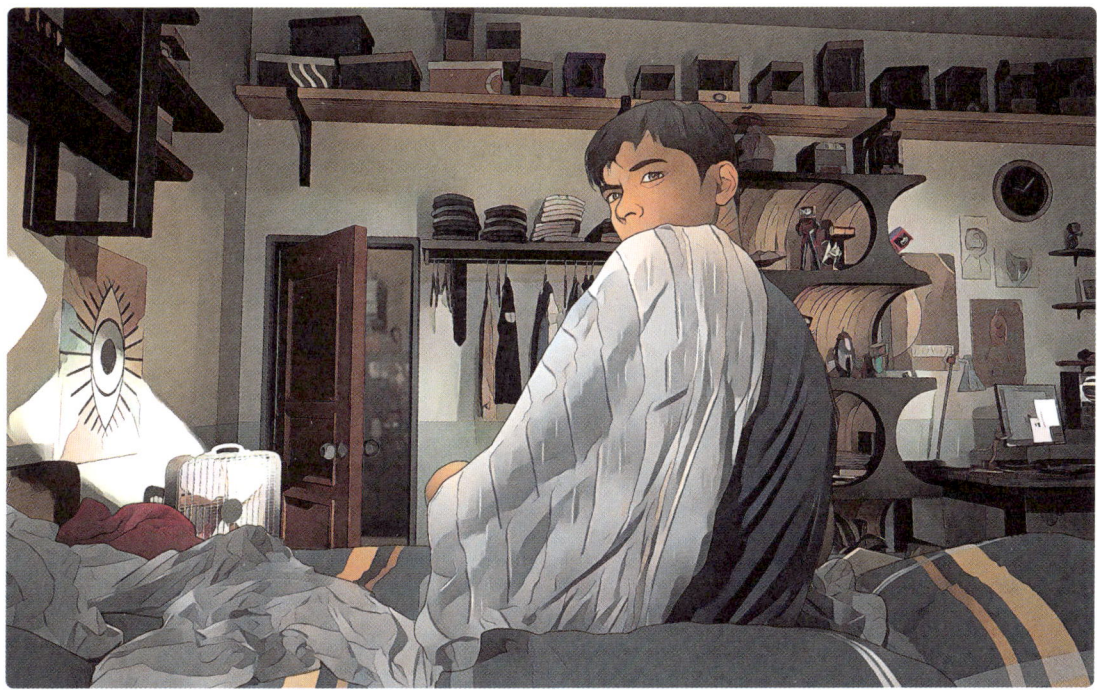

As memory and reality blur, the film's already distinct style becomes even more intriguing. Embracing digital creative language, elements of Eric's story appear with the grey and white chequerboard silhouette that signifies a transparent, or non-existent, layer of a visual file (pangs of pain as PNG). Through fear, or protection, these elements appear to have been erased, but they slip through from past to present and Eric's hand falls victim to the effect, the film's final act playing like someone's deleted a section of the protagonist. These various attempts at disintegrating Eric's body make for incredibly striking images, but as his physiological puzzle progresses, they become even more powerful, illustrating the multifaceted effects of abuse, of what it can steal from people's lives and how they might be able to find the parts that make them whole again.

Although undeniably intense in subject matter, there is some joy to *The Missing* as well. Supporting Eric through his journey is colleague turned romantic interest Carlo (Gio Gahol), whose blossoming relationship with Eric rings with authentic awkwardness, from bonding over pirated films, to delicate, tender first touches. Entirely, wonderfully supportive of her son and his romance is Eric's mother, Rosalinda (Dolly de Leon, fresh from global success with Ruben Östlund's *Triangle of Sadness*). Despite spending a lot of her screen time as a face on video calls, she offers a warmth, humour and brightness that's needed to cut through the weight of Eric's story. *The Missing* is not an easy watch, but it's a valuable one, a story that's expressively, engrossingly told and which has a voiceless hero who shouts about the animation talent coming from the Philippines.

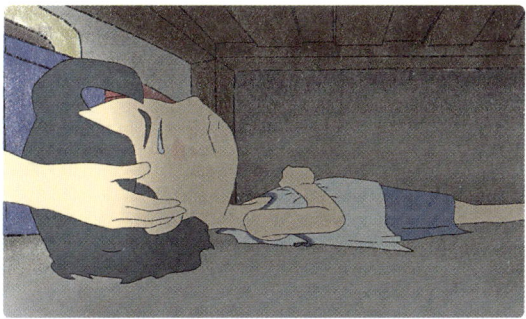

Opposite: Dolly de Leon (bottom) had recently starred in Best Picture Oscar nominee *Triangle of Sadness* before shooting *The Missing*.

Above: Eric, the protagonist of *The Missing*, who is intriguingly an animator himself.

Left: The cartoonish, disproportionate bodies in the film's flashbacks are markedly different to the realistic forms found in the present.

Elsewhere in Asia

Asia is by far the most populous of the continents, so even after six chapters looking at some of its bigger countries, we're still barely scratching the surface.

In a similar way to the former Soviet republics in Eastern Europe, animation was also a priority for film studios across Central Asia and the Caucasus, and many of these countries have rich traditions of animation that are worth exploring. We have to thank the Glasgow-based Samizdat Eastern European Film Festival for singling out some gems from the region, such as the delightful stop-motion short *Once Upon A Time* (1987), from Kazakhstan, in which a yeti steals a man's television set and takes it back across the snowy tundra – only to promptly return it after being confronted by the chaos and cacophony of the human world (including a surprise musical appearance by the B-52s). Unlike their counterparts in Eastern Europe, though, the animation output from these countries is less well known internationally. To explore further, we'd recommend checking out Klassiki's curated streaming platform, or diving into the deep end with the exhaustive database Animatsiya.net, which seeks to make "the full, rich tapestry of Russian and Soviet animation accessible to people all around the world". There's much to discover there, including Georgian artist David Takaishvili's gorgeous painted parable *Plague* (1983), a Cannes prize winner.

Another region worthy of further exploration is the Middle East. Stefanie Van de Peer's academic anthology *Animation in the Middle East*, published in 2017, sought to redress the balance, shining the spotlight on animation made across the region following a century of animated classics drawing inspiration from its folk stories and fairy tales (from Lotte Reiniger's *The Adventures of Prince Achmed* to Disney's *Aladdin*). When it comes to international awareness of animation from the Middle East, two films loom large. There's Marjane Satrapi's *Persepolis* (2007), which was adapted from her graphic novel and co-directed by French artist Vincent Paronnaud. Told in a visually rich, black-and-white comic-book style, *Persepolis* is a spirited coming-of-age film set against the backdrop of the 1979 Iranian Revolution and the rise of the Islamic Republic. *Persepolis* premiered at Cannes and picked up prizes around the world, as well as an Academy Award nomination – a

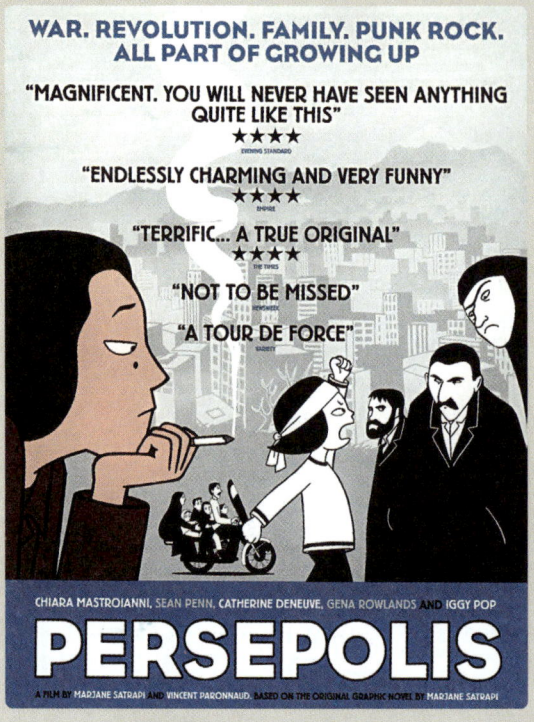

WAR. REVOLUTION. FAMILY. PUNK ROCK.
ALL PART OF GROWING UP

"MAGNIFICENT. YOU WILL NEVER HAVE SEEN ANYTHING QUITE LIKE THIS"
★★★★
EVENING STANDARD

"ENDLESSLY CHARMING AND VERY FUNNY"
★★★★
EMPIRE

"TERRIFIC... A TRUE ORIGINAL"
★★★★
THE TIMES

"NOT TO BE MISSED"
NEWSWEEK

"A TOUR DE FORCE"
VARIETY

CHIARA MASTROIANNI, SEAN PENN, CATHERINE DENEUVE, GENA ROWLANDS AND IGGY POP

PERSEPOLIS

A FILM BY MARJANE SATRAPI AND VINCENT PARONNAUD. BASED ON THE ORIGINAL GRAPHIC NOVEL BY MARJANE SATRAPI

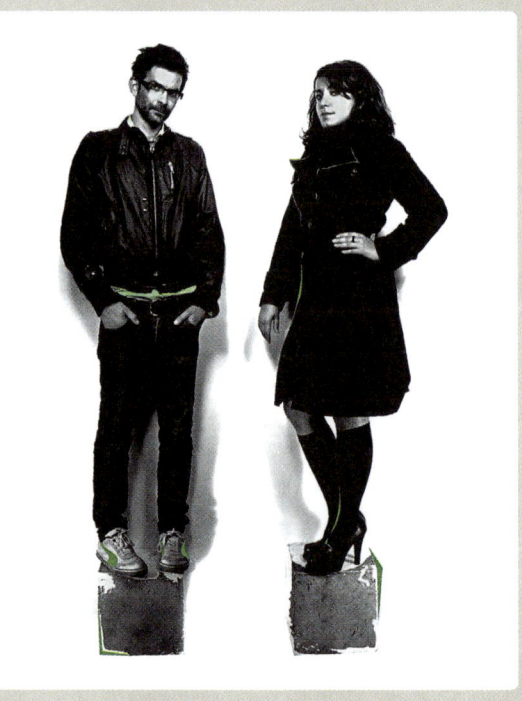

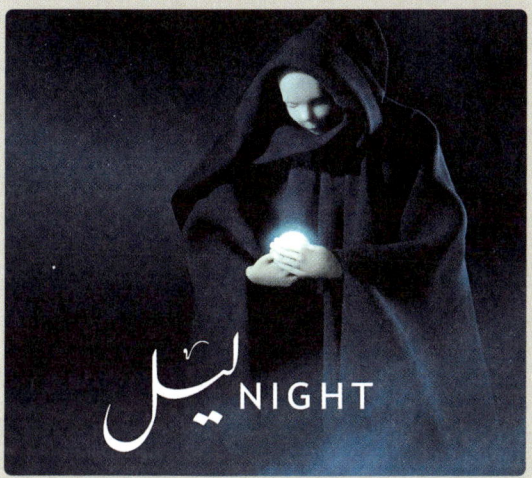

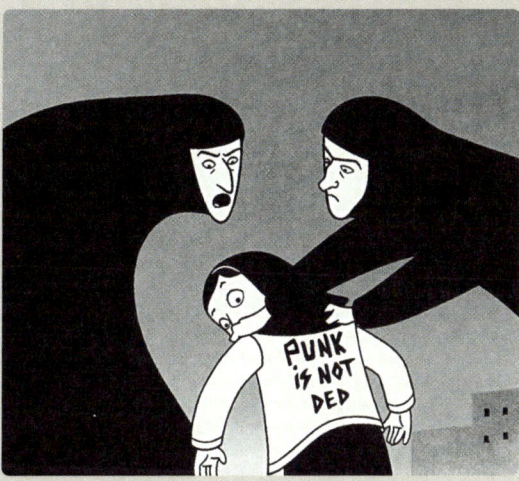

journey that was repeated the following year by Ari Folman's Israeli docudrama *Waltz with Bashir* (2008), a dark, psychological examination of PTSD and repressed memories of the horrors experienced and enacted by Folman and his peers as conscripts during the 1982 Lebanon War.

More recently, Saudia Arabia has heavily invested in its film industry, backing the Japanese anime co-production *The Journey* (2021). On a much smaller scale, there's Yegane Moghaddam's charming and highly creative Iranian stop-motion short *Our Uniform* (2023): a compact examination of the hijab and gender norms in Iran that uses the very fabric of clothing as its canvas.

If you want to venture beyond these films, we'd recommend reading Van de Peer's anthology, or Omar Sayfo's related work, *Arab Animation: Images of Identity*, which was published in 2021 and takes a broader look at animation from the Middle East and across North Africa. Much of this work wrestles with the region's turbulent history. Specifically, we wish to highlight the small but important tradition of animation from Palestine, which uses the art form to confront contemporary struggles and communicate them with the world. Ahmad Habash's *Fatenah* (2009) was billed as the first computer-generated film made in Palestine, and its simple 3D figures and low-key animation belie its devastating story of a Palestinian woman's search for adequate healthcare and cancer treatment while living under Israeli occupation. Elsewhere, Ahmad Saleh uses shadow-drenched stop-motion in the profound and poetic short *Night* (2021), a haunting tale of love and loss among the rubble of war, while May Odeh & Dia'

Azzeh animate the scratchy crayon drawings of actual children in the heartbreaking *Drawing For Better Dreams* (2015). Born out of workshops where Palestinian kids were encouraged to draw images of life in the Occupied Territories, *Drawing For Better Dreams* is presented as part of a process of easing their trauma and, hopefully, allowing them to one day dream freely. This is animation wielded with a humanist political intent. "While occupation kills and otherwise brutalises," writes Colleen Jankovic in *Animation in the Middle East*, "it cannot stifle the resilient, creative imagination of Palestinian artists, activists or their supporters."

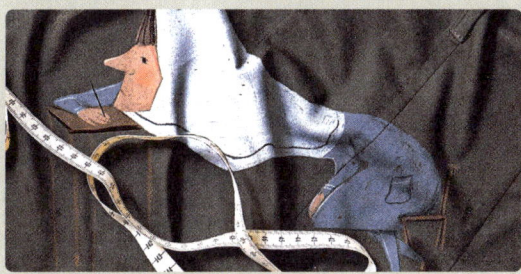

Opposite above: From the comics page to the Cannes stage, the graphic novel adaptation *Persepolis* was a crossover hit.

Opposite below: The directorial duo behind the film adaptation of *Persepolis*, Vincent Paronnaud and the original author, Marjane Satrapi.

Top left: The stop-motion short, *Night*, is one of a growing canon of films that capture the plight of Palestinians.

Top right: Unlucky Punk. The free-spirited pre-teen Marjane chafes against the strict dogma of Iran's Islamic Republic.

Above: Cloth cartoon. Innovative and insightful, the Oscar-nominated short *Our Uniform* incorporates the very textures of textiles into its animation.

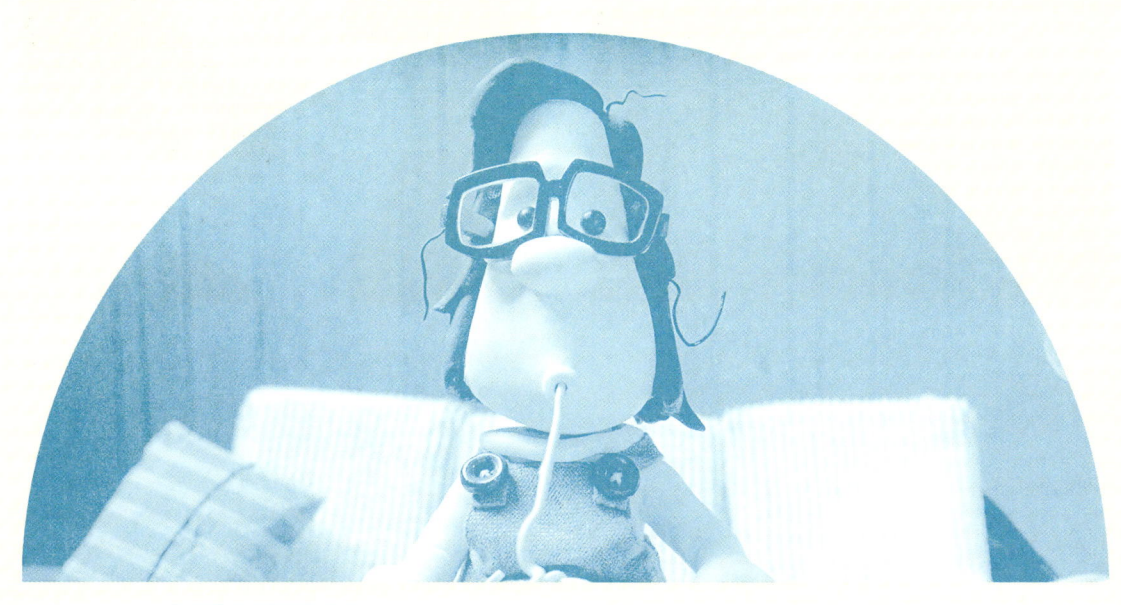
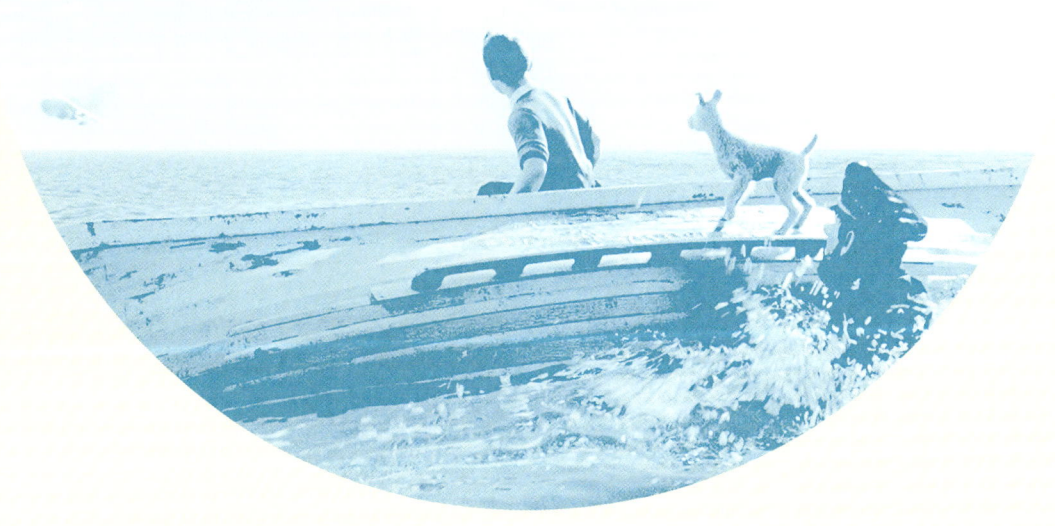

Oceania

Australia

Bittersweet Visions from a Clay Dreamer

🎬 Mary and Max

Director: Adam Elliot
Released: 2009

A wedding inside a cancer ward. It's a scene in Australian director Adam Elliot's 2003 Oscar-winning short film *Harvie Krumpet,* but it's also just a great symbol of what all of his films are about: human connection and optimistic faith in relationships, contained within the stark, draining, harsh walls of mortality.

Elliot's films can feel incredibly, almost overbearingly bleak, but by exploring the darkest corners of his characters and their sludgy black and brown lives and thoughts, they make the glimpses of light feel blindingly powerful, especially in his first feature film, 2009's *Mary and Max.*

Like many of his works, regardless of length, *Mary and Max* follows extended chapters of its protagonists' lives – Elliot, an avid reader of biographies, calls these stories "clayographies". In this case it's about eight-year-old Mary (voiced first by Bethany Whitmore, then later by Toni Colette) and her decades-long friendship with her pen pal, Max (Philip Seymour Hoffman, staid yet warm, gravel leafed in gold). Mary's a bespectacled

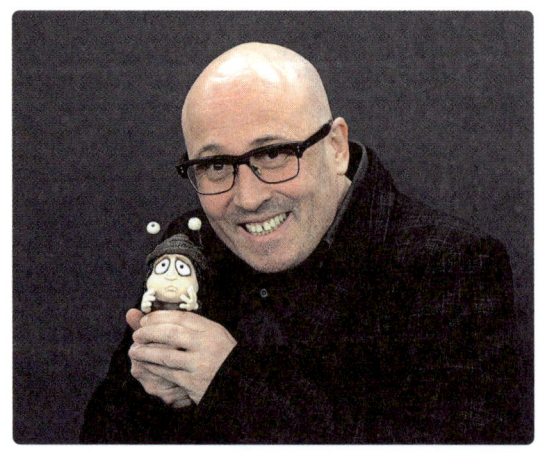

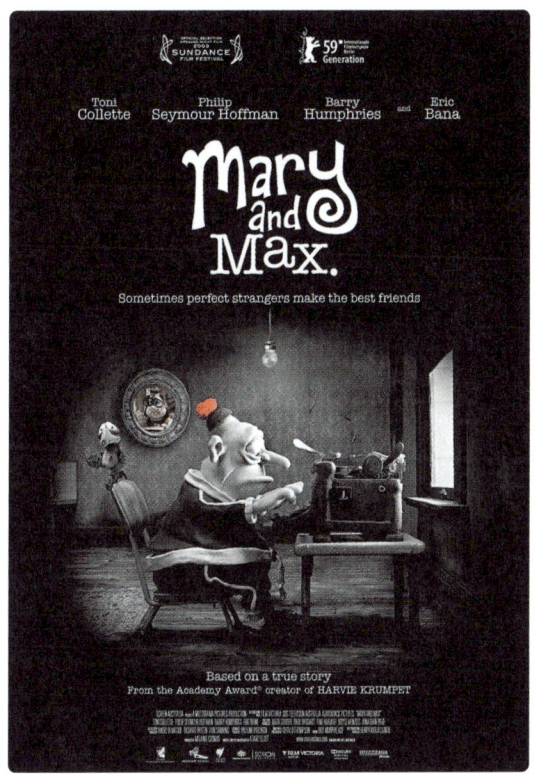

outsider with a pear-shaped head and a large birthmark at its summit. She's daughter to an alcoholic mother and a father obsessed by taxidermy, and she finds escape and solace in Max, a 44-year-old man from New York who has Asperger's syndrome (making him an 'aspie', to use Max's word). Overweight and anxious, he has a tiny yarmulke-topped pinhead, white butter bean eyes and a pumpkin-shaped torso. Journeying with Mary through adolescence, education and romance, and with Max through addiction, psychology and self-acceptance, is a tough but heartening thing. Splattered with hardships, the duo's letters help each other through the unpredictabilities of life, confusing as they are – or "confuzzling", to use another Maxism – but it doesn't come easy. Mary even betrays Max through ableism and hopes of "curing" him. Elliot, who has a physiological tremor, moulds disability deep into the clay of his tales, and Tourette's, deafness, cerebral palsy and OCD receive

Opposite: Adam Elliot and Grace Pudel, the director and star of *Memoir of a Snail*.

Left: New Yorker Max, seen here on the film's poster, was played by Philip Seymour Hoffman in his first vocal performance.

Below: Mary, here sucking up some noodles, was voiced by Australian actor Toni Colette.

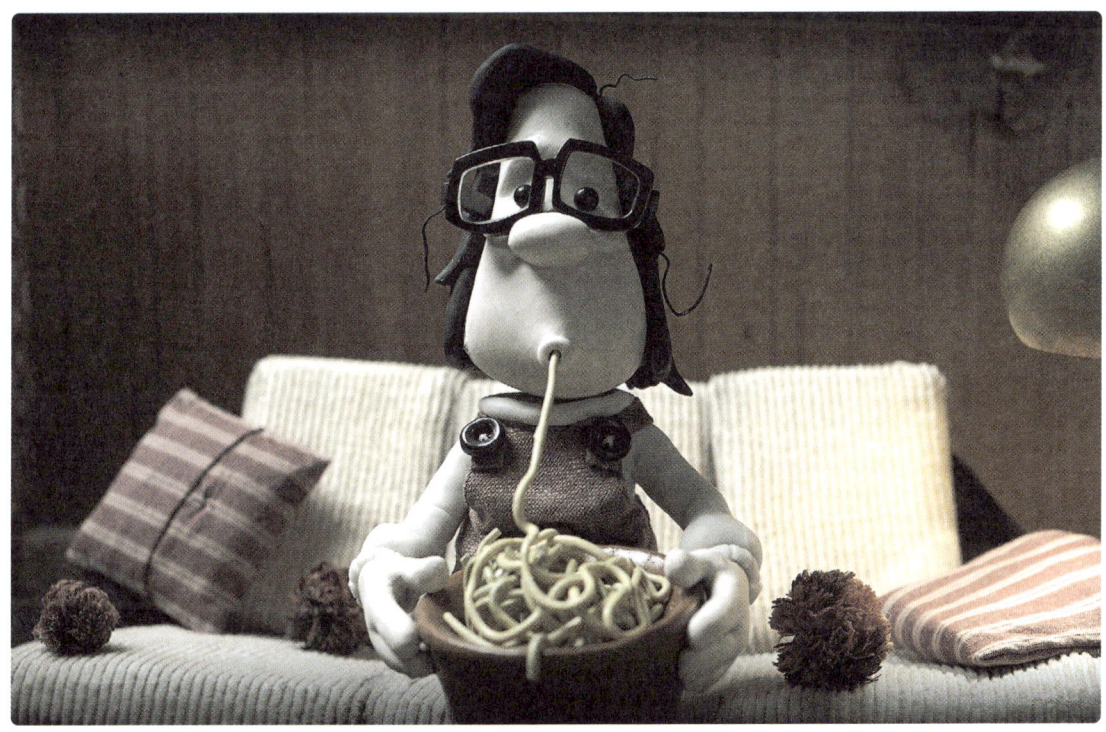

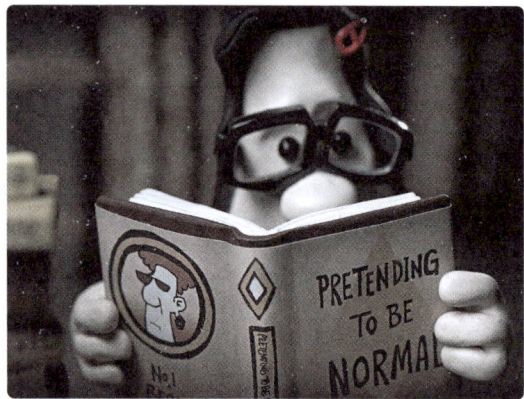

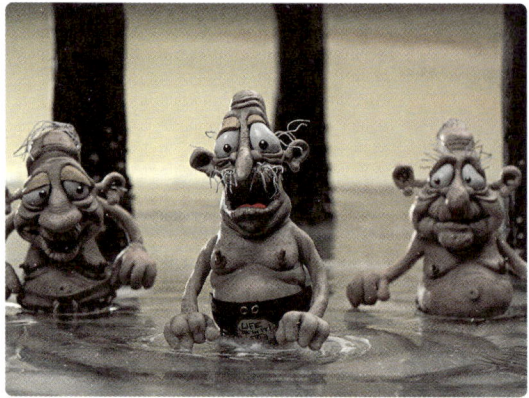

engaging but crucially funny exploration across his works. Rather than wrap differences in the cotton wool of saccharine, marginalizing inspiration, he respects them with the dark humour of reality, the embrace of being entirely everyday.

Elliot's films are predominantly presided over by warming narration – in *Mary and Max*'s case, grin-curling warmth comes courtesy of Aussie comic legend Barry Humphries, an early inspiration to the director. This voiceover-led approach was developed with three autofictional shorts in the 1990s: *Uncle* made in 1996, while a student in Melbourne, followed by 1998's *Cousin* and 1999's *Brother*, which both received funding

from the Australian Film Commission. He told animation-focused website Skwigly that there was "something really intimate and authentic and personal and real about" creating living snapshots of family, and the

Above left: Book and feel. Adam Elliot's films are full of miniature tomes, like this one, being read by Mary.

Above right: Body of work. Elliot's memorably realised characters always have a variety of shapes and ages.

Below left: *Memoir of a Snail*, Elliot's film from 2024, was a festival success but *Flow* (see page 90) would go on to beat it to the Animated Feature Academy Award.

Below right: Grace Pudel and Pinky, one always in her shell, the other fiercely out of it, both at the heart of *Memoir of a Snail*.

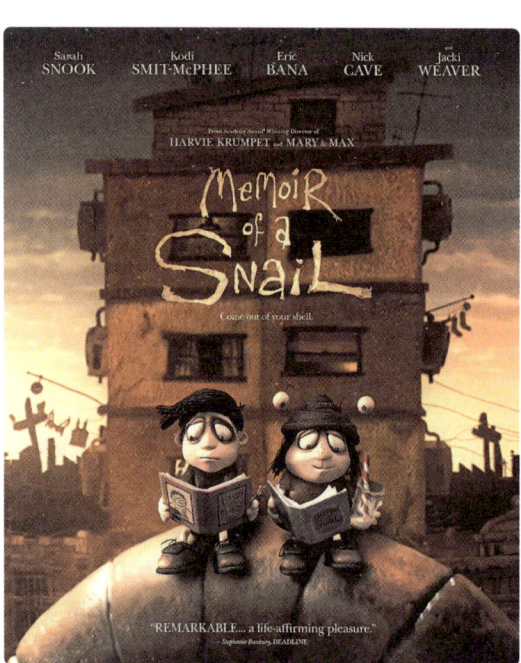

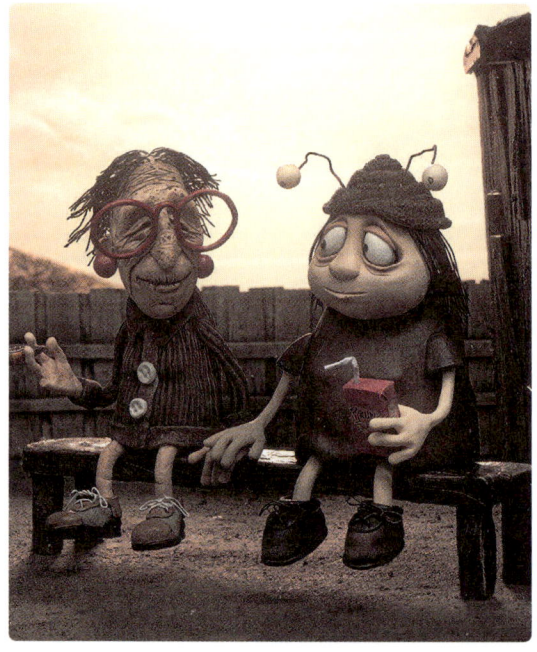

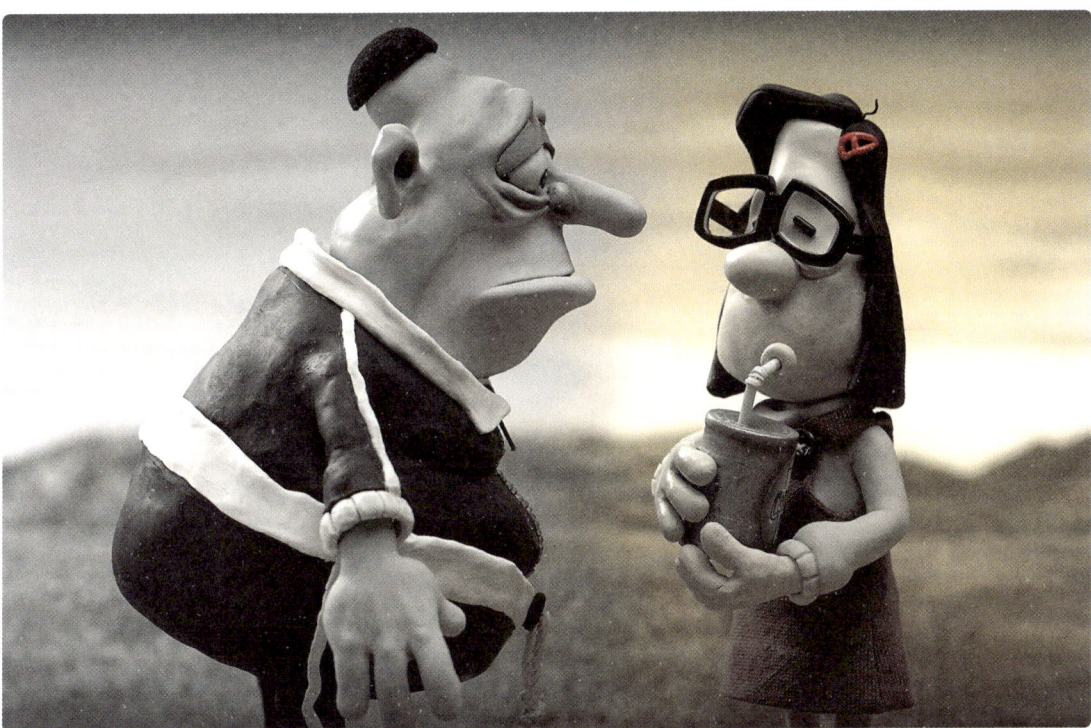

shorts signalled a storyteller fascinated by the foibles of personalities, the details of domesticity and the strength and power in simply existing outside of physiological and neurological norms. All of these preoccupations would develop further with *Harvie Krumpet* – a film whose Oscar win led to so many doors opening for Elliot that it got nicknamed a "golden crowbar".

Although mostly soaked in sepia or monochrome palettes, Elliot's stories are remarkably evocative thanks to his eye for detail in both his visuals and scripting. Focusing on the sensorial experience of life, his filmography regularly guides viewers towards people's scent – liquorice, pine needles and pickled onions have all been in the Elliot perfumery. The simplicity of his descriptions only makes them clearer. Take Mary's birthmark, which, despite existing in an all-brown world, is revealed to be "the colour of poo", not only capturing its aesthetics but her feeling towards it. The sights, smells and experiences of Elliot's worlds repeat on themselves: topics including immigration, consent, snails, animal rights, neckwear, trinkets, name changes, poison, death and many more ("things Disney and Pixar would never do") are returned to over and over again. The follow-up to *Mary and Max*, the short film *Ernie Biscuit* (2015),

even plays out like a romantic remix of *Harvie Krumpet*.

It would take another 15 years before Elliot made another feature, with *Memoir of a Snail*, a coming-of-age story about a young girl obsessed by a snail (there they are again) and the strange episodes of her life following the demise of her parents. Distinctly, unquestionably Elliot, the tragic and hopeful tale was released in 2024 and took home the top prize at both the Annecy International Film Festival and the London Film Festival, before being nominated for the Academy Award for Best Animated Feature, where it lost to *Flow*.

Although *Mary and Max* takes the chapter header here, the imagery, language and ideas from all of Elliot's films cycle through the film and beyond it. He's said that he hopes his works "are uplifting and nourishing and universal and hopefully, to a degree, timeless" – and almost three decades along from that first short, it's hard to argue with that.

Above: Max and Mary. Though separated by a vast distance, the two form a close bond.

◎ Bluey

Not since the early days of *The Simpsons* has there been a cultural phenomenon like *Bluey*: that rare type of series which cuts across generations and spills out of children's TV programming and into the mainstream of popular culture.

Created by animator Joe Brumm and produced by Ludo Studio in Queensland, *Bluey* is a "co-viewing" show that perfectly captures the attentions of kids and parents alike. While its primary audience of preschoolers are whipped up in the excitement of watching the everyday hijinks of Bluey and Bingo, the two hyper-imaginative daughters of the Heeler family of anthropomorphic dogs, the grown-ups in the room often find themselves taken unawares by a kernel of wisdom, or a deeply resonant observation, or an emotional gut-punch delivered with the lightest of touch.

Episodes such as "Rain", "Cricket", "Sleepytime", "Camping", "Onesies" and the extended special "The Sign" have already become firm fixtures in the *Mummy/Daddy, why are you crying?* Hall of Fame, and the programme has raised the bar on

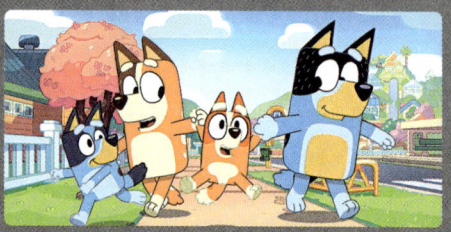

multiple fronts: for kids' TV, animation, and streaming series in general.

Make no mistake, *Bluey* is a big deal: at its peak, its weekly viewing tallies exceeded one billion minutes. And when the third series of the show premiered on Disney+ in 2022, voice actors Dave McCormack and Melanie Zanetti were welcomed as stars onto *The Tonight Show Starring Jimmy Fallon*, while a gigantic Bluey inflatable took pride of place in the annual Macy's Day Parade celebrations: an Australian giant, taking the US by storm.

Above: Heeler the World. The blockbuster animated series *Bluey* has brought Australian animation into family households around the globe.

◉ Further Viewing

If we haven't made it clear enough in this chapter already, we recommend exploring Adam Elliot's full filmography, right back to his earliest, shortest works *Uncle* (1996), *Cousin* (1998) and *Brother* (1999), a loose trilogy of bittersweet character studies narrated by William McInnes. As mentioned above, Elliot's *Harvie Krumpet* (2003) won the Academy Award for Best Animated Short, but it isn't Australian animation's only Oscar winner. Bruce Petty's odd, animated essay on the history of recreation, *Leisure*, won the same award in 1977, as did the adaptation of Shaun Tan's

dystopian picture book, *The Lost Thing* (2010). And then there's George Miller's bright, colourful, all-dancing penguin extravaganza *Happy Feet* (2006) – about as far as you can get from Elliot's delicate, desaturated handmade work – which beat Pixar's *Cars* (2006) and took home Best Animated Feature. The animation was produced by Sydney-based effects studio Animal Logic, who have since contributed animation work to Zack Snyder's fantasy epic *Legend of the Guardians: The Owls of Ga'Hoole* (2010) and the *Lego Movie* franchise.

Elsewhere in Oceania

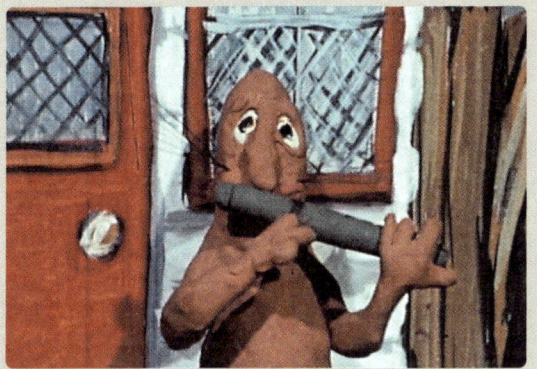

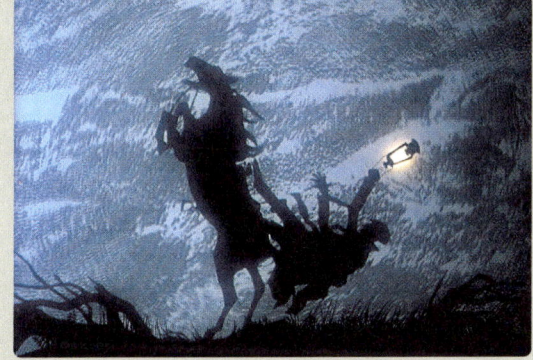

Much of New Zealand's animation history has been preserved and made available to view on the online portal NZOnScreen.com. Highlights include Fred O'Neill's fun and inventive 1964 short *Plastiphobia* (which predates Aardman's similar experiments with their plasticine character Morph by over a decade), the delightful adaptation of Lynley Dodd's children's picture book *Hairy Maclary from Donaldson's Dairy* (1996), and Bob Stenhouse's Oscar-nominated gothic fable, *The Frog, the Dog and the Devil* (1986). However, here's a fitting question for the end of our round-the-world trip. Does the digital technique known as "performance capture" count as animation? In many ways, it's no different to rotoscoping, a time-honoured process that has been used by revered animators such as the Fleischer Brothers and Ralph Bakshi, where artists paint over filmed footage of actors. And if it does count, we could point to Peter Jackson's New Zealand-based Wētā Digital, nominally a visual effects studio but one that played a pivotal part in animation of the twenty-first century, from the creation of characters such as Gollum in *The Lord of the Rings* (2001–2003), to producing Steven Spielberg's fully animated caper *The Adventures of Tintin* (2011).

Above left: Claying Around. Fred O'Neill's wildly inventive stop-motion short *Plastiphobia* is daft, playful and full of fun.

Above right: Demon Alcohol. Bob Stenhouse's Oscar-nominated *The Frog, the Dog, and the Devil* was inspired by the old New Zealand ballad, 'The Devil's Daughter'.

Below: Wet Wet Wētā. Steven Spielberg's mo-cap marvel *The Adventures of Tintin* was the product of New Zealand's world-leading VFX community.

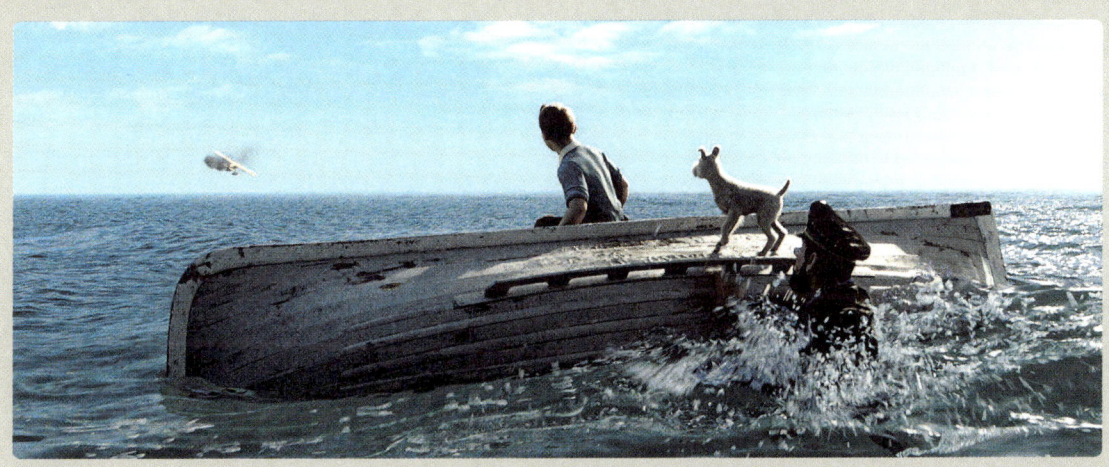

Further Reading

Over the years, we have been very lucky to speak with many animators from around the world, and in writing this book we drew from our interviews with Pablo Berger, Dorota Kobiela, Kenneth Ladekjær, Sebastien Laudenbach, Peter Lord, Chiara Malta, Tomm Moore, Nick Park, Henry Selick, Nora Twomey, Hugh Welchman and Gints Zilbalodis.

In addition to the below sources, we're also indebted to the work of the specialist home video labels that distribute animation from around the world, often with indispensable special features and booklets brimming with invaluable essays. Take a bow, Arrow Films, BFI DVD, Criterion, Deaf Crocodile, Eureka and Second Run. Long live physical media!

Books

Bendazzi, Giannalberto, *Cartoons: One Hundred Years of Cinema Animation* (London: John Libbey Cinema and Animation, 1994)

Clements, Jonathan, *Schoolgirl Milky Crisis: Adventures in the Anime and Manga Trade* (London: Titan Books, 2008)

Clements, Jonathan, *Anime: A History* (London: Bloomsbury, 2013)

Hames, Peter, ed., *The Cinema of Jan Švankmajer: Dark Alchemy*, Second edition (London: Wallflower Press, 2008)

Hieronimus, Robert R. and Cortner, Laura E., *It's All in the Mind: Inside the Beatles' Yellow Submarine*, vol.2 (Owing Mills, Maryland: Hieronimus & Co, 2021)

Kitson, Clare, *British Animation: The Channel 4 Factor* (London: Parliament Hill Publishing, 2008)

Kitson, Clare, *Yuri Norstein and Tale of Tales: An Animator's Journey* (Bloomington and Indianapolis: Indiana University Press, 2005)

Lord, Peter and Sproxton, David, *Aardman: An Epic Journey: Taken One Frame at a Time* (London: Simon & Schuster UK, 2018)

McCarthy, Helen, *The Art of Osamu Tezuka: God of Manga* (New York: Abrams ComicArts. 2009)

Mes, Tom and Sharp, Jasper, *The Midnight Eye Guide to New Japanese Film* (Albany: Stone Bridge Press, 2004)

Miyazaki, Hayao, *Starting Point: 1979–1996*, translated by Beth Cary and Frederik L. Schodt (San Francisco: VIZ Media, 2009)

Miyazaki, Hayao, *Turning Point: 1997–2008*, translated by Beth Cary and Frederik L. Schodt (San Francisco: VIZ Media, 2014)

Mitenbuler, Reid, *Wild Minds: The Artists and Rivalries that inspired the Golden Age of Animation* (New York: Grove Press, 2020)

Robinson, Chris, *Japanese Animation: Time Out of Mind*, (London: John Libbey Publishing, 2010)

Sanders, James, *Celluloid Skyline: New York and the Movies* (London: Bloomsbury, 2002)

Sayfo, Omar, *Arab Animation: Images of Identity* (Edinburgh: Edinburgh University Press, 2021)

Stewart, Jez, *The Story of British Animation* (London: Bloomsbury, 2021)

Van de Peer, Stefanie, *Animation in the Middle East* (London: I.B. Tauris, 2017)

Whybray, Adam, *The Art of Czech Animation* (London: Bloomsbury, 2020)

Williams, Richard and Sutton, Imogen, *Adventures in Animation* (London: Faber & Faber, 2024)

Articles, Interviews and Blogs

"Ask the Developer Vol. 10, Pikmin 4—Part 1", Nintendo.com, 2023: https://www.nintendo.com/us/whatsnew/ask-the-developer-vol-10-pikmin-4-part-1/

Boshoff, Irene, "Q&A: Ng'endo Mukii", Design Indaba, 2015: https://www.designindaba.com/articles/interviews/qa-ng%E2%80%99endo-mukii

Briggs, Raymond, "Art of the bomb", *Times Educational Supplement* #3524, January 1984.

Dudok de Wit, Alex, "Looping around limitations: the experimental shorts of Tezuka Osamu", *Sight and Sound*, 2019: https://www2.bfi.org.uk/news-opinion/sight-sound-magazine/features/experimental-short-films-osamu-tezuka

Felperin Sharman, Leslie, "Down the White Road", *Sight and Sound*, May 1994.

Gelder, Paul, "Lotte Reiniger at 80", *Sight and Sound* 48.3 (Summer 1979).

Hutchinson, Pamela, "Lotte Reiniger: animated film pioneer and standard-bearer for women", *Guardian*, 2 June 2016: https://www.theguardian.com/film/2016/jun/02/lotte-reiniger-the-pioneer-of-silhouette-animation-google-doodle

Jackson, Wendy, "The Surrealist Conspirator: An Interview With Jan Svankmajer", *Animation World Magazine*, Issue 2.3, 1997: https://www.awn.com/mag/issue2.3/issue2.3pages/2.3jacksonsvankmajer.html

Kaufman, J.B., "Disney's Folly", The Walt Disney Family Museum, 2007: https://web.archive.org/web/20081028032443/http://disney.go.com/disneyatoz/familymuseum/exhibits/articles/waltsfolly/index.html

Kizirian, Shari, "The Adventures of Prince Achmed", Silentfilm.org, 2008: https://silentfilm.org/the-adventures-of-prince-achmed-1/

Knight, Clare, "Pakistan's Oscar Hopeful", Animation Obsessive, 2024: https://animationobsessive.substack.com/p/one-of-2024s-best-films-was-made

León, Cristóbal and Cociña, Joaquín, "Cristóbal León & Joaquín Cociña Introduce Their Film 'The Bones'", Mubi Notebook, 2021: https://mubi.com/en/notebook/posts/cristobal-leon-joaquin-cocina-introduce-their-film-the-bones

Lord, Peter, "The Start of Stop-Frame: Animation's great lost pioneer", Guardian, 14 November 2008: https://www.theguardian.com/film/2008/nov/14/animation-ballet

Pichard, Hervé and Lémerige, Françoise, "Don de dessins de Paul Grimault", Cinematheque, 12 December 2014: https://www.cinematheque.fr/article/14.html

Poovaiah, Ravi, "Ram Mohan, The Legend of Indian Animation", D'Source: https://dsource.in/showcase/ram-mohan/interview

Reiniger, Lotte, "Scissors Make Films", *Sight and Sound*, 2020: https://www.bfi.org.uk/sight-and-sound/features/scissors-make-films-lotte-reiniger-creating-her-magical-animations

Saito, Stephen, "Anca Damian on Finding Empathy Through the Eyes of a Lost Dog in 'Marona's Fantastic Tale'", Moveablefest.com, 2020: https://moveablefest.com/anca-damian-maronas-fantastic-tale/

Sharp, Jasper, "Head Trip: the animated worlds of Yamamura Kōji", *Sight and Sound*, 2013 (Updated 20 June 2018): https://www2.bfi.org.uk/news-opinion/sight-sound-magazine/interviews/head-trip-animated-worlds-yamamura-koji

Sisterton, Dennis, "Magic Wilderness: El Apóstol & Peludópolis", Skwigly, 2017: https://www.skwigly.co.uk/magic-wilderness-el-apostol/

Vollenbroek, Tunde, "'My Life As A Zucchini' Director Claude Barras On The Hard Work of Simplicity and Minimalism", Cartoon Brew, 2017: https://www.cartoonbrew.com/feature-film/life-zucchini-director-claude-barras-hard-work-simplicity-minimalism-148395.html

Acknowledgements

Around the world of animation in 30 countries? A piece of cake. Well, only if you have help, and we relied on numerous friends and colleagues as we embarked on this ambitious trip. Thanks as always to our stalwart podcast companion Steph "Killer" Watts, and also the team at our publisher, Welbeck/Headline, specifically Ross Hamilton (who got us into this fine mess in the first place), Giulia Hetherington, Caroline Curtis, Marion Storz and Russell Knowles.

As we sketched out our globe-trotting itinerary, we were guided by invigorating and illuminating chats with many pals and peers, including Sam Summers, Steve Henderson, Jennifer Hall, Alex Dudok de Wit, Susie Evans, Kambole Campbell, Niall Geraghty, Bence Bardos, Sam Clements, Griffin Newman, Paul Williams, Ryan Gaur, Isabel Stevens, Justin Johnson, Andrew Osmond, Young Jin Eric Choi, Ravi Narayanswami and Aga Baranowska.

We were aided in our journey by filmmakers, distributors, sales agents, archivists and other front-line workers from the world of film: Lucy Rubin, Chance Huskey and Dave Jestaet from GKIDS, Kerry Kasim and Andrew Partridge from Anime Ltd., Léo Altmann and Xueyin Li from Charades, Kelly Powell and Jake Garriock from Curzon, Luce Grosjean from Miyu Distribution, Jessica Levick and Kate Robinson from Channel 4, Geo Lomuntad at Project 8, Dennis Bartok at Deaf Crocodile, Anna Lewis from Aardman, Jez Stewart and Will Swinburne from the BFI National Archive, Masaya Kaneko, and Mr Kōji Yamamura.

This is our sixth book in about as many years, and we're indebted to you, our readers, for joining us on these expeditions into animation and world cinema – but most of all, we couldn't do what we do without the love and support of Mim, Ivo, Louie and our newest fellow traveller, Gene.

Index

Credits

4 Photo 12/Alamy © Rita Productions/Blue Spirit Productions/Gebeka Films; 6 Album/Alamy © Walt Disney Productions; 7a TCD/Prod.DB/Alamy © Dream Well Studio/Sacrebleu Productions/Take Five; 7b Courtesy Ng'endo Mukii; 8a Photo 12/Alamy © Filme de Papel; 8b Everett Collection/Alamy © Cinelicious/Mushi Production; 9 Photo 12/Alamy © Comenius Film; 13a, 14 © Frédéric Back and Radio-Canada; 13b John Barr/Liaison/Alamy Stock Photo; 15l The Big Snit, 1985, 15r Inkwo For When the Starving Return, 2024 both © National Film Board of Canada; 16 Photo12/Collection 7e Art/Alamy Stock Photo; 17al Album/Alamy, 17ar Pictorial Press/Alamy, 17b Entertainment Pictures/Alamy, 18, 19 Allstar Picture Library/Alamy, all © Walt Disney Productions; 20a BFA/Alamy, 20b Album/Alamy, 21a Maximum Film/Alamy, 21b IFTN/United Archives/Alamy, 22 ScreenProd/Photononstop/Alamy, all © Touchstone Pictures/Burton/diNovi/Buena Vista/Disney; 23a PictureLux/The Hollywood Archive/Alamy, 23b kpa Publicity Stills/United Archives/Alamy, 24a Maximum Film/Alamy, 24b Entertainment Pictures/Alamy, 25 Album/Alamy, all © Walt Disney Pictures/Pixar Animation Studios; 26l © Suzan Pitt; 27a Courtesy Cinema Fantasma; 27b TCD/Prod.DB/Alamy © Netflix Animation/Double Dare You/ShadowMachine/The Jim Henson Company; 27r Courtesy Bitter Films; 30 Chris Pizzello/Invision/AP/Alamy Stock Photo; 31a, 32a, 33a Courtesy GKIDS © 2013 Filme de Papel; 31b, 32b Photo 12/Alamy © Filme de Papel; 33b Lifestyle Pictures/Alamy © Blue Sky Studios/20th Century Fox Animation/Davis Entertainment; 34 Esther Sanchez/AFP via Getty Images; 35a-37a Everett Collection/Alamy © Kimstim Films/Diluvio/Globo Rojo; 37b Collection Christophel/Alamy © Punkrobot Animation Studio; 38 Courtesy Archivo General de la Nación Argentina. AR-AGN-AGN01-AGAS-Ddf-rg-114406; 39l & r Courtesy ENERC (Escuela Nacional de Expermientacion y Realizacion Cinematografica)/Instituto Nacional de Cine y Artes Audiovisuales, Argentina; 40 Courtesy Santiago Caicedo; 41 Lifestyle Pictures/Alamy © Cinema Management Group/Cool Beans/Tunche Films; 44 Cecile Burban/Contour by Getty Images; 45a-46b Beast Productions/Vivement Lundi!/Pedri Animation; 47 Raoul Servais Collection, www.raoulservaiscollection.com; 48 Alexandr Hampl/CTK Photo/Alamy Stock Photo; 49a Everett Collection/Alamy © Studio Kresleného a Loutkového Filmu; 49bl-50a TCD/Prod.DB/Alamy © Ustredni Pujcovna Filmu/Loutkovy Film Praha/Studio Kresleného a Loutkoveho Filmu; 50b Josef Kubes/Alamy Stock Photo; 51a Sebastian Kahnert/dpa picture alliance/Alamy Stock Photo; 51bl © Condor Films; 52, 54a Courtesy of Film4; 53 Archives du 7e Art/Photo 12/Alamy © Condor Films/Film4; 54b © Condor Films/Film4; 55l Archives du 7e Art/Photo 12/Alamy © Kratky Film; 55r Archives du 7e Art/Photo 12/Alamy © MAUR Film; 56 Jonas Lindkvist/DN/TT News Agency/Alamy Stock Photo; 57a BFA/Neon/Alamy, 57b, 58b Album/Alamy, 58a, 59 TCD/Prod.DB/Alamy, all © Final Cut for Real/Sun Creature Studio/Vivement Lundi; 60 Jérôme Chatin/Gamma-Rapho via Getty Images; 61a Album/Alamy, 61b, 62l RGR Collection/Alamy, all © Les Films Paul Grimault/Les Films Gibe/France 2; 61c, 62r Photo 12/Alamy © Les Films Paul Grimault; 63l Keystone Press/Alamy Stock Photo; 63r TCD/Prod.DB/Alamy, 64a-65 Photo 12/Alamy, all © Films Armorial/Argos Films; 66a Aurore Marechal/Abaca Press/Alamy Stock Photo; 66b, 67b TCD/Prod.DB/Alamy © Miyu Productions/Dolce Vita Films; 67a, 68a Courtesy GKIDS © Dolce Vita Films/Miyu Productions/Palosanto Films/France 3 Cinéma; 68b TCD/Prod.DB/Alamy © Dream Well Studio/Sacrebleu Productions/Take Five; 69a Moviestore Collection/Alamy © Le Parti Productions/Mélusine Productions/Studiocanal/France 3 Cinéma/Les Armateurs; 69b Courtesy GKIDS © Everybody on Deck/Je Suis Bien Content/EV.L prod/Plume Finance/France 3 Cinéma/Shine Conseils/Gebeka Films/Amopix; 70 Keystone Pictures/Zuma Press/Alamy Stock Photo; 71a, 72 Photo 12/Alamy, 71b Archivio GBB/Alamy, all © Comenius Film; 73 kpa Publicity Stills/United Archives/Alamy © Fontana Filmproduktion/Senator Film Produktion/TFC Trickompany Filmproduktion; 74, 77r-79b Courtesy Film Archive/National Film Institute, Hungary; 75a-76b Everett Collection/Alamy © Pannónia Filmstúdió/Arbelos Films; 77l © Pannónia Filmstúdió; 81a Cinematic Collection/Alamy, 81b Everett Collection/Alamy, both © Les Armateurs/Vivi Film/Cartoon Saloon/France 2 Cinema/Buena Vista/GKIDS; 82a & b Album/Alamy © The Big Farm/Cartoon Saloon/Melusine Productions/Irish Film Board/Superprod/Norlum/GKIDS; 83 Courtesy GKIDS © Cartoon Saloon (Wolfwalkers) Ltd/Mélusine Productions; 84a Everett Collection/Alamy © AppleTV+/Cartoon Saloon (Wolfwalkers) Ltd/Mélusine Productions; 84b Collection Christophel/Alamy © Universal Pictures/Sullivan Bluth Studios; 85al Vittorio Zunino Celotto/Getty Images for BFI; 85ar Stephane de Sakutin/AFP via Getty Images; 85b Entertainment Pictures/Alamy © Aircraft Pictures/Cartoon Saloon/Melusine Productions/Canadian Broadcasting Corporation/GKIDS; 86 Marco Destefanis/Alamy Stock Photo; 87-88b Courtesy Bruno Bozzetto Distribution Snc; 89 Album/Alamy © Paul Thiltges Distributions/Aliante/JAM Media; 90 Elizabeth Goodenough/Everett Collection/Alamy Stock Photo; 91l BFA/Janus Films/Alamy, 91r & b TCD/Prod.DB/Alamy, all © Dream Well Studio/Sacrebleu Productions/Take Five; 92a-93a TCD/Prod.DB/Alamy © Subliminal Films/Bilibaba/Cinema Management Group; 93b Collection Christophel/Alamy © The Marriage Project/Studio Locomotive/Antevita Films; 94, 95r, 96al Everett Collection/Alamy © Good Deed Entertainment/BreakThru Productions/Trademark Films/Silver Reel; 95l Maurizio Gambarini/dpa/Alamy Stock Photo; 95b TCD/Prod.DB/Alamy, 96ar & b Album/Alamy, all © BreakThru Productions/Trademark Films/Silver Reel; 97 Courtesy Renata Gasiorowska; 98 Juan Gonzalez/EPA-EFE/Shutterstock; 99a & b, 100b, 101 Album/Alamy © Sacrebleu Productions; 100a Prod.DB/Alamy © Aparte Film/Sacrebleu Productions/Minds Meet; 101b Courtesy Romanian Film Archive © Romanian Film Centre, Romania; 102 TopFoto; 103 Heritage Image Partnership/Alamy Stock Photo; 104al & b Archives 7e Art/Photo 12/Alamy Stock Photo; 104ar PE Forsberg/Alamy Stock Photo; 105a Dmitry Kostyukov/AFP via Getty Images; 105b Photo 12/Alamy, 106l & r TCD/Prod.DB/Alamy, all © Soyuzmultfilm Studio; 107 Archives 7e Art/Photo 12/Alamy © Dentsu Tec/IMAX/Imagica Corp; 109a, 110b, 111a Album/Alamy, 109b TCD/Prod.DB/Alamy, all © Arcadia Motion Pictures/Lokiz Films/Noodles Production/Les Films du Worso; 110a Nacho Lopez/SOPA Images/Sipa USA/Alamy Stock Photo; 111b Cinematic Collection/Alamy © Abrakan Estudio/Basque Films/La Competencia Producciones; 112 Elizabeth Goodenough/Everett Collection/Alamy Stock Photo; 113a-114b Photo 12/Alamy, 115a Moviestore Collection/Alamy, all © Rita Productions/Blue Spirit Productions/Gebeka Films; 115b Courtesy Michaela Müller; 116 FlixPix/Alamy © Aardman; 117al Dave Donaldson/Alamy Stock Photo; 117ar Iounisphotography/Alamy Stock Photo; 117b Cinematic Collection/Alamy, 118 AJ Pics/Alamy, both © Aardman Animations/BBC Bristol/Wallace & Gromit; 119 AJ Pics/Alamy © Aardman Animations/Dreamworks Animation; 120 Shawshots/Alamy © Apple Corps/King Features Syndicate/Subafilms; 121 Everett Collection/Alamy Stock Photo; 122a Archives 7e Art/Photo 12/Alamy, 122c Everett Collection/Alamy, 122b Collection Christophel/Alamy, all © Apple Corps/King Features Syndicate/Subafilms; 123a, 124, 125a Courtesy Film4; 123b Ilpo Musto/Alamy Stock Photo; 125b RGR Collection/Alamy © Film4/Meltdown Productions; 126 Everett Collection/Animation Showcase/Alamy © Beryl Productions International; 127a Cinematic Collection/Alamy © Mikrofilm/National Film Board of Canada/Magnolia; 127b Album/Alamy © Animagrad Animation Studio/FilmUA Group; 130-133a Courtesy William Kentridge Studio; 133b Album/Alamy © Magic Light Pictures/Zweites Deutsches Fernsehen; 134 © Festival de Cine Africano de Tarifa; 135a & b © Moustapha R.; 136 Timothy Hiatt/Getty Images; 137a & b Courtesy Ng'endo Mukii; 138 a & b Courtesy Development & Executive Production, Disney Europe, Middle East & Africa Original Animation Team © 2023 Disney Enterprises Inc; 139 TCD/Prod.DB/Alamy © Agora Studio/Cinesite/Kugali/Road 14 Studios/Walt Disney Television; 142 Photo 12 © Shanghai Animation Film Studio; 143a, 143b Xinhua/Alamy Stock Photo; all 144 © Shanghai Animation Film Studio; 145a Photo 12/Alamy © Shanghai Animation Film Studio; 145a Prieto: Marie-Claire Kuo-Quiquemelle, Festival du Cinema Chinois de Paris. GFDL http://www.gnu.org/copyleft/fdl.html, via Wikimedia Commons; 145b, 146 Archives du 7e Art/Alamy © NeZha BrosPictures/Le-Joy Animation Studio/Perfect Circle; 147b Everett Collection/Alamy © Beijing Enlight Media/Chengdu Yingduoduo Culture Media/Coco Cartoon/Horgos Coloroom Pictures/CMC Pictures; 148 Source: https://w.wiki/57sz - CC BY-SA 4.0 via Wikimedia Commons; 149-151a Album © Nippon Ramayana film/Geek Pictures India/TEM; 151b Everett Collection/Alamy © Netflix; 152 The Asahi Shimbun via Getty Images; 153, 155 Photo 12/Alamy © Mushi Productions; 154 Everett Collection/Alamy © Alta Vista Productions/Toei Animation; 155 Photo 12/Alamy © Mushi Productions/Nippon Herald Films; 156a BJ Warnick/Newscom/Alamy Stock Photo; 156b AllStar Picture Library; 157a Album/Alamy, 157b Everett Collection/Alamy; 158 Courtesy GKIDS, all © Studio Ghibli/Tokuma Shoten/Nibariki; 160 Radek Petrasek/CTK Photo/Alamy Stock Photo; 161-163a Courtesy Yamamura Animation, Inc; 163b TCD/Prod.DB/Alamy © Surprise Red/Yamiken/Gaga; 164 Yonhap/Newcom/Alamy Stock Photo; 165a-167a Collection Christophel/Alamy, 165b Everett Collection/Alamy, all © The King Of Pigs Production Committee/Studio Dadashow; 167b TCD Prod.DB/Alamy © Yoo Productions/Seoul Donghwa; 168, 169b Courtesy Mano Animation Studios; 169a Album/Alamy © Mano Animation Studios; 170-171, 171a Courtesy Charades © Mano Animation Studios; 172 Leon Bennett/Getty Images for Critics Choice Association; 173-175 Courtesy Project 8 Projects; 176a RGR Collection/Alamy © Sony Pictures Classics/2.4.7Films/France 3 Cinema/Kennedy Marshall Company/French Connection Aniations/Diaphana/Celluloid Dreams; 176b Everett Collection/Alamy, 177ar Moviestore Collection/Alamy, both © Sony Pictures Classics; 177al Courtesy Fabian&Fred; 177b Everett Collection/Alamy © Yegane Moghaddam; 180 Ervin Monn/IMAGO/Alamy Stock Photo; 181a Archives 7e Art/Photo 12/Alamy, 181b AJ Pics/Alamy, 182al Cinematic Collection/Alamy, 181ar Moviestore Collection/Alamy, all © Melodrama Pictures; 182bl BFA/Alamy, 182br Everett Collection/Alamy, 183 Album/Alamy, all © IFC Films/Arenamedia/Screen Australia/Snails Pace Films; 184a Album/Alamy © Ludo Studio/Australian Broadcasting Corporation/BBC Studio; 185al & ar Archives New Zealand Te Rua Mahara o te Kāwanatanga; 185b Album/Alamy © Paramount Pictures/Columbia Pictures/Amblin Entertainment.